# HISTORY
## OF TEXAS CHRISTIAN UNIVERSITY

THE FACULTY AT THORP SPRING, 1891-93.

*Standing, from the left:* Mrs. E. C. Snow, Mrs. M. E. Wideman, Mrs. W. B. Parks, Miss Bettie Parker, W. B. Parks, A. C. Easley.

*Seated in chairs:* E. C. Snow, Addison Clark, Randolph Clark, A. Skidmore.

*Seated on steps:* Edwina Alsup, Sallie Cayce.

# HISTORY
## OF TEXAS CHRISTIAN UNIVERSITY

*A College
of the Cattle Frontier*

By
COLBY D. HALL
*1947*

Library of Congress Cataloging-in-Publication Data

Hall, Colby D. (Colby Dixon), 1875-1963.
  History of Texas Christian University : a college of the cattle frontier / by Colby
D. Hall. -- Anniversary edition.
    pages cm
  Originally published: Fort Worth : Texas Christian University Press, 1947.
  Includes bibliographical references and index.
    ISBN 978-0-87565-587-1 (cloth : alk. paper) -- ISBN 978-0-87565-588-8 (pbk. :
alk. paper)
  1. Texas Christian University--History. I. Title.
  LD5311.T382H3 2014
  378.764'5315--dc23
                                        2013043275

TCU Press
TCU Box 298300
Fort Worth, Texas
www.prs.tcu.edu


To order books: 1.800.826.8911


Cover illustrations by Erwin Sherman

# Dedicated

Dear Brother Addison,

I did not "go to" Add-Ran; Add-Ran came to me—to my home town, Waco, where I entered as (less than) a freshman in September 1896. My three years as a student there were mind-awakening, horizon-stretching years for me. The teachers were obscure, but genuine. You taught me Homiletics and Second Year Latin. Latin was not in your Department; you taught it because there was no other teacher available. Often that example has come to my mind when some instructor has balked on being asked to teach a class outside of his immediate specialty. One time I recalled it with gratitude when I was teaching a class in "War Aims."

Once, you almost expelled me from school. Guy Inman and I, young upstarts, had declined to attend any longer, the classes of the Professor of English, because he had insulted, in the columns of the *Collegian,* the State President of Christian Endeavor, a visiting speaker at the University. That Professor was your son, "Little Addie." This made it embarrassing to you. I'm sorry. That understanding attitude you took, despite your stern eye and rebuking words, has helped me to retain many a boy in T. C. U. through the years. You set the example of balancing the permanent good against the temporary bad.

What heartaching responsibilities and worries you carried through those lean years, of course, I did not then understand. Only as I have pondered the story in detail while writing about it recently have I come to realize the straining load you bore.

Somewhere along the road I have encountered this saying: "You are more comfortable than your grandfather, but are you a better man?" Sometimes, when I am inclined to take satisfaction in the vast improvement in plant and equipment which we enjoy in this generation, I can almost feel your eye penetrating me with that question. But even for some of these material acquisitions we are indebted to you. For did you not baptize Luke Brite? And was not the father of Mrs. Burnett your friend?

My first year of teaching was in 1902-3, which was the first year you were not on the faculty. As you went out, I came in. Throughout the years it has been my honor to be one of the ties with the old Add-Ran days, and now the figures say that I have served the school more years than any other individual. Perhaps these facts will justify my temerity in undertaking to write this history, and my boldness in dedicating it to you.

My chief desire in writing this story is to help pass on to succeeding generations, some measure of the spirit I found in you, the one man of all I have known, most supremely devoted to TRUTH.

COLBY D. HALL

*March 3, 1947*

# Contents

# EDITORIAL NOTE

TCU Press's approach in republishing Colby D. Hall's *History of Texas Christian University* was to treat the original 1947 book as an invaluable historical artifact. Except for new additions to the front matter and corrected page numbers, nothing has been changed, added, or amended, and therefore certain grammatical or stylistic constructions, spellings, phrasings, and references might be different from common contemporary usage.

LISA D. BARNETT
*Associate Editor*

pastor of Central Christian Church in Waco, which was the church of his youth, the church where he experienced his baptism and his call to ministry. Despite his desire for a settled life in Waco, TCU kept calling. In March 1911, Hall received a letter from trustee J. J. Hart asking about Hall's future interest in working at TCU with an upcoming vacancy in the "Bible Department." Hart also cited the possibility of the "Deanship of that Department" if Hall could "take a little further preparation, spend the next year in some of the leading theological seminaries and other universities of the country" to better prepare himself "not only for the classroom but for the executive duties."[10] Hall's two-page response indicated that financially he was not in a position to pursue additional educational studies, and though interested in future positions at TCU, he wanted to avoid the appearance of "place hunting" for the sake of "prominence, honor, or advancement." He wrote, "I am ready to cooperate with the trustees in any way I can to carry out the best things for TCU, yet I am not looking for any place, and am inclined to let the burden of proof that a TCU position is my duty, rest on others and not on myself."[11] Soon after his arrival as the new president of TCU in 1911, Frederick Kershner went to Waco to discuss Hall's future with TCU. Kershner persuaded Hall to come to Fort Worth to become a professor of Latin and provided some assurance that his role might expand in the future to become a professor of the Bible. Though he and Beatrice had started their family in 1912 with their first child, daughter Bita May, Hall accepted the offer and began another era of service at TCU in 1912. He also agreed to be the part-time pastor of the new University Christian Church, a position he held from 1912 to 1917.

Hall had been an avid supporter for a distinct College of the Bible to emerge at TCU, similar to his experience at the College of the Bible in Lexington. He noted in a letter sent to his father-in-law and TCU trustee T. E. Tomlinson in 1911, "I would like to see it [the College of the Bible] more than just a department of the University. It should have someone to build it up who would not be burdened with the affairs of the whole school, and someone at its head to stand with some strength for it, distinct from the President."[12] Whether or not Hall was aware of it at that time, ongoing conversations were occurring between Kershner, Chalmers McPherson, the endowment secretary for TCU, and Lucas C. Brite, a West Texas rancher, concerning a significant donation for the endowment of an English Bible Chair at TCU. On October 26, 1911, the trustees voted to accept $25,000 from Brite for the establishment of the English Bible Chair at TCU pursuant to terms stipulated in the contract expressing a conservative theological direction for the school. The terms of the contract stipulated that someone who does not deny "the supernatural birth of Jesus, His Divinity or His actual resurrection" occupies the chair.[13] In 1913, Hall assumed this position as professor of the English Bible, just as Kershner had promised him. More significant changes were to come affecting Hall's future. In 1914, the TCU trustees accepted Brite's proposal to charter and fund a Bible College.[14] The additional $37,500 toward the construction of a building to house the Bible College came with theological stipulations. Incorporated in 1914 as a separate institution, the charter of the Bible College provided a detailed four-point doctrinal statement that all trustees, staff, and faculty had to attest to in writing. The newly chartered Brite College of the Bible appointed Hall as dean of the school in 1914, a position he would hold for thirty-three years. In that same year, Hall was elected recording secretary of the International Convention for the Disciples of Christ at the Atlanta convention.[15]

Hall's family expanded in 1920 with the birth of their son, Colby Jr., and Hall's professional responsibilities grew when the TCU trustees named him dean of TCU in addition to his teaching and administrative work at Brite. The trustees created the office of dean in 1910 to assist the president during the relocation to Fort Worth, particularly stressful due to the temporary accommodations located in downtown Fort Worth.[16] Dr. W. B. Parks was the first to serve in this official capacity. Hall would become the second dean at TCU and remain in this administrative capacity until 1943. Hall often joked about this appointment, saying he "became dean on a 'temporary' basis, but it took them twenty-three years to find another."[17] One of Hall's first duties as dean of TCU was to elevate the academic status of the university by seeking accreditation. TCU was already a member of the Texas Association of Colleges, the American Association of Colleges, and the Board of Education of the Disciples of Christ, but Hall saw the value of accreditation status. The school submitted an application to the Southern Association of Colleges (SAC) for recognition. After filing reports, inspections, and adapting some policies to meet the educational standards, TCU gained official SAC recognition and became the sixth academic institution in Texas to receive accreditation.[18] Shortly thereafter, in 1928, the Association of American Universities placed TCU on their approved list of schools, and the Association of University Women approved TCU in 1930.[19] As academic dean of the university, Hall was responsible not only for the maintenance of educational standards at TCU, but he also served on several committees charged with the task of overseeing the academic integrity of other colleges. For thirteen years, Hall served as the chair of the Committee on Standards of the Association of Texas Colleges (1923-1936) and later as president of the Association of Texas Colleges (1933) and vice president of the Southern Association of Colleges and Secondary Schools (1934). He was also a member of the Committee on Classified and Accredited Schools, State Department of Education of Texas from 1935 through 1943.[20] This activity allowed Hall to become aware of the growing trend towards accreditation and the value of cooperation among institutions of higher education.

When the American Association of Theological Schools (first AATS, then later, ATS) formed in 1938, Hall, as dean of Brite College of the Bible, decided to seek accreditation status. This endeavor required a considerable amount of work, and on January 5, 1942, the AATS notified Hall that they had officially accredited Brite College of the Bible.[21] As a testament to the outstanding character and ability of Hall, the AATS appointed him to the Committee on Extension of Theological Education in 1941, before Brite's accreditation was official.[22] In his capacity as dean of Brite, Hall supervised the plans, construction, and financing of forty quadruplex apartments, which provided married ministerial students housing at an affordable price.[23]

In his commitment to raising TCU's academic standards to a nationally recognized level, Hall was responsible in the search for faculty members to complement those standards. He held himself to that same level of academic accountability. He spent the summer of 1928 in the Holy Land to supplement his knowledge of biblical studies, and in 1945, the Southwestern Society of Biblical Study and Research elected him president of the academic organization.[24] In 1931, Hall and three others assumed the editorial responsibility of the Christian Courier, the newspaper of the southwest region of the Christian Churches (Disciples of Christ).[25] In 1935, Transylvania University awarded Hall the honorary LLD degree for his work with the Southern Association of Universities and Colleges.[26] TCU and the Brite College of the Bible awarded him an honorary DD degree in 1951. Hall was a life member of the Texas State Teachers Association, the Texas State Historical Association, and the International Disciples of Christ Historical Association.

In 1954, Hall received recognition when named president of the Disciples of Christ Historical Society, an "honorary post to which the society annually elects an outstanding Disciple in honor of their contribution to the understanding of Disciple history."[27] The following year, the Disciples of Christ Historical Society awarded Hall a citation for distinguished service to the Disciples of Christ, calling attention to his distinguished career as preacher, teacher, administrator, and historian.[28]

Hall also maintained his ministerial service to the Christian Churches of Texas. He was a regular guest preacher in many congregations throughout the state, and did a two-month interim as supply pastor in 1922 at East Dallas Christian Church when their pastor, John Slayter, became ill.[29] Hall served as president of the Texas Christian Missionary Society for five years (1948-1953) and as president of the Texas Convention of Christian Churches for 1950-1951. Under the aegis of the Fort Worth area Council of Christian Churches, he worked to find and acquire sites for new Christian Churches in Tarrant County. Hall was affectionately nicknamed the "prime minister of University Christian Church" in Fort Worth by his former pupil, colleague, and pastor, Granville T. Walker.[30] In May 1953, the church dedicated its education and fellowship building to Hall.

Hall retired as dean of TCU in 1943 but remained on as professor and dean of the Brite College of the Bible. TCU officially named Hall Dean Emeritus for his years of service to the university. Though he suffered a stroke in 1945, he continued his work at Brite until 1947, when he asked the Brite trustees to allow him to retire as dean but continue as professor of church history.[31] Hall remained at Brite teaching church history and missionary work until 1955, when he retired as professor.[32] Retirement for Hall did not entail slowing down, but rather signaled a change in direction for his academic interests. As a Disciples of Christ historian, Hall turned to writing. He published the *History of Texas Christian University* in 1947 and *Texas Disciples* in 1953 with the TCU Press. Hall also wrote *Rice Haggard: The American Frontier Evangelist Who Revived the Name Christian* in 1957, *The New Light Christians: Initiators of the Nineteenth-Century Reformation* in 1959, and *Gay Nineties* in 1961. The establishment of a small museum at Brite with relics from Palestine gathered during Dr. William Reed's travels afforded Hall the opportunity to work on a project he envisioned for many years. He always wanted to make a map showing the missionary journeys of former TCU and Brite students, and the museum gave him the reason to make it and place to display it. Hall also served as curator of the Brite College museum.[33] Hall died at his home near the campus on August 26, 1963, having been bedridden for eighteen months with a broken hip.

An article about Hall in the 1929 TCU *Interpreter* noted, "Tradition in a college is an intangible asset of immeasurable value. Part of such tradition, and a most valuable part, is professional tenure of office extending through two, three, or more decades."[34] Hall's tradition with TCU extended beyond his professional career; TCU meant a great deal to Hall and his family. He was not the only one to value the tradition of the university. Hall had two brothers who graduated from TCU—Gordon B. Hall with a BA in 1908 and Clarence M. Hall with a BA in 1912. Hall's wife, Beatrice Tomlinson Hall, graduated with a BA in 1908. His daughter, Dr. Bita May Hall Compton, took BA and MA degrees from TCU in 1931 and 1936, and was a professor of French at TCU from 1938 until 1976, when she retired. His son, Dr. Colby D. Hall Jr., received BA and MS degrees from TCU. Hall's sister, Bertie H. Mothershead, began work at TCU as a librarian in 1923 and became head librarian in 1938, serving in that position until 1953.[35] Hall's father-in-law, T. E. Tomlinson, served as president of the TCU Board of Trustees, and many other Tomlinson in-laws attended and served the school. TCU was more than a job to Hall and his family.

One cannot think of TCU without thinking of Colby D. Hall. In 1957, TCU named a dormitory in his honor. His daughter, Dr. Bita May Hall, established a scholarship at Brite in 1971 to honor him. Hartwell Ramsey, the editor of the *Christian Courier*, wrote in September 1963, "Death will not stay the influence of Colby Dixon Hall. His writings remain. His name is set in perpetuity upon the facade of the dormitory which stands as a continuing testimony of his powerful 'conscious' and 'unconscious' influence."[36] Hall said in a speech to the Disciples Historical Society, "We are a part of history, despite our desire."[37] His work on the history of Texas Christian University is as much a history of his own life as it is of the institution that he loved.

[1]"Tribute to Colby D. Hall," *Horned Frog Yearbook*, 1947, 16. The reference to TCU as a "church-related University" refers to the association with the Christian Churches (Disciples of Christ), the religious affiliation of the founders of the school. When Addison and Randolph Clark founded Add-Ran College, they intended it to be a Christian college. In 1889, Add-Ran College became the property of the Christian Churches of Texas, and a new charter changed the name to Add-Ran Christian University. See Lisa Barnett, "Before Brite: Ministerial Education at TCU, 1873-1914," in *Institutional Change in Theological Education: A History of Brite Divinity School,* eds. Mark G. Toulouse, Jeffrey Williams, and Dyan M. Dietz (Fort Worth: TCU Press, 2011), 17-24. For information on the history of the Christian Churches (Disciples of Christ) and the Stone-Campbell Movement, see Mark G. Toulouse, "Christian Church (Disciples of Christ)," in the *Encyclopedia of the Stone-Campbell Movement,* eds. Douglas A. Foster, Paul M. Blowers, Anthony

L. Dunnavant, and D. Newell Williams (Grand Rapids, MI: William B. Eerdmans Publishing Company, 2004), 177-84; Lester G. McAllister and William E. Tucker, *Journey in Faith: A History of the Christian Church (Disciples of Christ)* (St. Louis: Chalice Press, 1975).

[2]Irene Rountree, "Dean Hall Reviews 50 Years as TCU Student-Teacher," *Skiff*, April 18, 1852, 5.

[3]"TCU Dean Emeritus Dies at Age 87 in Fort Worth," *Corpus Christi Times*, August 26, 1963, 3B.

[4]For more information about the Christian Endeavor see Christopher Lee Coble, "Young People's Society of Christian Endeavor (United Society of Christian Endeavor)," in the *Encyclopedia of the Stone-Campbell Movement*, eds. Douglas A. Foster, Paul M. Blowers, Anthony L. Dunnavant, and D. Newell Williams (Grand Rapids, MI: William B. Eerdmans Publishing Company, 2004), 795.

[5]Rountree, *Skiff*, April 18, 1852, 5.

[6]"Who's Who," *Christian Standard* 80, no. 35, May 30, 1925, 856.

[7]Robert B. Hall, "Colby D. Hall," in the *Encyclopedia of the Stone-Campbell Movement*, eds. Douglas A. Foster, Paul M. Blowers, Anthony L. Dunnavant, and D. Newell Williams (Grand Rapids, MI: William B. Eerdmans Publishing Company, 2004), 380.

[8]"Christian Education," *Horned Frog*, 1908, 28.

[9]Rountree, *Skiff*, April 18, 1852, 5.

[10]Letter from J. J. Hart to Colby Hall, March 10, 1911, in the Records of T. E. Tomlinson, Special Collections, Mary Couts Burnett Library, Texas Christian University, Fort Worth, TX.

[11]Letter from Colby Hall to J. J. Hart, March 15, 1911, in the Records of T. E. Tomlinson, Special Collections, Mary Couts Burnett Library, Texas Christian University, Fort Worth, TX.

[12]Letter from Colby Hall to T. E. Tomlinson, March 15, 1911, in the Records of T. E. Tomlinson, Special Collections, Mary Couts Burnett Library, Texas Christian University, Fort Worth, TX.

[13]Texas Christian University Board of Trustees Meeting Minutes (October 26, 1911), Special Collections, Mary Couts Burnett Library, Texas Christian University, Fort Worth, TX; and "L.C. Brite Bible Chair," *Christian Courier*, July 3, 1912, 10.

[14]Texas Christian University Board of Trustees Meeting Minutes (June 6, 1914), Special Collections, Mary Couts Burnett Library, Texas Christian University, Fort Worth, TX.

[15]"Rev. Colby Hall Gets Election in Church," *Fort Worth Star-Telegram*, October 12, 1914, 2.

[16]Texas Christian University Board of Trustees Meeting Minutes (November 29, 1910), Special Collections, Mary Couts Burnett Library, Texas Christian University, Fort Worth, TX.

[17]Rountree, *Skiff*, April 18, 1852, 5.

[18]"Texas Christian University Enters Southern Association," *Skiff*, December 12, 1922, 1.

[19]"Mechanic, Victory Gardener, Carpenter, Cook Retires as Beloved TCU Dean of 23 Years," *Skiff*, April 30, 1943, 6.

[20]Jerome Moore, "Retirement Years of Colby Hall," in the Records of Jerome A. Moore, Special Collections, Mary Couts Burnett Library, Texas Christian University, Fort Worth, TX.

[21]Blaine Hamilton and Dyan M. Dietz, "Accreditation and Change: From Brite College of the Bible to Brite Divinity School, 1939-1963," in *Institutional Change in Theological Education: A History of Brite Divinity School*, eds. Mark G. Toulouse, Jeffrey Williams, and Dyan M. Dietz (Fort Worth: TCU Press, 2011), 80-84.

[22]Letter from E. H. Roberts to Colby Hall, February 24, 1941, in the Records of the Brite History Project, Correspondence Files, Brite Divinity School, Fort Worth, TX.

[23]"Hall to Retire as Dean at TCU," *Fort Worth Star-Telegram*, January 3, 1947.

[24]*Christian-Evangelist*, March 14, 1945, 268.

[25]"Christian Courier Announces Editorial Plan," *Christian-Evangelist*, January 1, 1931, 19.

[26]George C. Stuart, "Colby D. Hall: A Pastor's Pastor," *Christian-Evangelist*, February 3, 1954, 105.

[27]"Dr. Colby D. Hall Named President of the Disciples of Christ Historical Society," *Christian-Evangelist*, December 1, 1954, 11.

[28]James M. Flanagan, "Disciples Neglect of History Discussed at Historical Society's Annual Dinner," *Christian-Evangelist*, December 21, 1955, 15.

[29]"Christian Minister Ill, Voted Leave of Absence and Supply Pastor Called," *Dallas Morning News*, January 31, 1922, 2.

[30]Moore, "Retirement Years of Colby Hall."

[31]"Dean Colby D. Hall to Retire at Brite College," *Christian-Evangelist*, February 12, 1947, 168.

[32]Dale Johnson, "Dean Hall, Thrice Retired, Still Works," *Skiff*, February 24, 1960, 8.

[33]Johnson, the *Skiff*, February 24, 1960, 8; "Fourth Book Written by Dr. Colby Hall," *Fort Worth Star-Telegram*, December 26, 1959.

[34]"Dean Colby D. Hall," *Texas Christian University Interpreter*, January-February 1929, 5, in the Records of Jerome A. Moore, Special Collections, Mary Couts Burnett Library, Texas Christian University, Fort Worth, TX.

[35]Betsy Colquit, *Prologue: The TCU Library to 1983* (Fort Worth: Mary Couts Burnett Library, Texas Christian University, 1983).

[36]Jerome Moore, "Information About the Tomlinson-Hall Families," in the Records of Jerome A. Moore, Special Collections, Mary Couts Burnett Library, Texas Christian University, Fort Worth, TX.

[37]Flanagan, *Christian-Evangelist*, December 21, 1955, 15.

# Illustrations

# Acknowledgments

A word of thanks from me (and the readers) is due to several friends who have graciously contributed encouragement, assistance and information to the making of this book. Several Professor-comrades have read the Manuscript and offered technical criticisms. Among these are Professor J. Willard Ridings of Journalism, Dr. Rebecca Smith Lee (formerly) of English, Dr. W. J. Hammond of History, and President Emeritus E. M. Waits, the friendly soul with whom, across the table, for more than twenty-five years, I shared the heart-beats of the old school. President M. E. Sadler, also took time out of his busy schedule to read the Manuscript and to give some valuable suggestions. His generous Introduction, is also very much appreciated. My good wife and our daughter, Bita May (both T. C. U. graduates) have offered inspiration all along and a high quality of criticism as well. The final round of editing was graciously done by that choice young professor of English, Dr. Paul Dinkins.

For some material not so easy to obtain, I am indebted to several ex-students: Jim McClintic, Archie Wood and W. O. Stevens (fellow students of the "Seven Lean Years") and L. C. (Pete) Wright, Douglas Shirley and Robert Badgett of later years. The members of the Clark family have been deeply interested and helpful in securing materials and photographs: Mrs. Randolph Lee Clark and her daughter, Mrs. Sypert Clark Lovejoy for rare photographs; most of all to Mrs. Louella Clark Holloway for letters, documents and photographs. Let me thank also, a present student, Francis Barnes, for locating and borrowing the only known copy of *The Life of Joseph Addison Clark* by his son Randolph, which we have had photostated and filed in the Library, returning the original to the family of Dr. Frank Clark.

The task of selecting the pictures for insertion proved to be delightful, difficult, daring and dangerous. Choices were made largely on the basis of rank, length of service and, occasionally, death in service, with a leaning, naturally, toward the earlier years. The matter of lifting a few samples out of the overwhelming abundance of the old *Horned Frogs* (43 of them) became almost a matter of chance.

May I venture to thank many of the participants in this story for their forgiveness, in advance, for the brevity of my references to them. Many encomiums have welled up in my heart, only to be compressed into moieties by limitations of space. In fact, the story was first written at greater length, then on the advice of friends, abridged. The longer version is typed, bound and deposited in the Mary Couts Burnett Memorial Library.

COLBY D. HALL

Fort Worth, T. C. U., March 24, 1947.

# Introduction

I N LARGE MEASURE, the history of Texas Christian University is the history of Texas. They grew up together. When this Institution was founded, seventy-five years ago, Texas was a very small state, except in land area and in the determination to do big things. This determination coupled with the vast possibilities, has made Texas first among all the states of the union in several significant respects. Texas Christian University has shared in this growth and development.

Those who founded this Institution had a two-fold compelling desire; they wanted to develop for this promising, undeveloped empire an educated, cultured, Christian leadership for all walks of life; and they wanted to produce the kind of ministers who could maintain for religion the place which it should have in a new and growing area.

The elaboration of these ideals; the explanation of the circumstances under which they had to be worked out; the description of some of the notable personalities around whom the life and work of the school have revolved; the pointing out of successes and failures; and the story of the growing realization of a great dream constitute the major task of this volume.

A meager story of Texas Christian University could have been told briefly by anyone acquainted with the main facts in its life. But to tell the story with insight, understanding, comprehensiveness, and real meaning, demanded a writer who has known, lived and loved Texas Christian University.

Dean Colby D. Hall has completed full forty years on the staff of this Institution, during which time he has served as field representative, teacher and Dean. It is fifty-one years since he entered as a student. He has been intimately involved in the life and development of the School for the major part of its existence. He knows what has happened and why it happened. To a degree far beyond anything indicated in this volume, Dean

Hall has been responsible for many of the most significant achievements the School has made. Those who read this volume should understand that in a very real sense they are reading the autobiography of the writer.

Herewith is the detailed, intimate, personal story of Texas Christian University by one whose life has been a large part of this Institution for a long time. Former students and friends, as well as those who are interested in the development of higher education in this part of the country, will read this story with abiding interest and appreciation.

McGRUDER ELLIS SADLER
*President,* Texas Christian University

*March 24, 1947*

# Milestones

1869—Clark family opens private school in Fort Worth.

1873—Add-Ran College opened, Thorp Spring.

1873-99—Addison Clark, President.

1874—April 11, Charter becomes effective.

1878—First building erected, displacing the original Thorp building.

1880—The first "Summer Term" conducted.

1882—The left wing of the Building added.

1889—October 5, Add-Ran Christian University name adopted and property taken over by the Christian Churches, J. J. Jarvis, Board President.

1892—The right wing completed, named "Jarvis Building."

1895—Christmas, moved to Waco, Col. J. Z. Miller, Board President.

1896—Thanksgiving Day, first (intra-mural) football game.

1899-1909—T. E. Shirley, President of the Board.

1902-06—E. V. Zollars, President.

1902—Name changed to Texas Christian University.

1906-11—Clinton Lockhart, President.

1909-16—T. E. Tomlinson, President of the Board.

1910—March 22, Main Building destroyed by fire.

—September, school opened in Fort Worth, downtown.

1911-15—Frederick D. Kershner, President.

1911-15—W. B. Parks became the first Dean of the University.

—September, school opened on present campus, with Main Building, Jarvis and Goode Halls.

—First Endowment, $25,000, by L. C. Brite.

1912—Fort Worth Medical College adopted as Medical Department.

—Becomes a charter member of the Association of Texas Colleges.

1913—Clark Hall completed.

1914—Brite College of the Bible founded, Brite Hall erected.

—Trustees voted to abolish the Academy, gradually.

1915—School of Law inaugurated, E. R. Cockrell, Principal.

1916-41—Edward McShane Waits, President.

1916-27—Sam J. McFarland, President of the Board.

1918—Medical College closed, due to radically rising costs.

—September, December, Student Army Training Corps.

1920—$300,000 in Endowment attained.

—Colby D. Hall, Dean of the University.

—Law School closed to concentrate funds on Liberal Arts.

1921—Academy finally closed.

—The Gymnasium building completed.

—Recognition and aid by the General Education Board.

—Elected to membership in the Association of American Colleges.

1922—Elected to membership in the Southern Association of Colleges and Secondary Schools, including accreditation.

1923—June: Jubilee celebration of the fiftieth anniversary of the founding of the school. $500,000 endowment achieved.

—December: Mary Couts Burnett Trust received.

1925—Mary Couts Burnett Library opened, February; East Campus.

1926—Graduate School organized, John Lord, Dean.

—Field House erected.

1927—General Education Board's gift of $166,666.67 received, debts cleared.

1927-40—Van Zandt Jarvis, President of the Board.

1928—Placed on approved list Association of American Universities.

1929—First Southwest Conference Football Championship.

1930—New $400,000 stadium erected, on West Campus.

—On approved list of the American Association of University Women.

1933—New University Christian Church erected.

—Depression causes 43 per cent cut in salaries.

1936—The Evening College made a distinct administrative unit.

1939—Brite College of the Bible celebrates Silver Anniversary and adopts standard Seminary Curriculum.

—June: First War training service begun; flying training under C. A. A.

1940-41—R. H. Foster, President of the Board.

1941—McGruder Ellis Sadler, President.

1941—L. D. Anderson, President of the Board.

—Brite College accredited by the American Association of Theological Schools, December.

1942—Foster Hall completed, May.

—Jarvis Hall assigned to Navy Air Patrol Training, later Navy V-5, September.

1943—Reorganization of the University Program into Seven Colleges.

—Navy V-12 program inaugurated, using Clark Hall, July.

1944—Jarvis Hall restored to girls. Navy V-5 closed, September.

1945—Navy V-12 program closed, Clark Hall returned to boys, October.

1946—The Financial Campaign, Fort Worth for $5,500,000.

—New Girls' and new Boys' Dormitories begun.

1947—Barracks from the U. S. Government for Boys' Dormitories and for Recitation Rooms.

1948—Celebration of Seventy-fifth Anniversary.

# The Southwestern Frontier and Its Schools

E NGLISH SPEAKING AMERICA spent her first three hundred
years growing frontiers. "The stern and rock-bound coast"
of the Pilgrims and the swamps of the James River made
the first frontier, hugging the Atlantic. Virginians leaped the
Cumberland mountains and opened the frontier of Kaintuck-ee.
The fat, flat lands of the Mississippi Valley became the
frontier when the current of migration flowed with Abraham
Lincoln's parents across the Ohio northward. Later, Lewis and
Clark opened the Northwest, which continued to provide one
new frontier after another. Only when Thomas Jefferson in
1803, with a bold stroke of the pen and a sense of destiny
purchased from Napoleon Bonaparte the swamps of Louisiana,
with all points west to Oregon thrown in, did the imagination of
Americans really begin to comprehend the dream of the United
States as being more than an Atlantic strip. On the tide of this
dream, the Anglo-Saxon stream poured through New Orleans
into the great prairies of the Southwest and clashed with the
long-planted Latin race at the Rio Grande. Then Texas came
into the picture as a new frontier.

There were two frontiers in Texas. The first was South
Texas. The route of entry other than the waters of the Gulf,
was from New Orleans, up the Red River to Nachitoches, Louisiana, and across to Nacogdoches, Texas, thence by trail to San
Antonio de Bexar. From that line South to the Gulf lay the
colonies of Stephen F. Austin and other impresarios. In this
Southern region were fought the battles for Texas freedom in
1836, the Alamo, Goliad and San Jacinto, the latter lapped by
the very waters of Galveston Bay itself. This is the land of the
mosquitos and swamps, piney woods and cotton fields, fragrant
magnolias and ancient live-oaks draped with the graceful Spanish moss. Old Texas is South Texas, and it still seems a sort of
effete civilization to some of the Western cow-men.

For there was another frontier in Texas. It was the dry

1

range country, with its cactus and mesquite, its long-horned cattle, its loping mustang ponies, its drought-resisting horned frogs, its long, rolling prairies and its truncated mesas; where for a long time there was no cotton, and where the fighting was between the white men and the Indians, then later between the cow-men and the sheep-men. This was West Texas, which became the frontier after the close of the War Between the States. It was the last of the borderlands, and a genuine frontier in its own right.

Naturally, the beginnings of college education were found in the Southern region, since it was the earlier region. Rutersville college, the earliest of the three schools which merged into Southwestern University, began in 1840.[1]

Baylor University was chartered in 1845 at Independence, near the spot where the Texas Declaration of Independence was signed.[2] Thus the more populous religious bodies—the Methodists and the Baptists—chartered colleges under the Republic of Texas. The Southern Presbyterians established Austin College in 1849 in Huntsville, hard by the home of Sam Houston. The Cumberland Presbyterians came farther north in the state, to Limestone County, and in 1869 opened Trinity University.[3]

College education made its beginnings also in West Texas, the cattle frontier, a region with its own problems and its unique flavor. The oldest surviving college of this region was born in September, 1873[4] at Thorp Spring, Hood County, to be known as Add-Ran College. It began before the railroads came through, before barbed wire fenced off the free wide-open ranges, and while the cattle trails to the Northern feeding grounds were still

[1]Catalogue of Southwestern University, April, 1942, pp. 7, 8. Rutersville College, located at Rutersville, was chartered in 1840 . . . other institutions of higher learning projected by the early Methodists of Texas were Wesleyan College, San Augustine, 1844; McKenzie College, Clarksville, 1848; Soule University, Chapel Hill, 1856. The right to grant degrees provided in the charters of (the others) was transferred to Southwestern, which opened in 1873, and was chartered February 6, 1875.

[2]Catalogue of Baylor University, 1942, p. 23. "Chartered in 1845 by the Republic of Texas, Baylor University is the oldest institution of higher learning in the Southwest."

[3]This information is from an article by James K. Thompson in the Fort Worth Star-Telegram, January 21, 1945. Sec. II, p. 6. This school also had predecessors: Ewing College at LaGrange opened in 1848, closed twenty years later; Chapel Hill at Daingerfield 1849-1861; and Larissa College, near Jacksonville. But each of these lapsed before Trinity was established. Trinity has made two moves: to Waxahachie in 1902, and to San Antonio in 1942.

[4]But see Ch. III, last paragraph, for evidence of 1869 as the beginning date.

2

in use. It grew up with West Texas. This book is to tell the story of that institution. It aims to portray some of the features of the life of the people who developed it, supported it and were influenced by it.

The cattle West was settled with vibrant energy in the swirl of the readjustments following the War Between the States. In that period, the birth rate of colleges was remarkably high, as was their mortality rate a generation or two later.[5] Both of these were caused by the changing conditions that belonged to the times.

Ambition for education was natural among a free people who boasted that any boy might be the President of the United States. Teachers were scarce; there must be schools to educate them. Preachers required schools also, despite the widespread prejudice against "educated preachers" which was naturally fostered by the unlearned as a sort of defense. But schools were hard to find. The Texas founding fathers had made opulent provisions for public education, but this was not yet implemented. The answer was private schools, worked up locally. Sometimes a few enterprising citizens with large families of children made up a subscription list and sent for a teacher. Often the teacher moved in and worked up the list himself. Out of these many local schools would develop, occasionally, one outstanding enough to attract students from other localities. There were two prevailing types. One, designed for school teachers, concentrated on review courses to prepare for examinations for Teachers Certificates. The other, of the older classical or Academy type, was usually presided over by a minister and had some connection with the church. Each school of either type was usually built around the personality of an unusual teacher. In nearly every case he used the members of his family as teachers with him. There was no concern about nepotism in those days. By no other method could such schools have been financed.

The number of schools was large, because the radius of travel was short. For instance, in the counties adjacent to Hood, where Add-Ran was located, there came to be such schools as Granbury, Eastland (Huckabee nearby), Weatherford, Whitt, Stephenville, and others not now known. When the radius of travel was lengthened by better roads, and public schools arose, most of these private schools lapsed. But some of them had qualities

[5]The author counted 156 names of colleges extinct, in the list of topics for the Hand Book of Texas and knew of many not therein contained.

3

or conditions that enabled them to survive. A few Normal Schools persuaded the State to adopt them, as at Huntsville, Denton, Stephenville, Arlington, and Commerce. Others secured the support of churches.

Add-Ran Christian University, later Texas Christian, is one of the survivors of the period following closely upon the end of the Civil War. Its history is a part of the general pattern of its time.

All of the flavor of the school traditions of America went into it. All the unique features of the range frontier belong to it. Moreover, it had, of its own, qualities that enabled it to endure and personalities who gave it a stamp of permanency. The story as related here is of interest to its friends, of course, to those thousands whose progenitors participated in it, and other thousands who inherited its blessings. It is rich in traditions and sentiment; it is a chapter of genuine history. But it is more. It is an epitome of the school life on the cattle frontier. It is a trail that will never again be traveled. It is the embodiment of education through an era that is gone.

# ∾ II ∾

# The Clark Family

WHEN LOUIS XIV SAT IN HIS LUXURIOUS PALACE on October 22, 1685, and signed the Revocation of the Edict of Nantes, he intended to convert by compulsion all the Protestants in France. Instead, he deflected a stream of the best blood of France into currents that enriched several of the states of Europe and many of the colonies of young America. One writer has said, "Every colony in America, from Massachusetts to South Carolina, extended them a welcome."[1] These Huguenots did not segregate themselves so much as many other European sects; they intermingled, and found themselves *en rapport* with the fresh release of freedom in the new world.

A part of this Huguenot stream was the D'Spain family, which had migrated to South Carolina, then Alabama, and finally settled in Texas soon after it had won its independence from Mexico in 1836. Their home was in the piney woods of East Texas near Nacogdoches.

Here this liberty-loving stream mingled with another of a different source but of kindred spirit. Randolph Clark expresses this spirit in referring to the lineage of his father, who was of the Scotch Irish stock. "Joseph Addison Clark came from that rugged stock of pioneers who colonized North Carolina, the first of the colonies to declare their independence of kings and state religions, and who have been prompt and united in defending their liberties."[2] These words reveal much of that pride in liberty so characteristic of the American frontier. He further states that he was born "Zachariah, but when he took control of himself he dropped this and took the name Joseph Addison." More American independence!

Joseph Addison Clark's wanderings were typical of the fluid frontier. Born in 1815, orphaned at twelve in Columbia, near

[1]Sweet, W. W., *The Story of Religion in America*, p. 37.
[2]Randolph Clark *Reminiscences*, p. 9, referring, no doubt to the Mecklenberg Declaration of Independence by the citizens of Mecklenberg County, N. C., May 31, 1775.

Clarksville, Tennessee, deprived of his patrimony by legal technicalities that left him wary of people, an editor at eighteen, a student for a year in the University of Alabama, he was skilled in law and surveying by the time of his majority. After teaching two years near Lexington, Kentucky, he took his mother and two sisters to Texas, landing at Matagorda when he was twenty-four.

From there they took the ox-cart route to Austin, the raw capital of the young republic, where he worked two years as a printer. On the death of his mother and the marriage of his sister, he started back to Kentucky, but was detained in Nacogdoches County by floods. His services as surveyor were in demand; he became widely acquainted in the county, and intimately acquainted with one family—the Huguenot D'Spains. Hettie D'Spain became his bride on January 21, 1842. Thus two families devoted to liberty met to keep the stream flowing.

He found, in this fortunate connection, more than love and home; he found religion. "At the time of his marriage J. A. Clark had no sure religious convictions. He had allowed himself to be classed with unbelievers."[3] Like many men foot-loose in the changing West, he had broken settled church ties, had become a little cynical of religious pretensions, and had imbibed some of the Tom Paine rationalistic philosophy which, in no small degree, had seeped into the reaction against tyranny in America. These French Protestants, to be sure, had been influenced by the great French Protestant, John Calvin, but it is obvious from the story of the D'Spains that some of them were far from being Calvinists in theology.

As far into the past as this generation knows of them they were zealous disciples of Christ taking no religious name but Disciple, or Christian; no creed but faith in the personal Christ as our Saviour, and God as an ever present Father; acknowledging no authority in religion but the Word of God. Before the Campbells started the movement for undenominational Christianity, before Christian Union was preached in America, a few of these people were settlers in Alabama and Tennessee. They nor their descendants were troubled with trying to harmonize church doctrines with the teaching of the Bible. They studied the Word of God to know the truth as it is revealed to common folk.[4]

[3]*Reminiscences*, Clark, p. 13.
[4]*Ibid*. p. 13.

6

It was this simple, sensible, scriptural interpretation of religion which he learned from the Huguenot family and saw in "the every-day life of his wife, by that beautiful faith that produced an ever cheerful, trusting personality,"[5] that clarified the Christian religion for him. "Brother Randolph," in his old age, often chuckled in saying, "They can call some of you brethern Campbellites, but they can't call me one. For I got my first principles from a different source, that goes 'way back of the Campbells."

If J. A. Clark had not heard of Alexander Campbell at that time, he was soon to learn that there were disadvantages in agreeing with him.

On becoming a Christian and refusing any denominational name or creed, he learned something of the power of religious prejudice. He had begun teaching school. On the morning after he was baptized, a concourse of citizens, led by the preacher of the community, assembled at the school-house and demanded that he give up the school.—He had joined the Campbellites.[6]

Hettie D'Spain was a woman of remarkable strength of character. It was a tradition in the family that she was a very beautiful woman, featured by naturally rosy cheeks throughout life. Her ability to become the school teacher of her own children, as she did, was the result of more than just good sense. As a girl she had attended an Academy under James Shannon, who later became the President of the University of Missouri.[7] She was one of the teachers in the early school of the Clarks while it was in Fort Worth, and served as matron of the girls at Thorp Spring.

Of the five sons and two daughters born to the couple, three of the sons, along with the father, labored together in developing the school known as "Add-Ran." One of the sisters too, Mrs. Ida Clark Nesbit, was in the midst of it and a most worthy contributor. Their training was under the limitations of frontier conditions but always in the atmosphere of the Christian faith, the loftiest of ideals and a genuine appreciation of true culture. The early schooling of Addison, the eldest (born December 11, 1842) was from the mother who "taught the fundamentals of good education, reading, writing, history, arithmetic,

[5]*Ibid.* p. 13.
[6]*Ibid.* p. 14.
[7]Interview.

and geography"; there was in the home a library of standard authors; and the paper edited by the father was considered a means of education in that home. His formal schooling included a primary school at Rusk and at Galveston, a year in an academy at Palestine, at twelve years of age, then one teacher after another whom his father sought—for it was difficult to find one much ahead of the lad, scarce as teachers were. It is probable that the other sons, Randolph and Thomas, followed a similar path. Randolph omits his own story from his volume. We know that on their return from service in the War between the States, May 22, 1865, both Addison and Randolph studied under Charles Carlton at Kentuckytown, later at Bonham, when Carlton College was coeducational. Randolph also spent six months in Bethany College, West Virginia, September, 1876 to February, 1877. His career there was cut short by the need for his presence at Thorp Spring to settle a dispute between his father and "Old Man Thorp" over the property.[8]

This final experience as student under Charles Carlton was most fortunate and influential. He was an Englishman of a unique character, a graduate of Bethany College under Alexander Campbell. Education, to him, was personal, and he was a great personality. He had a thorough grasp, too, of the principles of the Reform movement led by the Campbells, was a preacher of power, and gave the training to these young men both in pedagogy and religion which marked their careers.[9] Both Addison and Randolph were definitely committed to a career of teaching and preaching. Few preachers of that generation could depend on preaching alone for a livelihood. (Addison had become a teacher before going to Carlton College and served as an assistant there.)

A younger Clark brother, "Tommy," was the artist of the group. He contributed elements in Art, Music, Speech, Dramatics, and other fine arts which were not so popular on the frontier. He was different from any other member of the family, probably influenced by his mother, whose aesthetic tastes were well cultivated. The youngest brother, Frank Clark, became a physician, and educated at least four of his boys in that profession. He was a substantial leader in the church, too, at Iowa Park, Texas, for many years.

[8](Personal Interview) See Ch. IV.
[9]For a Biography of Charles Carlton see Kenneth Hay, *Life and Influence of Charles Carlton*, 1940, *Christian Courier*, Fort Worth.

8

Another woman who made her own distinctive contribution to the history and the qualities of the Clark family was Ella Blanche Lee, who became Mrs. Randolph Clark on July 5, 1870, at Bonham. Her father, Roswell W. Lee, was a cousin of General Robert E. Lee, a graduate of West Point and a classmate of General U. S. Grant. The traditions and the culture of the old Southland were her heritage; to transmit them in wholesome influence to the students was her privilege and life service. As will appear later in the story, her personal fortune was a factor in saving the institution financially at one time, and her personality was a gracious blessing in the home life of the student groups.

The following accords with the many stories of the hospitality of the Randolph Clark home and the remarkable management of the gracious Mrs. Ella Lee Clark. For some years

there was one big barnyard shaded by a grove of stately live oaks that furnished food and shelter for all who came. In the home was a cheerful woman, one of the elect, whose cruse of oil and measure of meal never grew less. Under all circumstances there was a glad welcome to every tired traveler. By some kind of magic there were rest and refreshment for all comers at any hour of day or night.[10]

This refers especially to the days when there was no boys' dormitory. Mrs. Randolph was not so much officially the matron of the boys; it was just the Clark home that received them when they came, and looked after them until they could be located. It seemed to be a kind of hospice, or voluntary dormitory for the boys. Mrs. Louella Clark Holloway writes of her:

"She (Mrs. R. Clark) possessed a cosmopolitan mind, the greatest poise of any woman I ever knew—never did I hear her raise her voice above a pleasant conversational tone in correcting any of her seven or any of the orphan boys and girls." She was a musician and artist. "She rode well, played the piano, danced, played chess, but best of all she was a real Christian. Until she came into the church she had never thought of dancing as a sin. She said that she always read the Bible and prayed after getting home from a dance but she looked at it differently after she accepted Christ as her Guide." She must have kept her youth well, for "so little did she change that she was able

---

[10]*Reminiscences*, Clark, p. 50, 51.

to wear, on her fiftieth anniversary, the wedding dress she had worn at their wedding."[11]

To trace the members of the Clark family who have attained distinction would lengthen this narrative beyond bounds. Two of Addison's sons proved to be brilliant scholars. Addison, Jr., who was on the faculty of Add-Ran, was a brilliant writer of promise, but his work was cut short by early death. Carlton Clark served as a professor in the University of Oregon until his death in 1940. Two of the sons of Randolph came to be well known in Texas educational circles. Lee Clark, the eldest, was Superintendent of Schools in Wichita Falls, Gainesville, and held a number of prominent positions. He died in 1941. Joe Clark has devoted a long career as scholar at the head of the Department of History of the Sam Houston State Teachers College. He was recognized by T. C. U. in 1941 by the conferring of the LL.D. degree. Mrs. Louella Clark Holloway not only aided her husband in many a school position, but proved herself to be, in school and church, a worthy projector of the tradition of her talented Huguenot grandmother in character, personality, and influence. It was she, Randolph's eldest, who became his protecting companion after his wife's death in 1921. For fourteen years he made his home with the Holloways in Comanche, Cisco, Ranger, and Dallas, where he passed away in 1935 at the age of ninety-one. During those octogenarian years, he suffered an automobile accident, a broken hip, and a rattlesnake bite, a cataract which left him blind, and an operation which aided his sight. Through this and his natural senescence, Louella above all others served as nurse, companion, secretary, and consoler.

Tommy Clark had only one son, Wallace. He inherited the love for art from his talented father, and became one of the outstanding leaders of Texas in the field of Music Education, serving as the Head of the Department of Music in West Texas State Teachers College.

The wide open spaces of the Western frontier, with its nomadic cattle herders and extreme individualism, gave rich opportunity for the exploitation of the meanness of scoundrels who had left the old states between suns to avoid the sheriff. Unfortunately this rough class has received undue attention in the popular stories because they were more dramatic and vocal than the great bulk of settlers who were serious minded seekers of homes for

[11]Louella Clark Holloway, in a letter to Colby D. Hall, 1944.

their families. Among these were many families of genuine culture with admirable esthetic taste, creditable libraries and nearly always a virile Christian faith. The Clark family is a conspicuous example of this better type of frontier folk who brought from the old states the best ideals and despite the crudities of frontier living led in building a social order of which America will always be proud.[12]

[12]This chapter is intended to present the Clarks as a family in Texas history. Their several participations in the story will appear in the following chapters, as will estimates of Addison and Randolph, separately.

The following list of immediate descendants was furnished by Mrs. Louella Clark Holloway: Children of Joseph Addison Clark and wife Hetty D'Spain Clark: Addison Clark, Randolph Clark, two boys who died in infancy, Ida Aurelia Clark, (Mrs. Alex Nesbit), Joseph Clark (Stamford, Texas), Thomas Marshall Clark, Mary Clark (Mrs. Billy Jones) died a young mother, Franklin Clark (Dr. Frank Clark, Iowa Park), Amelia Clark, called Minnie (Mrs. J. B. Rogers of California), Rachael Clark, died in infancy.

Children of Addison Clark and wife Sallie McQuigg Clark: Adran (on tombstone spelled Add-Ran) Clark, buried in Pioneer Cemetery, Fort Worth, Jessie Clark (Mrs. Lyman Russell) Rockport, Addison Clark, Jr., Walter Clark died a child, Carlton Clark, died a Professor in University of Oregon; Bessie Clark (Mrs. Mooney); Zemula Clark (Mrs. Farley), California; Roy Clark, California.

Children of Randolph Clark and wife Ella Blanch Lee Clark: Randolph Lee Clark, (Died in Cisco, 1941); Louella Clark (Mrs. Robert F. Holloway), Brownwood; Annie Clark (Mrs. F. H. Chandler), Stephenville; John Jarrott Clark, Joseph Lynn Clark, Huntsville; Mary Blanche Clark (Mrs. D. M. Harster), Stephenville; Esther M. Clark (Mrs. E. T. Chandler), Stephenville.

Son of T. M. Clark and wife: Wallace Clark, Canyon, Texas.

11

## ❧ III ❧

# The Beginnings In Fort Worth 1869

T HE REAL BEGINNING OF THE CLARKS' EFFORTS to establish a school, out of which grew Texas Christian University, was in Fort Worth, Texas, in 1869. Addison Clark, aged twenty-seven, just married to Sallie McQuigg of Bonham, and having completed his work in the "Academy" under Charles Carlton, was ready to begin his career as educator. His brother Randolph says,

> Where to begin permanent work was the first question to be settled. There was no lack of places and material to work with; it was not of first importance to find the place that offered the best inducements for the present, but the place that would be the best for all time. Citizens of Fort Worth invited him to locate there. Being on the border of the undeveloped West and the rich agricultural lands of the East with an enterprising citizenship, Fort Worth seemed to fill all the requirements.[1]

The Fort Worth School was one of those worked up by a group of interested citizens. In this case they were very distinguished citizens: "Major K. M. Van Zandt, Dr. Howard Peak, Judge Milwee, and Milton Robertson formed themselves into a general welfare committee."[2] Col. John Peter Smith and Major J. J. Jarvis became a part of the group.

The spirit of prejudice soon began to put snags in the way. The Masonic building, used at first, had to be given up in 1869, and also an old renovated cement house, both because of religious prejudice. Addison could have taught the public school at an attractive salary if he had been willing to take the "iron bound oath"[3] which was required by the Reconstruction State Government that was running things at the time.

Out of this disturbing condition of religious prejudice and political corruption was brought forth some order by the efforts

[1]R. Clark, *Reminiscences*, pp. 33-34.
[2]*Ibid*, p. 34.
[3]*Ibid*, p. 34.

12

of a group of influential citizens who were the leaders of the local Christian Church. They proceeded to build a church house of brick, on Main Street between Fourth and Fifth Streets, and use it for both church and school. In addition they erected a box house 24 by 36 feet for the use of the school. Thus even the private school in Fort Worth was sustained by the efforts and support of the church. But these were only temporary provisions. It was a permanent school of large proportions that was intended, as is evidenced by many signs. So Mr. J. A. Clark "secured a plot of ground in the east suburb of the town, on which it was designed, in the near future, to erect an academy building. This was near the territory that afterward acquired the significant title, 'The Half Acre'." Mr. Randolph in referring to it obviously could not bring himself to write "Hell's Half Acre" as it was actually known. The property must have been in the region of Calhoun and Jones, between Ninth and Fourteenth Streets. "Addison had already built a residence on a block near this place."[4]

Fort Worth was a starting place for the cattle trails to the northern feeding grounds, and the markets. These brought multitudes of people, and prosperous business. But they also brought the riff-raff of population that follow in the train of such prosperity, especially on the frontier. Those leeches of society, barrooms and gambling halls were unrestrained. Even some notorious outlaw bands such as sprang up after the Civil War roamed the hills near by.[5] Disturbing as this was, the coming of the new railroad, the Texas and Pacific, in 1873 made it worse. "A change almost as sudden as the change in Texas weather came over the quiet village" with the coming of the railroad.*

While the citizenry rejoiced in prosperity, the school teacher believed that the town was spoiled as a place for a college.

> The town boys, the boys from the farms and ranches, rough but clean were dazzled by the glitter of vice and caught up like insects around a street lamp. It might have been the better part of valor to have remained and fought

---

[4] *Ibid*, p. 38.

[5]Randolph says in *Reminiscences*, page 40, "The Sam Bass gang operated in this section." But that was probably several years later for *The Texas Hand Book* says he robbed stage coaches between Dallas and Fort Worth later than 1877.

*It was the *promise* of the railroad that caused the excitement in 1873; it did not arrive, actually until 1876. The story is told in Paddock's *Early Days in Fort Worth* and in Donald Day's *Big Country Texas*.

the flames in an effort to prevent the fire from spreading but we thought more of saving those who could be kept out of the burning, and of building a place to prevent others from being caught. One thing was clear, that was not the place to build a school to bring students from abroad.[6]

For men to whom a school was primarily a character building project, this was no place for a location. So, it came to pass that the early home of Add-Ran was to be in the quiet and beauty of the Texas countryside, rather than in the future metropolis.

Did Add-Ran University really have its beginning in Fort Worth? Was it born in 1869? The history has not so been written, but a most excellent case can be made out for this contention. Addison Clark picked Fort Worth as "the place that would be best for all time."[7] The father, J. A. Clark, had faith enough in the place to purchase a plot of ground— "on which it was designed to erect an academy building."[8]

Addison "had selected Fort Worth as the place to do his life's work and had put three years of his life into it. Part of his life was planted there."[9] It was very difficult to persuade him to make the move.

Now that colleges are old enough to take some pride in their longevity, it has become customary to count the birth date as that of the earliest stream that flowed into its making. In many cases the persons who started the separate schools never had to do with the final collected institution. The early leaders were temporary, and the connection with the surviving school was rather tenuous. Much stronger than that is the claim of Add-Ran. The same leader, the same family group, the same purposes and ideals, the same administration with which the school began in Fort Worth in 1869, remained in charge until some time after it had come to be recognized as a distinct and distinguished University. True, its name, Add-Ran, was new at Thorp Spring, but even that name came out of Fort Worth, and the child for whom the name was coined lies buried there. Moreover, Fort Worth became again its home after a lapse of only thirty-seven years. In a very genuine sense Texas Christian University was born in Fort Worth in the year 1869.

[6]R. Clark, *Reminiscences*, p. 41, R. C. gives a vivid picture of the conditions and the coming of the railroad to Fort Worth.
[7]*Ibid*, p. 33.
[8]*Ibid*, p. 38.
[9]*Ibid*, p. 44.

14

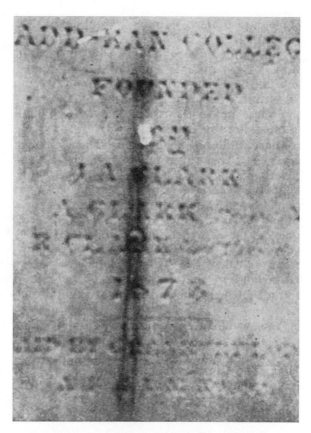

*Copy of the Cornerstone of the Main Building
at Thorp Spring, erected in 1878*

## ❧ IV ❧

# Add-Ran College at Thorp Spring 1873-1889

T HE LONG ROLLING PRAIRIES, reaching to far-stretching horizons, inspired many a sojourner in early Texas to write
panegyrics of praise to the folks back in the old states. The
darker green strips that traced by their lines the courses of the
streams, and the cross timbers that streaked athwart the land
like strips of lean in bacon sides, formed variety and framing
for the charming picture. It was in those nests of woods that the
camps of the Indians and the earliest homes of the settlers were
located. There were to be found wood and water, the first essen-
tials for primitive living. If some shady nook could add to these
necessities the luxury of a bubbling spring, it became famous on
the frontier.

The Comanche Indians had long used such a spot ten miles
east of Comanche Peak, three miles from the Brazos and forty
miles southwest of the U. S. Army fort named Fort Worth on
the banks of the Trinity. There was a never-failing creek (later Stroud's Creek), a perennial spring of clear cold water, also
a sulphur spring, which perhaps nature, and certainly imagination, could use for healing. What the Comanches named it is not
recorded, but by 1873 it had come to be known as Thorp Spring[1]
because "Old Man Thorp" had land certificates for nearly all the
land in that region, and Captain Milligan had persuaded him
that he could make a profitable health resort out of it.

A school, too, would attract people and it was needed, since
there was no public school. So Mr. Thorp erected "what was
at that time quite a commodious building,"[2] then sought out a
good teacher. The Clark's private school in Fort Worth must
have attained a goodly reputation by now, along with the name

[1]The spelling in the first catalog was Thorp's Springs (in the charter and in
an ad); the next three, Thorp's Spring; many later ones, Thorp Spring. This follows the natural tendency of language to wear off the difficult pronunciations.
The U. S. Post Office uses Thorp Spring.
[2]R. Clark, *Reminiscences*, p. 42.

ADDISON CLARK, Co-Founder, First President, 1873-99.
Total Years of Service, 29.

RANDOLPH CLARK, Co-Founder, Vice-President and Professor,
1873-95.

of Addison Clark as a teacher, for "interested parties from Thorp Spring came to try to induce him to move the school to that place." They were disappointed to discover that Addison was spending the summer "in different parts of the state, preaching, and incidentally making known the plans and purposes for building the school." He "could not be reached; this was before the days of railroads and telegraph lines."

So Randolph, junior to Addison by a year and a half, went with the messenger to

> look over the situation and advise for or against the move. The location was more ideal than I had pictured in my imagination. The Brazos River, the mountains, the valleys, the matchless never-failing Stroud Creek filled the requirements for student life. The people were not there to furnish the boys and girls for the school, but the rich valleys and prairies would invite settlers who would want the school and the children from the farms, ranches, and cities would come in numbers.[3]

Mr. Thorp was a good salesman, and "Mr. Randolph"[4] was a vivid dreamer, so the latter agreed to take the property at the price of $9,000.00[5] "subject to Addison's approval allowing time for us to realize from the Fort Worth property." The father, J. A. Clark, now fifty-eight years old and in vigorous health, next visited the beautiful vale, and was likewise charmed. He it was who drew up the papers and settled all of the business details.

When Addison returned from his summer round of meetings, and received the glowing reports, he

> did not become enthusiastic but showed mingled feelings of pleasure and disappointment. The financial part of the business gave him little concern; he left that to others, but he had selected Fort Worth as the place to do his life's work and put three years of his life into it; part of his life was planted there. He had taken his stand and was slow to retreat; he would have to take the matter under advisement.

---

[3]All quotations in this chapter which are not otherwise accredited are from R. Clark, *Reminiscences*, as is most of the information.

[4]About the campus, the brothers were usually addressed as "Mr. Addison" and "Mr. Randolph," or as "Brother Addison" and "Brother Randolph," partly to distinguish, partly with a flavor of respect and affection.

[5]Interview with the author.

Addison obviously felt under obligation to maintain the school in Fort Worth because he had advertised to do so. His sense of obligation was deep and unwavering always. So it was finally agreed that he, along with his father, would remain to conduct the school in Fort Worth for the entire session, employing an assistant, while Randolph should open up at the new site that September. Their reluctance was real, despite the fact that the untoward conditions had already led them to consider a move.

It was Randolph who had the more venturesome spirit. He it was who opened the school at Thorp Spring on the first Monday in September, 1873, with the very modest beginning of thirteen pupils.[6] But in those days admission to College did not close on a fixed date; there was no late registration fee. Each student could enter when he arrived and begin where he was in the book. "The beginning of the second month found an increase in numbers; students enrolled from the four adjoining counties. The session closed with an enrollment of seventy-five." The catalog of 1874 lists the names of 117 who attended during that first session.

The year's experience confirmed their faith. Addison moved to the grounds that summer. The father followed in the spring of 1875. A charter from the State of Texas was obtained, becoming operative April 11, 1874. Obviously they had in mind a permanent and large institution rather than just a local school. And the type of institution in their minds was clear.
This indicated their purpose:

The model in the eyes of educators of that early period was the Academy of Colonel Bingham in Georgia. He was an English officer who stayed in this country after the Revolutionary War. His Academy was known for thoroughness. When a man was known as a Bingham man, he was known to be thorough. . . . When General Lee left the army he was importuned to sell his name to several business enterprises, but he spurned them all and decided to give his life to education. He said 'The best thing any man can do for the South is to build it with citizens.' Addison Clark made

[6]His spirit was as modest, 47 years afterward when he wrote: "I was not surprised at the small attendance for that was about the number in the community who felt any interest in the school and we were not expecting boarders. In fact, there was no school; it was only a purpose formed in the mind, a matter of faith. It was a vision of things yet in the future. It was there to open the door of opportunity for any ready to enter."

the same statement about the same time without knowing that
Lee had taken that stand.[7]

The Academy was their model.

The house had been named a college when built and the
school had fallen heir to the title but Addison was very reluctant
to assume the responsibility of making it a college. He wanted to
take no chances of increasing the number of 'Soonover colleges,'
that had paraded before the public in Texas. The purpose was to
make a strong academy in which boys and girls would be taught
how to study, would be given a purpose in life, and a foundation
on which to build character. He finally consented to obtain a
charter for a college at Thorp Spring with the name Add-Ran
in memory of the little boy for whom the name was coined. . . .
In every catalog he promised less than he expected to do.

Addison's thoughtful discrimination raised another objection:
"He would not consent to its being called a Christian College; if it became Christian, it would be so by Christian teachers and would be
known by its fruit. He said to call a school Christian in contradistinc-
tion to other church schools in the state, was to denominationalize
the name."[8]

His avoidance of the title Christian as being denominational did
not mean any neglect of church affiliation. During that first year
when the school was only four months old and while Addison
was still in Fort Worth, they secured the endorsement of the
church body.

At a Convention of Delegates from congregations of the
Christian Church in different parts of the state, held at
Plano, Collin Co., December 30, 1873, Add-Ran College was
adopted and endorsed by an unanimous vote, as a College for
the Christian Brotherhood of Texas. The building and grounds
are, as yet, individual property; but it is none the less a Christian College, and the brethren are earnestly solicited to exam-
ine strictly into its merits.[9]

This is full evidence that they recognized the school as a "Church
College," if not belonging to, at least appealing to the "Christian

[7]R. Clark in Interview.
[8]His objection can better be appreciated when it is observed that throughout the
Add-Ran catalogs the particular communion was referred to, generally, as "the
Christian church," never as the Christian churches, as became general later, never
as the Church of Christ or Churches of Christ. "Disciples of Christ" was used once,
1894, p. 8 and "Disciples in Texas" once, 1890, p. 4.
[9]Catalog, 1874, p. 3.

21

Church" in Texas. This was seventeen years prior to the formal transfer of ownership and control of the property to the church, at which time the term Christian was incorporated in the title. The charter name adopted was "Add-Ran Male and Female College." Add-Ran was the name of Addison's first born, who had died and was buried in the Pioneer Rest Cemetery in Fort Worth. The name was coined from the first syllable of each of the brothers' names. The original spelling was Adran.[10] The "male and female" expression was a sign of progress, for practically all of the older colleges were for men or women separately. To admit both sexes was a bold adventure; to call attention to the fact in the title was to recognize its newness; to omit completely any further use of the title in this form shows how quickly they became accustomed to it. The "male and female" never appeared in any catalog at any time except this first one quoting the charter. That same catalog, although containing only 16 pages, devoted two of them to the quotation of an article by President Giltner of Eminence College (Ky.) in defense of co-education.

The faculty announced for the second session (1874-75), was A. Clark, Teacher in the Department of Ancient Languages and Mental Philosophy; R. Clark, Teacher in the Department of Physics, Chemistry and Mathematics, blank lines for English, Modern Languages and Primary; J. A. Clark, "Proprietor and General Business Manager," Mrs. Hettie Clark, Matron.

The panic was still having its effect, but the printed roster lists 164 students, 43 of whom were from 14 counties outside of Hood. The third session, 1875-76, had about the same total enrollment, but there were 82 students from 18 counties outside of Hood. The Clarks were circulating among the churches over the state preaching and announcing the College, especially during the summertime.

The fourth session, 1876-77, proved to be a critical one. It started off so well that Randolph thought it was opportune to take a leave for further study. He enrolled that September in Bethany College, W. Va., where his former teacher, Charles Carlton, had graduated. His stay was disappointingly brief, however; he was called back in February, 1877.[11] A head-on clash had occurred between J. A. Clark and Mr. Thorp over the

[10]So says Mrs. Louella Clark Holloway in a paper read at Brownwood, Texas, in 1944. A copy is in the T. C. U. Library.
[11]Interview; J. W. Holsapple, *Autobiography of an Octogenarian*, p. 55.

debt on the property, and there was "every prospect of eviction at once." The notes which the Clarks had given for the property were now due, but the panic had so reduced the value of their Fort Worth holdings that they could not pay the debt on time. They felt that Mr. Thorp had so profited by the deal that he could well afford to extend the time.

> Mr. Thorp did not offer us a bonus to have the school moved there, but offered to sell the building for what it had cost . . . considering the advantage of the location sufficient induce- ment . . . the school would enhance the value of the property and otherwise benefit the new country.

This feeling and their faith that "There was reasonable prospect that in the near future our property there would more than pay the debt, even with accumulated interest," made them expect an exten- sion of time. Randolph's view was that "we could have teased along with him and got on without a break."[12] But the diplomacy for "teas- ing along" was not forthcoming. Randolph was in Bethany, W. Va., and Addison, as previously indicated, left to others the financial part. So the negotiator in this case was the father, Joseph Addison Clark, and doubtless his best friends would not have classified him as a diplomat. As Randolph mildly put it: "The parties chosen to set- tle the business were not very careful each to please the other; not much effort was made to harmonize and settle to the interest of all." The very diplomatic quality of that sentence would make one wish that Randolph had been in charge. Neither was Mr. Thorp diplo- matic; so we judge from Randolph's quotation that he was incensed and demanded that they "get out and get out right now."[13] But Ran- dolph was careful to withhold blame.

> Mr. Thorp decided he had rather have the school building than to take chances of the Fort Worth property's paying for it. His proposition was accepted; the deeds were cancelled and the notes returned. The school was to pay rent at the rate of fifty dol- lars per month to the close of that session.

Mr. Thorp probably was the loser because he had a building on his hands which he could not use. The College was benefited because it proceeded to secure a property of its own and conse- quent permanency. It was, even then, in the excellent position,

[12]Interview.
[13]Interview.

with its "reputation of money value," to accept favorable offers to move elsewhere. And that very move might have been made but for the sense of obligation of Addison Clark.

Citizens of Granbury offered to build such a house as we would designate and give Addison a residence, to have the school moved only three miles. Other places offered buildings, some offered land of value that would have insured the erection of buildings and a foundation for an endowment.

"Two men from Fort Worth offered ten acres, the ground that was afterward given to the Methodist College."[14]

But against all these tempting offers was Addison's word that he had settled at that place permanently. On that assurance, several persons had moved there, bought property and made homes. Unless he could remunerate them for all the losses he would remain; besides he had no intention of adding to the number of failures.

He might not counter or control his associates in matters financial, but when he judged it was a matter of integrity, he was adamant. That was Addison Clark!

Here was crisis indeed! It was spring; by September there must be a school house. Randolph Clark recalled:

A plot of 6½ acres was secured at a cost of $650.00. Addison gave little attention to this phase of the enterprise. Father attended to the details of making contracts with workmen, paying for material and superintending the construction. The task of getting the money fell to one poorly qualified for such work. I had an architect make a draft of the building that we would try to erect. Father made a contract for the stone walls, agreeing to pay for each story as finished. The money for the first payment was obtained by the sale of Addison's home and my home in Fort Worth. These were sold at a price just equal to a year's rent on them in 1873. Another sale was of 320 acres of land belonging to my wife. This land is in Collin County, and the location tells its value, but not what was received for it. Another was wife's childhood home in Bonham—improvement and five acres of land within two blocks of the courthouse square. I do not look back on these transactions with any feelings of pride or assurance of having acted wisely. The only palliation is the purpose for which the sacrifice was made.

[14]Interview.

24

Randolph graciously recognizes the generosity of his wife:
"It is often the case that men get the credit and their praises
are sounded for doing things, when the reward and the praise
was due to the silent partner who toiled in the home. In the Great
Day, who will hear the Master say, 'Well done'?"
These sacrificial sales of family lands were not sufficient to pay
for the new building.

What these sales lacked of furnishing the money was raised
by the sale of scholarships covering tuition and board for four
years. This entailed a heavy burden and proved to be a continuing liability. To pay tuition and feed boys when the money for these things was in stone walls was more than a hardship—somebody had to suffer.[15]

Randolph said that this scholarship plan was his father's. If so,
he must have suggested it to the committee of the church convention which had inspected the property and had given a favorable
recommendation to the brotherhood in 1875, for they said, "We
have advised the proprietors to sell scholarships, full, perpetual,
to be sold for $500.00 to act as a lien on the property."[16]
But the plan was not original with any of these men. It was
one among the many strange schemes, unsafe financially and
unsound economically, which churches and schools in those
days frequently substituted for straight out donations. Alexander Campbell resorted to the "Scholarship Sale" plan in building Bethany College.[17] Kentucky University (Transylvania) sold
tuition scholarships with face value at fifty dollars, which kept
coming in for redemption for fifty years after. The market value
reduced to two dollars and the tuition was changed to two dollars,
while a matriculation fee was added at fifty to save the school
from ruin.[18] These scholarships at Add-Ran were worse, for they
included board as well as tuition, and must, therefore, have made
a terrific drain on the budget, a fact which the Clarks later came
to realize, distressingly.

[15]*Reminiscences*, p. 53.
[16]Catalog, 1875, p. 13.
[17]"Bethany College expects to sell 2500 scholarships at $50. a piece.
Each purchaser will be able to support one student in college successively from
fifteen to twenty-five years, which will reduce the tuition fees per annum to from
Two to Three Dollars. The scheme is original with Alexander Campbell and it
will make our college extensively useful." Millenial Harbinger, March, 1847.
[18]The author used one of these two dollar scripts when he enrolled in
K. U. in 1899.

By such strenuous efforts and costly sacrifice the new building was erected, not, indeed, by the promised September, but in time for the following spring term, temporary arrangements being made meanwhile. The new structure, even this first section of it, surpassed in size and impressiveness the original Thorp building which had been described as "quite a commodious building."

An unusual feature appeared in the life of the school in the year 1877, an Orphan Department. It appears to have been a combination of an effort to help finances and to serve the unfortunate. Scholarships of $133.33 were solicited, the interest on which was to pay the tuition of an orphan. "General R. M. Gano was appointed trustee and financial agent . . . all donations should be made through him." The General was a preacher and land promoter of that generation, who was probably the proponent of this idea. The plans went so far as to announce[19] that "the Board of Directors of the Christian Orphan Home have purchased the buildings and grounds of Add-Ran College and have added to the College the Orphan School." This proved to be only a paper plan. It terminated with the Home being "near the College and the children having the benefit of the tuition in the college."

After the first five years of a struggling start, the next decade was one of steady growth in students, in faculty, of ever widening recognition and prestige—and of continued financial struggle. "The school had made some reputation for thorough work and high moral standards. Emphasis was placed on doing well every task undertaken and on clean living."

This reputation, and the continuing contacts with the churches over the state through preaching, had increased the attendance. There were hundreds of local schools, each drawing from a horse and buggy radius. The Clarks had no such restricted aims, despite Randolph's modest statement of the start. And it did not long retain its local appearance. The counties represented were nine the first year, fourteen the next, and then eighteen, twenty-four, thirty-four, thirty-one, twenty-six, and in 1882-83, fifty-four counties. After that it was about "sixty or more," as the catalog itself often announced.

By the eighth year the number of students from outside Hood County surpassed the number of locals, 166 to 133. This is really surprising, especially in view of the fact that the public school

[19]Catalog, 1880, p. 9, 1881, p. 13.

was included in the local enrollment, being a part of the total attendance. And only forty-four of the 166 came from "adjoining counties." To draw 122 students in that day from distances more than forty miles was a notable achievement. It gives evidence of the high prestige the school so early attained. The banner county was Collin, as it was, on the average, through all these early years. The next was Parker, then came Tarrant and Dallas. It is safe to say that during the first ten year period more than seventy-five counties were represented in the attendance, and the record shows that the list increased each year. Add-Ran took on the proportions of a state-wide institution early in its career. The enrollment climbed steadily till 1883 when it reached 435, then hovered about 300 to 400, reaching 445 in 1892-93, the largest year.[20]

The Board of Trustees, during the years of private ownership was selected by the Clarks, and served in advisory capacity only. Its membership was not stable. Beginning with 1883-84, men outside the local ones were used: J. H. Caruthers of Palo Pinto; Chalmers McPherson and J. B. Gibson of Waxahachie; W. K. Homan, Caldwell; C. C. Couch, Italy; G. D. Harrison, Longview. The next two years all of these were left off except Homan, and all members were local except R. L. Ragsdale of McKinney, an ex-faculty member. The next year most of the Trustees were teachers on the faculty.

The Presidency of the Board was kept in the family, and the secretaryship also except that in 1884 Chalmers McPherson served as Secretary and in 1888 F. O. McKinsey. An entirely new group appeared in 1889 when the change was made to church ownership.[21]

During these years of private ownership, life went along under typical frontier conditions. Conveniences for living were scarce, luxuries unknown. The accounting for an institution that was a family affair was necessarily simple, and the struggle to make ends meet was constant. At first there were no dormitories, the students living with teachers preferably, or with approved families.[22] Beginning with 1883 the girls were required to board in the dormitory and the boys were privileged to board with the matron or not. By 1888 "neat comfortable cottages for boys and young men have been erected on the col-

[20]The annual enrollments are tabulated in Appendix II.
[21]A complete list of Trustees and officers appears in Appendix.
[22]Catalog, 1275, p. 11.

27

lege grounds."[23] The popular name for this housing was "the sheep shed." Boarding, shifted about as it was between the school and the homes, was not counted on as a source of income. The Clarks' generosity with impecunious students would have consumed any profit, at best. Student fees were a poor source of income, as is indicated by the rates. College tuition for nine months was, at first, $50, dropped in 1876 to $40.[24] For the Intermediate it was usually $40, and for Primary $20. The lower grades served as the public school for which tuition was paid by the State. This fact never appears in the catalog, but is evidenced by some actions of the Trustees.[25]

The consciousness of building a school for the brotherhood led naturally to a call on the brethren for contributions. This call, however, was to individuals rather than to the churches. In that day no conscience or custom of the churches had been developed toward contributing to organized work. The Texas Missionary Society was not organized until 1886, and it ran on a very small budget and against a tide of strong and bitter opposition to all organization.

The appeals to individuals was, at first, a matter of personal contact by the Clarks, as they went about holding meetings among the churches. "Large hearted brethren are showing their appreciation by coming to our help in the erection of new buildings. There is yet opportunity for others to do likewise" is the modest language of the "Greeting" in the 1882 catalog.

That some of the large hearted brethren actually did come to the rescue is evidenced by a cheerful report in the "Greeting" of 1884.

> The sweetest music that has fallen on the ears of our friends was the statement made by Add-Ran creditor, Mr. Bush of Plano. At the close of the session just ended, he arose and said, 'I have heard since my arrival that the college is greatly embarrassed by debt; I wish to say to one and all that satisfactory arrangement is being made for paying all that is owed except $800, and that will not be due 'til next January. The college is unembarrassed and will go on nobly.'

[23]Catalog, 1888, p. 35.
[24]In 1880 it was $31.50 for a seven months term, which was a temporary experiment.
[25]Minutes, September, 1892: Ordered the Secretary to collect tuition from "students who remain in college before and after the free school term expired."

Despite this optimistic note in 1884, debts accumulated and the financial strain was increasing.

It was the encouragement of such devoted friends and their profound faith in the purpose which dominated their lives that enabled them to invest such sacrifice and keep going through these hard pioneer years of their beloved enterprise.

*The Spring*

## ∞ V ∞

# Add-Ran Christian University at Thorp Spring 1889-1895

THE YEAR 1889 marked a definite epoch in the life of Add-Ran. In September of that year, on the initiative of the Clarks, it came under the ownership and control of the Christian Churches of Texas, and at the will of the new Directors its name was changed to Add-Ran Christian University. The process by which this transfer was made seemed very simple to a typical Disciple, J. W. Holsapple, in his *Autobiography of an Octogenarian*, says:

> It was during this Convention (1889 in Fort Worth) that the Clarks turned over Add-Ran to the brotherhood. Addison and Randolph both addressed the Convention in making the presentation. They recited the history of the school up to the time, telling, among other things, of its beginning in Fort Worth when the city was only a village and of their struggles and troubles when it began to grow into a city.

No need was felt by him to refer to any contract, any resolution of acceptance or any machinery set up for the management of the school, for the Convention was a mass meeting of the brethren, not delegated, and at that time not incorporated. This was in accord with the tradition of the congregationally organized communions. Truly their validity is spiritual rather than legal.

Proper legal steps were taken, however. The Clarks made a deed "to a board of trustees for the church." So, in place of the old advisory board, selected by the Clarks, there came in now a new board with full control, being trustees for the churches. There were twelve members, nine provided at the time of the Convention, the other three selected by the Board itself at its first meeting, September 27, 1889. Under the leadership of its lawyer-president J. J. Jarvis, the Board got right down to business at its first meeting, the minutes of which, fortunately, are preserved.[1]

The minutes reveal that the Trustees took matters in hand. They met to elect a faculty; they set salaries, employed solicitors, planned an endowment campaign. Once they over-ruled a recommendation of A. Clark on a matter of salary and the selection of a teacher. They even tackled thorny disciplinary problems, and finally voted down the recommendations of the President and Vice-President by relaxing the rule on the use of tobacco.[2] They voted that the Executive Committee be "instructed to overhaul the books and get them in proper shape and meet once a month."[3]

The new charter, approved October 5, 1889, was doubtless written by the new President of the Board, who was an eminent lawyer of decisive disposition, but his wife, Ida Van Zandt Jarvis, probably gave him some suggestions, for according to information given by Mrs. Mason in an interview with Mrs. Jarvis she "wrote the charter."[4]

Actual operation under the new charter, therefore, began in the autumn of 1889, but there was no opportunity for catalog

---

[1]"The Trustees of Add-Ran Christian University met by agreement at the University office, September 27, 1889, with the following names present: J. P. Smith, J. J. Jarvis, J. N. Votaw, J. J. Collins, A. Clark, T. A. Wyth, A. Irby, R. Clark. J. J. Jarvis was elected Chairman.

"The committee, J. P. Smith and J. J. Jarvis, appointed to prepare a charter for the University, reported. The charter reported by them was read, discussed and adopted, article by article.

"The By-laws for the government of the Board of Trustees were read and adopted.

"It was resolved that all money or property, whether received by donation or otherwise, be held by the Board in trust and not as capital stock.

"It was decided that all donations and paid-up subscriptions shall be used only to secure necessary grounds, for putting up necessary buildings and laboratories, and to secure an endowment fund.

"The Board went into permanent organization by electing J. J. Jarvis, President and R. Clark, Secretary.

"The following persons were elected to be members of the Board of Trustees of Add-Ran Christian University: J. J. Jarvis, President, J. P. Smith, J. J. Collins, W. H. Lemmons, E. C. Smith, A. Clark, R. Clark, Secretary, Charles Carlton, H. M. Bandy, T. A. Wyth, A. S. Henry, Alf. Irby."

"A. Clark was nominated and elected President of Add-Ran Christian University. The present faculty and employees of Add-Ran College were elected to fill like places in Add-Ran Christian University."

(Minutes of the Board of Trustees for Sept. 27, 1889.)

[2]Minutes, March 6, 1891.

[3]Minutes, June 6, 1890.

[4]*The Beginnings of T. C. U.*, p. 63.

announcement of it until the catalog of 1890, which recognized the new arrangement with the following hearty "Greetings":

> Add-Ran Christian University greets you with her first annual catalogue—the eighteenth of Add-Ran College . . . The University is not so much the outgrowth of Add-Ran College as it is the development of a long felt desire among the Disciples in Texas to have an institution of higher Christian education. The cause of the great brotherhood of our great state demands this. There is not an endowed institution of learning in our brotherhood in Texas. Add-Ran College has been given with all its experience of seventeen years and all its possessions, to the University. A new Charter with a new board of incorporators and directors has been obtained, and the University has been launched—the omens favorable, and the winds inviting. The directors are planning for an endowment of $100,000, and something has already been done in that direction.[5]

Aside from this "Greetings" and the use of the word "University" instead of "College," the catalog gave no indication of the change in status. The faculty, administration and other routine of the school went on as usual. In the 1894 catalog a "Brief History" stated simply, "In 1890[6] the proprietors of Add-Ran College made a donation of all buildings and property to the Christian Church of Texas."

That "something already done in that direction" referred to in the "greeting" above, was the employment of two Financial Agents, "Randolph Clark at $100 a month, and H. M. Bandy at $75, but he is to get his salary out of the funds that he may collect." The appeal of the Trustees was obviously and frankly to the church brotherhood, as shown by their messages in the catalog. "This is a University for and by the Disciples of Christ.[7] Every trustee, as provided in the charter, must be a member of the Christian Church in good standing; so must all the professors and teachers." Again, "They (the churches) are determined to make it one that is equal to the best denominational Universities in the South, and that they will endow it."[8]

[5]Catalog of 1890, p. 4.
[6]The date was really 1889; others since then have made the same error, doubtless due to the fact that the first announcement appears in the 1890 catalog.
[7]Catalog, 1894, p. 8, "Disciples of Christ" is used to refer to the church communion; in Catalog 1890, p. 4 "Disciples in Texas" was used. So far as observed these are the only times these expressions are used. See foot-note in Chapter IV for further remarks on this subject.

At that time there was no systematic plan of gathering financial support from the churches for the general interests of the church program, and very little conscience had been aroused among the members for such giving. The frontier was still in the attitude of individualism. They were just beginning to suspect that a "free church" implied freedom to support its program. The appeal to the emulation of their religious neighbors was natural. The neighbors were in the same state of progress and were making similar appeals. All of them, no doubt, were stimulated by the rapid rising of the young University of Texas, which had just started in 1881.

One of the best accomplishments of the new order was the securing of Major J. J. Jarvis as a supporter and leader. His chairmanship of the Board, being the first under church control, initiated the policy of a strong personality, and a rather long term of service, for this position. He was one of the group of pioneer citizens (including his brother-in-law, Major K. M. Van Zandt) who had fostered the school in Fort Worth. A distinguished attorney, a man of education and of some means, he did not look on his position as merely honorary but as one of responsibility.

He seldom missed a meeting. His financial contribution was as generous as his devotion of time. "He at once began the work of erecting new and large additions to the building. This he put up practically at his own expense." The addition, a four-story stone with seven good rooms is known as "Jarvis Building".[9] For his contributions and leadership the Trustees passed formal resolutions naming the third wing (East) after him. The name was perpetuated in the girls dormitory on the Fort Worth campus.[10] "He pledged $500 (at the Fort Worth Convention in 1889) to the work and where it was to come from he didn't know. Before five years were over he had not only given that sum, but $35,000 more for improvements, debts, and teachers' salaries." So runs the testimony of his wife, Mrs. Ida Van Zandt Jarvis.[11]

In later years, again he personally financed the Clark Brothers in the Add-Ran Jarvis College on the same old site in 1904-1909.

---

[8]Catalog, 1894, p. 7.
[9]Catalog, 1894, pp. 6-7.
[10]Minutes, 3-24-1892, p. 28.
[11]Mason, p. 117.

How much of his interest was stirred by his good wife, Ida Van Zandt Jarvis, cannot be ascertained; but it is certain that if he had not been interested on his own account, she would have inspired him into some activity. For her unique and capable personality became a vital factor in the school in Thorp Spring and continued long after his death till her own end in 1935. She was a frequent visitor on the campus, especially during the years when her son, Van Zant Jarvis was a student (B. A. 1895), and became an unofficial adviser. She delighted especially, as she related years after, in loosening up the rigid discipline of the times.

Her own story of his enlistment in this enterprise shows she had something to do with it.

The first serious quarrel between Mrs. Jarvis and her husband was over the question of which school their son, Van Zandt Jarvis, should attend. Major Jarvis was in the Senate at Austin that year and had planned to put his son in the State University to study law. Mrs. Jarvis wanted him to go to Thorp's Springs. The discussions were many and no decision had been reached when the State meeting of the Christian Church met in Fort Worth. When Mr. Jarvis came home he said he supposed it was decided. The church had accepted the gift of Add-Ran College and he was President of the Board.[12]

It was through her influence years later as a prominent leader in Church Missions that her husband donated a section of land near Hawkins, Texas, for negro education, out of which grew Jarvis Christian College. She humorously told often of giving the land which her husband had received as an attorney fee and "wasn't worth anything any how but to pay taxes on."

What were the causes which impelled the Clarks to donate their school to the church? Several currents were flowing in this direction, the simplest of which was expressed by Randolph thirty years later in his *Reminiscences,*

If the college was to continue beyond the lives of the present workers it must have endowment. These might toil till worn out and others might not be found to take their places. It was decided to give the property to a board of trustees for the church. This was thought to be the surest and quickest way to get the college endowed and firmly established . . . All assets, visible and invisible, were a free gift to the cause of Christian education.

[12]Mason, p. 117.

The title to the property was held by J. A. Clark, A. Clark and R. Clark. Their inventory appraised its value at $43,000, besides two tracts of land 640 acres in West Texas, and 160 acres in Kaufman County. "There was a $5,000 indebtedness." Thus went into the donation all of the accumulations of the several Clark families' savings and inheritances—with one exception. The father, J. A. Clark, had "not given any money but he had given his time and his labor while the house was being erected and for many years later without any compensation." The brothers paid him $2,000 for his share and "he joined in making the deed to the trustees."

To secure that much desired endowment was one of the first moves of the new trustees, as we have already observed. It proved to be many years before this objective was accomplished, yet the move then made was doubtless necessary to this end.

That the $5,000 indebtedness increased rapidly is evidenced by a motion in the Board "that the executive committee be authorized to make a loan of Seven Thousand Dollars, or as much thereof as may be necessary to discharge the indebtedness of the university."[13] In fact the annual deficit was doubtless more threatening than the amount of the debt itself. One cause of this deficit is shown by the remark, "We kept a crowd of boys. She (Mrs. Randolph) made a home for them and the money for this board expense went to build and equip the college."[14] Very likely the claims for the scholarships were still coming in and had to be redeemed although the money received for them had long since been used in rock walls. Moreover, the teachers were underpaid and often tardily paid. "As the world estimates pay for work done, these teachers received little compensation for their labors. Sessions passed in which the janitor received more than the president of the University."[15] When the new Board took over it was voted to "allow board and tuition for one student for what the University owed" Professor R. L. Ragsdale for his teaching for the session of 1889-90. It was discovered that other teachers were in similar situations so it was voted "to allow teachers to whom the University owes as much as Five

---

[13]Motion by C. N. Boynton, Minutes, September 9, 1890.
[14]Mason, p. 88.
[15]*Reminiscences*, p. 50.

Hundred Dollars to enter one student and receive board and tuition thereon."[16]

Another long desired objective was accomplished by the new administration: the completion of the College Building. The design had been already prepared. It was to balance off the structure with a new right wing. It was on its way in 1891 and was completed in the fall of 1892.[17] As stated before, it was largely financed by Major Jarvis. The completed structure was indeed a magnificent one for the time. A fire later (after 1895) and a restoration, gave it a final form somewhat different from the architects drawings in the catalog. For over half a century it loomed, a glistening pile to the eye of the traveler coming up the highway from Stephenville to Granbury. In 1941, because of the crumbling of the mortar, two of the wings were razed leaving standing only a token of its old self.

After all, the donation of the school to the church was following the trend of the times. All private colleges were under similar pressures and were seeking permanency by the support of either the church or the state. Moreover, to turn over their beloved institution to the church was the most natural thing for the Clarks to do. We fail to take the true measure of these men unless we recognize that theirs had to be a Christian school because Christianity was so prominent in their lives and in their philosophy of life. They were more concerned to build character than to teach books. They had returned from the War with the recognition that the Southland had to be rebuilt. As Randolph put it:

> There were opportunities for young men in various fields of labor; there were temptations for gain in lawful and unlawful ways. The need was for men to give unselfish service in rebuilding on better foundations, all the business of the country.[18]

The Jarvises had a great admiration for the Clarks, believing them to be giants in religion, but babes in finance.[19] Randolph modestly confessed his limitations in financial lines and testified that "the financial part of the business gave (Addison) little concern; he left that to others."[20] "As the world estimates pay

[16]Minutes, June 19, 1891.
[17]Catalog, 1891, 1892.
[18]*Reminiscences*, p. 29.
[19]So the son Van Zandt Jarvis frequently testified.
[20]*Reminiscences*, pp. 43, 44.

for work done," to borrow a Randolph phrase, they were doubtless impractical. They had undertaken to earn enough off the school to pay for buildings and equipment in addition to operation. Further, they were caring for a considerable number of impecunious students and frequently accepting barter in lieu of cash. Then there was the scholarship money that had gone into stone walls, while the students still had to be fed and taught. On the other hand it should not be forgotten that they did not calculate on a profit-making basis. "As the world estimates" was different from their way. The world would not have sunk its own private fortune in a school in the first place. And the world would not estimate the value of an awkward youth so highly as to make it minimize debts and deficits. Such was the spirit of sacrifice and service that went into the founding of Add-Ran.

*The Live Oaks on Thorp Spring Campus.*

# ∾ VI ⊱

# The Features of a Frontier College

MODERN SCHOOLS OWE MUCH to the experience of those schoolmasters who labored under primitive conditions Such stories as that of Add-Ran become a thesaurus of experience from which educators may draw, and doubtless have drawn more than they are aware. Incidentally, much of the history and especially the personnel will be revealed in this study of "features." For it is observed that personalities can best be presented along with the studies which they taught. This combining of the study and the teacher is especially fitting for a generation in which the personality of the teacher counted for so much.

It would be strange to find a college of that period whose curriculum was not based on the classics, and Add-Ran was not strange; it was normal. The classic pattern is recognized in the names of the six departments announced in the first catalog: "1. Ancient Languages 2. English Language 3. Mathematics 4. Physical Sciences 5. Mental and Moral Sciences 6. Social and Civil History."

The Department of Mental and Moral Sciences introduced the student to the schools of thinking in philosophy, the technic of logic, the new field of psychology, and the evidences of Christianity. Whom did these frontier lads have to interpret to them the accumulated wisdom of the ages? No less than Addison Clark, a man of towering intellect, open mind, insatiable reading, balanced character, sufficient to rank him among the great in education.

The basic field of mathematics was taught by J. E. Jarrott until 1877 and by Ed Milwee until 1882, both of them having graduated in the first class, 1876. Then followed E. C. Snow, quiet, steady, forceful teacher, master in the field, who held the chair, with some intermissions[1] until his retiring age, and during 1899-1902 served as Acting President. As the head of

[1]In 1892, Professor Snow was granted "a leave of absence for one year to restore his health," without salary. Minutes, 3-24-92. He returned in 1899.

Mathematics in 1892, came a recent graduate, Robert F. Holloway, who was to play a large part in the life of the school at Thorp Spring and in public school circles later. Having married the eldest daughter of Randolph Clark, Louella, he had the privilege of teaching nearly all the younger children of both families. He served also as Business Manager of the school in the last years at Thorp Spring, as he did with R. Clark years later at Lancaster, Hereford, and in the Add-Ran Jarvis College.

The Department of Ancient Languages was one of the foundation stones in the curriculum. Addison Clark himself taught this at first, and occasionally filled in through the years. Two of the Add-Ran graduates, trained under him, carried these subjects: G. E. Carpenter in 1880-82, F. O. McKinsey 1884-89. Although these were young men, home products, and without experience, they proved by their later records to be men of superior ability. The former made an outstanding record as a business man in Plano, the latter attained distinction as District Judge, and later Assistant State Attorney General. He was honored by his Alma Mater with the honorary degree of LL. D. in 1935, three years before his death.

In 1894 they called to the Chair of Ancient Languages, Professor T. Louis Comparette, thus expressing their desire to draw into the faculty graduates of the Eastern universities. He was an accomplished scholar, a gentleman of genuine culture, a bachelor, a man from the east who made himself congenial in the unaccustomed west.[2]

The field of the natural sciences was just coming into recognition at this time in college curricula.[3] Randolph Clark handled these subjects with the aid of the College Physician, Dr. J. S. Poyner (1880-83) until 1886, when another product of Add-Ran, W. B. Parks, who had made this his field, was put in charge. He was of the class of 1886, began teaching science in 1887 and continued, with seasons out for graduate study, and a few years with R. Clark, until he resigned in 1916.

Two other "departments" were less continuous in scope and leadership. These were English, and Social and Civil History. The latter listed such sub-heads as "Church History, Bible Manual, Carter's General History, Wayland's Political Economy."

[2]The author received his introduction to the Greek language from this excellent scholar and with it a lasting inspiration for the study of philology, and an appreciation for the charm of the classics.

[3]Bacon College, organized in 1836 by leaders in the Christian Church, revealed by its name their interest in science.

In 1884, they began to call these "schools" instead of "departments." For a while there was no "school" covering the social sciences, although some courses were named, as "General History" and "History of England." In 1880-82, Ed Milwee was teacher of Political Economy and Mathematics.

The Department of English Language in the beginning catalog described its scope chiefly by listing the textbooks used. These included Webb's *Model Definer*, Webb's *Etymology*, Pinneo's *Grammar and English Teacher*, Quackenbos' *Composition and Rhetoric*, Hart's *English and American Literature*, also Holmes' *U. S. History* and Goodrich's *History of England*. No doubt the same teacher taught both English and History but the teacher is not named. When the term "schools" was used in 1884, there was no "school of English" but English Grammar and Composition appear in the list of subjects taught. English and History were taught by J. E. Jarrott (1875-77), Ed Milwee (1880-86) and R. L. Ragsdale (1887-89). By this time the "school" of English and History had a steady place, but yet as one. It was a much later generation that separated them into two fields.

These six departments constituted not only the bulk, but the total of the curriculum. Other subjects were taught, but they were not considered as a part of the college curriculum. They were extra, both in course and in cost. While there was a gradual evolution from this rigid separation, which we shall soon notice, in the beginning the bar was put up in no ambiguous terms. For the second catalog warned the girls (only it said "females"),

As lessons in drawing, painting, and embroidery, encroach upon the time necessary to the studies of the regular course, it is advised that the regular course should first be gone through, or that it should be partially dispensed with during the time devoted to these ornamental branches.

The previous catalog had mentioned another subject that seemed to have a vogue in many girls schools of that day: wax-works. It was announced: "Special contract with the teacher in the Department of Drawing, Painting and Wax-works, Embroidering and Cutting." These "ornamental branches" were not only extra, they had to be contracted privately with the teacher. Obviously, Add-Ran was making moves to get away from some of the frills of the female finishing schools of the day, for wax-works was not mentioned after the first catalog.

The department of Modern Languages was definitely outside the fold. Add-Ran was probably forward, rather than tardy in offering it and later in accepting it for credit. But at first it was among the "extra branches" at an extra fee of ten dollars a month, or "at the teacher's price," payable to the teacher. It was taught by a succession of teachers: Lucy Rutherford in 1876, Emma Bruhn in 1877 (she also taught needle work), Clara Wilmeth in 1882, Mattie Schultz in 1889-90 and finally Miss Mattie Wade, after it had become a "department," and a few years before she married one of the professors, W. B. Parks. After that Modern Language was accepted as a substitute for the classic language, if a student took the B. S. degree.

It was really Tommy Clark who laid the foundation for this department. At first he taught instrumental music, then added vocal, and in 1880 began to teach French and German, as an extra course without credit toward a degree. When Mattie Schultz came in 1889-90 he enrolled for these subjects as a student under her and received his B. A. degree in 1893. Tommy Clark was a true pioneer, not so much interested in felling trees and breaking prairie as he was in blazing a trail of recognition for fields not yet accepted, and awakening his fellows to an appreciation of the beautiful. He taught instrumental music when it was unpopular, the modern languages when they received no credit, and laid the foundation for early recognition of both of these fields. He was the founder of the college magazine, "The Student," later known as "The Collegian." He even established a print shop which printed the magazine. And the catalog from 1880 through 1892 (except two years) was printed in that shop. "Tommy Clark Printer" appeared on the 1880 issue.

He had some unorthodox ideas of education and labored to make them orthodox. Whether his position as a younger brother in the family helped him or hindered him in his effort at progressiveness, we cannot tell. After 1892, his name does not appear in the catalogs. About that time, he established a school for girls, "Bay View College" at Portland, Texas, which became a center of culture for many decades, until it was destroyed by storm, and he retired. He was truly a man ahead of his time.

Another field that was hesitatingly entered was the Commercial School. There was some hesitance in incorporating mere business training in a college, and definite criticism of a "Business College" was expressed in an article on "Practical Education" in the catalog of 1884 from the pen of J. A. Clark. But in an effort to adapt this field to college teaching, courses in Bookkeeping were announced that year under Professor R. B. Whitton, followed in 1890 by A. M. McKinney. In 1891 a new personality entered this field, fresh with his B. A. in 1890 and destined to build a place for business education in the College. This was A. C. Easley, a redheaded dynamo of energy and a Christian impregnated with all the high idealism of the Clarks. Within two years the "School of Commerce" had three pages of space in the catalog and a list of graduates who afterward had distinguished careers in business.

After the initiation given to it by Tommy Clark, the Fine Arts teaching blossomed out in 1884 with Mrs. Anna D. Bradley teaching music and Miss Ola Thompson, art. Mrs. Bradley had with her at the time her young son, Kenneth, who in later years became the founder of the Chicago Music Conservatory and of the American Association of Schools of Music. She was followed by Miss Dessie Pickens, who continued until 1895, even after she had married Professor E. C. Snow. On the untimely death of Miss Thompson, the teaching of Art was done by her cousin, Miss Sallie Cayce.

It should not be overlooked that the Preparatory, Intermediate and sometimes Primary departments were going on all of the time. Obviously, public school children were included among these, by some arrangement, for on one occasion the Treasurer was instructed to collect the tuition from the children who stayed after the public school term had closed.

The "Industrial Department" was a dream that recurred. The idea was incorporated in the Orphans School. It was advocated by J. A. Clark in the catalog, and cherished by Randolph Clark all his life. In 1893, an "Industrial Department" was announced with the statement that "present facilities are by no means meager—expect to be increased. Donations are asked," etc. It is not clear just what was covered by the "Industrial Department"; it probably afforded employment for boys to earn a part of their expenses.

The efforts to establish teacher training appear more than once. In 1875 comes the statement "And then we have a Normal Department."[4] In 1892 the Trustees voted "to prepare a course for Teachers Certificates." It was at this time that the Add-Ran work was recognized by the State Department of Education for certification. A full Department of Education in the school came later.

[4]Catalog, 1875, p. 4.

42

Although the second catalog announced, "The College has a large faculty" (it numbered nine), emphasis was really on quality:

Those who compose it are earnest in their work, and spare no pains for the moral and mental improvement of those committed to their charge. . . . As permanency is our aim, we shall make no changes in teachers except when absolute necessity or the welfare of the institution demand it. Frequent changes of teachers is the great misfortune with the schools of our State.

Then follows a plea for the spirit of consecration to the profession.[5] Here we sense the very points which are being stressed in educational circles in our own times: individual guidance, character education, and devotion to the profession. Perhaps it was because the Clarks desired to perpetuate this spirit that they called into the faculty their own graduates, with frequency.[6]

There is one feature stressed by modern schools, however, that was entirely lacking in Add-Ran, namely, degrees. Only a diploma was promised "when a student has passed an approved examination in the regular college courses."[7] Two years later "appropriate degrees" were promised, but not named.[8] This naming was done for the first time in 1888, as Bachelors of Arts, of Science, and of Literature, and these degrees were added to the names of the graduates in the catalog. Eighty-one per cent of the degrees granted were the B. A., which required Greek and Latin; the B. S. required a little more science, the B. L. more literature; both omitted the foreign language requirement. Up to 1899, twenty-three B. S. degrees were given (the last one in 1899), and three B. L. degrees, two in 1894, one in 1896. The accumulated "Alumni List" began to be printed in full in the catalog from 1891, but no degrees were listed with the names until beginning with 1903.

Degrees were granted, however, earlier than they were listed in the catalog, and it is probable that the graduates themselves did some urging for their recognition, for it is observed that the names of three of the early graduates appear as faculty mem-

[5]Catalog, 1875, p. 4.
[6]Among these Add-Ran alumni who taught were: J. E. Jarrott, '76; Edwin Milwee, '76; G. E. Carpenter, '77; F. O. McKinsey, '82; W. B. Parks, '86; R. L. Ragsdale, '87; A. C. Easley, '90; R. F. Holloway, '92.
[7]Catalog, 1875, p. 10.
[8]Catalog, 1877, p. 16.

bers, with degrees.[9] The teachers were even more slow in securing the printing of degrees after their names for this was not done until 1893.

There is ample historical explanation for this minimizing of degrees; it was no disparagement of learning. These were men of the frontier, where a man's worth was reckoned by his own individual record, without regard to genealogy, rank, or distinctions bestowed. Also, these men belonged to that generation whose normal years for schooling were claimed by service in the Civil War; they were at a disadvantage and would be inclined to disparage any superiority claimed by those who studied while they fought. It is probable too, though not certain, that the spirit of the Disciples Movement affected them. Alexander Campbell in his earlier period, up to 1830, severely excoriated all emphasis on titles, ranks and distinctions among the clergy, even the title "Reverend." This was in harmony with the spirit of the American Constitution in forbidding titles to governmental personages. It was a part of the spirit of the frontier. The prejudice against educated preachers on the frontier is common knowledge. This general spirit took the form among some leaders, of opposition to college degrees. For instance, the College of the Bible at Lexington, Kentucky, under such influential personalities as Robert Graham and J. W. McGarvey, refused to grant degrees to graduates, awarding only "diplomas." This persisted to the passing of the last of these men in about 1910.

With such a background, it was natural, almost inevitable, that these Add-Ran pioneers should minimize degrees, even if they did not oppose them. Having accounted for the neglect of degrees by the influence of the environment, we must reckon with the fact that the founders and first faculty were themselves without degrees. That fact, however, is a product of this same environment and not a sign of lack of learning. Charles Carlton, himself a graduate of Bethany College under Alexander Campbell, restrained announcement of degrees, Addison Clark completed all the requirements at Carlton College, and even became an instructor there; but he was given no degree. Randolph Clark, who did not advance as far as his brother, went to Bethany but returned shortly on account of family conditions, and had no degree. J. A. Clark studied in the University of

---

[9]These were Milwee, '76; Carpenter, '77 and Miller, '81, in the catalog of 1880, 1881, 1882. Another, Jarrott, '76 taught three years but died before 1880 when they first printed these degrees.

Alabama and used his schooling to make himself a surveyor. His ability as lawyer, editor and teacher was acquired largely by his own efforts, in keeping with the spirit of self-reliance native to pioneers. He belonged to the home-spun era and disdained all frills; natively, he would oppose degrees. T. M. Clark, the youngest, more open-minded to innovations, earned his degree by 1893, but he had been a member of the faculty from its second session. The subjects he taught, however, were all those "extras," music, elocution, and modern languages, which did not regularly count toward degrees.

It was only speaking the language of the day on the frontier, therefore, to minimize degrees. What counted with them was actual achievement. When we express it this way, we recognize a twentieth century sentiment that is even now struggling for adoption.

Since degrees were so minimized, it seems clear that it was not a thirst for more degrees, either by students or by teachers, that motivated the announcement of a "Postgraduate Course" in 1881.

> In order to encourage our students in thoroughness of preparation for the chosen work in life, we have selected a course of study requiring the time of one session to be pursued by those who may have taken the regular course. No charge will be made for tuition for the course.[10]

It was not for more income either. It appears to have been an opportunity, offered to graduates, to take some courses they had not had time to take in their four years. A peculiar touch of the English idea of "ripening a degree" appeared in the announcement in 1890:

> A Bachelor of three years standing in any one of the courses may receive the honorary degree of Master of Arts in that course, provided he shall have maintained, during the interval an exemplary character, and pursued studies related to the degree.[11]

On the background of this tardiness of the recognition of degrees came an innovation which, to our modern minds, seems to veer far in the opposite direction. This was brought in by Dr. James W. Lowber, B. A., M. A., Ph. D., LL. D., Litt. D.,

[10]Catalog, 1881, p. 12.
[11]Catalog, 1890, p. 29.

F. R. G. S., R. A. S., R. S. G. S., R. S. A., A. A. A. S., M. R. A. S. Many of these were Fellowships or Memberships in the Royal Societies of England or Scotland. The extensive collection of his diplomas and certificates will probably be entrusted by Mrs. Lowber to the Texas Historical Collection.

The coming of this unusual personality, together with the new control by a Board representing the church, doubtless had much to do with the new interest in degrees. Dr. Lowber, the pastor of Major Jarvis, the newly elected Chairman of the Board, appeared in the Board meeting of April, 1893, recommending "to confer the degree of LL. D. on Addison Clark, and the degree of A. M. on Randolph Clark." This was done, obviously as honorary. At the same meeting he was elected as "Chancellor," an office created for him. His duties were stated: "to deliver two courses of lectures before the students of the said University annually, and to travel and solicit donations for the endowment fund,—to solicit attendance, make monthly reports" etc., with much detail emphasizing the raising of money.[12]

The Trustees naively and hopefully assumed that a man with much learning could easily raise money, pretty much as many assume that because a man becomes a famous scientist, or a successful captain of industry, he can speak that last authoritative word on religion or philosophy or anything else. There is no evidence that the good Doctor even tried to raise funds; he was a busy pastor, at Fort Worth (1888-1893), then Galveston, and finally at Austin. For five years (1892-1897), he delivered the annual lectures, but his most extensive and unique contribution to the life of the University was his direction of the "University Extension Course" providing graduate credit by reading and correspondence flavored with the English pattern of tutoring and examination.

The catalog announcement, under "Post Graduate Courses," was

I. There is a special course requiring one year's work on the part of those who have received the A. B. to obtain the degree of A. M. This work is different from that mentioned elsewhere of resident graduates who continue an extra year in a department for the A. M.

II. It will require a two years' course on the part of those who have received the A. B., B. S., or B. L., and a

[12]Minutes, 4-5-93, pp. 34, 35.

thorough examination to obtain the degree of Doctor of Science.

III. A similar course will be required for the degree of Doctor of Laws.

IV. A two years' course in philosophy will be required of all who have taken the degree of A. B., B. S., or B. L., to receive the degree of Doctor of Philosophy.

The work can be done at home, but the candidate must pass a thorough examination at the University. This University confers no honorary degrees.[13]

It appears that about thirty-eight degrees were awarded under this plan for non-resident work under Dr. Lowber. The Master's degree for resident work had been awarded already to two in 1891 and five in 1892. Between 1893 and 1899, inclusive, twenty-eight Master's degrees were awarded, but only two of these were in residence during that time.[14]

Three Ph. D. degrees were granted: W. B. Parks, 1894; Frank H. Marshall, 1895 (while he was in Japan); I. M. Cline, 1896, the director of the Weather Bureau in Galveston, where Dr. Lowber was pastor. Eight LL. D. degrees were granted. One was honorary, to Addison Clark, 1893, on vote of the Trustees, and recommendation of Dr. Lowber; one was to J. B. Sweeney.[15] A third was to G. A. Lewellyn, at that time a teacher in Kentucky, later joining the faculty of T. C. U. in 1909. The other five LL. D.'s were to Britishers, living in London, Hull, Brighton and Exeter, England. This latter fact may be a clue to the inspiration of Dr. Lowber's plan, for the English are accustomed to doing their "reading" away from the campus. How the word got around is not known, but it is a fact that occasionally through the years, even as late as in the 20's, letters came to the University from England and Australia asking for Doctor's degrees by correspondence. Among others to receive these degrees were four faculty members, Dr. Lowber's wife, and four residents of Galveston where Dr. Lowber was pastor at the time.

[13]Catalog, 1893, p. 23.
[14]These were 1894, seven; 1895, eight; 1896, five; 1897, one; 1898, two; 1899, three; 1900, two. These last three years were after Dr. Lowber was no longer officially Chancellor, but there is every evidence that these were not in residence, so students must have been allowed to complete the work begun under him.
[15]The record of this appears first in the 1904 catalog, stating that the degree was awarded in 1905. Sweeney died in 1901. It is likely that this was a typographical error intended for 1895. The later catalog copied it.

This plan of his should be freed from the suspicion of being merely a scheme for satisfying, by easy measures, the thirst for higher degrees. It had some precedent among the English, as observed. The Doctor was quite in touch with the British scholars, and a member of a number of their learned societies. His was a genuine effort to bring to the few who longed to go further in learning, the opportunity for the guidance they sought. There was in it something of the evangelistic zeal of the Chautauqua movement of that period, later observed in the adult education and extension education moves, aiming to keep people studying after their formal school days are past.

Among the Items in which the old school pioneered and experimented was the form of the school year. At first the session embraced ten months, then (1876) the thirty-six weeks was divided into two "terms of eighteen weeks each." After trying for several years to "solve the problem of what is the best length for a school session in this climate and country" (including seven months to save expense) Add-Ran decided on two terms of six and four months each, then (1893) three terms of twelve weeks each, next (1896) the two semester plan was restored.[16]

The beginning of summer terms in college has often been accounted as of the 1910's or a few years earlier. It is observed that Add-Ran was trying it out as early as 1880.

Two strains of thought concerning play appear on the frontier. Many of the early letters from Texas describe the gala days when the neighbors gathered to play, rope cattle, run horses, and have lively sports. On the other hand, there was the anxiety of the patriarch that every member of the household must work, from the least to the eldest. "Holidays" is the title of a section in the catalog with an attractive title but forbidding message:

There will be two during the session, Christmas and one day in April. Parents will please not encourage nor expect their children to return home Christmas, nor anytime till close of school. It is impossible to have children do good work when they lose time from their studies.[17]

Three years later this attitude was stiffened by: "Holidays, We promise none—Parents and children must learn that school life is one of work; and just so much work and so much play

[16]Catalog, 1884, p. 24; 1893, p. 2. Later changes are 1903 term plan, 1925 semester plan.
[17]Catalog, 1881, p. 19.

must be allowed as is helpful and healthful." Yet a slight relaxation was hinted: "if in the judgment of the faculty one is needed it will be given without reference to custom or youthful fancy." Custom, however, claimed a little gain the next year: "We promise only two, Thanksgiving and Christmas, to be observed 'with proper decorum'."[18]

That expression "and one day in April" is intriguing. Did the stern old Roman choose to recognize April Fool's day? No, the answer is given in Mr. Randolph's story:

> Vacations were taken as they were needed. When the long winter of hard work was passed, and the green prairies and trout brooks began to call, the President would appear in chapel and say, 'I am going to take a three days trip to the Paluxy. All who want to walk the eighteen miles with me be ready at a certain hour. A wagon will follow to carry camp equipment and to pick up the stragglers and those who fall by the way.'[19]

And any student of that generation glows with precious memory in telling of the spring picnic at Comanche Peak. "Play while you play" even though it be seldom.

Of "athletics" as later known, there was none, in those days. That is, no organized athletics, or intercollegiate contests. But let no one suppose from this that the men themselves were not athletic. President Addison Clark walked those miles to the picnic and invited all who would and could to follow him. He was recognized as the best long distance walker among them, even after he was up in years. The story of his conversion to athletics in the form of football and the beginnings of sport is told in the chapter on the Athletics.[20]

The recreational life of old Add-Ran was distinctly in the literary field. This statement needs to be interpreted in the light of the experience that when the gate of literary companionship is opened, an abundance of social life slips through. This heritage of the old "Lyceum" and Friday afternoon "Declamations" or "Exhibitions" of American School history, must have been the basis at the beginning, and soon blossomed into Literary Societies. For the catalog of 1877 lists among the "Advantages" what every issue repeats, with embellishments later on: "Literary Societies. There are several of these. They meet once a

[18]Catalog, 1884, 1885, p. 26.
[19]*Reminiscences*, pp. 55-56.
[20]Chapter XXI.

week. There are rooms especially prepared for these exercises, and one of the College faculty presides over the labors of each society."[21] Space in the building was assigned to each society on condition that the society furnish it at its own expense and the furnishings become the property of the school after two years. The Walton Society,[22] at first for young women, then for both sexes, was for juniors and seniors who were recommended by the faculty. The Add-Ran Literary Society was for juniors and seniors, and the Add-Ran Biblical Society (later the Watts) was for ministerial students. The Eclectic Star for younger pupils was under the supervision of the teachers.[23]

Publication was another means of literary expression, as early as 1882, when the "Add-Ran Student, the Paper for the Times" had a page ad in the catalog. The editor named was R. Clark but tradition has it that the "Local Editor, Tommie Clark" really operated it. His name appears as the "printer" of the Catalog in 1880, so it is assumed that there was a print shop there too.

The high ideals and the lowly trials of a publisher are revealed in a paragraph from the ad. "Reliable business men are selected to advertise in the Student. None other need apply, as we are determined to rid our paper of all objectionable advertisements. Some have crept in, but greater caution will be exercised in the future."[24]

Modern colleges have many media for the exploitation of their excellencies, but Add-Ran had only one—the catalog. So the catalog had a strain of salesmanship, dignified but definite. The first issue of sixteen pages was compact and somewhat restrained. The location is praised as possessing "advantages perhaps superior to any in the state." There was usually an expression of high aims, and occasionally a burst of gratitude for the achievement of goals already attained, or confidence of success. "We feel prepared to meet fully and faithfully any educational want of our brotherhood in Texas." "It is the determination that the College shall be second to none in the state for the accommodation and benefit of the Christian brotherhood."[25] "Departments: These embrace more than is found in any University."[26] And the climax: "We congratulate ourselves that every-

---

[21]Catalog, 1887, p. 4, and each catalog.
[22]Named for John T. Walton of Waco, who gave an annual medal.
[23]Minutes, 6-19-91, 9-22-91, Catalog, 1893, pp. 30-31.
[24]Catalog, 1882, last page.
[25]Catalog, 1875, p. 3.
[26]Catalog, 1890, p. 35.

**JOSEPH ADDISON**
CLARK, Co-Founder

**MRS. HETTIE D'SPAIN**
CLARK (Mrs. J. A.)

**MRS. ELLA BLANCHE**
LEE CLARK (Mrs. Randolph)

**THOMAS MARSHALL
CLARK**
(Taken in later life)

**MRS. LOUELLA CLARK
HOLLOWAY (Mrs. R. F.)**

**RANDOLPH LEE
CLARK**

JOE L. CLARK

ROBERT F.
HOLLOWAY

ADDISON CLARK, JR.

FRANK CLARK, M.

Others of the Clark Family (whose pictures are available).

The Thorp Spring Building, erected 1877, reconstructed after the fire, 1905, demolished 1946.

*Below:* The original Thorp Building, purchased 1873, reverted 1877; still standing, used as a storage house.

*Below:* The Girls' Home at Thorp Spring.

G. E. CARPENTER, A. B., '77 Planter, Plano

D. F. GOSS, A. B., '77 Lawyer, Seymour

LOU CARR, A. B., '79, Mrs. S. J. Bass, McKinney (for years, the oldest living graduate)

LEWIS B. MILLER, A. B., '81 Author of early Texas adventure stories, St. Louis

F. O. McKINSEY, A. B., '82 ; Professor, 1884-91 ; District Judge, Weatherford; LL. D., '35

JOSEPHINE SCOTT (Mrs. F. O. McKinsey) A. B., '82, Weatherford

DR. W. M. CAMP-BELL, B. A., '82, M. D. Weatherford, (living at 83)

FRANKLIN G. JONES, B. A., '90, Professor (See Appendix for details.)

*Above:* A FEW OF THE EARLIEST GRADUATES.
*Below:* The graduates of 1896 in reunion in Fort Worth, May 14, 1947. After 51 years all ten were living, nine were present.
*Top, left to right:* W. H. Penix, J. T. McKissick, Mrs. Mary Lipscomb Wiggins, J. F. Kemp, J. M. Campbell.
*Seated, left to right:* Mrs. Julia Easley Robinson, Mrs. Lottie Beard Wright, Mrs. Louella Clark Holloway, Mrs. Bertha Mason Fulier, Mrs. May Miller Simmons, the one absent, lives in Houston, was represented by her daughter.

DEAN J. B. SWEENEY     DR. J. W. LOWBER     CAPTAIN T. M. SCOTT

COL. A. C. EASLEY     PROF. W. T. HAMNER     PROF. E. C. SNOW

VICE PRESIDENT     COLBY D. HALL,     DR. G. A. LLEWELLYN,
J. F. ANDERSON     Educational Secretary,     Professor and Dean
                1906-'09

Some Leaders in Thorp Spring and Waco.
For Details see Appendix VI, p. 359 ff.

thing is as it ought to be in the Department."[27] This referred to one department, was repeated once, then eliminated, as was the preceding quotation.

But most of the appeals for patronage were couched in dignified and fitting language; the points advertised were constructive. It is worthwhile to observe what these were in that day. The fact that the school was co-educational was stressed from the first. In the first catalog, two of the sixteen pages were used in printing an article arguing for co-education.[28] To counteract the idea that college education could be had only in the old states, it was announced "We can assure them (the parents) that they need no longer send beyond the limits of the state to be educated." A feature favorable for patronage evidently was that "Add-Ran is adopted and endorsed . . . as a college for the brotherhood of Texas." Much more definite, however, was the appeal to the high standards of character building and lofty ideals of life and service.

The announcement of new features, as they were added, was highly commendable, and occasionally arguments for them were extended. Once this took the form of satirical remarks about other types of education in a six-page article by J. A. Clark on "Practical Education." It ridiculed certain types of "Business Colleges" and referred to the "extravagance of State Schools."[29]

In the early years the College seemed not to be anxious about attendance.

Add-Ran College has prospered and is prospering beyond the most sanguine expectation of its founders. It has not sprung up and grown in any enthusiastic impulse. There have been no ad capitandum efforts for patronage. Its founders have pursued the even tenor of their way, laboring faithfully and incessantly. The increase in patronage has been gradual.[30]

In the later years, after the numbers had grown, but were not mounting sufficiently, there was definite straining to increase the enrollment. Several times Randolph Clark was put in the field for money and students. The visiting of the Clarks among the churches was, of course, a continuous influence for recruiting students. After the church took over, the Trustees voted to

[27]Catalog, 1886, p. 17, and 1887, p. 16.
[28]Catalog, 1874, pp. 15, 16.
[29]Catalog, 1884, pp. 30-35.
[30]Catalog, 1884, p. 34 by J. A. Clark.

pay Addison Clark one hundred dollars a month to solicit students during the summer months.[31] At the same meeting it was resolved that anyone securing students "from outside the state" should be credited fifteen per cent of the tuition. In 1893 this offer was extended to the securing of any students at ten per cent.

There was a definite military note in the discipline of Add-Ran in the early days; military terms often appear. In the roster of students for the session of 1887-88 one name is marked "deserted." The 1883-84 list has three marks to note those "dead," "deserted," "expelled." In the list of 1891-92, the record is even more severe. The footnote reads: "These are not desirable pupils. We do not wish them back at this school; neither do we commend them to others." This, after all, means just what many a note says on a modern transcript, but it is more direct.

Discipline was necessarily a difficult problem on the frontier. The students, mostly adolescents, brought undisciplined, adolescent ways with them, coming as they did from isolated communities, without well directed high school experience and with limited group contacts. Physical prowess was at a premium and the spirit of adventure was strong. Cultured homes there were, to be sure, but they were in the minority and even in these the exterior was rough and conveniences were crude. It is with this frontier background in mind that the "Rules of Conduct" should be read. In practically every catalog they appeared, from 1876 through 1897.

It is presumable that every student will have some knowledge of the first principles of morality, propriety and decorum, and that it will therefore be unnecessary to prescribe a complete code of specific rules and regulations. But it will be expected and required of all students:

1. That they be diligent in their study, punctual in their attendance upon worship, recitation, examinations and all other college exercises, and that they promptly render a valid and satisfactory reason to the proper officers for any delinquency.

2. That they treat all persons, and especially the students and teachers of the college, with becoming respect.

3. That they do not trespass upon the premises of any person, and they in no way deface or injure the property of the college.

[31]Minutes, 6-19-91.

4. That they attend no exhibition of immoral tendency; no race course, theatre, circus, billiard-saloon, bar room, or tippling house.

5. That they neither introduce upon the premises of the college, nor use there or elsewhere, any kind of intoxicating beverage; and that they abstain from the use of tobacco in the buildings of the college.

6. That they neither keep in their possession nor use any firearms, a dirk, a bowie-knife, nor any other kind of deadly weapon.

7. That they abstain from profanity, the desecration of the Lord's day, all kinds of gaming for a reward or prize of any kind, and from card playing even for amusement; and also whatever else is inconsistent with good order, good taste, and good morals.

8. That they attend public worship every Lord's Day.

9. That they do not leave the college until regularly dismissed at the close of the session, without the special permission of the Faculty.

10. That they do not change their place of boarding without the permission of the Faculty.

11. That they shun and discountenance all disorderly combinations and associations of students or citizens; and that they co-operate with the Faculty in every honorable way to promote the interest and reputation of the college.[32]

The use of tobacco was then quite general, especially chewing. Few farm boys failed to indulge. Here is a point in which the ideals of the founders and the habits of their clientele clashed. Addison and Randolph Clark were teetotlars in tobacco as well as intoxicants. And they set that standard for their young men students. It was a hard rule to enforce. The fathers of the students were chewers, also, many of them. So in addition to the general rule, the 1888 catalog had a paragraph.

The use of tobacco in any form is forbidden in this college. Let all concerned take notice of this, and if they cannot or will not stop the use of tobacco, they are requested *not to come here to school*. The pernicious effects of tobacco smoking, especially of cigarette smoking, upon the young, impell us to this decision. It may be considered a great hardship upon young men of mature years not to allow them to exercise their pleasure in this matter, but we cannot correct the habit among younger boys while we allow it with young

[32]Catalog, 1876, p. 13, "Conduct of students."

men. We may lose some students on account of the restriction, but we shall retain a *good conscience*.[33]

The difficulty increased. So long as the school was a private institution, the Clarks consulted no one about their rules. They were staunch and rigid in their convictions and brave in enforcement. But after the Church took over ownership and the Trustees assumed final authority, there were appeals beyond the President to the Board, and it broke out in this tobacco problem. The first Minutes after the new charter was in operation March 18, 1890, recorded a motion that "the law in force against tobacco be continued." The division of sentiment and the delicacy of the situation were such that it was dodged. Decision was deferred and the secretary was instructed to secure the sentiment of other members of the Board. During the next year and a half, there must have been much agitation and division, for on September 22, 1891, a motion was made "to take up, discuss and decide the tobacco question." Letters were read from three faculty members, Skidmore, Snow, and Parks, advising modification. The resolution that passed provided that boys could use tobacco only in their rooms and that every effort should be made to avoid it entirely. The Board must have voted solidly for this—but not the Clarks. The minutes record two negative votes: Addison and Randolph Clark. It may be added that this regulation remained alive until about the time of the World War in 1917, not much mentioned but well known.

That the ex-soldier stern disciplinarian was not without his human side, appreciative of humor, is evidenced by several stories that gained wide circulation among the ex-students, and have been recorded in Mrs. Mason's "Beginnings."

Some unpleasantness had occurred between the faculty and boys. The humiliation of a public reprimand had seemed to them to be too much, and a deep plot was laid to get even. The new two-seated surrey, which belonged to the President, was kept behind doors without locks.

Under cover of darkness the conspirators crept into the little buggy house, lifted the shafts from the rests, and pulled the vehicle out into the road toward the creek. Only when they reached a safe distance did the boys begin to exult over the seeming success of their prank. Hilarious laughter, and remarks about what would happen when the surrey was found in the creek the next morning, filled the rest of the way. They did not dream that a leak had occurred in their plot until they began to shove the surrey in the water, in a secluded spot under the trees.

The tightly closed curtains parted, and Mr. Addison quietly remarked that he had enjoyed the ride, but he thought they had taken him far enough, and he was ready to go home.

Another story proves that tolerance and even humor lay beneath the mask of sternness which Mr. Addison so often wore.

The boys were fond of stealing hours from study to indulge in a chicken roast, usually at night in some secluded part of the woods.

Near the dormitory stood a tree that was the roosting place of a large flock of chickens. One night several boys were sent for supplies while others went on to prepare the fire. As usual one boy climbed the tree and gently lifted each bird down to waiting hands. He was so intent on the work he did not know that the boys had slipped away as a tall figure came among them. Reaching down with one he asked if it were fat enough. When Mr. Addison's quiet voice answered that it seemed to be but he believed they had enough for the roast, the shock was so great the climber fell to the ground. He was not seriously hurt but was confined to his bed for several days.[34]

Extravagance of any kind was discouraged. From the first this was stressed. "Parents are advised to prepare their children for this school with plain, neat but comfortable clothing. It is thought best that no encouragement should be given to gaudy or extravagant dress."[35] At this time no uniform was prescribed, but in 1884 quite a lengthy argument was published in favor of uniforms. The required uniform was:

For girls, gray woolen goods.—This for every day wear to be worn with check, gingham aprons. For Sunday, black woolen goods with apron. For head wear, bonnets of check gingham for every day; Hats for Sunday. Shoes of sensible style. Jewelry not allowed. For boys, gray jeans or cassimere, black hats.[36]

This was later relaxed to "Leave off all jewelry except one ring."[37] A little more yielding is observed through the succeeding catalogs, but always a grudging one.

[34]Mason, pp. 54, 55, from an interview with Mrs. Fannie Broiles Cook. Also, these two stories were told by an ex-student of Add-Ran to the author, in 1895, more than a year before he entered the school.
[35]Catalog, 1875, p. 12.
[36]Catalog, 1884, p. 17.
[37]Catalog, 1888, p. 29.

In conclusion we will say that we regard love of dress and devotion to fashion as one of the greatest temptations to the young to be vain and frivolous, absorbing mind and time that should be devoted to the earnest work of life. Viewing this question from every standpoint, physically, financially, morally, we think a reformation is needed. This reformation can come only through education.[38]

Anyone who has opportunity to observe is aware that the restrictions thrown about college girls were much tighter two and three decades ago than now. It must have been tighter the further back one goes, judging by the rules at Add-Ran.

All students, who are boarders here, are forbidden to engage in written correspondence with any one but their parents and their own folks at home, except by special consent of the President. It is presumed that parents will appreciate the importance of this rule without an argument in its behalf.[39]

The next year it was stated: "The kind of students wanted in this college: Those who have neither the time nor the desire for miscellaneous gallantry or letter writing." And even this: "Those who never dream of matrimony until their education is finished."[40] This extreme statement is simply an indication of the depth of conviction that was characteristic of the Clarks. What they believed they proposed to back up at any price. But that expression was not repeated; it appeared in only one catalog. Maybe it was engendered out of an experience with some provocative case. Their concern about courting is not surprising when we recall that they were pioneering in co-education, and that in that day of farm life and large families, marriages were unusually early.[41]

---

[38]Catalog, 1890, p. 35.
[39]Catalog, 1875, p. 11.
[40]Catalog, 1876, p. 13.
[41]Two stories recorded by Mrs. Mason in her "Beginnings" are too good to be lost:
The watchful care given the girls in regard to their dress and conduct is shown in the story of the two girls who were reprimanded for cutting their hair to make bangs. They were told that they had disobeyed the teachings of the Scriptures by cutting their locks.
Another girl was called before the Faculty for walking across the campus with a young man. When she explained that he was her brother, she was told that others wouldn't know he was a relative, and she "must avoid the appearance of evil." Mason p. 73, an interview with Mrs. Ida V. Jarvis.
Mrs. Jarvis was a visitor at Add-Ran College for Commencement week in

The ambition of every administrator is to develop such an atmosphere on the campus that cases of discipline will not arise. In a very high degree this was achieved in that segregated and unified community.

It has already been observed that much prominence was given to lists of textbooks in the catalog. Doubtless classes depended upon texts rather fully, and upon library very little, for that was the custom of the day, and the library was not available. The extenuating circumstance was that great teachers can teach successfully by either technic. But there was not lacking an appreciation of the library. The Walton Literary Society was named after Major John T. Walton of Waco, because he had

---

1882. There was a musical concert in the college chapel on Monday night. The next morning an anonymous note was sent the President saying that a young man from the boy's dormitory had walked home with a young lady who lived in town. This open disobedience of rules was the subject of the chapel talk. The offender was asked to stand that all of the audience might see the student to be expelled for breaking the rules.

When one of the finest young men of the senior class quietly arose, it astonished the faculty, but did not change the sentence. Before an hour had passed a petition was brought from the student body asking for pardon and stated that the offenders of the evening before were to be married in two weeks. The petition also stated that nearly all of the students had stolen privileges at some time during the year. An assembly of students and visitors was called. The president stated the decision was final; there was no excuse for breaking rules, and all students who had done so during the year must consider themselves expelled.

Mrs. Jarvis walked slowly to the girl's dormitory where she found all in confusion, girls in nearly every room were packing trunks and weeping. The matron, almost frantic, said: "Something must be done, call a faculty meeting." Mrs. Jarvis replied: "Faculty nothing,—there has been too much faculty now. Give me my umbrella, and I will attend to this." She tied a large white handkerchief on top of the umbrella and went to the home of Mr. Addison. He was in the cow pen with Mr. Randolph and both were in earnest conversation, seated under a live-oak tree.

Mrs. Jarvis marched up to them, waved her flag of truce and said: "Good morning, you seem to be in trouble." Mr. Randolph said: "I've been trying to talk some sense into him." Mr. Addison replied: "We are in deep trouble, and I wish you could tell us what to do." Mrs. Jarvis had come prepared to do just that, and readily outlined the situation. It meant breaking up the school over a trifle, in the presence of hundreds of visitors from all over the country. She ended by saying there was only one thing to do: "Take back what you have said and forgive them." Mr. Addison looked down in deep thought for some moments, then the humor of the whole situation appealed to him, he threw back his head and laughed heartily. He called an assembly at once and not only revoked the sentence, but gave the students full privileges for the entire week. Mrs. Jarvis was a heroine.

Mason, p. 115, an interview with Mrs. Ida V. Jarvis.

donated a library.[42] But even more rejoicing was expressed in that same catalog that

> One of the most timely and generous gifts to the University was that of one thousand and forty-five volumes of well selected books, donated by Mr. Edwin J. Toof of New Haven, Connecticut. These books were all selected, arranged and catalogued by his son, that noble man of God, J. T. Toof, former pastor of the Central Christian Church, Dallas, Texas.[43]

Through this, and many other of the features portrayed in this chapter it is observed how these foundation builders in the new West marked out the lines of growth and development which have been followed and enlarged by the succeeding generations. As they said of the gift of the Toof Library, we say of them: "We owe a lasting debt of gratitude, a debt of love too large to be paid off in this world."

Students and Faculty Spring 1896

[42]Catalog, 1893, pp. 31, 35.
[43]Catalog, 1893, pp. 31, pp. 31, 35.

# ◈ VII ◈

# The Range and the Railroad Make Friends 1895

JAMES I. MOORE        RANDOLPH CLARK

T HE STORY IS TOLD OF A POOR FARMER FAMILY in the days of Ranger oil boom of 1917: On their rocky heavily mortgaged hillside farm was discovered oil in gusher proportions; prospect for wealth was intoxicating. But the lady of the family deplored thus: "This dirty oil soils the clean white feathers of pretty White Leghorns." A similar dubious welcome greeted the railroads of the frontier. The promoters raved with enthusiastic joy over the coming of the twin rails, but many settlers perceived the curses among the blessings. It was in such a mood that the Clarks had moved their school from the village of Fort Worth when, as they thought, the railroads brought its influx of riff-raff population to multiply the iniquities of an already rowdy cow-country headquarters.

One of the advantages of the Thorp Spring location claimed in the catalog was that "It is retired . . . away from the alluring vices of the city, free from the evils about railway stations, the nearest being Granbury, three miles distant."[1] There was, indeed, a recognition of the value of the Railway as a means of getting there, but the Clarks were glad it was not too close, for the first catalog stated, "The situation is retired, yet sufficiently near the T. & P. railroad line to receive the advantages of that road." For years the slogan was published, "Railroads on every side but none near the village."[2]

It must have been a concession, therefore, when the 1890 catalog carried an advertisement of the Missouri Kansas Texas Railway.[3] It was a concession, indeed, to the onward march of the railroad era, and not a direct result of the ad, when the school as a whole, faculty and students, rode that same M. K. T. train into Waco on Christmas, 1895, to their new home. And among the reasons given for the choice of the new location was

[1]Catalog, 1888, p. 32.
[2]Catalog, 1874, p. 14, 1886, p. 28.
[3]Page 41.

63

that Waco had "seven railroad outlets," of which the same Katy Road furnished two. The day had arrived when it was more important to have a ready means of travel than to have abundance of wood and water at your door. Thus did the frontier bow to the inevitable approach of the railroad era.

The idea of moving to a city must have been brewing for some time, for it was consummated rapidly after a plan was proposed. It was at the Trustees meeting of September 4, 1895, that the President (Jarvis) appointed T. E. Shirley, Scott Milam, and T. M. Scott, "a committee of three members to investigate and make report on the proposition made by Brother James I. Moore of Waco as to the removal of Add-Ran Christian University to Waco, Texas."[4]

Nine days later "the largest Board meeting for several years" (ten present) assembled in Fort Worth in special called session to hear the proposition of Mr. Moore for Waco, as follows:

> We the undersigned brethren submit the following proposition to wit: In consideration of the transfer of Add-Ran Christian University, with the Board of Trustees, faculty and students to Waco, Texas, on or before January 1, 1896, we will deed to the said University, the Waco Female College and fifteen (15) acres of land situated in the northwestern suburbs of the city of Waco, and we further agree to complete said building except the fourth, or dormitory story, and to build a dormitory for boys not to exceed in value the sum of five thousand dollars, ($5,000) or such other buildings as may seem necessary for the accommodation of the University, provided that in no case we be bound to erect buildings to exceed in cash the aggregate, the sum of five thousand dollars ($5,000), and to move the faculty and students and their effects to Waco, free of cost. The Executive Committee from the Christian Church at Waco. (Signed) J. I. Moore.

Papers were also presented from the Waco Commercial Club as evidence that the people of Waco were in earnest in desiring the transfer. "The Board was unanimous in accepting the proposition," stated the minutes.[5]

That seemed to be moving rapidly in a big matter. But it proved to be not so simple after all. On November 22, at Thorp Spring, F. N. Calvin, the pastor of the Central Christian Church at Waco, appeared with modifications in the proposition. He explained in writing that "For many reasons, we found that it

---

[4]Minutes, 9-4-95, p. 56.
[5]9-13-95, p. 58.

would be impossible for us to do unaided what we first thought we could do." An appeal had been made by the Waco brethren to the Brotherhood in a called meeting "of four or five hundred of the leading members of the Christian Churches in Texas," at the time of the State Convention which had just met in Dallas. There, "it was decided on account of the sectarian hostilities and other difficulties encountered by the Waco Church, making it impossible for them to raise the money required" etc. "to raise $16,000 in the state, $8,000 to help the Waco Church and $8,000 for liquidating Add-Ran Christian University's debts." This meeting had been presided over by Col. J. Z. Miller of Belton, with J. H. Banton of Waco as Secretary. "Brother Calvin" reported this at the November 22 meeting, promising "to put the Waco college buildings in suitable repair to accommodate the school we take there, . . . also two and a half acres of land to the President and to his brother, provided they move there, and to get citizens to erect boarding houses for the boys."

Letters were presented also from J. W. Mann of Waco, representing the creditor purchases of the Waco property, stating that they had sold the property to James I. Moore, et al, for $30,000 and would deliver title when $18,000 was paid and notes made for the balance. There was also a statement from Mr. Mann agreeing to accept for that balance a certain note for $9,000 signed by certain men. These were, indeed, the elders of the Central Christian Church of Waco.[6]

The Trustees, the Waco brethren, and the representatives of the Texas Christian Churches in Convention were all anxious for the move to be made and were of a mind to go their limit in meeting the conditions and difficulties which they faced. No one group seemed to be more eager than the other, although, naturally the Waco group was in the position of the aggressors. A formal resolution was drawn and passed unanimously by the Add-Ran Trustees on November 23, and that session closed with the resolution, "That the Christmas holidays . . . begin December 22, ending January 1, 1896, and that all students who go home for the holidays reassemble at Waco, Texas, after the holiday vacation."[7]

Action followed promptly. Despite the many complications that were necessarily involved in transferring not only an estab-

---

[6]The author cherishes the fact that his father, R. M. Hall, was one of these signers and that both his father and he, then in his teens, contributed to the cash fund at the time.

[7]Minutes, 9-22, 23 and 11-22, 23.

lished institution but practically an entire village, the move was made. In two days more than a month from the official vote, a company of about a hundred professors, families and students marched in procession down the streets of Waco, to the welcome cheering of fair-sized crowds who looked up from their Christmas shopping to view with curiosity and interest the pilgrimage from country to town.

A formal program of welcome was held in the convenient down-town auditorium, a tabernacle of the First Baptist Church on South Sixth Street. Cordial welcome was expressed by representatives of the Waco Commercial Club, of the churches and of the schools. The most distinguished voice on the program, no doubt, was that of the venerable President of Baylor University, Dr. Rufus C. Burleson, this being among the last of his appearances in a general public assembly.

It cannot be claimed that the city of Waco was greatly stirred by its acquisition. It was just beginning to be awakened to the spirit of expansion by its Commercial Club, with such slogans as "ten railway outlets," and "the seventh largest suspension bridge in the world." The townspeople had been drawn into the move by the vigorous leadership of James I. Moore, the most aggressive and venturesome personality among them, who was the more interested because it was the school of his own church. This very fact may have given some feeling that, after all, the raising of money for this school was primarily up to the Christian Church. Waco had already "the oldest college in Texas," in Baylor University, and the Baptists led in church population in the city. The welcome was courteous, cordial and sincere, as Waco people always are. Add-Ran had a new habitation; it must build its own place in the life of the community.

Waco may not have been very deeply stirred; that could be a matter of opinion. But there was no doubt about Thorp Spring. To that pioneer village the move was a death blow. To the credit of the remaining citizens it can be said that through the following years they struggled time and again to maintain a college and to recapture the dream that had given glory to their village. But the sylvan dell of beauty had had its great day. Thorp Spring became one of those many historic spots left by the wayside by the new day of railways and highways, scores of them in the Southwest, with an honored past but no future. Many a one now has the sentimental charm of the "Deserted Village."

There was disappointment, of course, in the hearts of many of the residents of the village. But among the faculty and students such a spirit was rare, to say the least. In the old Minute Book is recorded a list of the entire faculty at the time of the move, with their salaries rated (totaling $940 a month). Only two on this list failed to move to Waco. These were Randolph Clark and his son-in-law, R. F. Holloway.

It is remarkable that opposition to the move was not stronger. There was opposition among the more conservative church brethren, who favored the anti-organ group. These found their expression some sixteen years later, in an effort to utilize the plant for a school of the Church of Christ, the anti-organ communion. This story is told in another chapter.[8]

The struggle that went on in the soul of Addison Clark must have been worthy of a master dramatist to express. He had vowed never to leave the old site in the country, and despite much pressure he kept that vow so long as the school was in the family control. But after he yielded control to the church, he acquiesced in its decisions; he was a democrat. He went graciously, led faithfully, met new conditions bravely; but he never found himself fully at home in the city. He soon began to relinquish the vigor of his leadership. But prophet that he was, he insisted that the school increase while he decreased. His loyalty was perfect.

If there was opposition within the Board it does not appear in the records and was not voiced where it would be remembered. Major J. J. Jarvis would have been the logical objector, for he had invested several thousand dollars in the building that could not be moved. He did insist on dropping his Presidency of the Board, but retained membership on it and attended the meetings at Waco. Even after his resignation from the Board he manifested interest in the school when it moved to Fort Worth.[9] Three years after his resignation his son, Van Zandt Jarvis, came on the Board, actively, and served on it the rest of his life. When T. C. U. moved to Fort Worth, Major Jarvis was elected on the Advisory Board in July 1910,[10] and was reelected as such annually until his death in 1914. His wife, Ida Van Zandt Jarvis, continued her unabated zeal through all these changes and even to the end of her own career.[11]

[8]Chapter XXIV.
[9]Minutes Book, 6-6-99, p. 134 and 7-6-99, p. 136, also 191.
[10]Minutes, 7-14-10, p. 216.
[11]See also Chapter XIX.

A division in the ranks of the Christian Church over the question of the use of the organ and of missionary societies came into an open break at Thorp Spring in the fall of 1893, during a meeting held by B. B. Sanders and E. M. Douthitt. This has been cited by some as a cause of the move; it was definitely charged by Prof. C. W. Howard in a letter written about 1930. He describes the incident and draws his conclusions in these words:

As the strains of the organ struck up, so did J. A. Clark and half the congregation arose amid tears and groans and marched forth to battle. Add Hall and a bunch came to me and wanted me to advise them to go and get the devilish machine and cut it up with an axe and throw it in the creek. I told them they could not afford it. It would ruin their cause. They withdrew. The next morning Mr. Randolph said to me, 'It will ruin us. These old brethren in the country won't let us preach in their school houses.' And it did. They only lasted one year more and the school having fallen off so, they took it to Waco, where it burned, then to Fort Worth.[12]

The schism was serious enough, and had enough evil effects, but that it had much to do with the decision to move is not plausible. Mr. Howard himself, was obviously, a prejudiced witness. His language betrays his feelings. He left the faculty that year, himself, having been there only two sessions.

As a matter of fact this decline in the attendance was not so extensive as it seemed, probably not more than would be accounted for by the financial panic of 1893-94. The figures were: 1889-90, 425; 1891, 360; 1892, 315; 1893, 445; 1894, 370; 1895, 270. Even the notable drop, the year following the schism, 1894-95, to 270, was confined to the local attendance, for the attendance from outside of Hood County was 207 that year and 197 the following year. This is only to say that the move would have occurred whether or not the split had come. It is not to minimize the seriousness of the division itself. That grew, became permanent, and seriously weakened the growth of the communion. This conservative group, which came to be known as the Church of Christ, found an expression, some sixteen years later in an effort to utilize the property for a college under its direction, the Thorp Spring Christian College.[13]

[12]Mason, p. 111, 112.
[13]See Chapter XXIV.

As already stated, only two faculty members chose to remain at Thorp Spring: Randolph Clark, who personally had opened the doors of the school twenty-two years before, and his son-in-law, Robert F. Holloway, who continued to team with his father-in-law all of his days, and whose wife, Louella Clark Holloway, became her father's chief dependence for care and nursing in his later years. Mr. Randolph's decision against going to Waco was not because he was not encouraged to go. He was offered a home there, and later on was invited to a position as canvasser for students.[14] Twice they, together, proposed to the Trustees to lease the old site for use as a school and both times the Trustees accepted. Evidently a school was operated there in 1896-97, for reference is made to it in the Collegian, naming R. F. Holloway as the Secretary.[15]

Inasmuch as this period was the closing of Mr. Randolph's official relationship with the University, it seems a fitting place to trace the rest of his career, such as does not naturally fall into the story as it goes on. Never did his pacific spirit give any indication of opposition to the school. Many of his years were spent in attempting to build Junior Colleges (there were four), but he always regarded them as "feeders" for T. C. U. He felt that his philosophy of education did not fit well into an urban environment. His ideal of an educated person was one who would become versed in books, then return to the farm to establish a cultured Christian home. He deplored the tendency of college education to wean the boys and girls away from the farm. His favorite phrase was "the three-fold education of the heart, mind and hand."[16] It is said that he started the teaching of manual training before it was begun in the public schools. His distinguished son, Dr. Joseph Clark, long time Professor of History in the Sam Houston State Teachers College, in his *"History of Texas, a Land of Promise"* pays this tribute to his father,

My first and most effective teacher of Texas History was my father. He was born in the Republic of Texas and was a soldier of the Confederacy. His acquaintance included many of heroes of early Texas and his comprehensive knowledge of the geography of the state was acquired at the time when there was leisure for horseback riding and stage coach travel.[17]

[14]Minutes, 3-17-96, 12-29-97, 3-15-98.
[15]Collegian, September 1896, p. 16, November 1896, p. 56. Also see p. 332.
[16]Letter from Mrs. Holloway, 12-7-43.
[17]p. 111.

The relationship between the two brothers, Addison and Randolph, was very intimate and always cordial. When Randolph wrote his Reminiscences at the age of seventy-five (he was born in 1844) it turned out to be largely a biography of Addison, his elder by a year and a half. He was wont to comment, "Addison was always the leader; I was content to follow." Yet he was the more venturesome, and possessed qualities of social ease and personal persuasiveness that were lacking in his more austere, reticent brother.

During all the years at Thorp Spring, his home was the one most frequented by the students. For this generous hospitality he gives his wife credit, but his genial personality fitted well into the picture. They had a large family of mentally able and socially alert children, and when the Orphan School was closed in 1885 they took into their home nine orphans and kept them until they could be placed. Later they took in "two Armenian children brought to this country by a kinsman when the Turks were killing the Armenians. They were named Ruth and James Dolkranian."[18]

He was preacher as well as educator, busy through the years especially as an evangelist, beginning his first resident pastorate at Stephenville when he was sixty-six years of age. In 1923 he was among those receiving the Honorary Doctor's degree from T. C. U. on which occasion he was led on the platform with eyes bandaged from an operation to relieve his blindness. Other afflictions vexed his old age. An automobile wreck caused a concussion of the brain, and a rattlesnake bite put his life in jeopardy. From these he recovered and became able again to use his pen and typewriter, and even served a term as Chaplain of the Texas Senate. He passed away in the home of the Holloways in Dallas in 1935.[19]

His greatest capacity was for making friends. He genuinely loved people, especially his brethren. He loved God, he loved the truth, he loved his kin, he was devoted to the soil, to his country, to his church; but the love that dominated his life was the love of the brethren. He may well be characterized as *philadelphos*.[20]

[18]From the letter by Mrs. Holloway.
[19]The story of Randolph appears throughout these pages, especially in the Chapter XXV on Related College. A fuller chapter was written concerning him but had to be condensed here for the sake of space.
[20]This is the word used in Rom. 12:10; Heb. 13:1; I Pet. 1:22, II Pet. 1:17.

# ∾ VIII ∾

## The Seven Lean Years 1895-1902

ADD-RAN IN WACO        COL. J. Z. MILLER

THE NEW HOME OF ADD-RAN IN WACO was again on the
Brazos river, nearer than before. The cedar brakes on
Blue Branch began only a block away and extended
along the chalky limestone ledges to the river bank a mile distant. Included in this stretch was the famous Proctor Springs,
later a part of Cameron Park. Two miles a-foot, where the
beautiful, clear Bosque met the sprawling, muddy Brazos, was
legended Lover's Leap, a favorite picnic ground. These wood-
land beauty spots atoned somewhat for the loss of the sylvan
scenes of the old country site, and wove themselves into the
sentiment of the new generation of students as they came on.

But that band of four score trail-blazers who hailed the new
Add-Ran home that Christmas day in 1895 had no eye for the
woods. What they saw was the campus itself, a bleak hill-top
of 15 acres, unrelieved by tree or shrub, the more stark by
the immensity of the single massive brick building in its center. The school was again three and one-half miles from the
railway station, though in the city. The campus faced North
18th Street, extending between Lyle and Alexander Streets. It
was reached by a half-hour ride on the street car, which was
later reduced to fifteen minutes when the route was changed
to North Fifth Street.[1] After several years a barbed wire fence
enclosed the grounds, with stiles for entrance.

The single large building which now became the home of
Add-Ran had been recently erected for the Waco Female College,
a Methodist school, founded in 1857,[2] which had operated on
South Third Street until Mrs. R. O. Rounsevell, the President,
undertook to expand by erecting this impressive building in
North Waco. Obviously, the plans were extended beyond available

---

[1]This change was made in the fall of 1898 when funds were scarce and the
Trustees had to contribute $1,800 to build the track out Herring Avenue. Minutes
6-3-98, 9-7-98.
[2]According to Roger Norman Conger, *Highlights of Waco History*, p. 56.

71

resources, for the First National Bank took over the property and sold it to the Trustees of Add-Ran. It was, indeed, a magnificent structure, with ample rooms for Dining, Library, Chapel, Gymnasium and Parlors, as well as recitation and living rooms, all in one large building. It was constructed of solid brick, with the lower walls some 18 to 24 inches thick, brick walls between all rooms, but with wooden floors, stairways and roof. The first two floors were finished; the Waco people, according to promise, completed the third. The fourth, partially dormer, remained, for years, a shell. Toilet facilities were entirely primitive and bath tubs were few. Side-walks were lacking; black waxy soil was sticky and abundant. These limitations to comfort were little felt; it had been the same at Thorp Spring and was so at other schools. "As to location and building there is no school in the South more favorably situated" so they felt about it.[3] They were quite accurate in advertising "one of the largest school buildings anywhere." Certainly Baylor had none so large, and that was something tangible.

During that first spring, 1896, in addition to all the girls and some of the boys, nearly all of the faculty members roomed and boarded in the Building (at $12 a month, half of that to be credited by back salary).[4] In the course of the first year homes were built by Professors A. Clark, W. B. Parks, J. W. Froley and J. B. Sweeney, and several large homes were erected as boarding houses for boys. During the next fifteen years, groups of boys, one generation after another, collected fond memories and fancy tales about such good homes as the Hunter House, the Singleton House, Wortham's and Schafer's. When erection of the new Girls' Home made it possible for the boys to live in the Main Building, the social spots were Brown's and Ford's stores, not to overlook Doc Bell's Drug Store, where he kept his old T. C. U. sign long years after the school had moved to Fort Worth. The growth of the community of North Waco (called Hermosen P. O. for a few years after 1900) was enhanced also by the migration of families who moved in to school their children, as was done at Thorp Spring.

When the students assembled in the fall of 1898, the question was freely passed about, "Will we have enough students to open school?" They did. The leanness of these years showed up in the attendance record. There was definite struggle to build

[3]Catalog, 1896, p. 8.
[4]Minutes, 12-5-95.

72

up the attendance, and there was confidence that it would be done. "We desire to make this the largest institution in the Southwest. . . . To any one sending a new pupil who would not otherwise have come, we will allow 20% of the regular tuition fees."[5] This was considered a better proposition to the ministers than free tuition.

It is observed that the local attendance in 1896-97 was the same practically as the local attendance at Thorp Spring in 1894-95. It was the boarding enrollment that was harder to get.

For seven years in Waco, the annual attendance was less than for any year after 1876; the only year it exceeded 200 was 1897-98, when it was 230. In the number of those graduating, there was also a lag. During the seven years previous to the move the number of bachelor's degrees granted was 46; in the seven years after the move, 32. By stretching this test over eight years the number is even, 50. The largest graduating class at Thorp Spring was 12 in 1893; the class of 1904 was 18, and thereafter always larger. The period of the seven lean years was required to overcome the effects of the transplanting; after that the growth was steady and rapid, thus justifying the wisdom of the move.

The two vacancies in the faculty, caused by the failure of Randolph Clark and R. F. Holloway to move to Waco, were supplied by J. W. Froley as Professor of Mathematics and Addison Clark, Jr., as Professor of English and History. The latter had received his B. A. (1890) and his M. A. (1895) from Add-Ran and had done some graduate work at Michigan University.[6] He was a gifted writer, a brilliant student, a sincere Christian, devoted to scholarship and to the institution. He made a distinct contribution to the founding of an athletic program, having had much to do with converting his father to the idea, and even more to the stimulation of student interest. He suited up and played rough and tumble with the students, despite his diminutive size.

He was innately awkward in social contacts, though keenly anxious to be gracious. He initiated and largely produced the first Annual, that of 1897-98, and was influential in the selection of the name "Horned Frog" for it, recognizing the useful little lizard as typical of the Southwest, its habitat.[7]

[5]Catalog, 1896, p. 59.
[6]The faculty at Thorp Spring is listed in the Minutes of 1-2-96, p. 63.
[7]For the story of the origin of the Horned Frog title see Chapter XXI.

As editor of *The Collegian*, the monthly magazine, he found it a joyful outlet for his penchant for pungent paragraphing. Into that vigorous style of his came the influence of W. C. Brann, of the famous Brann's Iconoclast, which was flourishing in Waco in those days. Through this style of writing he offended many of the students and some Waco citizens. In December, 1898, the Board, after criticizing him, accepted his written apology for certain articles which they deemed "injurious to the institution and critical of religion," etc. At the March meeting following, he volunteered his resignation, which was accepted. In a larger institution, he might have survived and have gained a better balance; Add-Ran was a close-knit group, too close to avoid offense.[8]

In addition to these replacements, the main faculty started off with the five who came from Thorp Spring: President Addison Clark, Professor of Mental and Moral Science; W. B. Parks, of Natural Science; J. B. Sweeney, of the Biblical Department; T. Louis Comparette of Latin and Greek; and A. C. Easley, Principal of the Commercial Department.[9] Professor Comparette of Ancient Languages, served only a year and a half in Waco, being followed in 1897-98 by Franklin G. Jones of the Add-Ran class of 1890, then by J. B. Eskridge, who served from 1898 through 1912.

A. C. Easley made the Commercial Department about the most flourishing of all. He was partly on a commission basis, and was overlooked in a move to raise salaries. In polite, but vigorous language, he wrote the Trustees of their oversight, and called their attention to the growth in his department, the financial returns of it, and to the many tasks he was performing. In their eagerness to cover all the points, and with somewhat of a facetious twinkle, they voted to "elect A. C. Easley as Principal of the Business College, as Bursar, Treasurer, Bookkeeper, Steward, Commandant, Assistant Physical Director, and General Roustabout."[10] The only exaggeration in the motion was the last title, for he actually did cover all of the other duties mentioned, and in a most efficient manner.

The Preparatory Department was of much importance in those days, the enrollment outnumbering that of the college. Miss A. Taylor, who had headed it last at Thorp Spring, was placed at

[8]Minutes, 9-7-98, 12-20-98, 3-14-99.
[9]Minutes, 3-17-96.
[10]Minutes, 6-4-10.

the head of Modern Languages, and Professor R. P. Kirk of La-Grange was called to this place. He was an old time Public School Superintendent and a practical teacher of worth.

His successor, who came with the fall of 1898, proved to be a beloved figure on the campus for many years. W. T. Hamner headed the Preparatory, later taught English in the College, but his richest service lay in his supervision of the boys in the dormitory through several generations (with an intermission), till 1916. This genial Christian gentleman, a bachelor, whose love was reserved for his boys, awakened many a lad to the finer values of life. His little reed organ gathered them about him to sing until the deeper springs of the heart were aroused. It was his influence that started the tradition of good male quartets and glee clubs in T. C. U. It was his custom to have one boy room with him, whose cost and career were his peculiar charge.

The Department of Fine Arts was kept up to good standard, but with faculty turnover more than normal. All of these teachers were on commission, usually 80 per cent. Music was headed first by Mrs. Josephine Haywood, 1896; Miss Stella Pierce, of Belton, 1897; then Miss Emma White of Connecticut[11] for two years to 1899. Voice teachers were Miss Byrdie Holloway and Miss Laura Yates. Those who taught Art were Miss Sallie Cayce, Miss Eugenia Price, 1896-98; Miss Laura Yates, 1898-99, then Mrs. Dura Brokaw Cockrell who began in 1899 her twenty-four year career. Miss Theodora Cayce, sister of the Art teacher, and an assistant in the Preparatory, offered to establish a "School of Elocution" in the spring of 1896. She married one of the graduates* of the next spring class, and was succeeded for a year by a vigorous personality, Miss Greenwood Hardy, then in 1898-99 by Miss Alice M. Grannis of charming personality and rare skill. Thus was started the tradition for outstanding teachers in speech, which has not been broken.

The matron in those days was of exceedingly great importance. Mrs. M. E. Wideman, sister of the well known minister, A. J. Bush, served in this capacity at Thorp Spring and came on to Waco. She was followed by Mrs. Martha Taliferro, who also had previously served at Thorp Spring.

The life of the students was a happy one, probably enough to harmonize with the expression, the "Gay Nineties." The limitations in numbers contributed to the homogeneity and fellowship.

---

[11]Miss White became Mrs. Clement Wilson, died April 1904. *Skiff*, 4-30-04.
* J. M. Campbell, B. A. '96.

75

Everyone knew everyone else. "No caste—no secret societies, no hazing, no plutocracy."[12] The social and expressional life of the students centered largely about the Literary Societies even more than about athletics. These were considered a requisite, for the sake of self-expression. Each student was free to select the society he preferred, but was required to join one. For the few who neglected to do so, a "Company Q" was appointed, to assemble in the study hall during society time.[13]

School was held, in those days, five days a week. Monday was utilized mostly for laundry and literary societies. On the top floor, amid rafters and beams, every Monday morning the societies gathered at ten o'clock, the Waltons in the southwest wing, the Add-Rans in the northwest, in neat halls which they had fitted up at their own expense. After a half hour of program, both societies recessed, and woe be the performer who chanced to be performing when his audience heard the other society turn out for recess. For the urge to sociability was running strong. After a time, a varying time, the program was resumed, or a joint program held. It is tradition that the time for recess kept getting longer and the programs shorter. Some of the students, especially the ministerial, ambitious to exercise their speaking powers more frequently, organized, in 1897, a new society named after T. E. Shirley, the "Shirley Bible and Literary Society." This continued the work of the former Watts Society, which had lapsed. One of the honors of the school life was to win the Walton Medal given by Major John T. Walton of Waco, or the Shirley Medal donated by T. E. Shirley. The Add-Rans also got up a medal. The spirit of the Shirleys was expressed in the complaint made by one of its members on one occasion, because there was not time for each speaker to take part more than once a fortnight. He complained, "Mr. President, I can't afford to tramp through the mud and dark and come here at night just to hear the other fellows talk; I want on the program at every meeting."

A vigorous Student Volunteer Band was also alive on the campus; many of the students were active in the Christian Endeavor, some prominent in state-wide offices.

The medium of literary expression was The Collegian, a monthly magazine. Advertising business was not sufficient yet to support a weekly newspaper. That was to come in 1902.

[12]Catalog, 1896, p. 13.
[13]Annual, 1897-98.

Although "dates" were scarce and the young ladies were carefully chaperoned, there was abundant social enjoyment. Parties in those days were called "soirees."[14] Even with some of the professors there was a spirit of camaraderie. Otherwise an incident like this one could not have occurred. Professor Froley, in a mathematics class, was finding it difficult for the students to comprehend the meaning of asymtotic lines. So he gave a human sort of illustration. Knowing that Claude McClellan was somewhat sweet on Bess Sims, he said to him: "If you were standing against this wall, and Miss Sims were backed against the opposite wall, you would step half the distance to her, then again half the distance remaining, then again half the distance remaining, then again half the distance still remaining, and so on. Since you go only half the distance each time, you would never really reach her." "Yes, Professor, but I'd get close enough for all practical purposes" was Claude's reply.

The discipline of the school was quite the same as in the former days, at least in the catalog. The same ten paragraphs on "Conduct of Students" was still printed there. And they still prohibited "race course, billiard, saloon, bar, or tippling house—fire-arms, dirk, bowie knife, or any knife or deadly weapon, profanity, card playing," etc. The old rule "Abstain from the use of tobacco" was modified to "Do not smoke in any public place" and a new paragraph "Efforts will be made to discourage the use of tobacco among the students by showing them its evil effects and to secure a pledge from each young man that he will not use it in any form."[15]

It was in the financial struggle that the leanness of these years was felt most keenly, most dramatically—even tragically—at least it skimmed tragedy on thin ice. There were four elements that edged like a swollen river with constant threat of submersion during all of these seven years. First was the debt brought over from Thorp Spring, then the failure of the Waco citizens to back up the Waco church brethren in the amount anticipated, the accumulating deficit under reduced enrollment, and finally, the absolute necessity of spending some money to complete and furnish the building.

The old indebtedness amounted to more than $13,000.[16] Not so much, we moderns may think, but it was genuine danger in

---

[14]Horned Frog, 1897-98.
[15]Catalog, 1897, p. 63.
[16]According to a report by the President of the Board in the Catalog of 1895.

those days when the habit of donations was but little formed. Moreover, the nature of those obligations made them annoying to the Trustees. In the summer of 1896 Mr. Cogdell threatened suit for his account of $4,170.20 unless he were given a lien on the Waco property. But the Trustees could not get a deed to the Waco property until the Thorp Spring campus was cleared. He declined a lien on the latter. They were disappointed in the autumn of 1898 when the Masonic Grand Lodge of Texas declined the request of the Granbury Lodge to purchase the Thorp Spring property as a site for an Orphanage, at the price of $10,000.[17] At a later date, the Board requested J. J. Jarvis to accept bonds in payment of the account he held against the school. A lien on the Thorp Spring property was offered to him also, in settlement, as it was, again, to him and to Mr. Cogdell the following March.[18]

At a meeting, February 1, 1900, it was reported to the Trustees that the First National Bank of Granbury proposed "to take $2,500 cash for their debt, or that we give them deed to the Thorp Spring property and three other pieces of land." These pieces were 320 acres in Trinity County (one-third interest), 160 acres in Red River County, and 640 in Lynn County. The latter offer was accepted; the land was deeded and the debt cancelled.[19]

The record does not make it appear that the claim of J. J. Jarvis was included in this settlement, nor how it was settled. The fact is that Mr. Jarvis later secured possession of the old campus, leased it to the Clarks for Add-Ran Jarvis College to 1910, then sold it to the Trustees of Thorp Spring Christian College for the Church of Christ brethren about 1911.[20]

The second financial burden was the shortage in the amount expected from Waco. This disappointment caused no small amount of feeling between the old trustees and the "Waco brethren." But it appears to have been just another one of those cases of rosy promises from the mass, and poor collection from individuals. The church men had the promise of backing from the commercial group in general, and when the collections fell short the church brethren did not have the resources to make it up.

[17]Minutes, 10-12- and 12-28, 97 pp. 111, 113.
[18]Minutes, 3-16-98, p. 116.
[19]Minutes, 2-1-00, 3-12-00, pp. 142, 143.
[20]But see Chapter XXV, pp. 339, for accurate details on this.

In spite of these debts, the leaders were hopeful. For in March, 1896, they voted to restore some salary cuts that had been previously made.[21] The threat of an accumulating deficit on current operation continued to mount, despite the modesty of the monthly pay-roll. This consisted of two salaries of $100 per month (President, and Business Manager-Commercial Teacher), three at $85, four specials and matrons at $65—total, $715 month. Others were on commission. J. B. Sweeney was to get $100 a month, out of his collections, for the Endowment Fund. Modest as was that pay-roll, the income from the student fees was even more meager. The enrollment figure of 153 for 1896-97 included all the part-time, part-year specials, and those with jobs. And the faculty was always generous with jobs for student expense. The ministerial students did not then receive any concessions on tuition; they were offered commission on students they solicited and secured, but few cashed in on this. There was little hope for profit from the boarding department to help out.

The faculty were the ones who were feeling the pinch most; they met the issue with initiative and generosity. Eight of them made a written proposal to the Board in September, 1896, to join a total of twenty persons in guaranteeing the salary of a capable solicitor for funds, for a period of five years, allowing twenty-five per cent of the funds he raised to apply toward his salary and expenses if necessary, etc.[22] This did not materialize. The next spring, 1897, the faculty made a more drastic proposal which the Trustees accepted and operated for the two sessions of 1897-98 and 1898-99. The "Big Four," as the students dubbed them—Addison Clark, J. B. Sweeney, W. B. Parks, and J. W. Froley—leased the property, operated the school, paid the salaries and all expenses out of the income from students and board. The faculty selection had to be approved by the Trustees, the lessees were limited to a maximum salary of $100 a month, and were to pay to the Trustees seventy-five per cent of the profits (!) after all expenses were paid.[23] This lease arrangement was terminated by agreement made at the Board meeting March 16, 1899; two of the lessees were leaving: A. Clark and J. B. Sweeney.

[21]Minutes, 2-17-96.
[22]Minutes, 2-2-96.
[23]Minutes, 3-16-97, 6-1-97, 3-15-98.

79

A meeting had just been held in the chapel at which pledges of $10,000 were made. Perhaps this prospect of new funds, and the paucity of their salaries thus far, moved the teachers of "the literary department" to ask for a "supplement to their salaries" at this time. The Trustees responded by issuing to each teacher a note of $50, due the following May 1, and by passing a resolution of "hearty thanks," great appreciation, regrets and sympathy, recognizing that "they deserve much more than we are now able to do."[24] Provision was further made that day that the salaries for the next session should be $70 a month, plus fifty per cent of the surplus income from the literary departments proper, up to $90 a month.[25] Thus it was clearly recognized that the brunt of the sacrifice in those lean years was borne by the teachers.

The fourth financial concern was for the obvious need of an improved plant and living conditions. To complete the building would make more room for students, and to improve the grounds and equipment would make it more attractive to them.

Burdened by these four harassments the Trustees were torn between the fear of being swamped by debt and the challenge to put the school on a new basis of attractiveness to draw a larger enrollment. All of this called for more money. In order to raise it, the first attempt was to issue bonds. Three times in the spring of 1896 they voted to authorize a bond issue of $30,000, then $50,000. Against this policy was a strong popular sentiment which found expression in a resolution in the State Church Convention, June 1896. But this was reversed a year later. In December 1897, an agent was employed to sell $30,000 of the bonds. There seemed to be no market for the bonds among the banks, so in 1899, the members of the churches were appealed to, to purchase them.[26] But the brethren were also shy.

Prior to that time, however, the tide of sentiment had turned toward direct solicitation of gifts to clear the debts, rather than depending on bonds merely to defer them. So in the spring of 1898, the Board selected one of its own number to go among the churches and solicit contributions. This was A. S. Henry, a merchant of Blooming Grove, a capable church leader and an ex-state senator, who moved his family to North Waco, put his children in school and remained there several years longer than

[24]Minutes, 3-16-99, p. 127.
[25]Ibid.
[26]Minutes, 3-17-96, 4-25-96, 3-14-99.

the two years he served as Financial Agent. His work marked the turning of the tide for better conditions. By the following September he reported pledges amounting to $21,000.

The policy of solicitation received an impetus by a rally in the Chapel in the spring of 1899, addressed by the eloquent and persuasive Granville Jones. The amount pledged was $10,000, but the pledges were made largely by students who were more zealous than pecunious; the occasion was mostly a breath of encouragement. This effort was followed by the organization of a campaign among the churches started at the Church Convention in June 1899. Fourteen ministers were selected to canvas under the direction of a Committee. In July at a Trustees meeting a total of $1,375 was reported, of which $1,035 had been raised by Addison Clark. A. S. Henry, summing the collections and prospects, estimated that, in order to open school that fall, they must have $10,000 on hand and the prospect was for $8,500. Mingling their little cash with their large faith, they voted that a catalog be printed, that school should open in September, and "that A. S. Henry should keep on raising money."[27] So close to the margin of disaster did the school come that fateful summer of 1899.

The realm of finance was not the only one to suffer crisis that summer. The turn-over in leadership was at its peak in all the history of the institution. It was almost as if there were a sensing of the gliding of the old century into the new. In March 1899 two of the "Big Four" resigned, J. B. Sweeney, and Addison Clark; a third, J. W. Froley in July; the fourth one, W. B. Parks, withdrew the following February. A. S. Henry, the money raiser, withdrew in September.

The significance of Addison Clark and the spirit of his withdrawal is discussed, as it deserves to be, in a chapter of its own.[28] His dropping out had much influence on the situation at this juncture. For some time he had been seeking release, and the hand of his strong control had become slackened. As early as June 1897, J. B. Sweeney had been appointed as "Chancellor," obviously to share responsibility. That the move was on his own initiative is evidenced by the vote of March 1899, that "Addison Clark be instructed to conduct the correspondence for a new president," and the further fact that he continued on the faculty for three years after the termination of his presidency in 1899.

[27]Minutes, 7-6-99.
[28]Chapter IX.

81

Interesting to later generations is the name of the first person approached for this new presidency: Clinton Lockhart. He had but recently accepted the presidency of Christian University, Canton, Missouri,[29] and was not induced to change at that time.

The Trustees were not slow in filling these vacancies in the ranks. At the same meeting (March, 1899) a new Chancellor was selected in the person of Dr. Albert Buxton. A little later he was appointed as Chairman of the faculty. About the campus it was generally assumed that he was the new President or was to become so. He may have thought that himself, but obviously the Board was doubtful as late as January 1900, when they voted that "the election of a President be postponed." Dr. Buxton wrote from his home in Fairbury, Nebraska, in April 1899, asking that a clear statement of his relationship with President Clark be expressed.[30] He was a man of many degrees, well earned, for he was a genuine scholar. In public address he was at times brilliant, in personality friendly, in devotion to the cause, unquestioned. But his best friends could not class him as an executive. He submitted a rather grandiose scheme for the organization of the University, one that would fit a school with thousands of students but quite impracticable for a struggling small college. He had difficulty with discipline, due to his diffidence in dealing with people. It soon became apparent that he was not the man for the place of responsible leadership, so in March 1900, he requested that he be relieved of his duties as Chairman of the Faculty. He was retained as Professor of Ancient Languages and Chancellor, but at the end of the semester he withdrew entirely.[31]

When the Board met in September (1900) the election of a President was again postponed and E. C. Snow was elected as Acting President. He was just returning to the faculty as Professor of Mathematics.

During this interim without a permanent president in charge, the Trustees necessarily had to assume more than ordinary responsibility, and therefore, authority. In some instances they encroached unwittingly on the prerogatives of the faculty, and this faculty was far from being a spineless non-entity. The differences appeared in the matter of athletic control[32] and came

[29]Now Culver Stockton.
[30]Minutes, 4-11-99.
[31]Minutes, 3-12-00. Dr. Buxton died August 24, 1930, according to a report in the Interpreter at the time.
[32]See Chapter XXI for this story.

to a culmination in a communication from the faculty to the Board in September 1901, expressed in very courteous terms, yet definitely claiming a field of its own. "It is only fair to say that the faculty ought to know better than any other person or body of persons how to govern the student body, and the internal machinery of the school. To manage such affairs and to teach their respective classes is the life work of your faculty, their first and only business. . . . In our judgment the proposed ruling of the Board relative to Senior privileges will not be an encouragement for the best young men and women to attend Add-Ran. The faculty made the rule after most careful deliberation, and has not been consulted relative to the proposed change . . ." The faculty was invited to come in person for a conference with the Board. The resulting action was that "All questions of discipline not covered by rules by the Trustees be committed to the faculty." Thus was felt the lack of a strong administrative head, between presidencies.

Other new teachers called in at this period to fill the vacancies were: Egbert R. Cockrell in History and Political Science, his wife, Dura Brokaw Cockrell, in Art; Frank H. Marshall as Dean of the Bible College, and a little later, C. I. Alexander, in Mathematics. E. V. Zollars was invited to come as a lecturer, but he did not accept, until he came in 1902 as President.[33]

It was a time of changes in the Board of Trustees also. In June, 1897, the Convention took over the responsibility of electing the Trustees, on nomination of the Board, but in September 1899, the charter of the University was amended to return this power to the Board of Trustees itself. This was done with the understanding and approval of the Convention.[34] The members of the Board from Waco were very active, spending much time in making friends among the local citizens and handling the business matters of the school. The most active of these were James I. Moore, who had led in securing the move to Waco, and the pastor, F. N. Calvin. Three of these Waco brethren served successively as Secretary of the Board: W. B. Hays, Dr. F. W. Burger, who lived near the campus and sent his children to Add-Ran, and S. M. Hamilton, an ex-student of Thorp Spring days, and a most energetic devoted young man. Others were W. S. Blackshear, whose wife served a while as Matron, and Major John T. Walton, a friend from the older days. All of

[33]Minutes, 6-8-99.
[34]Minutes, 6-3-97, 9-12-99, 6-3-98.

these were leaders in the Central Christian Church. Prominent among the Trustees from over the state were W. K. Homan, Editor of the *Christian Courier*, lawyer and preacher; Chalmers McPherson, minister at Waxahachie; G. V. McClintic; and Judge A. E. Wilkinson of the State Supreme Court. Charles W. Gibson of Waxahachie, who became one of the eminent men of the Board in later years, began this year, 1899. The Alumni spoke up for the first time, asking to be represented on the Board. In June 1901, this request was recognized by the election of J. J. Hart (B. A. '97) and Van Zandt Jarvis (B. A. '95). When the responsible place of President of the Board was vacated in June 1896 by Major J. J. Jarvis, a strong leader was found in Col. J. Z. Miller of Belton, a devoted churchman, a banker, a courteous Southern gentleman.

That summer of 1899, which saw so many changes and skimmed so many dangers, brought into recognition another of those outstanding personalities who have served as Presidents of the Trustees. T. E. Shirley of Melissa had joined the Board in 1893, but had dropped out a little later. But that first summer in Waco he was reelected as a member, and in 1899, when Col. Miller retired, the Board recognized T. E. Shirley as the strong man to carry on the tradition of consecrated and able leadership. For ten years he glorified that office, fulfilling, during a part of that time, the duties that usually fall upon a college president, and, at time of crisis, those of the financial secretary.[35]

A number of influences converged to make that summer of 1899 the depth of the valley and the start up the hill. The doubts, the debt, the changes, the losses were altogether enough to have effected disaster in any ordinary group or undertaking. But this was not ordinary either in purpose or in personnel. Many believed that Providence was back of it.

The policy of raising money instead of selling bonds met with favor. The whittling down of the debts by the funds raised by A. S. Henry and the Convention canvassers gave hope and encouragement. Then there was the galvanizing faith of the new chairman of the Board, T. E. Shirley

With this modest gain and immeasurable faith, the spring of 1900 witnessed the next venture of faith—a new building. Up to this time the boys had boarded out in the community, the girls

---

[35]Minutes, 6-30-96, p. 85; 6-6-99, p. 135.

living in the Main building. Once it was proposed to run a wooden wall through the building so as to use it for both boys and girls.

It was in a memorable meeting on March 12, 1900, when they agreed to a settlement of the Thorp Spring debt, elected nine new teachers, deferred the election of a president, appointed a committee to clear the title to the campus, and declined any further concessions to the athletic group, that they also passed this blunt motion: "That we build a Girls Memorial Hall to accommodate fifty girls—carried."[36]

They went a step further at their next meeting in June; they decided who the "we" should be. "Moved and carried that the proposed Girls Home be built by the ladies of the Christian Church in Texas."[37] One might remark that these men were certainly very courtly gentlemen, so to yield to the ladies. As a matter of fact, Mr. Shirley had discovered in his rounds that there were several ladies in Texas who were able and willing to give and others who were devoted to the school. Sixteen of them were appointed to "meet and formulate their plans at the Paris convention," which was soon due.[38] By the following March, construction was under way, and, by the next fall, nearing completion.[39] They were so much in the mood of advancement and building that they voted in November "to encourage the community in the building of a house of worship near the University," but not on the campus.[40]

So through these seven lean years from 1895 to 1902, the story is marked by fears and faith, sacrifice and success, the dark valley and the bright sunshine. Enough is revealed in the lines and between them to assure that the very limit of endurance was closely skimmed more than once. Evidence, too, there was of much heroic sacrifice, and hard labor on the part of some. There is a tradition, and it is well authenticated though documentation is not possible, of a certain meeting in the Church in Fort Worth when a climax was reached. It is told that, after the canvas was made among the churches and the results were too meager to give assurance of continuing the school, the Trustees were of a mind to give up the struggle. It is said that T. M. Scott made a motion to notify the brethren that they had given

[36]Minutes, 3-12-00, p. 144.
[37]Ibid. 6-3-00.
[38]Ibid., p. 155.
[39]Ibid., 3-3-01; 9-4-01, p. 174.
[40]Ibid., 11-27-01, p. 178.

full evidence that they did not want the school continued, and that the Trustees had decided to close it. His brother-in-law, T. E. Shirley, was in the chair. He refused to put the motion; hence it could not carry. That might have led to an impasse, if it had stopped there. But it did not. Mr. Shirley volunteered to devote his full time to the job of raising that money himself, starting the subscription with a thousand dollars. That proposition was accepted.

On the request of Mrs. Frankie Miller Mason, for her Early Beginnings, Mrs. Pauline Shirley Haile wrote of her father's experiences in this period, as follows:[41]

It was at this critical time that Mr. Shirley asked for a leave of absence from the H & T C Railroad Company, and sought to raise the money for the school. He began by making a liberal pledge himself and stating that he would pay his own expenses and charge nothing for his time so that every dollar given would count on the indebtedness.

Many there were who had given again and again to pay on indebtedness of the school, only to learn the debt was increasing instead of diminishing. These friends had become discouraged but Mr. Shirley's statement restored their confidence. Colonel J. Z. Miller, of Belton, always a friend to T. C. U. said, when first approached by Mr. Shirley, "I do not care to put another dollar into a sinking ship." After Mr. Shirley explained his plan and told Colonel Miller that every cent of the money to pay the entire debt must be in the Waco bank before any was paid at all and that if the entire indebtedness could not be wiped out none of the money was to be paid, Colonel Miller said, "There never was a safer proposition made," and gladly signed his name as one of the ten men giving $1,000 each. This was the first time that as much as $1,000 had been given at one time by any person except that given by Major Jarvis. Altogether there were three hundred and one persons who gave.[42]

The Trustees Resolved:

Their thanks to T. E. Shirley, their chairman, for his unwearied effort in raising the money to discharge the indebtedness, . . . in devoting his time and great personal influence without compensation and in addition to his own liberal contributions, meeting the expenses of his canvas . . . and in a great Christian University for the state of Texas, now free from indebtedness, meeting its expenses and hope-

[41]Mason, p. 103.
[42]Mason, p. 103, an interview with Pauline Shirley Hale.

Random samples
of students in
Waco days :

*Top, from Left :*
  Myrtle Tomlinson
  Leslie Procter
  Burl Hulsey
  Mercy Perkins
  Noah (Cy) Perkins
  Pauline Shirley
  Thurman (Hoss)
    Allen
  Gordon B. Hall
  Lucile Wolford
  Roy Tomlinson
  Mary Bain Spence
  Bess Coffman
  Paul Tyson
  Bryant Collins
  Leia Tomlinson
  Nona Boegeman
  Beatrice Tomlinson

Some More Random Samples from Waco Days.

*Top left :* Mrs. W. B. Parks, Mrs. M. Taliferrio, Miss Tyler Wilkinson, Miss Harriet Frances
Smith, Bonner Frizzell, Ed "Chicken" McKinney, (Founder of The *Skiff*), Frank Elkin,
Olive Leaman McClintic
*Military Group :* Franklin Kinnard, Ivan Harbour, Odell Elliot, Hardy Grissom,
(seated) Douglas Shirley.
*Baseball Team 1907–Top Left :* A. C. Carnes, 3rd B., M. O. Thomas, 2nd B., Bert Bloor, C.,
E. R. Randle, P., P. W. Witt, 3rd B.
*Second Row :* Paul Tyson, P., Douglas Shirley, Mgr., Leslie Proctor, Cpt., 2nd B., Ellis Hardy,
Coach, Marshall Baldwin, 1st B.
*Third Row :* Cy Perkins, J. B. Frizzell, RF., R. G. Williams, Utility.  Chas. Carlton, teacher of
the Clarks ; Tom Gallagher, baseball, 1904
*Fourth Row :* A bluebonnet view of the Waco campus ; E. R. Randle, P. "Fuzzy" Baldwin, 1st B.

Main Building, Waco, 1897.

Main Building after the fire, 1910.

MAJOR J. J. JARVIS, 1889-95        COL. J. Z. MILLER, 1895-99

THORNTON E. SHIRLEY, 1899-1909        THOMAS E. TOMLINSON, 1909-17
Total Service, 24 years.                           Total 37 years.

THE FIRST FOUR PRESIDENTS OF THE BOARD OF TRUSTEES.

fully launched upon a career of prosperity worthy of the name which it bears.[43]

It was at this same meeting that the Trustees were called upon to express, out of their hearts of sorrow, resolutions on the death of J. B. Sweeney. Although he had given up his allotted task of endowing the Bible College two years before this, remaining a Trustee, they sensed the true measure of his value to them:

While the loss has been upon the whole church in all its departments of work, the blow has fallen hardest upon our beloved University, in whose service he spent the best years of his life that was all too brief. . . . Giving all, as he did in the days of dark adversity, it is a matter of deep regret to us that he is not present in body to rejoice with us in the day of prosperity.[44]

Their hill of difficulty ran in small figures, as later generations count figures. How could a school be in danger of its life from a $17,000 indebtedness? But it must be remembered that those days were still on the border of the frontier, and the frontier was largely a barter age. Cash was a minor portion of the living. The man with the farm was wealthy. It gave him and his large family a living. A few sold crops enough for a minimum of cash to buy luxuries. But all cash transactions were in small terms. The large end of the living was in kind. As late as the nineties, Chalmers McPherson used to say that only three preachers (of the Disciples) in the state were on regular salary from one church and that they were dubbed "stall-fed preachers." Indeed this was a pioneer school, emerging from the frontier period.

It was not the size of figures that counted. Men who could pull through such times, under such difficulties, and express the optimism and hope of those resolutions about Sweeney and Shirley, were men of spirits indomitable. Theirs was a mighty challenge, and they met it nobly and successfully. They breathed the spirit of the indefatigable pioneers into the school, for the generations to come.

With the coming of 1902, better times arrived. But it was not yet to be the seven fat years. Three times seven years had to pass before any such appellation could be imagined. But the seven lean years were over.

[43]Minutes, 11-28-01, p. 179.
[44]Ibid., p. 180.

ADDISON CLARK
*(The picture that appeared in the 1897-98 Horned Frog)*
*Compare with his bearded picture in the group on page 62*

# ❧ IX ❧

# Addison Clark, Philalatheian, 1842-1911

A T A MEETING OF THE ASSOCIATION of Texas Colleges in the 1920's, Dr. William S. Sutton, the Dean of the University of Texas School of Education, and its founder, one of the wisest and wittiest of Texas sages, included in an address words which may well be paraphrased in the following paragraphs:

Two college presidents on the western frontier guided their respective schools from small beginnings to substantial growth through the 1890's, both leading brilliantly, devotedly, with general honor and acclaim. They were pioneers, to the frontier born, with its spirit in their souls; for it, they worked out a technique that succeeded brilliantly.

Then times changed. Travel became easier, the urban trend set in, new standards arose, and a new technique for college was demanded. One of these presidents, venerable, honored, beyond seventy, was invited by his Trustees to an emeritus status at generous salary and honorable distinction. He not only declined, but resisted continuously, to the hurt of the institution, devotedly determined to "die in the harness."

The other, not yet sixty, perceived the situation and required his Trustees, over their protest to secure, as he said, "a young man, trained in the great Universities of the East, who can carry on the school in the new generation." "I am a pioneer," he pleaded; "get some man who can fit his day as I have done mine. My work is done; let the institution grow greater with the new day."

Thus did one good man allow his devotion to blur his judgment, while the other exercised the rarest of wisdom, by effacing himself for the sake of the cause. Few men rise to such heights of greatness as did this humble giant of the frontier days.

After Dr. Sutton's talk, the writer of these lines went up to him and correctly identified both of the distinguished presidents, whom he naturally had left unidentified. That pioneer of such rare wisdom and self-effacing greatness was Addison Clark. His strength was well known to all educators of that generation. The shortest acquaintance with Addison Clark would impress one with his quality of humility.

But it was the humility of greatness, as illustrated and recognized by Dr. Sutton. It was inbred; not a consciousness of any weakness of his own, but a recognition of the worth of others. That this respect for others was not confined to any age or rank was proved to this writer on one occasion, much to his abashment. It was while the Clarks were conducting Add-Ran Jarvis College at Thorp Springs, about 1906, that the writer, as Education Secretary[1] for T. C. U., visited the school. This was nine years after he had been a student under "Brother Addison." He was received with genteel treatment and far more than expected honor. The visit concluded on Saturday afternoon, when both of us had to catch a train at Granbury, three and a half miles away, for Sunday appointments. "Mr. Addison" went out to get a horse and buggy. He was gone for some time, then was overheard out on the porch trying to locate a conveyance, and not having much luck. His visitor, sensing the situation, stepped out on the porch and said, "Brother Addison, you have always been quite a walker; if you are still able to make it, I shall be glad to walk with you to Granbury." That simple-hearted, noble reply will never be forgotten: "Well, now, Brother Colby, I *always* walk, but I couldn't think of allowing my guest to walk."

That from the veteran to the stripling! We walked!

His brother's testimony to this quality of humility is valuable:

On public occasions he avoided platform reservations and conspicuous seats.—On one occasion, when W. J. Bryan was to deliver an address, the committee on arrangements informed Addison that a seat was reserved for him on the speaker's platform; but when the crowd assembled, he was found in the audience, in front of the speaker. At the Centennial Convention in Pittsburgh in 1909, there was a special time and place for the assembling of pioneer preachers. They were seated according to seniority; representatives were called to give *Reminiscences* of their times, places, and work.—A brother arose and asked to be permitted to introduce the distinguished pioneer educator of the great Southwest. Addison saw the trend of the introduction and whispered to one sitting by him, 'If I am not here when the

[1]*Skiff*, November, 1906, Editorial.

94

audience is dismissed, I will be just outside the door.' When his name was called, there was no one to answer.[2]

Mr. Randolph sometimes remarked that Addison had had the responsibilities of maturity thrust upon him so early in life that he never experienced a normal youthhood. He was barely twenty when he became a soldier and only twenty-two when mustered out of the army. "He was soon asked to take the office of Orderly Sergeant of the company, and in a short time was given a commission as a lieutenant.—On occasions he was given command over men his senior in years and rank."[3] Even before that, he was inclined to take life seriously and calmly, for, to one who was excited about the prospects of military glory, he wrote: "It is a good time to be calm and to take one's reckoning. The people will soon know who are the unsafe advisers. Some Washington may arise and lead the people to safety, but just now the political fools are in appearance."[4]

After the war he was so absorbed in his life purpose of securing an education, and teaching to build character for the New South, that he had no time for play and very little for sociability. In the formalities of social contacts, restricted as they were on the frontier, he had little experience, so he was always somewhat diffident on social occasions. Everywhere he would impress one as a refined gentleman, gracious as a courtier. But the refinement came from within. He was unskilled in the artifices of correct social bearing; his was the artless expression of a genuine soul.

Addison's wife, Sallie McQuigg, whom he had met as a member of the household of Charles Carlton, while a student, and whom he married at the time of his graduation, was even more retiring than her husband. A mother supreme, she was devoted to her children but adverse to public appearances. Their children, in a large measure, were serious in disposition, studious in habit, brilliant in books, indisposed to sociability, some of them even ill-at-ease in social groups. Would that space permitted the tracing of the careers of the illustrious lives of the children of both these homes of Addison and Randolph. All have proven worthy of their cultural heritage; not a few have made notable contributions to education and religion.

[2]*Reminiscences*, p. 61.
[3]Ibid., p. 26.
[4]Ibid., p. 25.

Addison Clark had a mind that was at home with the giant intellects of the ages, a design of life that soared above the pettiness which dulls the days of most people. He must have been, often, a lonely soul. Yet he had a way of getting through the barriers of persons into their inmost beings, and of making them sense the glorious worth of integrity which he loved, lived, and embodied. One cattle man, whose speech betrayed the paucity of his gleanings from books, declared, "I didn't make my grades, and I gave Brother Addison a lot of worry, but my time wasn't wasted. What I got from the character of Addison Clark was worth more than all the books; it made a different man of me. I've always tried to be true to the standards of integrity he lived." Thus have testified hundreds of others.

Addison appeared to be stern, for he was serious. Sometimes he was stubborn, for he had convictions. He was reputed to be unrelenting, but he had none of the face-saving of smaller men who never like to admit an error. Many a student had the experience of seeing that steel-gray eye soften into winsome yearning for his good and a willingness to help. Mrs. Jarvis delighted to tell how she saved the school when she tied a handkerchief to her parasol and approached him as if with a flag of truce, and moved his sense of humor into a change of sentence. That was not the only time he relented.[5]

He had been a soldier, accustomed to strict discipline. Military terms came readily to his tongue. He lived in rough times when boys needed to learn discipline. But he did not delight in punishment. He loved the bad boy, but sent him home for the good of those left behind. It was his custom to let boys withdraw and save the stigma of expulsion. Many a chapel talk concluded by advising the recalcitrants to "fold your tents like the Arabs and silently steal away."

"The noblest Roman of them all" was the way many of his fellow-leaders felt about him. In a sense he was an aristocrat, though he would have been the last to agree to such an idea. He was in many ways a man apart. Others instinctively expected him to do the deciding. In any group, his native dignity was obvious to all except to himself. "Cussing" was common on the frontier; some men were pridefully eloquent at it, others were slavishly vulgar. It is safe to assert that not even the most hardened would have ventured to cuss in the presence of Mr.

[5]This story is told in Chapter VI.

Addison, any more than they would before ladies. No man who looked at him, unless drunk already, would have dared offer him a drink of liquor.

Despite this distinction and the deference men accorded him as President through many years, he was genuinely a democrat. He respected the opinions of others, as he demanded respect for his own convictions. He may not have preached on "the high value of the human personality" so much as the generation that followed him, but he must assuredly have practiced this basic tenet of his Master. Randolph reveals that Addison was opposed to naming the school a "college," and afterward a "university." But he yielded to the majority opinion of the group with whom he labored. His soul was tied devotedly to the location at Thorp Spring, and he declared he would finish his life's work there. But he respected the judgment of the men on the Board of Trustees, and recognized that he had given the proprietorship to the church, so he yielded to the move to Waco, though his heart yearned for the rural quiet. His pioneer's disdain for waste of time made him constitutionally opposed to play, at least to organized time-consuming play. Aside from military drill, he could see no place for college athletics, especially in the form of football. It looked rough. It was rough; too rough for the untrained. So he was opposed to football when it began to come in. Yet he yielded, after evidence and persuasion. It required the influence of some of his fellow-teachers whom he respected, and especially the persuasions of his son, Addison, Jr., whom he adored. But he yielded and became a "fan." He was a democrat.

Busy as they were with teaching and administration, the Clarks never lost the habit of preaching, nor the fervor of it. They spent their summers in holding "protracted meetings." It was in one of these in 1897 that Mr. Addison baptized Luke Brite of Marfa, who in later years became the benefactor of Brite College. Randolph was, in some ways, the more popular preacher. He was sociable and cordial. His sermons were practical and human; in his later years, rambling and reminiscent. Addison's sermons were profound, dignified, graced with a native eloquence, flowing with a beautiful sense of rhythm, clarifying with apt figures of speech, and convincing by a deep devotion to truth. Anything he said was because he believed it, not because it might please the audience. He dealt with great concepts. Those who had not the background to grasp his thought were nevertheless drawn irresistibly to strive for higher ideals.

Surprisingly, Addison Clark succeeded as a pastor. After twenty-six years as a college president, he served several years as pastor of the Central Christian Church at Waco; then at Amarillo, before returning to Thorp Spring for the last school, Add-Ran Jarvis College. His parishioners felt that they were living on rare feasts to hear his preaching. They loved him tenderly as he mingled in their homes, never sparing himself in serving the needs of his flock. Any intricate planning for the machinery of a city church was entirely out of his range. He realized this and doubted his fitness for a city pastorate, but his people were content to grow on his great preaching. Those were high days for these fortunate churches.

It is a temptation to lengthen this chapter into a biography of Addison Clark, instead of just an estimate and appreciation. And the author would greatly delight in that assignment, for to no one man does he owe more for ideals of character and of education. But any such biography would have to lean too heavily on Randolph's *Reminiscences*, and no one could ever catch the tender flavor of that writer as he poured out his tribute to his beloved brother.

This sketch should close with a recognition of the one trait of character, which, above all others, made Addison Clark distinctive. That was his love of truth. At least that is the humble conviction of one who knew him well, and many would share the estimate. This characteristic stood out through many experiences, most of them difficult to describe. On returning from a trip one time, he was told that a certain boy had won in a debate and another had lost. "That boy," he remarked, "will always win in the long run because he is devoted to the truth; the other is not"; which dictum revealed much more about Addison Clark than it did about the boys. Once he heard the story of a T. C. U. representative who had been asked to referee a football game between T. C. U. and A. & M. on the latter's grounds. (Officials for football in those days were unofficial, unpaid, and scarce.) The T. C. U. "referee" saw a T. C. U. offside, then saw T. C. U. make a touchdown on the play—their only one. Still he called the foul, though he could have overlooked it.[6] It greatly delighted Mr. Addison to hear of this integrity; he told of it immediately in chapel.

He was a constant reader of the latest theological publications. He kept abreast of the new theories, disconcerting though they were to the older conservative views that were native to him. He remained conservative, but he was never frightened, never hostile to free investigation, and often accepted new views sooner than his junior brethren. He believed in liberty of thought; he was far from the spirit of the heresy hunter. There have been occasions in the history of this brotherhood when some men were cornered and compelled publicly, either on the platform or in print, to express a sort of confession of faith to prove themselves sound in the faith. That sort of treatment he not only abhorred; he thought it subversive of the very plea for freedom which the Disciples made. He said as much one time in a public discussion, and afterwards wrote: "I said that a man who was that well known and with as good a record as he had made must take the witness stand before the brotherhood and be catechized as to his faith in the fundamental truths of the Christian religion, is a shame." Also: "I am sorry that he suggested it or submitted to any such proceedings. It sets a bad precedent."[7]

During a lectureship at Waco about 1907, he was called upon to express his view in the open discussion. (He rarely joined in unless invited.) His remarks revealed familiarity with the most recent writing upon a controversial subject, and some sympathetic understanding of the new and suspected viewpoint. One young minister, his former pupil, was heard to remark: "Dear, dear, I'm afraid Brother Addison is slipping." It was rather the integrity of an open mind which would recognize truth when he saw it, and hold to it at any cost if he believed it to be truth. There have been souls in every generation whose devotion to truth was notable, but surely there could never have been one more devoted than Addison Clark. Eternity will recognize him as Philalatheian—Lover of Truth.

He was one of those rare souls to whom one feels impelled to apply the encomium which John Drinkwater in his play reserved for Abraham Lincoln, on his too early passing: "Now he belongs to the ages."

[6]This game was T. C. U. vs. A. & M., October, 1906.
[7]Private letters in possession of the author, signed by A. Clark.

## ❧ X ❧

# Trail Blazing For A Bible College, 1895-1914

## J. B. SWEENEY, 1895-1899

I N SEPTEMBER, 1895, a horse and buggy drove into the village of Thorp Spring, wended its way across Stroud's Creek, down the lanes of that sylvan dell of beauty, and stopped under the shade of one of the giant live oaks that lined the campus of old Add-Ran Christian University. There this country college, the oldest in West Texas, the fifth oldest in Texas, had stood for twenty-two years, but for only five years had belonged to the church and borne the dignified title of University. The session previous had enrolled 300 students from 60 Texas counties, besides 4 "foreigners" from Tennessee, Arkansas, and Indian Territory. The faculty that year had consisted of an even dozen: 6 in Liberal Arts; 1 each in Art, Music, Commerce, Preparatory and Primary; 1 listed as "Teacher of Elocution and Guitar."

It was the thirteenth teacher, a believer in pluck rather than luck, that unlimbered his long legs out of the buggy that September day, straightened out his Prince Albert coat, and probably smoothed his fair crop of chin whiskers, and looked out on the campus of the old school whence he had graduated just ten years before. This man, J. B. Sweeney, was the second preacher to be graduated by Add-Ran, the sixth enrollee to become known as a preacher. In his middle thirties, he had just resigned the pastorate at Taylor to become Professor of Sacred Literature in Add-Ran. He came with the sanction of the "State Meeting" and a salary from the Trustees of $1200, provided he could collect it from the brethren in the field.

Before his coming, two names had appeared as teacher of Bible: Addison Clark, and his father, J. A. Clark. Both of these had other duties, and to them Bible teaching was secondary. But to J. B. Sweeney it was the sole purpose of his coming. It was more; it was a romantic adventure for a longtime, lofty purpose. He was coming as more than just another professor. That summer, a charter[1] had been obtained for "The Bible Department" of the University; the title to which he had been elected[2] was "President of the Bible College"; one catalog listed him as "Principal" another as "Dean,"[3] and before he left the University four years later he was "Chancellor."[4] The term "Bible Chair" was frequently used in the effort to raise endowment.[5]

Incidentally, the next motion following his election was to appoint a committee to investigate the proposition to move the school to Waco, and the actual move was just about three months later. So Mr. Sweeney's work was mostly done at the Waco location.

From the first, the announcements indicated a serious purpose to establish a distinct, worthy and permanent Bible College. The President of the Board, J. J. Jarvis, had printed in the catalog of that session a "report" including the following:

"By inspection of the catalog it will be seen that a plan is on foot to establish and endow a Bible Chair in the University. We hope this will be accomplished at an early day, there being at this time pledges to establish such a Bible Chair amounting to about $10,000, and it is earnestly hoped that the brotherhood will increase this amount to $50,000 before the opening of the next session."[6]

The Bible College Faculty consisted chiefly of Professor Sweeney, utilizing the services of the Professor of Greek, T. Louis Comparette, later Franklin G. Jones, for the language, and the President of the University, A. Clark, for the philosophy. The content of the teaching followed that of the College of the Bible at Lexington, Kentucky, where Mr. Sweeney had gone to study after having completed his B. A. at Add-Ran in 1885 and his M. A. under Dr. Lowber. The scope of the course was expressed thus:

We do not confer nor encourage the title of B. D. or D. D. Omitting from the regular University A. B. course the large part of the Junior and Senior year and substituting therefor the two above years of Bible College Work (which is more

[1]Authorized by the Board. Minutes 6-10-95, p. 53.
[2]Minutes, 9-4-95, p. 56.
[3]Catalog, 1897, p. 35.
[4]Minutes, 6-3-97, p. 106.
[5]Catalog, 1895, p. 6.
[6]Catalog, 1895, p. 6.

than equivalent), gives us, on the elective system, a regular four years' college course for Bible students, which creditably completed, confers the A. B. degree.[7]

This differed from the Lexington pattern in covering four years and granting the Bachelor's degree.

A post-graduate course of one year, leading to the M. A., was announced, but was never operated.[8] An English Bible course was also announced, covering two or three years.[9] This, likewise, was seldom used.

The example of the College of the Bible was followed in refraining from granting the B. D., in the strong emphasis on the Bible as a text, and on the classroom texts used. In fact, Professor Sweeney used the texts which were written and printed by the College of the Bible at Lexington, the very notes which he had himself used as a student. A list of textbooks used is suggestive of the content of the courses; "McGarvey's Class Notes, Everest's *Divine Demonstration*, Milligan's *Scheme of Redemption*, Dungan's *Hermeneutics*, Broadus' *Homiletics*, Fisher's *Church History*, et al."[10]

In addition to the teaching load, Professor Sweeney had to keep constantly at the task of raising the endowment. Every week end he was out preaching and soliciting funds. Often he spent two or three weeks at a time in the field, leaving his classes to be taught by a student. When he came in from trips like this, he had little time to freshen up his own knowledge. Much of his time was devoted to the business of the school, too, for he was one of the "Big Four" who took over the operation of the University's finances[11] when the Trustees found the going hard. At one time he was elected as "Chancellor," indicating that he was looked to as the leading person to take over some of the responsibilities that were being loosed by the President.[12]

The brethren did not respond readily to his appeals for donations to the endowment. The financial "panic" was strong in that particular period; the University was making its appeal also. It required as much as he could raise, almost, to keep

[7]See chapter XX for a fuller discussion of the curricula compared. Catalog, 1897, p. 37.
[8]*Ibid.*, p. 39.
[9]*Ibid.* p. 39.
[10]Catalog, 1895, p. 39.
[11]Minutes, 3-16-97, pp. 98, 99; Chapter VIII.
[12]Minutes, 6-3-97, p. 106.

the current expenses going. His family was young and growing. Considering all of these conditions, it is not surprising that even so dauntless a soul as J. B. Sweeney should decide that the time was not ripe for the completion of the project of endowing a Bible College. So he resigned March 14, 1899, and that summer became the pastor of the Dixon Street Christian Church at Gainesville, where he died of typhoid fever contracted while holding a meeting at Honey Grove.[13] It is quite safe to say that no preacher in Texas has rendered a more consecrated service to the brotherhood, exercising more good sense, balanced judgment and practical wisdom than J. B. Sweeney.

A fruit tree blossoms in beauty, bears its fruit in its season, then sheds its leaves and seems to die. But this is only for the winter. The fruit abides to feed the hungry and the tree lives on to bear more fruit the next season. The Bible College tree, planted in the hard, droughty soil of the decade of frequent panics, nevertheless lived, had many fruitful seasons ahead, and finally grew into the Brite College of the Bible. The net sum of endowment realized from his labors was $4,939.78, which was doubtless absorbed in the general expense.[14] But its fruitage was well worth all of the investment of funds and devotion of toil that had been put into it.

There are five distinct, permanent contributions which this seeming failure made. First, that adventure turned the tide of ministerial attendance in Add-Ran. In the twenty-three years previous to the coming of J. B. Sweeney, six preachers had graduated, and not more than twenty-one enrollees can be counted who became preachers, and this includes four women who married preachers. That was an average of one a year. The first session of the Bible College, 1895-96, enrolled five new ministerial students, in addition to the six remaining; the next session nine; the next sixteen; and 1898-99, twelve. Of this thirty-one, twenty actually spent their lives as preachers, three spent several years, or part time. Eight of these did not stay with the ministry. Except for the three years immediately following Sweeney's resignation, the number never fell lower, and soon rose much higher.

Second, the program he undertook and the publicity that attended it turned the attention of prospective preachers to college. In this middle of the 20th century, we assume that a lad

[13]Minutes, 3-14-99.
[14]Minutes, 3-9-1900, p. 147.

who aspires to preach plans to go to college. Not so in the frontier days. Schools were scarce; sermons were plentiful; those who were moved to preach them did so. Schooling was not regarded as essential; indeed, there was some prejudice against the educated preacher. Not so, after 1900, at least, not much.

Third, this effort dramatized the fact that this college training could be had in Texas. J. B. Sweeney himself had gone to Lexington, Kentucky, to the College of the Bible, after graduating at Add-Ran. R. C. Horn, veteran of Collin County, had made this trek; also his son-in-law, Eugene Holmes, and a few others of that generation, perhaps a dozen. But they realized that only a few could or would go that far; that no supply of professional men, preacher or other, has ever been or could ever be kept up by education at long distance. The adventure of Sweeney was worth its cost to prove that point in Texas.

A fourth fruitage of that period of adventure which must not be overlooked is the personnel it enlisted. Among those callow youth with roughhewn dreams who studied under Sweeney and served with power in later years are such names as J. T. McKissick, J. N. Wooten, Virgil Graves, R. H. Simmons, J. J. Ray, W. O. Stephens, Macon Howard, Walter S. Knox, Bertha Mason Fuller, C. E. Chambers, J. Crocket Mullins, J. F. Posey, W. Frank Reynolds, S. Guy Inman, E. J. Bradley and Colby Hall. Even Patrick Henry, though a small boy in knee breeches, was about the campus at the time.

Some of the ministerial students prior to Sweeney's teaching period were: H. M. Bandy, 1874-76; W. H. Bagby and W. E. Stamps, 1876-77; J. D. Stamps, 1880-81; R. H. Bonham, 1883-84, B. A. 1884; J. B. Sweeney, 1883-85, B. A. 1885; George L. Bush, 1884-86, B. A. 1886; Franklin G. Jones, 1886-93, B. A. 1893; George Morrison, 1891-95, B. A. 1895. Through the years 1892-95: E. C. Boynton, B. A. 1906; W. W. Phares, B. J. Forbes, J. H. Clark, W. F. Sanders, Bertha Mason (Mrs. J. H. Fuller), S. B. 1896; Flora Pinkerton (Mrs. George H. Morrison), S. B. 1895; Frankie Yarborough (Mrs. Walter S. Knox), May Miller (Mrs. R. H. Simmons), L. B. 1896; D. A. Leak.

A fifth result of that fateful but fruitful adventure of J. B. Sweeney, and perhaps the richest fruit of all, was the fixing in the consciousness of the Disciples of Christ in Texas the policy that there must be, as a part of its University, a College devoted to the education of the ministry. After that period, there was

*Also Walter S. Knox.

104

never any doubt about this policy. Every catalog carried an announcement of the Bible College, even though the faculty allotted to it often justified only a "Department." The brotherhood, in convention, has always been ready to vote resolutions of support, even if often tardy in translating these into funds.

Not only was the germ of the later College of the Bible developed in this period; a source of funds was stirred by these leaders in this time. In the summer of 1897, while J. B. Sweeney was "shelling the woods" for funds, Addison Clark was evangelizing, as usual. He was invited by one of his former students, Willie Moore, to hold a meeting at Marfa, where another student had preached the previous summer, but where there was no organized congregation. That summer, Addison Clark had the joy of baptizing a stalwart cattleman by the name of Luke C. Brite, also his beautiful, cultured young wife, who had a Disciple background in Missouri. She had come to teach school in the Davis Mountains and had been won by Mr. Brite. It was fourteen years later that this conversion came to bear financial fruit for the College. That story comes in a later paragraph. But it was out of the strenuous efforts of Clark and Sweeney that the message came to the Brites, as well as to many others.[15]

On the retirement of J. B. Sweeney, there was no slackening of purpose to keep the Bible College going. The catalog for the ensuing session of 1899-1900 printed quite an imposing list of Faculty for the "College of the Bible." It contained nine names, headed by Addison Clark as Dean, and Professor of Philosophy and Christian Evidence. Albert Buxton, the new Chancellor and Chairman of the Faculty, was listed as Professor of Hebrew and Old Testament History and Pastoral Care; Frank Marshall, A. M. and Ph. D. (from Dr. Lowber), was the new teacher on the faculty, just returned from a service as missionary in Japan. He was Professor of Church History and Missions, but became the one who gave more time than any other to the teaching of Bible. Professor W. T. Hamner of the English faculty was listed as Professor for Voice Culture and Elocution. The three "Lecturers," who doubtless were expected to visit the campus occasionally, were J. W. Lowber, J. B. Sweeney, and surprisingly, E. V. Zollars, the later President. There is no evidence, however, that he ever came to the campus until he came to look into the presidency in 1902.

[15]Letter from Noel Keith, while pastor at Marfa on information from Mrs. Brite, 1942.

105

There were seven ministerial students enrolled that session (1890-00), and eight the next. There was one preacher in the graduating class of 1901, and two in 1902. Obviously, the loss of Mr. Sweeney, and especially the little time devoted to the classes in the previous years, had caused a slump in attendance. Definitely, several went to Lexington rather than delay their full course in the ministry.[16]

Practically the same faculty was carried for the next two years. In 1901-1902 Addison Clark was Professor of Bible and F. H. Marshall was Dean. The following summer, 1902, the new president, E. V. Zollars came, and found a spirit of optimism and hopefulness. The debts had just been paid, the Girls' Home was in process of construction; they were out of the valley of despair. A part of the resolutions passed in November, 1901, concerning the death of J. B. Sweeney was, "Giving his all as he did in the days of hard adversity it is a matter of deep regret to us that he is not present in body to rejoice with us in the day of prosperity."[17]

The Bible College was fortunate in finding in President Zollars, a zealous advocate of ministerial training. In fact, the finding and financing of preacher boys was the thing nearest to his heart. In his rounds of visits to the churches, he met and encouraged many a lad to come to T. C. U. and study for the ministry. The funds he collected from his Sunday lectures and sermons, he kept under his personal control and used them generously in loaning or giving to the support of the preacher boys. He brought several students from Australia, and New Zealand, helping them financially. The enrollment of ministerial students during the four years of his administration was 17, 19, 22, and 23.[18]

The "Course of Instruction" continued to be a four year undergraduate course leading to the B. A. degree, with the option of an English Bible Course without the degree. The former pattern of the College of the Bible at Lexington was no longer apparent, in texts and terminology. There was even a larger portion of the curriculum devoted to ministerial subjects. The only "literary" subjects assigned were Mathematics 5 hours, and English 15 hours, in the Freshman year; and in the Senior year,

---

[16]At least two were Guy Inman and Colby Hall.
[17]Minutes, 11-28-01, p. 180.
[18]The catalog shows a larger figure for the second and third year, but this was the number of students enrolled in Bible classes.

Psychology 4, Logic 2, a total of 28, out of 180.[19] The next year provided a little more room for "electives from the College of Arts and Sciences," but left only a little time for taking them.

All of these courses were taught by the two teachers, President Zollars and Professor Marshall, with the aid of the Professor of History, Walter Lee Ross. President Zollars used several of his own texts, and was a zealous instructor. His method emphasized the drilling of Bible facts. He was quite enthusiastic, too, in drawing into the Bible classes numbers of non-ministerial students. With them he was very popular; he had a charm of teaching. There was great disappointment among the ministerial students when the announcement of his resignation was made; some of them followed him to his new school. The story of his break with the T. C. U. Trustees is told in Chapter XI.

Although President Zollars was Dean of the Bible College, he planned to have a man of special scholarship devote his entire time to this post. So, before his resignation was planned, he had already arranged to have Dr. Clinton Lockhart elected as Dean of the Bible College. But before the latter arrived President Zollars had resigned, and Dr. Lockhart was elected as Acting President also. His background is told in Chapter XII, showing how fitting a scholar he was for this work. He, too, exercised his teaching functions in the Bible field, and served as Dean and President.

The place of Professor Marshall, who followed President Zollars to Oklahoma, was filled by a former schoolmate of the new Dean, Professor Walter Stairs, as Professor of Greek and New Testament Literature. Members of the Liberal Arts faculty used were Ellsworth Faris, in Sacred History and Philosophy; J. B. Eskridge, Professor of Homiletics and Church Ministries; Egbert R. Cockrell, Church History; and Miss Olive McClintic, later Miss Clyde Reaves, in Public Speaking. Quite a list of "Special Lectures" was announced, to be given by Texas ministers.[20]

In harmony with his training in the Eastern Universities, Dr. Lockhart introduced a spirit of high scholarship, and offered for the first time the Bachelor of Divinity degree. The Bachelor of Arts degree was required as a basis for it, but the two curricula were intermingled. The close figuring student could obtain both degrees within five and a half years. Three students

[19]Catalog, 1904, pp. 73, 74.
[20]Catalog, 1906, p. 54; 1907, p. 55; 1908, p. 71.

took the B. D. degree in 1907: Ralph V. Calloway, J. F. Quisenberry, and Frank C. Buck; one, H. R. Ford, took it in 1909. The larger number were satisfied with the Bachelor of Arts degree, including much Bible. Although the English Bible Diploma was offered, few sought it. Several of the ministerial students dropped out after the break with President Zollars, and returned to T. C. U. eight or ten years later and completed the degree work. It required several years to build back the attendance of preachers to the level of 1903-1906. During the first four years of President Lockhart, 1907-1910, the attendance of preachers was 17, 17, 13, and (probably) 13.[21] The number of preachers graduating in 1903-1906 was 17, from 1907-1910 was 8. The next four-year period graduated 10.[22]

In the fourth year of Dr. Lockhart's presidency, 1909-1910, he brought to the Faculty of the Bible College Professor G. A. Llewellyn, another product of the College of the Bible at Lexington, a schoolmate of Dr. Lockhart's there. He received his B. A. in 1885, his M. A. 1886; then, while serving as President of a Tennessee college, took the correspondence work offered by Dr. Lowber through Add-Ran, and secured both his Ph. D. (1896) and his LL. D. (1897).[23] He was not so highly trained in technical scholarship as was Dr. Lockhart, but he had a similar sense of appreciation for high scholarship, was a forceful and popular teacher, and a man of practical sense. On the resignation of Dr. Lockhart from the faculty in 1911, he was elected as "Head of the Bible Department," and later in September this title was changed to "Dean."[24]

His greatest contribution, however, was in lines other than teaching. He had been a college president, and he saw the needs of the situation in general. The old problem of the cost of living was keeping preacher boys out of school. Dr. Llewellyn believed that the people would respond to a call for funds to build a dormitory for ministerial students, to reduce the cost of rooms. He presented the plan to the Trustees. They contracted with him on June 9, 1910, the next meeting after the decision to move to Fort Worth, promising to pay him 7 per cent for gross funds raised, up to $10,000 and 5 per cent for funds above that amount.[25] Mrs. M. A. Goode, of Bartlett, was one of the

[21]The figures are not given separately the fourth year in the catalog.
[22]A closer study of the attendance will be found in the Appendix.
[23]Catalog, 1909, shows his record, p. 7.
[24]Minutes, 4-19-11, p. 259; 9-19-11, p. 272.
[25]Minutes, 6-9-10, p. 214.

good women who had previously encouraged T. E. Shirley by a Thousand Dollar donation, in 1901. She responded to Dr. Llewellyn's plea also, giving the largest sum of any one individual to the dormitory, $5,000. Hence it was named "Goode Hall," in her honor.[26] The cost of the building was about $34,000. It served as the men's dormitory, in 1911 and until Clark Hall was built in 1912. It was then devoted exclusively to the use of ministerial students as planned, including several married couples. A Dining Hall and Club Boarding House was operated in the basement. This arrangement reduced the expenses of the students, and was quite satisfactory until the cost of food rose during the World War I period. The building was only partly occupied, and there was need for the space. Moreover, there had grown up a severance between the Bible students and the other boys on the campus, which was not very welcome to the ministerial boys. This sentiment was expressed in a *Skiff* editorial while Nimmo Goldston, a ministerial student, was the editor. From all of these conditions it was agreed about 1925 to use Goode Hall for Junior and Senior men, and Clark Hall for Freshmen and Sophomores, placing the ministerial students in either, according to the rank of each. At the same time, the benefit of the gift of Goode Hall was maintained by giving a reduction in room rent to each ministerial boy, in whatever dormitory he lived. Hence the preacher boys have received a reduction in room rent through the years.

In his rounds of solicitation in 1910 and 1911, Dr. Llewellyn called upon L. C. Brite of Marfa, and Mrs. Brite, both of whom had been baptized in 1897 by Addison Clark, as already related. The record does not show the size of their contribution to Goode Hall, but it does record a gift of $25,000 to endow a Chair of English Bible in T. C. U. which grew out of this visit. For, although this gift was received later by President F. D. Kershner, it was the result of the conversation with Dr. Llewellyn. Mr. Brite told the author in personal conversation that it was Dr. Llewellyn "who first opened my eyes to the good that could be done by educating preachers." The continuation of that story, of course, comes in the chapter on Brite College.

The contract with L. C. Brite, accepting the funds for the endowment of the Chair of English Bible, was authorized by the Trustees on October 26, 1911. Before the next annual meet-

[26]Catalog, 1915, p. 24, and other catalogs.

ing on February 14, 1912, Dr. Llewellyn had died, and the Board took action expressing their appreciation of his services. In less than three years the good Doctor had made a contribution which is seldom equalled in a score of years.[27]

A teacher was not immediately elected to occupy the newly endowed Chair of English Bible. President Kershner taught the courses during the session of 1912-13. Dr. Lockhart, who had completed his services as President in June, 1911, was called to be professor of Greek and Hebrew, beginning in September, 1912.[28]

Thus, through a period of forty years, a succession of devoted teachers had been blazing the trail for a thorough, permanent College of the Bible. What an array of teachers: J. A. Clark, Addison Clark, J. B. Sweeney, Frank Marshall, E. V. Zollars, Clinton Lockhart, Walter Stairs, E. E. Faris, G. A. Llewellyn, Frederick D. Kershner! Men of staunch faith, rich traditions, clear minds, profound faith, attractive personalities, all filled with the Holy Spirit, and devoted to the Church and to preaching of the Gospel of Christ. What mountains of difficulty and indifference they climbed! What ideals of service and accomplishments they dreamed! What strong foundations they laid! Such men are the salt of the earth. The institution to which they blazed the trail, the Brite College of the Bible, will have a separate chapter of its own.[29]

[27]Minutes, 2-14-12, p. 279.
[28]Minutes, 2-11-11, p. 255; 6-11-12, p. 288.
[29]Chapter XX.

# ❧ XI ❧

## The School Becomes An Institution

### T. E. SHIRLEY, E. V. ZOLLARS, 1902-1906

D URING THE SEVEN LEAN YEARS, the pioneers of Add-Ran had never lost their dream of a great University. They had now achieved one essential characteristic of a permanent institution: the school would go on despite drastic changes in personnel. It was not a one-man enterprise, not a family affair; it was an institution. It was now their responsibility to shape their policies in harmony with this more permanent stature. And there is evidence in the record that they consciously did this very thing.

There was the deliberate purpose, for instance, to secure a president, with the broad training afforded by the Eastern Universities. Addison Clark had strongly recommended this policy. It was one of his arguments for his withdrawal that the era demanded such leadership. This principle was applied also to the faculty. The Thorp Spring faculty, as previously observed, was made up of the family, or of the graduates of Add-Ran itself. That began to change with the coming of T. Louis Comparette, a cultured classical scholar. This change was no doubt in mind in the exploiting of the Graduate School under Chancellor J. W. Lowber, who "had enough diplomas to cover the walls of his study." The abundance of degrees seemed to have been the one argument in favor also of Albert Buxton as Chancellor and prospective President, for he had no experience as an executive, and no national reputation as a leader. Brilliant as he was, his degrees did not put him over. Because of this disappointment, the Trustees were perhaps more cautious, but they lost none of their determination to make Add-Ran a university of the broadest educational culture. Yet they recognized other aims as equally essential.

One of these aims was to make the institution positively a church school. It had been officially adopted by the Church Convention in 1889, but that was only a recognition and a permission. To make this relationship function, it had to be accepted by the local congregations, or more accurately, by the individual churchmen locally. So far, the Christian churches had not developed any large sense of responsibility or any habit of contribution of funds to the causes of the church. The attendance of students had been built up on the confidence which the people had in the Clarks, and, increasingly, in the other teachers. Now, in 1902, one of the founding brothers was operating another college, less than a hundred miles away;[1] the other was retiring on his own insistence. A new loyalty had to be built up. That loyalty was to be to a church institution. This would not be easy, for the Disciples were notoriously independent and, as frontiersmen, individualistic. The new president, therefore, should be eminently a church man, well acquainted with the history, traditions, and psychology of this particular movement.

That is the kind of a President that was secured in the person of E. V. Zollars. His messages sounded a strong plea for church loyalty. This plea was reiterated by others, by those preachers who exerted themselves at all for the support of the school, by the financial solicitors, and by some of the Trustees. This was particularly true of T. E. Shirley, President of the Board. He, as well as his brother-in-law, Captain T. M. Scott, and his cousin, Andrew Sherley, a later Trustee, were all products, educationally, of Texas A. & M. But they sensed the need of the Christian philosophy and oversight in education, and were strong advocates of it. It must be recalled that there were only two State educational institutions of collegiate rank in Texas in 1902, both young: the University, nineteen, A.&M., twenty-six years old. The two other state schools were Normals (at Huntsville and Denton), not of collegiate rank. There were some who thought of State colleges as interlopers, since the college field had been built up by the churches—though no one would have used so strong a word as that. In public address, T. E. Shirley was wont to go rather far in criticising the lack of religion in those schools. This was based on the experience of some individuals whom he had observed. There was, on the other hand, a tendency on the part of some "State" faculty and administrators to minimize the value and educational respectability of church colleges in general. Doubtless, there was material for argument, from cases, on both sides. Fortunately the mutual respect and cooperation of the

[1]Randolph at Lancaster, Texas. See Chapter XXV.

two types of colleges has greatly improved since that day, for reasons too extended to be discussed here. This element was a live one at the period under discussion, and the choice of the new President was doubtless influenced by it.

The adoption of the new name, Texas Christian University, was, without doubt, a part of the consciousness of the new era. The catalog announced the change "as suitable to the greatly enlarged purposes and work of the school."[2] It is impossible to ascertain just what was in the minds of the men who made the decision. The Minutes record merely the motion put and passed. No arguments were recorded, no time for discussion among the brethren allowed for. There followed a strong criticism on the part of some of the Thorp Spring students and disappointment, if not resentment, among some branches, not all, of the Clark family. Some loyalties were lost, some later regained, some never. To all such there was some satisfaction in the fact that the very next motion was "That the Department of Arts and Sciences be called the Add-Ran College of Arts and Sciences." (The next motion after that was "That the President of the University be authorized to employ a stenographer and a typewriter." Things were becoming modern rapidly!)

Although the change in the name was made at the time of the coming of President Zollars, and was favored by him, he was not the initiator of the idea. For the same name had been proposed at the time of the removal from Thorp Spring. Indeed, at a meeting at Thorp Spring on November 22, 1895, it was voted to change the name to Texas Christian University. But on December 5 following, this action was reconsidered by a four-to-three vote, and "the subject of naming the institution was open again for consideration." T. E. Shirley then moved to name the school "Addison Clark University," but there was no second. Later in the evening a motion carried 6 to 1 to adopt the name "Clark University," but it was only a straw vote, there being no quorum.[3] Discussion without action obviously continued, for the Alumni Association voted "thanks to the Directors for their refusal to change the name of our University, and an expression of desire that it never be changed."[4] It is possible that the dynamics of President Zollars brought into action the idea that had been simmering thus for seven years.

2Catalog, 1903, p. 11.
3Minute 12-5-95.
4*Collegian*, November 1896, p. 56.

The new name intimated the institutional rather than the family characteristic of the school. The retention of the beloved term "Add-Ran" for the College of Arts and Sciences was a gesture of appreciation of the family which fathered the school. And that appreciation was genuine. There was no lack of loyalty to the retiring president. The change was strongly advocated and defended by T. E. Shirley, Chairman of the Board, who had been a Trustee in the Thorp Spring days and very loyal to the Clarks. As the one who had raised the money to clear the debt, he was then the most influential person in the Brotherhood, in the affairs of the institution.

The new name attempted to express the scope of the school. That this type of name was favored by President Zollars is shown by the fact that he later named "Oklahoma Christian University," the college which afterward became Phillips. This was, of course, to rely on description rather than psychology. It is the college, with its wealth of history, that makes a name meaningful. Kentucky University, resuming its pristine name Transylvania, redolent of the memories of the frontier days, was happy and fortunate. The name "T. C. U." has long since come to have a flavor of its own, entirely apart from the descriptive prosaic title. The word "Add-Ran," like old rose petals, will gather fragrance and attractiveness with the years, many believe.

President Zollars seemed to fit into the needs of the school in this period very definitely. He was strong-willed, with full confidence in his own ideas and no compunctions in making changes to conform to them. He was preeminently a church man, an ordained minister with some pastoral experience. He was saturated in the traditions of the communion, the Disciples of Christ, having been educated in Bethany College, and having grown up in southern Ohio and North Middletown, Kentucky, a few miles from Cane Ridge, regions of the beginnings of the Reformation Movement. In this very environment had grown up, also, the one President of the United States who was an ordained,* actual preacher, James A. Garfield, who was a predecessor of Zollars as President of Hiram College. Coming from such a distinctively Disciple atmosphere, and widely recognized nationally as a strong leader in the communion, E. V. Zollars was an ideal man to lead in a new era as a church school.

*Ordained in the sense of the general recognition as a preacher by the churches, the customary practice of the Disciples then.

When the new President arrived he was presented to the brotherhood, in convention and lectureship, with extreme laudation, and was received with approving enthusiasm. He was a man of great dominating power over an audience. He fell into the free, easy bantering approach of the Western men, who were at home in that type of humor later made famous by Will Rogers, which was native to the cow-country West. It was in this humor that Granville Jones, eloquent and witty, introduced him to the Ministers' Lectureship in Weatherford in 1902:

> "Heretofore among our Texas preachers, we have had three preachers so ugly that they are in a class by themselves: V. R. Stapp, G. A. Faris, and myself. We have longed to make it 'an ugly man's quartet,' but we have never been able to find a fourth man ugly enough to qualify. Now our problem is solved. We have found our man. E. V. Zollars qualifies abundantly. We welcome him to make complete the 'Ugly Man's Quartet'."

President Zollars was indeed blessed with craggy features. He proved a good sport. His reply was:

> "I am honored to accept the invitation, but you do not need me. Back in Ohio, we had a 'Liars Quartet.' When one of the members was asked to name the four men who made it up, he replied: 'Bill Jones is one, Tom Brown is another, and Sam Smith is such a big liar he is the other two.' Now any of you can look at Granville Jones and see that he is ugly enough to make the other two of the ugly man's quartet."

So President Zollars was accepted as a good fellow, not an effete Easterner. He had the ruggedness of the pioneer that fitted into the West, and the dream of greater things for the future which met the mood of the Texas brethren. He had everything coming his way.

As indicated, the turn in affairs for the better had already begun before the arrival of President Zollars. This was evidenced by the clearing of the old debt, the completion of the new Girls' Home, the gathering of an excellent faculty, and the adding of a $10,000 central heating plant,[5] and by the gift for the newest building, Townsend Memorial Hall. This latter was secured largely through the influence of Granville Jones with the Townsend family of Midland. The cornerstone bore the following inscription:

[5]Catalog, 1903, p. 119.

This building is dedicated to the cause of Christian Education by Mrs. Ella Townsend, as tribute of a loving wife and mother to the memory of her husband, S. E. Townsend, and her son, Irye, who died September 10, 1895.[6]

Its erection during the fall and dedication in February, 1903, furnished material evidence of growth which made for enthusiasm for the new administration.

President Zollars utilized fully this optimistic turn and supplied plenty of vigorous moves of his own to enhance greatly the enthusiasm and to make the progress substantial and continuous. His first move was to improve the sanitary provisions of the plant and tone up the buildings in several ways. A large lumber company was persuaded to donate some lumber for board walks; the black waxy mud was not so tolerable to newcomers as it was to the natives.[7] He took the initiative in getting the community incorporated as North Waco in March, 1903.[8] It was later merged with Waco. The Post Office had been, until then, called "Hermosen."

Among the new aims was that for a gymnasium. When it did not soon enough materialize, some one through *The Skiff* rationalized that the balmy Texas climate made an "open air gymnasium much to be preferred."[9] The spirit of aspiration must have been strong in the air, for the second number of the newborn *Skiff* enthused with the expression "We are beginning to think in T. C. U. these days that we can get anything we want."[10] Many of the new features bore the unmistakable marks of the unyielding decisions of the new President. For instance, the generally accepted principles of landscaping were violated in setting out the trees in geometrical rows, criss-crossed as hard and fast as double checked corn rows.

By 1904, $40,000 had been spent on plant improvement. The fourth floor of Main Building had been finally completed, a laundry and a lighting plant erected, and ambition enough engendered to announce intention to build some concrete walks, which were several years in coming, and to finish the towers on Main!—which never came.[11]

[6]*Skiff*, 2-21-03, Vol. 1, No. 21.
[7]*Skiff*, October, 1902, Vol. 1, No. 3.
[8]*Skiff*, March 24, 1903.
[9]*Skiff*, 9-26-02, Vol. 1, No. 1.
[10]*Skiff*, 9-02, Vol. 1, No. 1.
[11]Catalog, 1904, pp. 138, 139.

The new spirit of hope made possible the birth of the weekly newspaper, The *Skiff*, a fixture in the life of the school ever since.[12] Credit for this venture goes to an enthusiast who came down from the days of J. B. Sweeney and Addison Clark, one Ed S. ("Chicken") McKinney. He had come in 1897, wedded to preaching, poetry, and poverty. His struggle with the latter kept him hustling, and out of school for a while. He returned in the fall of 1902 with another dream and the necessity of making ends meet; The *Skiff* was the answer. It was Ed McKinney who put it over with enthusiasm and sweat, encouraged and aided a little by two of his former fellow-students who were now fledgling faculty members, Olive McClintic and Colby Hall, associate editors.[13]

A much more vigorous policy of advertising the school was inaugurated. The *T. C. U. Bulletin* was started, featuring pictorial numbers. An effort was made to have the churches establish an annual Assembly on the campus.

On the background of the discouraging seven lean years, it was natural that this new spirit should tend to increase the enrollment. In 1902 this was 302, then 428, 470 and 412.

In 1904 the term (or quarter) system replaced the semester plan. This was a part of the influence of the newly flourishing University of Chicago. The semester plan was restored in 1925.

Some new names appeared on the faculty at the time the new President came. Bruce McCully, a Hiram graduate, headed the Department of English for six years, with a brilliant record and with the respect and loyalty of the students. The urge for higher scholarly preparation induced Professor Eskridge to take leave of absence in 1902-03. He arranged for one of his former students, Colby D. Hall, to supply that one year. Abdullah Ben Kori, a temperamental Turk of fine character and loyal devotion, also a Hiram product, taught Modern Languages for three years.

For a period of two years, 1904-06, the school had the blessing of the presence of Lee Clark, as Head of the Preparatory Department. He was an alumnus, the son of Randolph Clark, devoted to the school and beloved by all. But for the demands of a growing family, he might have remained as a permanent fixture.

In 1904 came a jolly soul who meant much to the school in the years just ahead. He was Professor J. F. Anderson, founder

[12]This did not replace *The Collegian* which was a monthly literary magazine.
[13]*Skiff*, Vol. 1, No. 1, September, 1902.

and President of the small, local, but excellent Grayson College at Whitewright, Texas. He came as Vice-President and Professor of Biology, and served as Business Manager until 1911. Walter L. Ross came in 1903 as Professor of History and Political Science, E. R. Cockrell being then in New York for several years.

That year saw also the return of one of the old standbys from the early days. W. B. Parks, who had followed Randolph Clark to Lancaster, then to Hereford, now returned. A. C. Easley, also from the Thorp Spring days, continued as Head of the flourishing College of Business until 1905, when he turned to the business world as teller at the Citizens' National Bank of Waco. Other delightful personalities on the staff were Miss Harriet Frances Smith, piano, and Miss Gussie Ward, voice, both coming in 1904. Also Martha K. Miller, invaluable in Business and as Registrar.

A man of President Zollars' strong individuality would naturally take the discipline into his own hands. He started by a rigid system of monitors enforcing study hours in the dormitories. That met with unfavorable reaction. But before Christmas The *Skiff* announced "President Zollars has given permission for the young men in the dormitory to make their own rules and govern themselves."[14] The control was not so loose as that statement sounded, but it met favorable response and worked fairly well, depending on the strength of the student leaders; and that varied. By 1906, it had developed into a form of municipal government, in which the students elected a set of officers known as Mayor, City Judge, City Attorney, and such.[15] A strong hand was really back of the discipline without seeming to be so. A student caught in mischief might receive a thorough tongue lashing in chapel. On one occasion, the victim was called to the front seat to receive his verbal castigation and to hear his expulsion announced. However, there was a soft spot in the heart of the President for the boys. In that very case he relented and the boy was reinstated.

This genuine love for students, and his obvious intellectual ability, made him popular with the students. Their life was a happy one. The higher aspirations were encouraged. Socials (called "soirees"), were carried on with much elation and eclat. Students, then, as always, were constantly clamoring for more privileges. Athletics had come out of the "doghouse," as is

[14]*Skiff*, December 6, 1902.
[15]*Skiff*, January, 1906.

shown in Chapter XXI. The Quintet was much announced by The *Skiff*, keeping up the tradition for good singing.

Perhaps the primary devotion of President Zollars was to the idea of the Christian emphasis in education. Chapel came every day, and was compulsory for all students and teachers. There he spoke often on the ideals of Christianity, and even used the occasion for drilling on some phases of Bible teaching. His favorite was *Bible Geography*, on which he had written a small text.[16] The national leaders of the Brotherhood of Disciples were his intimate friends; he had them often to visit the campus and to speak to the students. He was gracious in having, early in his term, the retired President, Addison Clark, as a chapel speaker, while he was yet pastor of the Central Christian Church in Waco.[17]

His special love was for the preacher boys. To discover and send out Timothies was the chief joy of his life. His own struggles in early life had made him sympathetic with the financial predicaments of these students, so he was generous in providing aid for them. He obtained some funds from the prominent Disciple T. W. Phillips of New Castle, Pennsylvania[18] and collected much from his lectures among the churches. These funds he handled himself rather than through the office, and used them for loans and donations to the ministerial students.

It was this individualistic way of handling affairs, as contrasted with institutional practices, that led to the final break between the President and the Trustees, and his resignation. But prior to that break came a rift between him and the faculty which attracted by far so much more attention that many had the two confused. The rift between the President and the faculty developed during the session of 1904-05 and came out in the open in the meeting of the Board of Trustees in February 1906. A group of students, fond of the President, demonstrated noisily, to the discomfort of the Trustees, but most of the students held aloof as being unacquainted with the facts. The *Skiff* reported nothing and the Trustees adopted a policy of silence. The Minutes for that period are not available, so no official record can be consulted.[19] But the facts are clear. The writer

---

[16]*Bible Geography*, Standard Publishing Company, 1895.
[17]*Skiff*, December, 1902.
[18]Catalog, 1906, p. 65.
[19]Minutes from August, 1902, through March, 1910, were destroyed by the fire.

of these lines became an advisory member of the Board in March 1906, was present at every one of the Board meetings[20] that spring, except the February meeting, and is therefore well acquainted with the facts.

The friction between the faculty members and the President was largely a matter of attitudes. Two definite factors, rubbing constantly, aggravated whatever feelings arose over details. One was the disparity in salaries. The same Board meeting of March 14, 1902, which contracted with President Zollars for $3,000 a year, raised the top professors' salaries from $600 to $720. The other claim was that the President was too domineering, dictating even to the details within the departments, leaving little room for either initiative or dignity to the teachers, or to the faculty as a whole. Be it said to the credit of the Trustees, that, with patience and persistence, they brought the two parties together, wrought out the grounds on which they became reconciled and secured an agreement for peace and harmony for the future. That was accomplished in a meeting in April.

But, unfortunately, in that same meeting another rift developed, this time between the President and the Trustees. This rift was over financial policies, as already hinted. In addition to the continued solicitation for funds for buildings by T. E. Shirley, President Zollars, naturally, gathered money from the churches for the use of the school. These funds, as already stated, he handled himself, through his own office, rather than through the office of the Treasurer of the school. There was no official record even, of these loans and grants to students. This was not pleasing to the Trustees. The point which concerned them was that the indebtedness was steadily growing, the cost of operation mounting, and they were unable to ascertain exactly the financial status of the institution. After long discussion on this point among themselves and with the President, they came to a definite conclusion, and instructed W. K. Homan to make their decision clear to the President in the next session of the Board. Mr. Homan graciously, but quite clearly, stated that the Board had decided that the institution must hereafter be operated on a budget, with income and expenditures agreed to in advance, as customary in such institutions.

The reply of President Zollars was that he had never operated on such a basis and was unable and unwilling to do so, that

[20]The files of the *Skiff* reveal that there were four extra Board meetings that spring before the regular one in June.

he had always had freedom to control all funds himself, without accounting to any one. The discussion on this point was lengthy, in good spirit, but determined on both sides. Mr. Homan made it clear that the Board would not recede from its decision. President Zollars agreed to take the matter under advisement for a month, or thereabout, and give his answer at the next meeting. Before that next meeting he made a trip through Oklahoma and Kansas, sounding out the possibilities of another college. When the Board met in June, he announced his resignation, stating that he could not accept the condition to work under a budget. The result is history. His resignation was accepted, and he proceeded to organize Oklahoma Christian University.*

The local results at first seemed almost disastrous. President Zollars was very popular with the students. A score of them followed him to Oklahoma, together with two faculty members, Marshall and Dyksterhuis; two of the Trustees, E. J. Mantooth and A. D. Milroy (advisory members), dropped out of activity. They had been absent from all of the meetings, and knew only from hearsay of the matter.

The Trustees agreed to pursue a policy of absolute silence, on the theory that the hurt would heal quickest with the least talk. If they should tell their side, it might seem to be shifting blame. So no explanation was ever issued. It is quite probable that the majority of people thought the resignation was due to the break with the faculty. But that was not true. That break was patched up. The real break was because the Trustees demanded a budget. The Trustees had come to the faith that T. C. U. had attained the status of an institution, able to persist, despite the coming or going of individuals. They, therefore, kept silence and bent every energy to the building up of student attendance for the fall, and winning the confidence of the people.

One of the most universally recognized traits of the pioneer is individualism. The frontier makes more for self-reliance than for team work. President Zollars was a frontiersman at heart. He was a mastodon in strength. But he must work alone. This episode was perhaps a part of the passing from the frontier individualism into the period of the institution.

---

*It should go without saying that there never was any question as to President Zollars' fidelity in handling finances; his integrity was above questioning. The difference was over fiscal policies.

121

# ⊱ XII ⊰

# The Glory of the Small Church College

CLINTON LOCKHART—J. F. ANDERSON, 1906-1910

HE SUDDEN AND SURPRISING WITHDRAWAL OF PRESIDENT
ZOLLARS in the spring of 1906 left matters in somewhat of a
state of confusion. Fortunately, he had, himself, unwittingly arranged for a fitting successor to be on hand, ready to step
into the leadership. For, several months previously, on his recommendation, Dr. Clinton Lockhart had been elected as Professor
of Bible and Dean of the College of the Bible, to begin the following September. The Trustees were familiar with Dr. Lockhart's
record, and knew that he had just completed a term as President
of Christian University in Canton, Missouri, so, confronted thus
suddenly by the vacancy, they promptly elected him as Acting
President.

Foresight rather than fortune may be credited with his selection, for at that critical Board meeting of March 1899 (when the
resignations of Addison Clark and J. B. Sweeney were received
and that of W. B. Parks and J. W. Froley, the "Big Four," were
imminent), they sent this telegram to Clinton Lockhart: "Will you
accept the presidency of Add-Ran University, twelve hundred dollars first year; what chairs can you fill." He had, at that time just
accepted the presidency of Christian University, and was not in
a position to change so suddenly. But he was remembered, seven
years later, when the Trustees were seeking a man of outstanding
scholarly attainments to become the Dean of the College of the
Bible. It was the "Acting President" part that was fortuitous.

His acceptance of the larger responsibility was delayed, slightly, by reason of his absence from America on a tour of Palestine.
But the efficiency of his good wife made the delay brief, and by
late summer he was on the campus, dignity residing in his schol-
arly-looking "mutton chop" beard and confidence and optimism
beaming through his sincere brown eyes. It was soon discovered that the President's wife was a personality to be counted

DR. ELY V. ZOLLARS,
President, 1902-06.

DR. CLINTON LOCKHART,
As he appeared in 1906.
President, 1906-11.
Total service, 36 years.

DR. FREDERICK D. KERSHNER,
President, 1911-15.

DR. EDWARD McSHANE WAITS,
(From the 1917 Horned Frog.)
President, 1916-41.
Total service, 31 years.

The second, third, fourth and fifth Presidents of the University.

upon as well for helpful suggestions and a cultured atmosphere of much value. Writing now from the perspective of the later years, when those same brown eyes of the Doctor still twinkle, but with the soberness (not the weight) of eighty-eight years of service, it is the more obvious that he fulfilled the two-fold desire of the Trustees for a leader who is as devoted to the church as gifted in scholarship. For Clinton Lockhart was a double pioneer. His family of Lockharts had furnished a dozen or more pioneer preachers for the Reformation Movement of the Disciples of Christ, as it moved into the virgin lands of the Mississippi Valley. He was a farm boy from the black land of Illinois, who did not stay on the farm long because from childhood he was marked for scholarship.

He was a pioneer in education, too, among the Disciples. It was a Disciple college that gave him his education—Kentucky University (later Transylvania) with its College of the Bible. That was in the days when Robert Graham was the leader and J. W. McGarvey was coming along, with Charles Louis Loos to give him the great opportunity for technical training in the languages. There he received his B. A. (1886) and M. A. (1888). In those days there was no theological degree in Disciple colleges. The Bible was taught in the undergraduate years; the M. A. was for the rare scholar. Following the precept of Alexander Campbell, those who went through college were strong in a broad general and classical education, well versed in the Bible, but with little training in technical scholarship or theology. The treasures of learning in the great universities on the Eastern border were not for them; partly because they could not afford it, more because they did not expect it, and somewhat because the leaders would have frowned upon it. They would incur suspicion in some quarters for having had their education, as one of the elder statesmen felicitously phrased it, "topped off in the uncongenial atmosphere of a sectarian theological seminary."

As early as 1891, this school (Yale Divinity School) thought it worth while to advertise in Disciple papers, but the returns were slight. Not until 1894 were there as many as three Disciple students there at one time, and there were not so many at any other similar institution.[1]

Dr. W. E. Garrison, who wrote that statement, was one of those

[1] W. E. Garrison in Religion Follows the Frontier, p. 258.

pioneers in going to Yale. He received his B. A. degree the same year that Clinton Lockhart received his Ph. D., 1894. Herbert L. Willett was one of the first to go there, and was a fellow student of Clinton Lockhart (1890-91), receiving the benefit of the rich tradition of Semitic scholarship planted by the great teacher William Rainey Harper, who left Yale in 1891 to become the famous President of the fledgling University of Chicago. Pioneer, indeed, was Clinton Lockhart in the higher education among the Disciples, and a fitting man to fill the desire of the frontier sage, Addison Clark, in his dream for the future of his child, Add-Ran.

It was to the office of "Acting" President that Dr. Lockhart was elected. The Trustees forgot about the "Acting" part, and when, at the next February meeting he reminded them that this was a temporary title, and dignity expected it to be changed one way or the other, they made him President. His efforts were concentrated on the academic phases of the work, gathering a faculty, developing the cultural atmosphere, and teaching classes himself. Sundays were spent among the churches, lecturing, preaching, and making friends. The financial "hustling" usually demanded of a president was not a part of his nature or of his program. His responsibilities were carried with his accustomed graciousness, greatly aided by his capable and devoted wife, through the trying years of the fire and the move, and the planning of the new structures in Fort Worth. Then after 1911, he was allowed to concentrate on the more congenial field of teaching, except for the period of 1916 to 1920, when he served as Dean of the Add-Ran College of Arts and Sciences.

That the situation was very critical in that summer of 1906 was as painfully felt then as it is clearly apparent from the later perspective. Many of the students were estranged. The policy of silence by the Trustees left many of the real facts unknown, and some feelings unsatisfied. Yet the Trustees had the confidence of the brotherhood; they were men whose motives were unquestioned, whose wisdom had been proved, and who had themselves sacrificed in time and money for the institution. This helped to give balance. A vigorous canvass for students was made during the summer by the new Educational Secretary, whom President Zollars himself had selected. Those who were disaffected were especially visited and warmed up. There proved to be a substratum of genuine loyalty which held the hearts of most of the group to the old school; so the attendance did not fall so much as anticipated. The loss was only 17 per cent (from 412 in 1905-06 to 340 in 1906-07). In fact the last year of the previous presidency had seen a drop of 12 per cent. The drop in the Liberal Arts College for 1906-07 was only 23 students. The attendance stayed under 400 until 1912 in Fort Worth.[2]

One of the factors that gave stability at this juncture was the strength of the faculty. Only three main places were vacated by the shift in the summer of 1906, and these were promptly filled by strong men. In addition to the old standbys, Professors Anderson, Parks, Snow, McCully, Hamner, Dacus, Miss Harriet Smith, there were added Ellsworth E. Faris in Philosophy, Orie W. Long in Modern Languages, John W. Kinsey in Education, Walter Stairs and G. A. Llewellyn in Bible. Three former teachers also returned at this time, Miss Olive McClintic and Professor and Mrs. Cockrell.

The last four years in Waco witnessed a continuous, vigorous, versatile struggle to get the school out of debt and to start a surplus for endowment. The burden of this fell upon the Trustees; the President was not a money raiser, and recognized that his contribution was academic. T. E. Shirley, who had so generously devoted his time to solicitation, with such gratifying results, had by this time contracted a severe asthmatic condition which required him to remove to and remain in the Panhandle region. He made his home thereafter at Hereford, coming to Board meetings at the cost of much suffering.

Letters sent out at the time show that the indebtedness brought over from the building program up to 1906 amounted to $60,000, a very sizable sum for the time. This was carried in various forms by the Citizens National Bank of Waco, together with individuals connected with it, on the endorsement of the individual Board members. Trustees meetings in those days meant a time for signing up again. The pressure for payment of these obligations, therefore, was heavy.

Several devices were provided for the raising of this needed money. "Education Day" was inaugurated as a date on which the churches were to make an offering annually. The Educational Secretary was charged with this responsibility, along with his cultivation of the churches, solicitation of students, and affiliation of high schools. Vigorous advertising of this "Day" was sent out, through the T. C. U. Bulletin, the *Christian Courier*,

[2]Catalogs, in loco.

and special letters and appeals. The first Education Day offering, January, 1907, had but little time for preparation, but it yielded $1,348. The second, 1908, brought from the churches $5,853. In addition to these church offerings, other collections through these same efforts made a total collection of actual cash during that fiscal year of $17,578.95.[3]

This gain was made partly by the use of a "T. C. U. Endowment Company" with shares of $100 each with the idea of keeping the money as it came in until all the debts were paid, thus clearing the way for endowment.[4] To solicit large gifts for endowment, Chalmers McPherson was called to be Endowment Secretary. As pastor at Waxahachie and as Trustee he had been active for years, and had recently secured a gift of $2,000 from Mrs. Davis of Italy. His purpose was to cultivate friendships for large gifts rather than to raise money fast. It worked out that way. In 1909 Education Day yielded about the same as in 1908. In the fall of 1909 the Educational Secretary, who had now become the pastor of the University Church, was detailed for a special trip among the churches of West Texas for an urgent solicitation leading up to the next Education Day. This trip resulted in raising about $3,000 in cash. Soon after Education Day 1910 came the fire and a new slate for finances.[5]

It was during this period that a spirit of cooperation among the Texas Colleges in general began to develop. The cordial spirit of President Lockhart helped in this and the field contacts of the Educational Secretary were pointed in this direction. It was customary for each college to send visitors to the high schools and to make a sort of formal affiliation, while the University of Texas, through the splendid work of Professor J. L. Henderson was definitely affiliating them with the University of Texas.[6] The other colleges appreciated the services of the State University but felt that the affiliation should be with all of the colleges alike. It was finally worked out that the "accreditation," as it came to be named, should be handled through the State Department of Education for all, being advised by a Committee of Classified and Accredited High Schools. This plan has operated through the years with satisfaction.

[3] From Announcements of the time on file in T. C. U. Library.
[4] *Christian Courier*, November, 1907; Announcements.
[5] Fire was March 22, 1910. See Chapter XIII.
[6] The T. C. U. catalog published a list of affiliated High Schools in 1907 through 1912; it was renewed in 1923 through 1930.

The relationship of T. C. U. to other colleges of the same
church became a problem about this time. Up to 1900 Add-
Ran had had the field to itself, for Carlton and Carr-Burdette
were small and for girls. When new Junior Colleges began to
appear two different policies developed among the T. C. U.
Trustees. T. E. Shirley and President Zollars were heartily in
favor of fostering Junior Colleges, as feeders for the University, and the revised Charter of 1902 had provided authority for
so doing. The contract with Hereford College was such that
T. C. U. was sued for some of the debts of that school, and
some hard feelings were caused, when the school had to close.
The opposite policy, supported by T. E. Tomlinson and C. W.
Gibson, was that the resources available to the Trustees were
so limited that they should be concentrated on the one school.
The latter attitude prevailed in 1908 when the Trustees declined to join in establishing a Junior College at Midland,
agreeing only to provide, as a matter of courtesy, a "locating
committee" to help in selecting the local site.[7]

The following schools were listed in the T. C. U. catalog
at some time between 1908 and 1919, in varying degrees
of relationship: Panhandle Christian College (later Hereford),
Midland, Carlton, Add-Ran Jarvis, Jones Academy, and the
Christian Institute (Monterrey, Mexico).

The pages of the student publications sparkle with many
names that have become known to the world of leadership in
later years. Some of them have already been mentioned in this
story, all too briefly. The name of Houston Foster, 1904, appeared frequently, as President of the Christian Endeavor Society, in debate, and elsewhere. It appeared later as President
of the Board of Trustees in 1940-41 and in the memorial name
of Foster Hall. Paul Tyson, 1908, later famous coach of the
Waco High School football team; Bonner Frizzell, long time
Superintendent of Public Schools at Palestine and a Trustee
of the University; Douglas Tomlinson, 1909, Fort Worth publisher, founder of the All-Church Press; Joe L. Clark, Head of
the Department of History of Sam Houston Teachers College,
fine flower of the Clark family—these are samples, out of the
many who could be named.

Among the expressions of enthusiasm in this period was the
T. C. U. Band, organized in 1905 with Arnold Kirkpatrick as

[7]This committee was C. W. Gibson, Chalmers McPherson and Colby Hall.

Director. Among the few members of the band were Dan Rogers, trap drummer and Tom Gallaher, bass drummer.[8] T. C. U. never had any difficulty in getting up a good male quartet so long as dear old Professor Hamner was around, for he could drill them, inspire them, and sing first tenor. Each succeeding quartet was the T. C. U. Quartet if one listened to such members, for instance, as Bryant Collins, Thurman Allen, Miles Bivens, Grits Anderson, Bill Massie, Clois Greene, Dan Rogers, and so on.

Then there was the goodly influence of the Y. W. C. A., with such gracious leadership as Mercy Perkins, Beatrice Tomlinson, Mary Bain Spence, Jennie Vic McCulloh, Mary Riter as presidents. The religious atmosphere was most vigorous in the life of the campus. Notable was the going out to India as a missionary of one of the group, Miss Nona Bogeman. The University Church, by the financial assistance of the Trustees, acquired a full-time pastor in 1909. The Literary Societies continued traditionally as the focus of expression and social life. The social phase became so prominent by 1908 that the faculty requested the Add-Ran and Shirleys to admit no more ladies, and the Waltons to admit no more men, thus separating the sexes in the hope of more serious literary work.[9] Oratory was a major activity, with local contests of keen rivalry and representations to the State Oratorical Contests with high honor. The State Prohibition Oratorical Association flourished for a while. Because the story of athletics during this period, so full of thrills and memories, forms a part of a longer history it is reserved for a separate chapter.[10] Miss Tyler Wilkinson, assisted by Miss Lottie Watson, won the enduring love of the girls as the matron, and, despite the sometimes seeming strictness, numbers of happy homes were established by "campus couples" of the period.

The *Skiff* continued its weekly messages, mostly constructive, and the *Horned Frog*, having started again in 1905, continued without intermission its annual picturization of student life, with the exception of the year 1910. Everything was ready for publication when the fire destroyed the copy. Some of it was rescued and was published in the 1911 annual.

[8] "Introducing the T. C. U. Horned Frog Band," p. 10.
[9] *Skiff*, December, 1908.
[10] See Chapter XXI.

This mention of the *Horned Frog* is very fortunate, for it suggests a way out for the distressed author, who has been led irresistibly into the recognition of some of the multitudes of exceptionally worthy personalities of that day, quite aware that a limit must be reached, and that to stop is dangerous. The *Horned Frog* is the thesaurus of personalities. To the *Horned Frog*, we commend the reader for the rest of this charming personality story.

It is safe to say that no period in the life of the institution afforded a more intimate, integrated, inspiring body of students than this one, unless it be the old Thorp Spring days, so full of sentiment. Here at Waco, the student body was small, living mostly in the dormitories, very homogeneous, with opportunity for that intimate acquaintance that made for mutual friendship and happiness. A like degree of this family closeness was never regained in the later environment, which was quite different. Truly the extra-curricular (a word not then used) activities contributed richly to the moulding of character. Such is the glory of the small college. It was never more completely expressed than on the T. C. U. campus in the Waco days.

A Typical T. C. U. Glee Club, 1935-36

## ∾ XIII ∾

# The Fire and the Third Move 1910

CHARLES W. GIBSON     T. E. TOMLINSON

A CATASTROPHE AND A CHALLENGE came down with shocking suddenness on Tuesday, March 22, 1910, at 8:30 p. m.—a fire of unproven origin that destroyed the magnificent fire-proof (?) Main Building and resulted in the removal, that summer, from Waco to Fort Worth.

Two students on the fourth floor, Roy Tomlinson of Hillsboro and Carl Melton of Allen, discovered the fire near the roof in an unoccupied room in the northwest wing, and gave the alarm to the others who were leisurely wending their way to their rooms for the evening study hour.

> In an incredibly short time the entire roof was ablaze and the boys . . . had to flee for their lives. Practically all of them lost their personal effects. It took the flames but a few minutes to eat their way back to the lower floors, and within two hours . . . naught remained of the magnificent building but the charred and blackened walls.

The speed of the spread is explained by the wooden roof and stairs together with the suction produced by the stair wells. The theory of a "fire-proof" building with these features was well exploded.

Traditions of the students include multitudes of incidents, tragic and amusing, which were exploited in The *Skiff*. The *Horned Frog* for 1910 was one of the casualties. Roy Tomlinson exerted himself carrying out goods until he fell exhausted and was carried two blocks to the pastor's home—by a girl—Ada Culpepper. Earl Gough—or was it Bob Abernathy—threw his mirror out the window and carried his mattress carefully down the stairway. The campus was strewn with trunks and odd effects, as old photographs testify. Many friends, including some Trustees, received their first intimation of the disaster by the sight of the blaze on the horizon, many miles away.

The shock was taken by students and management with commendable poise. Even while the walls were still falling, arrangements were made for housing the boys in neighboring homes and classes were resumed Thursday morning in Townsend Hall, Girls Home and professors' homes. The Dining Hall served for chapel and church services. The severest loss was the Library, nearly all of which was destroyed. No records were lost from the Business Offices except the Trustees' Minutes, 1902-1910. Even the old Student Enrollment book from 1889 to 1901 was preserved.

The insurance money was very small and could make only a contribution toward paying the debts against the property. The prospect of Waco's providing funds for rebuilding was so doubtful that several ambitious Texas cities sent in prompt invitations for the school to move. The *Skiff*, three days after the fire, printed a list of these bids, and a week after it, March 29, in special session in the Business Men's Club of Waco, the Trustees received representatives from Fort Worth, Dallas, and Waco concerning the matter of rebuilding. The promises of Waco were hearty but vague, so much so that the Board voted "we much prefer that the people of Waco make us a definite proposition, which we will give due consideration."[1] On April 1, they voted

that Messrs. Shirley, Tomlinson and Gibson constitute a committee to continue the investigation of possible locations, and to decide upon location of the school; and that their action shall be final in such matters without further ratification.[2]

Despite this expression of supreme confidence, these men modestly planned, at the final action on May 9, to report the facts and leave the decision to the Board. Whereupon the Board passed a lengthy resolution including, "Having heard it has been decided by these brethren to refer the question to the Board for . . . decision . . . we must earnestly urge them to carry out the instruction given them to act in all matters connected with the location of the University" and pledging their support. Whereupon the committee "reported that they had accepted the offer of the city of Fort Worth for the location of the school," and the report was immediately, unanimously "received and the action ratified."

[1]Minutes, 3-20-10, p. 207.
[2]Minutes, 4-1-10, p. 209.

It would be dereliction on the part of any writer to omit a personal introduction of these men who so held the confidence of their brethren and who so thoroughly and satisfactorily completed within six weeks such an onerous and delicate assignment, so that no opposition was expressed and not a ripple of criticism was ever heard. T. E. Shirley has already been presented as the financial savior of the school in the early 1900's and the President of the Board from 1899 to 1909. Since his ill health kept him confined to the Plains, the work of the committee was done by the other two, with his final review and approval. Charles W. Gibson, a planter and banker of Waxahachie, had been enlisted as a supporter of Add-Ran when T. E. Shirley solicited a donation about 1901. He agreed to give, and asked how much was expected. As he told the story later, "When Brother Shirley suggested a thousand dollars I thought he was crazy. I never knew anybody ever gave away that much money." And his earnest eyes twinkled with happiness as he recalled that he recovered, gave the thousand and later some more. He became a Trustee July 6, 1899, and continued actively until his death in 1919, having sent three of his children to T. C. U. meanwhile. He was also chosen as a Trustee of Brite College when it was organized in 1914. He had but one good eye, and his hearing was impaired, so that he could not preside at a meeting. His devotion, his seasoned judgment, and his unquestioned integrity were highly prized by his brethren.

T. E. Tomlinson, a hardware merchant of Hillsboro, started his children in T. C. U. in 1904, became an advisory Trustee in 1906, an executive member in 1907, and, on the resignation of T. E. Shirley in 1909, was selected as the President of the Board. He served thus until 1916, and as a Trustee until 1941, when, at eighty-four years of age, he insisted on retiring and was elected Trustee Emeritus. Incidentally, his six children (except one who was prevented by illness and early death) continued in T. C. U., one or two or three at a time, until 1916; then, by nephews or grandchildren, his line has been represented among the students ever since, numerously, without interruption. Like "Brother Gibson," his interest was early clinched by his donation of a thousand dollars, most of which he borrowed on his life insurance, to help in a crisis in 1908. His very sound judgment in business affairs and his unselfish devotion won the admiring confidence of all who dealt with him, as it had always done in the home town. The University recognized his contributions in 1942 by conferring on him the LL. D. degree.[3]

Of such stuff was the Board made which led T. C. U. through its crises, and the fire was one of these testing periods. Mr. Tomlinson and Mr. Gibson gave practically their entire time to the task of location, for two months or more and much to the actual building operations for longer. Mr. Gibson did more of the latter, as Chairman of the Building Committee, Messrs. Tomlinson and Van Zandt Jarvis being the other members. Later additions were J. L. Cassell and James Harrison.[4]

Waco citizens made a valiant effort to retain the school, John S. Fall the most persistent, but forty thousand dollars was the height of their hope, and it was not enough. McKinney and Gainesville made bids, but these were not large enough to give promise of success. Dallas made a serious effort, despite the fact that it was at the time completing negotiations for the planting of Southern Methodist University there. A numerous and influential colony of T. C. U. Ex's in Dallas and a group of outstanding Christian churches were disappointed when President T. E. Tomlinson broke the news at the Texas Christian Convention in Dallas, on the evening of May 11. After learning the propositions of the two cities, and reviewing the entire situation, it was clear that the Fort Worth bid was superior to that of Dallas. There was general, if not unanimous, praise for the wisdom, ability, and efficiency of the locating committee, as well as appreciation for the genuine and generous offer from Fort Worth.

Waco was disappointed, but by this time had come to realize the inevitable. The May 11 issue of the Waco Times-Herald, which announced at the bottom of the page: "Fort Worth will get Texas Christian University"; carried a three inch streamer headline on page one: "Waco gets the Hebrew University—The establishment of this school somewhat softens the blow of the loss of T. C. U." Thus did the loyal editor do his patriotic part in helping his city to meet the loss graciously, although the Hebrew University never materialized. Be it said that the old Waco friends have maintained a gracious spirit through the years and the Central Christian Church has loyally supported T. C. U. in its new home, both in students and in finances. Naturally, some of the Waco Trustees dropped off the Board.

[3]T. E. Tomlinson's death occurred February 1, 1946.
[4]Minutes, 6-8-10, p. 213.

Two of them had moved to New York: James I. Moore and W. S. Blackshear. S. M. Hamilton continued active until he moved from Waco a few years later. Frank M. Miller and Dr. H. W. Gates maintained, without any decrease, their warm affection and tangible support for many years. F. M. Miller sent his daughter to T. C. U. in Fort Worth. Dr. Gates, and his unusually capable wife, Dr. Rosa B. Gates purchased the spacious home-place of J. F. Anderson on the corner of 18th and Herring, and through all the following years kept this spot of T. C. U. atmosphere going on "the hill."

Several futile attempts were made by Waco to utilize the old campus. The city petitioned the Trustees in November 1910, that the property be held for a Girls' Christian Orphanage, Waco to assume all of the indebtedness. In 1911 an effort was made to locate a State Normal College; for this the Trustees promised to contribute $15,000 if as much as $60,000 could be had for the property. The two buildings were used temporarily for a hospital, one of them suffering from a fire. The whole plot was finally sold for $38,000 to a Real Estate Company, in February 1912, and cut up into residence lots.[5]

The contract with Fort Worth provided for a campus of fifty acres, $200,000 in money with assurance of connections with city utilities and street car.[6]

The "money" was to come from two sources. One hundred thousand dollars was to be raised by the Board of Trade and the Christian Churches of Fort Worth by July 1, 1910. The net realization of this effort was $75,000. The other $100,000 was to come, and did come, from the sale of lots through the Fairmount Land Company. Four hundred lots valued at $500 a lot were held by two special trustees, one for each party. The Land Company then purchased $65,000 of these lots, paying for them in installments of $10,000 a month, this to be used exclusively for the erection of the new buildings on architects' estimates. The next $35,000 from sales of lots went to T. C. U.; after that all income from sales were divided 65 per cent to the Land Company and 35 per cent to the University. All agreements were carried out faithfully, including the University's

---

[5]Minutes, 11-29-10, p. 229; 2-21-11, p. 253; 2-14-12, pp. 283-285.
[6]This contract was with the Fairmount Land Company signed by B. L. Waggoman, President, and C. W. Gibson and T. E. Tomlinson, locating committee, and again by T. E. Tomlinson as President of the Board. Minutes, 11-29-10, p. 233.

promise to "maintain the institution upon said site for a period of at least ten years." The county officials cooperated in grading and filling a roadway, including the concrete bridge just south of Forest Park. The City extended its boundaries from the Park in a strip two blocks wide (from University Drive to Wabash), to and including the campus. These arrangements were completed just in time for the opening of school in September 1911, for it took a year to transform the old Johnson grass field to a campus.

This was a land deal of large proportions, wrought out in full detail most carefully by men of business ability and integrity, actuated by lofty motives. Both parties did some adventuring and both found themselves abundantly rewarded for their faith. The contract was made with the Fairmount Land Company, but it included the land of at least two other parties with whom it had made its own dealings. The Fairmount land consisted of the blocks north of Cantey (then named Gibson, after C. W. Gibson) and east of University Drive (then called Forest Park Boulevard), including the Park Hill section, which was bought from B. B. Bobo and C. P. McGaff, who had dairies there. This company included William Bryce and William Capps. The latter testified years later that it took lots of nerve to put up so much cash on raw lots, but that it was returned several times over.

The blocks immediately east of the campus, to Lubbock Street, were a part of the Smith estate, including Miss Lucy Smith and her sister, Mrs. Robert M. Green. This was handled by Dr. Green, who became a neighbor to the campus, took a vital interest in its constant improvement, gave his home[7] on the annuity plan, and finally willed much of his estate to T. C. U., subject to life interests of others of the Smith family. The block on which the Library stands, he sold to the University about 1920, for a modest price, $15,000. A lesser portion of land was that lying south and southeast of the campus in which T. P. Wilkes and others were interested.

In the sale of these lots in the early years, W. A. Darter was the Trustee representing T. C. U. Later, many lots were sold to pay for paving costs, which began to come on after the main thoroughfare was paved in 1923. It was not until then that the Fairmount Land Company opened up for sale its section of lots.

[7]The Smith farm of 160 acres lay south and east from the corner that is now University and Cantey: Miss Smith and Dr. Green jointly gave the home at 2929 Princeton to T. C. U. on an annuity basis.

137

In amending the Charter to provide for the new location, provision was also made for twenty-one Trustees instead of thirteen. Naturally, some Fort Worth men were added and the number of Waco men decreased. The new members elected July 14, 1910, were: Dr. Bacon Saunders, John L. Cassell, H. M. Durrett, and James Harrison of Fort Worth; R. L. Crouch and J. J. Hart of Dallas, William A. Wilson of Houston, and F. G. Jones of McKinney. Also, Dr. R. H. Gough and W. W. Mars of Fort Worth, in 1914.

The continuing members were: T. E. Tomlinson, C. W. Gibson, T. E. Shirley; S. M. Hamilton, F. M. Miller, and Dr. H. W. Gates of Waco, VanZandt Jarvis of Fort Worth; George W. Cole of Belton; G. A. Faris of Dallas; S. P. Bush of Allen; T. W. Marse of Taylor; H. H. Watson of Longview; and Morgan Weaver. The last named was succeeded in January 1912 by H. W. Stark of Gainesville, thus bringing in one of the stalwarts of later years.

Not the least among the many complicated problems incident to such a massive move was that of securing quarters for operation until the new buildings could be erected on the Hill. By July 15, a contract was closed leasing the "Ingram Flats" at $5000 for the year. This was a series of two-story brick buildings on the corner of Weatherford and Commerce streets diagonal from the County Court House. The Commerce Street building contained class rooms, chapel, music rooms on the first floor and boys' rooms on second. The Weatherford Street side housed the offices, print shop, dining room, and Business College on the ground floor and girls' rooms on second. On nearby streets were homes of the teachers, one additional home for girls and several for boys. These "dormitories" downtown were hallowed one year by the vibrant life of college youth: Dacus House, 213 W. Pecan, Alexander House, 712 E. Belknap, Daggett House, 607 E. Cliff, Lockhart House, 1000 W. Weatherford, Adams House, Pecan at E. Weatherford, Pitts House, 119 Jones, Smith Annex, 415 Belknap, and the Adams House, 601 E. Weatherford. That downtown site the first year had its drawbacks that are obvious, but by its very location it constituted live advertising.

It was generally understood that the insurance money and the sale money cleared all of the old indebtedness, giving the fresh start in Fort Worth a clean slate, but no accumulation and no endowment.

An old saw says that three moves are as disastrous as a fire. Counting the first move from Fort Worth to Thorp Spring, the old school had endured both calamities; three moves and a fire! Its mettle was thoroughly tried; it faced the challenge with hopefulness and great expectation, on its return to its original home in Fort Worth. It remained to be seen how the city of cattle fortunes and the big packing houses would take to the exponent of Christian culture.

Fort Worth was distinctly "Cowtown." It was the coming of the packing houses that had put it in the city class. But the University gradually edged its way into the interests of Fort Worthians. Van Zandt Jarvis, himself a ranch man, while President of the Board, made a speech in chapel one day lauding the worth of T. C. U. to the city. In his exuberance he exclaimed, "T. C. U. is the most valuable asset Fort Worth has - - ug ug - - next to the packing houses . . . next to the packing houses, T. C. U. the most valuable asset in Fort Worth."

# ❧ XIV ❧

## New Roots in Old Soil

### F. D. KERSHNER—W. B. PARKS—Fort Worth, 1910-1916

T HE CITY OF FORT WORTH into which T. C. U. began to grow its roots in 1910 was a very different community from that frontier cattle village from which the roots of Add-Ran had been torn in 1873. Its population had grown from less than 4,000 to more than 30,000[1]. In addition to the one T. & P. Railroad, whose prospect in 1873 had so disrupted the moral situation that the school had fled to the country for refuge, six other roads had come. The bulk of the business section was on Main Street, extending about eighteen blocks from the magnificent red Texas granite Court House on the Square to the old T. & P. red-brick station with its prominent tower, at sixteenth and East Front streets[2] (demolished in 1932). Two beautiful structures, the old white stone City Hall and the dark red brick Carnegie Library, were attractive and were (foolishly) demolished in 1940. "Hell's Half Acre" was still running rampant, and the business men of the city were still cherishing that foolish delusion that a flourishing liquor trade was good for business. Appreciation of education, arts and culture there was in the city in many homes of refinement, and expressed in a few clubs; but these were not the dominant notes. It was still "Cow-town."

Fort Worth gave the school a genuine welcome. The commercial interests advertised generously in The *Skiff*. "Burton's" claimed to be the leading store. There were such familiar names as Stripling, Washer's, The Fair, and Fishburn.[3] In the very midst of the summer, the sum of $75,000 was raised by subscription as a part of the bonus. Fort Worth University gave a special party to welcome its new neighbor and competitor. It was the two Christian Churches, however, who most bestirred

---

[1]U. S. Census of 1910.
[2]Now Lancaster.
[3]*Skiff*, July and August, 1910.

themselves to attract students and the teachers. The First Christian Church, then in its old stone building of considerable grace and ecclesiastical charm, was within a few blocks of the temporary campus. J. E. Dinger, the pastor, and S. W. Hutton, the assistant, then a T. C. U. student, made the welcome very clear and insistent. The Magnolia Avenue Church, which had just completed its Spanish style building on Magnolia Avenue, under the leadership of Pastor E. M. Waits, provided special chartered cars to take the students out in a body to the Sunday School and Church. This invitation went out in the name of Superintendent George S. Adams.[4]

There was no escaping the fact that T. C. U. was in the town, when more than three hundred students had no other campus than the Court House lawn and the sidewalks about Commerce and Weatherford streets.

The summer of 1911 was marked by feverish activity. The *Skiff* was published all summer,[5] advertising the rather complete Summer School going on downtown, urging the payment of all pledges to James Harrison, Treasurer of the Building Funds, and repeatedly assuring the public that the three buildings would be ready for work in September. The latter clarion call was so vigorously expressed that one article, denying the rumors "given out by other schools that T. C. U. could not open this fall," etc., was headed "Imposters." The City and County officials were rushing about getting the roads and utilities stretched out to the southwestern Johnson grass hill that was to be a campus, and the Traction Company managed to get the first car there on the opening day, September 16, 1911.

By October, 1910, the architects' drawings were published.[6] By Thanksgiving, the bids were in for two buildings, and so the contracts were let to the Texas Building Company, for approximately $160,000 for Main and Jarvis. Additional amounts were added which do not appear in the records.[7] The funds for these came from the Fort Worth bonus. Goode Hall was erected the following spring out of money raised for the specific purpose of reducing the cost of living to ministerial students.[8] As a part of the program of the Texas Christian Convention held in the

---

[4]*Skiff*, 9-16-10.
[5]The Editor was B. B. Hulsey; Business Manager, Grover Stewart.
[6]*Skiff*, 10-12-10.
[7]Minutes, 11-19-10.
[8]See Chapter XVI.

Magnolia Avenue Church in May, 1911, a cornerstone-laying exercise was held on the new raw campus, involving quite a problem in transportation, for no car line was yet available. The crowds took the street car out Summit Avenue, as far as the point where the present Windsor Place crosses the Frisco Railroad. From there, the group tripped by foot or buggy to Forest Park Boulevard and out the road to the Johnson grass field which was soon to be a campus.

A few automobiles were included in the procession. The period can be dated by this incident: C. W. Gibson, long skilled as a driver of a fast team of horses, was quite unskilled in steering his new open-topped, heavy seven-passenger automobile. In the press, he almost ran into some of the pedestrians, whereupon he pulled back on the steering wheel as hard as he could and yelled, "Whoa, Whoa."

Throughout all this process of transition and transplanting, the continuity of the institution from its early days was alive in the hearts of the leaders, and was made apparent to the public. The name of Jarvis, which had been given to a building at Thorp Spring, was carried over and given to a new one in Fort Worth, by action of the Trustees.[9] The name of Townsend Memorial Chapel was assigned to the new chapel in Main Building. This wing of Main was a structure as extensive as the smaller building at Waco which bore the name Townsend Hall. It must be admitted that the name for the chapel never did come into popular use, but the Trustees were faithful to their obligation.[10]

The presence of the old in the new was assured when the Fort Worth citizens and the school body assembled on September 16, 1910, for the formal opening of the session of 1910-11 downtown, in the old limestone City Hall, with its odd, corkscrew steps, and its rather commodious auditorium. The old Add-Ran spirit was surely present. For besides brief words of welcome from County School Superintendent J. S. Hammond, City Superintendent J. W. Cantwell, and President of the Board of Trade H. T. Edgar, and the main address by the Mayor, Honorable W. D. Davis, with appropriate responses by President Lockhart, and President T. E. Tomlinson of the Trustees, there was a word, also, by the old war-horse himself, Addison Clark. Thus was the veteran President able to pronounce his blessing upon

[9]Minutes, 6-11-10.
[10]Minutes, 7-8-13, p. 333.

142

the old school in its new home. It was the patriarch's parting blessing indeed, for this was his last general public appearance.[11] The following March, an invitation to write a word for the anniversary of the Clark Society brought from Mineral Wells a reply of affection and appreciation, which he was barely able to pen, for his mortal illness was upon him.[12] His message and his picture were printed in The *Skiff*.

Again was the historical continuity symbolized at the cornerstone laying, May 8, 1911, to which previous reference has been made.[13] Here, with Judge Anson Rainey presiding, the hands of the Board Chairman, T. E. Tomlinson, were grasped in fellowship with those of J. J. Jarvis, who was the first President of the Board in 1889 when the church assumed ownership. Likewise, the President of the University, Dr. Lockhart, was greeted in fellowship by the Veteran Randolph Clark, whose presence graced and blessed the occasion,[14] and who loyally loved and supported the school for another quarter of a century thereafter.

Another genuine gesture of recognition was made in naming the newly projected dormitory for boys, "Clark Hall." This name and the campaign to raise the funds were announced at the Convention the next day after the cornerstone laying. Soon thereafter W. M. Williams was employed as Financial Agent to lead in the campaign.[15] It was just a week after the Clark Hall name was announced that Addison Clark was called to his long home, May 13, at Comanche, Texas. All who ever felt the vibrancy of his noble spirit pray for its ever abiding presence in the institution to which he gave such worthy tone.

A vigorous effort was made to maintain the attendance in the new location. That spirit of solidarity and loyalty so characteristic of the "small college" at Waco proved substantial in a surprising way. There was no drop in enrollment, such as was shown at the time of the move to Waco. The total attendance in these years beginning with 1908-09 was: 379, 367, 362, 414, 495, 497, 507, and after that a continual increase. The fact that Fort Worth was a larger city had something to do with this increase. Also, the local attendance which in Waco had been 17 per cent became 24 in Fort Worth that first year.

[11]*Skiff*, 9-23-10.
[12]*Skiff*, 3-9-11.
[13]p. 146.
[14]*Skiff*, 5-18-11.
[15]*Skiff*, 2-14-12.

At least five other Texas colleges were moving about the same time as T. C. U. and some of these touched on its history. The Southwestern Baptist Theological Seminary, emerging out of the Bible Department of Baylor University under the leadership of the Moses-like B. H. Carroll became a neighbor two miles south. Dr. A. H. Newman, well known church historian, was the seminary's representative at the cornerstone laying. Fort Worth University, founded in 1881 by the Methodist Episcopal Church, after a year of over-lapping with T. C. U. moved to Guthrie, Oklahoma, as Epworth University, and later became Oklahoma City University.[16] The Southern Methodists, too, were endeavoring, at this period, to concentrate their strength on the newly established (1910) Southern Methodist University in Dallas. They failed to get Southwestern University moved from Georgetown, and although Polytechnic College in Fort Worth was coalesced with it, the old campus was used two years later for Texas Woman's College. During this interim, President Kershner graciously used three of the faculty members of Polytechnic at T. C. U., S. A. Boles, Dr. C. C. Gumm and S. A. Myatt.

The fifth school on the move at this time was the Fort Worth School of Medicine which became a part of T. C. U. for six years and played a tragic part in a most dramatic chapter of medical education in America. Its story is found in Chapter XV.

An unusual spurt of activity occurred in the Alumni Association in 1913, under the presidency of the vigorous and versatile Dan Rogers, '09. It was marked especially by the issuance of a monthly magazine, "The Grad," in handy coat-pocket size. Besides Rogers, as the editor-in-chief, and Grover Stewart, '13, business manager, the assistant editors included such stalwarts as Bonner Frizzell, '09, Clarence M. Hall, '12, and E. E. Faris, '94.

It was Dr. Faris' article on "Let's Change the Name for the Last Time" that furnished the pabulum for about half of the discussion in the year and a month of the life of "The Grad."[17] He advocated the adoption of the title "College" in lieu of "University" as more in harmony with the facts. The columns were prolific with discussion of the proposal, a majority favoring the change. Some of the older grads pleaded for the restoration of the earlier name, "Add-Ran College." Several argued for retaining the name "University," and growing to it. After a

[16]Catalog, June, 1913, p. 168.
[17]A file is in T. C. U. Library.

year of discussion, the editor admitted that the negative had won; the name was to stand.

"The Grad" also sponsored the proposal that more alumni be elected as trustees of the University, calling attention to the fact that F. G. Jones was the only alumnus "re-elected" that year, 1914. As a matter of fact, there were on the Board at the time J. J. Hart, '97, Van Zandt Jarvis, '93, and H. H. Watson, an "ex." In 1915, Dan Rogers was added to the Board, in 1916, T. C. Morgan, and in 1920, Dave Reed.

Another plea made by this keen-eyed journal was for a recognition on the Fort Worth campus of the "Memorial" that had perished by the removal from the Waco campus. Especial sentiment was expressed for the Memorial Arch around which clustered the memories of significant occasions at Waco, and that "Townsend Hall" at Waco should be recognized in the naming of some structure on the Fort Worth campus.

"The Grad" was sponsored and financed by the Dallas chapter of the Association, and an editorial carefully explained that this was not a matter of presumption but of practicability. The hope was expressed that the Association would adopt and perpetuate it. Obviously the financial load was too heavy. Its final number was November, 1914.

The untimely death of Dr. G. A. Llewellyn on February 4, 1912 ended a most promising career. He had just completed the canvass for the funds for Goode Hall, and was elected as Dean of the Bible College. Dr. J. B. Eskridge closed his term on the faculty in 1912, going to the presidency of three colleges in Oklahoma successively. The chair of Latin was handled then by Colby D. Hall, but that was temporary; his real mission was in Bible.

Patrick Henry, the son of A. S. Henry, appeared on the campus again in 1914. For a while he operated the Business College as Principal, then devoted his entire time as a student, preparing for the ministry. He was to become a strong factor in the life of the school in the years ahead.

The second year in Fort Worth saw the closing of the T. C. U. career of one of the strong figures for the previous nine years, J. F. Anderson, Business Manager. Having made quite a success in the establishment of Grayson College in the small town of Whitewright and being a loyal churchman and a teacher of science, he had been called as Business Manager of T. C. U. in 1903. He was a man of action, able to manage multitudes of details readily and in good humor. The multiplicity of duties left him little time for keeping keen and fresh his scientific facts, yet he was an inspiring teacher, stirring many a boy to the spirit of investigation and research.

In the hard financial years at Waco, and through the maze of difficulties involved in the fire and the move, he was the one on whom fell the details of management. He was very popular with all of the faculty, as were all of his lovely family. His ingenious devices for meeting hard situations and providing necessities when there was no wherewithal, were most surprising and often amusing. Physically, he was built like President Taft, though not so large, and his characteristic resounding laugh, though not delayed like that of the jovial President, was far more hilarious and much more contagious. After the work of the session of 1911-12 was completed, he resigned to accept the Presidency of Carr-Burdette College at Sherman, Texas. There he served until his death in 1914. The Business Management fell to J. A. Dacus, who had been for some years Head of the College of Business.[18]

President Lockhart, having been called originally as a teacher, for which work he was best fitted, had carried the executive load for five years, and in his annual report to the Trustees in February 1911 recommended: "That in the election of a President for the next year, a man be chosen to give his whole time to administration, and especially to the raising of funds to meet the necessities of the institution." The President of the Board had knowledge of this move and the Board concurred by accepting his resignation. He was called into executive work again in 1916-20 as Dean of the College of Arts and Sciences, but found that work uncongenial. The glory of his career lay in his work of teaching, as a great scholar. His unique mastery of the technical phases of Oriental languages and culture was perhaps best phrased by genial President Waits in his encomium: "Dr. Lockhart knows the color of every Egyptian mummy's eye."[19]

During the summer of 1911 the Trustees were making a rather wide search over the Brotherhood for a president, while W. B. Parks served as Acting President. On September 19, 1911, they elected as the new president, Frederick D. Kershner (B. A. Transylvania, 1899, M. A., Princeton, 1900) a minister with a good Disciple background and an unusual classic style of ex-

---

[18]Minutes, 7-29-12, p. 296; 9-10-12, p. 298.
[19]Chapters XII and XX contain more of the story of Dr. Lockhart.

pression, who although only thirty-six years of age at the time had already served as a college dean and president, last at Milligan College.[20] Perhaps the outstanding achievement of his administration was the establishment of Brite College of the Bible. At the same meeting in which he was elected President, the Board formally received the gift of $25,000 from L. C. Brite, solicited by Dr. G. A. Llewellyn. President Kershner followed this up by arranging with the Brites to pay for a building of the new Bible College which was named Brite College of the Bible.[21] He was largely responsible, too, for selecting the faculty and arranging the curriculum.[22] He was highly respected by the faculty and students and recognized generally by the public as an able scholar and an inspiring teacher. In June, 1915, he was granted a year's leave of absence for study in Washington, D. C., with full intention to return, as he declared in a letter[23] to the Trustees. But this same letter was also his resignation. He had been persuaded, for the good of the Brotherhood as a whole to accept the editorship of the Christian Evangelist, in the hope of settling a feud between that paper and the Christian Standard. It appeared a rather promising hope since he was trusted and admired by both sides. Yet the plan failed, and he later became Dean of the School of Religion at Butler University.

The following spring (1916) while Dean Parks was serving as Acting President and the Trustees were looking around for a permanent executive, the Dean announced his resignation from the faculty. W. B. Parks was one of those erect souls whom Addison Clark had recognized for his love of truth and had placed in the faculty in 1887. He was, therefore, the one figure who reached farthest back into the life of the school and who embodied so much of its spirit. He was also the first person ever to serve as "Dean" in the faculty. The need for a dean had become felt during the year spent downtown where the temptations were abundant for loafing or even for mischief. The Trustees therefore elected Professor Parks as the Dean, "to have full control of all matters pertaining to the discipline of the school, relieving the President of that duty."[24] For six years W. B. Parks had so graced this position with dignity, firmness,

---

[20]Minutes, 9-10-11, pp. 269, 275; 2-14-12, p. 277.
[21]Minutes, 9-19-11; p. 275; 6-6-14, p. 347.
[22]This story is told in Chapter XX.
[23]Minutes, 10-24-15, p. 399.
[24]Minutes, 10-15-10, pp. 228, 229.

leadership and love that all other appellations that may have gathered about him through the years had faded away, leaving him in memory as "Dean Parks." It is clear that two motives prompted his resignation. One was financial. For thirty years he had invested his all for Christian Education, at a meager salary, ever hoping for a better day. Now his family of four children was growing up, needing advantages he could not afford, and his salary was still not more than $2,000 for twelve months. His second motive, as he expressed it to some of his intimates was, "I am tired, just tired, of discipline problems."[25]

This attitude of Dean Parks suggests that he represented a type of discipline which he had inherited, to which he was faithful, but which was on the way out. It was the semi-military type which counted infractions of rules in terms of demerits, and when the number reached fifty the student was automatically suspended. Often when mercy mitigated a penalty, the boy was given forty-nine. Then he could be suspended for a minor infraction. Such a case did occur. When the girls, according to a tradition, all stole out of the dormitory early on April Fool's Day, all of the boys followed. One boy who had forty-nine demerits came to the Dean, dolefully explaining, "I'm the only boy on the campus today. Must I stay to avoid that one demerit which will send me home?" The Dean gave the permission but it added wrinkles to his brow. Then one dark night a company of fine boys in a playful mood "lifted" a few chickens and held a clandestine feast in the bottoms. That surely was a case for fifty demerits. It would have been easy to assess that if the boys had been a tough gang and the chickens had belonged to a stranger. But they were the Dean's chickens, and the boys were among the finest in school. The boys graduated with forty-nine demerits, but the case added to the Dean's worries.

The seriousness of discipline cases in those days can scarcely be appreciated by a modern faculty. It was the business of the Dean to gather the evidence, but the faculty still held the prerogative of sifting the evidence and pronouncing the penalty. The cumbersomeness of this plan was proved concretely in 1913-14. According to custom, the Junior class was giving the annual banquet to the Seniors. The latter class had grown sufficiently sophisticated to venture out in formal dress for the occasion. As the self-conscious boys were gathered on the south steps of Main Building, white shirt bosoms glistening in the

[25]Minutes, 2-10-14, pp. 343, 378, 379; 2-22-17.

twilight, there came from a room in Clark Hall a shower of eggs. At least one of them found its target—the bosom of the President of the Senior Class. Now it so happened that that senior was also an instructor in the Academy, a nice looking fellow who was quite aware of the fact, and was none too popular with either students or faculty. So when suspicion fell heavily on a certain sophomore, the question was not, "Is he surely guilty?" but "How much shall the dignity of this cocky senior be avenged?" The faculty met in full attendance, daily, for two weeks, without a decision, while the students were merrily repeating each evening what had been said in the faculty meeting that afternoon. Finally the Dean called for a vote. It was a tie! Two weeks of confusion, then a tie! The Chair decided by his vote. He also decided another item: discipline is a job for an executive, not a faculty.

It is surprising how many items which once were matters of the most serious concern are now regarded as within the student's prerogative to decide. A few years after the above incident, the girls increasingly rebelled against wearing a uniform. Gradually the requirement was relaxed. Any white blouse and any blue skirt would do! Finally all regulation was removed except one: they had to wear a regulation hat. These were ordered, delivered and each girl must purchase and wear one. There was nothing the girls could do about it—except lose them. And lose hats they did. How could a girl wear a hat if the hat was lost? That ended the whole uniform affair forever.

If the times had not compelled dear Dean Parks to take so seriously the multitude of smaller items of behavior, he might have lasted the years through on that job. Who knows? But the division of labor has brought us specialists for this as for other duties. And the man trained for the task works with efficiency rather than worry. Deans of Men and of Women trust young people more and help them grow up faster—we hope. The conception of personnel guidance is slowly coming into its own, with growing favor. This is not to ban discipline, but it is to leave the old military discipline behind.

## ❧ XV ❦

# The Colleges of Medicine and Law
# 1900-03 1911-20

## DR. BACON SAUNDERS—EGBERT R. COCKRELL

**"M**ANY A COLLEGE HAS CRIPPLED OR KILLED ITSELF by undertaking, regardless of its strength, everything that any other college is doing," warns Trevor Arnett,[1] who has passed on much wisdom to American colleges. Thus, T. C. U., like most colleges, was tempted to encompass the schools of Medicine and Law within its scope, tried the scheme and passed over it. The story is so typical of a period of development in the college world that it is deemed worthy of a chapter.

Perhaps no phase of education has ever experienced such rapid and drastic metamorphosis as that of medicine in the early decades of the Twentieth Century. The preparation of physicians in our country, as of lawyers, had begun by the apprentice system. In a city where doctors were sufficiently numerous, they organized their students into classes with laboratories and group lectures, and called it a "Medical College." Many of the Colleges served efficiently, nobly, even sacrificially. The doctors with the highest conception of the profession felt an obligation to pass on their traditional lore in good form; those with active minds felt the stimulation for investigation which teaching stirred; all welcomed the prestige which an organized institution brought. This prestige, obviously, would be enhanced if the college were a part of some university, even though only nominally related. The older medical colleges had been inaugurated by private practitioners, then adopted by Pennsylvania (1765), Columbia (King's, 1767), Harvard (1782), Dartmouth (1798), and others.

In this tradition came the worthy record of the Fort Worth School of Medicine, which in 1911 became the College of Medicine of Texas Christian University. Its spirit and history can better

[1]In *College and University Finance*, passim.

be appreciated against the background of a sketch of the grand man whose dream-child it was. Dr. Bacon Saunders came from the same spiritual lineage as the Clarks. His family at Bonham, Texas, was one of the many nurtured on the powerful preaching of the stalwart Charles Carlton, who was for several generations the President of Carlton College, the pastor of the local Christian Church, and practically the spiritual guide of most of the households of the town![2] Hence Dr. Bacon Saunders possessed, in large measure, the two features so much admired in Addison Clark: a lofty sense of integrity of character, and a deep devotion to the "plea" of the Christian Church, as taught by the fathers from the days of Alexander Campbell. He was an elder in the First Christian Church of Fort Worth as long as he lived. He was selected as the Chairman of the Board of Trustees of the Brite College of the Bible when it was chartered in 1914, and served in that capacity until his death in 1924.

The spirit of the pioneer was in him. Dr. I. J. Chase, the Dean of the College of Medicine, used to delight in telling of the venturesomeness of Dr. Saunders in performing operations. The following is an expression from his own profession of medicine, concerning Dr. Saunders.

In October 1879 he performed the first recorded operation for acute appendicitis in Texas, probably in the South . . . During his active years he probably did more surgery than any other physician in Texas . . . He was a charter member and ex-president of the Texas Surgical Society; fellow of the American College of Surgeons; member and ex-president of the Southern Surgical Association; member and ex-president of the Texas State Medical Association; member of the county, district, state, and American Medical Associations; member and vice-president of the International Surgeons Associations, etc.[3]

It can be understood, therefore, that the purposes expressed in the following history of the Medical College are very genuine.

The Medical Department of Texas Christian University was organized in 1894, as the Medical Department of Fort Worth University. The first degrees of Doctor of Medicine were conferred in 1895.

At that time there were no medical schools within a radius of 350 miles, a territory of 380,000 square miles,

[2]See Kenneth Hay, *Life and Influence of Charles Carlton*, for his life.
[3]*Texas State Journal of Medicine*, XXXVII, 1941.

containing over four million people. Many of the nearest schools were poorly equipped, gave two-year courses of instruction, furnished inefficient laboratory training and no bedside teaching. The right to practice medicine in Texas at that time rested on certificates from District Examining Boards, to obtain which practically no medical knowledge was necessary. The country was rapidly filling up with physicians who had poor, or almost no medical college training, and, in addition, there were no accessible anatomical, surgical, bacteriological, or pathological laboratories to which the medical profession in this vast territory could resort.

The first faculty consisted of fifteen full professors, with adjuncts, assistants, and demonstrators. The scientific branches were for some years taught in the laboratories and buildings of Fort Worth University. In the school's second year, a special building was erected on the University campus. Later a medical building in the heart of the city, the site of the present Seibold Hotel, was secured and occupied for ten years. The demand for more modern equipment was met in 1905 by the erection of a new modern medical building, today one of the best structures of its kind possessed by any Southern Medical College.[4]

After the removal of the academic and college departments of Fort Worth University and their union with the Epworth University at Guthrie, Oklahoma, the Medical Department was known for some years as the Fort Worth School of Medicine. In 1911 it became affiliated with Texas Christian University. In 1913 the University acquired possession of all buildings and properties of the Medical School, which became one of its departments. The faculty is elected by the University Trustees and the Department financed by the general funds of the University.[5]

That "affiliation" with T. C. U. in 1911 was on the basis of mutual courtesy and exchange of prestige, as described in preceding paragraphs, "without either department in any way assuming the financial obligations of the other or interfering with its management or control."[6]

---

[4]On the northeast corner of Fifth and Jones.
[5]Catalog, 1916, pp. 119, 120. This history appeared in the catalogs from 1911 through 1916. That of 1917 (announcements for 1917-18) announced the Medical College but gave no catalog: that of 1918 (announcements for 1918-19) gave the number of Medical students for the previous session as 62, but made no other mention of the Medical College.
[6]Minutes, 6-9-11, p. 265.

This action was consummated in good faith on June 28, without the awareness of the cloud on the horizon no larger than a man's hand which was to blow out of existence, within a decade, one hundred of the one hundred and seventy-five Medical Colleges of the United States. This cloud was the campaign of the Education Committee of the American Medical Association, which began by demanding that the University with which a Medical College was related must assume full responsibility for the financing and operation of its Medical College, actually, not nominally. Dr. Saunders presented this situation to the T. C. U. Trustees at their meeting in February, 1912, and they voted "to look with favor on the proposition of assuming full ownership, management and control of the Medical College," and appointed a committee to carry this project out.[7] They then elected the faculty for 1912-13,[8] and later fourteen-fifteenths of the stock held by the Directors of the Medical College was transferred to Texas Christian University.[9] The Medical Association meanwhile was tightening the requirements. Not only should the doctor-teachers be free from any personal interest in the fees collected, but there must be at least six teachers employed for full time and at specified minimum salaries which chanced to be more than that of the T. C. U. professors.

These regulations and the entire policy of the Medical Association were based on the assumption that the sponsoring University would be able to spend on the Medical College far more than it received in tuition fees. Obviously T. C. U. was not in a position to do this. The catalog of 1916 announced "a liberal appropriation of $7,500 from the general fund to be assigned to the Medical Department."[10] Of course the general fund could not spare such an amount; it had a deficit of its own. The appropriation consisted of donations made by the doctors themselves. Efforts were made to raise funds through a canvass of Fort Worth citizens and commercial interests, but without sufficient results. Most of the money raised was from the doctors.[11]

On receipt of a warning letter from the Association dated February 16, 1917 the Board appointed Professor W. M. Winton,

[7]Minutes, 2-14-12.
[8]Minutes, 7-3-12.
[9]Minutes, 2-11-13, p. 305.
[10]Catalog, 1916, p. 120.
[11]Minutes, 2-12-14; 6-23-14, p. 350; 7-22-14, p. 351; 3-19-16, p. 370.

the Head of the Biology Department of the University, who was serving as counsellor to the Trustees in the matter, to investigate and recommend. He reported on February 22:

> A fixed income of at least $25,000 a year must be provided for . . . . The present hospital facilities must be doubled (they were using the City County) . . . the full-time staff must be enlarged and salaries raised . . . the Medical College cannot continue to secure students unless it is raised to an A grade.[12]

On the basis of the report as sifted by Professor Winton, the Board voted that "it is financially unable to meet the requirements of the A. M. A. and that a clear understanding of our position in this matter should be conveyed to all interested parties." A resolution of similar import was passed the following June by the Faculty of the Medical College addressed to the Holding Board.[13] The session of 1917-18 was operated by the Holding Board (Physicians), and enrolled 62 students. The Medical College was closed the spring of 1918 and the student records were turned over to the young Baylor Medical College in Dallas.

During the twenty-four years of its life the Medical College had faculty of high worth and graduated 350 doctors, including some of the best known practitioners in Fort Worth and in Texas. The school fell before the line of march of the A. M. A. with its determined purpose to reduce the number of medical colleges. Since that time it has come to be understood that only millions of dollars of endowment can make possible such a school. Whether the A. M. A. was extreme in its methods and its figures, is a matter of opinion. Whether its program encouraged it or not, the numbers of schools of healing of lesser grade surely multiplied following its slaughter of the orthodox medical colleges. One fact has become apparent through the years: T. C. U. was wise in its policy of concentration upon the scope of work it could handle with high quality.

The first attempt of Texas Christian University to establish a school of Law was in one of its leanest years, 1900-01. The school was announced in the catalog of 1900, offering a full curriculum of Law for the following session, with a faculty of three teachers and six "Lecturers." Two of the teachers were practicing lawyers in the city of Waco, Sam E. Stratton and

[12]Minutes, 2-22-17, pp. 415, 416.
[13]Minutes, 6-4-18, p. 467.

John J. Foster. The other was Professor Egbert R. Cockrell, who also carried the full responsibility of teaching all classes in the Department of History and Political Science. The five Lecturers were prominent men: Judge A. C. Prendergrast, Judge J. E. Boynton, Judge Sam R. Scott, all active judges in the Courts at Waco; Judge A. E. Wilkinson of Austin, Clerk of the Court of Civil Appeals; and Judge W. K. Homan of Dallas, Editor of the *Christian Courier*, clergyman, and a strong lawyer. The LL. B. degree was promised on the completion of the two years' course. Courses were available, as elective, to Arts College students.[14]

This was during the interim between the presidency of Addison Clark and that of E. V. Zollars. The enrollment of the University the previous session had been 161, and that year, 148. The majority of these students were Preparatory. The response to the announcement of a College of Law obviously was not promising. The announcement was not repeated after the 1903 catalog. Circumstances were not yet ripe for the expansion.

The second venture for a Law School was urged and headed by the same enthusiastic, optimistic personality as in the first instance, Professor E. R. Cockrell, Head of the "Department of Political and Economic Sciences." The Trustees in 1915 authorized the opening of the Department of Law, but assumed very little financial responsibility. Milton Daniel and George M. Conner taught part-time, and Professor Cockrell added to his load of Social Sciences. Each of these was obligated also to secure as many as fifteen students.[15] There were five "Special Lecturers" also, including Judges Marvin Brown, Ocie Speer, F. O. McKinsey, and R. M. Rowland. The second year R. E. Rouer was added to the faculty and the third year (1917), Morris Rector and Harold Stearns. By 1918 the LL. B. degree was promised at the completion of the three years' course, and in 1919 it was announced that ". . . graduates will be admitted to the bar without further examination." A combination B. A. and LL. B. was announced, and many courses were used as elective for the B. A.[16] At the February, 1920 meeting of the Trustees the Law School was included in the budget by a special vote but in June it was resolved that

[14]Catalog, 1903, pp. 40, 41.
[15]Minutes, 3-10-15, p. 362.
[16]Catalog, 1918, p. 87; 1919, pp. 70, 71.

155

on account of the advance in standards in maintaining a law school in Texas, as well as being requested to bring the Law Library up to 10,000 volumes (there were 2,500) . . . together with a well paid faculty, something like $25,000 would be required. Not being able to finance same under existing conditions, we deem it best to discontinue the Law School.[17]

This decision was reached despite an encouraging enrollment. The total number of students taking law ran to 30 the first year, 50 and 62 the last two years. Most of these were Arts College students; the strictly law students numbered 17 or 18 each year, but the last year it appears to have been 41. Since the number of graduates was small they may be named: 1918: Jewell H. Bauldwin, William E. Bauldwin, Jesse Arna Raley, Jesse Martin; 1919: none; 1920: David Rubenstein, P. M. Scardino.[18] The list of matriculates includes such other names as: Morrow Boynton, Cedric Hamlin, Dewey Lawrence, Ralph Martin, Frank Ogilvie, John Sturgeon, and Howard Vaughn. Willis McGregor had completed his second year when the school closed.

The Trustees were convinced that the Education Commission of the American Bar Association was planning to follow the pattern of the A. M. A. in its policy toward medical colleges. Having just tasted the experience with the one, the Trustees did not care to go further with the other. In the case of law, it would have been possible still to get students; other non-standard schools did so later. But the University had wisely adopted the policy that it would operate a school first class, or not at all.

After this decision was made and the Law School was closed, another pressure in favor of this conservation policy was encountered. That year, with the coming in of a new Dean of the University, a constructive policy was inaugurated of gaining the recognition of all the highest accrediting agencies. The first of prime importance was the Association of Colleges and Secondary Schools of the Southern States, and one of its standards required that any professional school which a university operated must be accredited by the national rating agency for that profession. Hence it came about that the University itself could not attain its proper rating if it had retained either the Law or the Medical College. Such professional schools must await the day when income could be fed into them from the

---

[17]Minutes, 6-8-20, pp. 523-529.
[18]Catalog, 1921, p. 156; Minutes, 6-4-18, p. 462.

DR. BACON SAUNDERS, M. D., President of the Faculty of Medical College, Trustee T. C. U., 1910-25 : B. C. B. President of Trustees, 1914-25. 15 years

EGBERT R. COCKRELL, Professor, Dean of School of Law. 18 years.

W. B. PARKS, Professor, Dean, 1911-16. 24 years.

CHALMERS McPHERSON, Professor, B. C. B., 1914-27. 16 years.

COLBY D. HALL. Dean of the University. 1920-43 ; Dean, B. C. B. 1914-47. 40 years.

W. C. MORRO, Professor, B. C. B., 1927-43. 16 years.

CLINTON LOCKHART, Professor, B. C. B., 1906-43. 36 years.

GEORGE CUTHRELL, Trustee, B. C. B., 1937-43 ; President, 1941-43.

ELMER D. HENSON, Trustee, B. C. B., 1942– ; President, 1943– .

Some Executives and Professors in Fort Worth.
For more details consult the Appendix.

*First Row :* Willis McGreggor, '17 ; Clifton Ferguson, '13 ; Jess Martin, '18 ;
Nabunda Oda, '27 ; "Mother Ross," a happy visitor.

*Second Row :* Joe Frederick, '31, B.D., '43, won title "Ugliest man on the campus";
Loy Ledbetter, '20 ; Milus Little, '14-'17, killed in World War I ; Milton
Daniel as Coach ; Main, viewed from the Arch.

*Third row :* Mary Beth Waits, '21 ; Homer Tomlinson, '17 ; John Allen Rawlins,
'14 ; Lloyd Burns, '30 ; Valin T. Woodward, M. D. '16, B. A. '26, (representing
the Medical College).

*Fourth Row :* A (much condensed) group of Trustees, 1922 ; a World War I
bi-plane that landed on the campus ; the old First Christian Church that
welcomed T. C. U. in 1910.

Some samples of Fort Worth Days, with snatches from Law and Medicine.

general revenues of the University, either by endowment or larger current donations. In 1920 there was no prospect of such a day.

It was not lack of a mission, but a dearth of money, that made the career of the College of Law so brief.

The aspiring, cordial personality who was the mainspring of both of these adventures into the Law School was Egbert R. Cockrell, who had come on the faculty in 1899 as the Head of History and Social Sciences and, but for two leaves of absence for further study, had remained with it continuously.[19] He had specialized in the study of Municipal Law and Administration, so in order to apply his knowledge he announced as a candidate for Mayor of the city of Fort Worth in 1921. He requested a leave of absence for the campaign, to retain his place if not elected.[20] Despite the opposition to him as a theorist and a novice in campaign tactics, he was elected. Political clouds obscured his accomplishments at the time, and experienced political manipulators plied all of their devices against him, but the perspective of the years makes it clear that his term of office marked the turning point of Fort Worth from an easy-going ultraconservative town, to the progressive ways and equipment of a modern city. Up to this time the City was on the Commission form of government, the Mayor possessing but limited power. In order to facilitate the transfer to a city manager form of Government he resigned before his term expired, and soon afterward, accepted the presidency of William Woods College at Fulton, Missouri. There he served with his talented wife, until the hand of death[21] removed from earth one who was unexecelled in the art of making friends.

In the years to follow, other professional schools grew up in T. C. U.: Education, Journalism, Business and Theology. But the more expensive ones of Medicine and Law, having made their adventure, were laid aside for the time. Thus far the counsel of Mr. Arnett had been followed; wisdom had won over adventure. It was to be class A or nothing.

[19]One in 1903-08, another in 1911-12, the latter spent in England.
[20]Minutes, 2-5-31, p. 536.
[21]Egbert R. Cockrell died September 13, 1934.

# ❧ XVI ❧

# Struggles With War and Finance 1916-1923

## E.M. WAITS—SAM J. MCFARLAND

WHILE DEAN PARKS WAS SERVING AS ACTING PRESIDENT in the winter of 1915-16 the Trustees were scanning the far horizon for a new president, then finally found one near by. They elected L. D. Anderson, an alumnus, and pastor of the First Christian Church in Fort Worth; he left the decision to the members of his church and they pleaded with him to remain as their pastor, which he did.[1] Then the board found another close by. It had been assumed that the presidency would go to a preacher, although there was no preacher on the Board. But the Secretary of the Board was a preacher, E. M. Waits, Pastor of the Magnolia Avenue Christian Church, Fort Worth. His five years of experience as secretary had made him familiar with the affairs of the institution. Being one of the group, he was easily overlooked in the search for a president. He was well known, however, to the recently elected President of the Board (Sam J. McFarland), having been his pastor at Ladonia some years before. Mr. Waits had just passed through the deep waters of sorrow in the death of his wife, leaving him alone with his young daughter, Mary Elizabeth; because of this he had resigned his pastorate and had accepted a call to a church in California. From this he secured release when, on September 20, he was elected President of the University.

He came into this responsibility as a minister rather than as a school man. A graduate of Transylvania University (then Kentucky University) in 1896 (LL. D. from the same, 1923), with a native culture broadened by travel in Europe and the Holy Lands, he was a pulpit speaker of forceful language, a devotee of beauty and a personality gifted in making friends. His first Annual Report in February, 1917 reveals the condition of the institution as it appeared to him at the time, and expresses the

---

[1]Minutes, 3-8-16; p. 371; *Skiff*, 3-10-16; 3-17-16.

spirit of those reports which he made annually and between times for a quarter of a century, glowing with optimism, glittering with beauty and challenging with problems and opportunities.

The history of the institution during its six years of residence in Fort Worth can scarcely be duplicated in the whole history of Christian education. To rise in six years from ashes, disaster and almost bankruptcy to the possession of the best material equipment in the brotherhood, valued at approximately $1,000,000, to occupy a place of cultural influence equal to the best in so short a period, sounds like fiction rather than a page of sober history . . . This does not mean that we are at the end but rather at the beginning.[2]

The first seven-year period of his administration, which will be covered in this chapter, was marked by such highlights as the demise of the Medical College, the coming and going of the Law School, the strengthening of the Board of Trustees and of the University Christian Church, World War I with its kindred disciplinary problems and several financial campaigns climaxed by the Jubilee Celebration in June 1923.

The Board of Trustees lost at this time three substantial members: by death, C. W. Gibson (1920), George W. Cole (1922), and by illness J. J. Hart. Some valuable additions were made to the group: D. G. McFadin, 1917, Dan D. Rogers, 1915, Dave C. Reed, 1916, Andrew Sherley, 1920, L. D. Anderson, 1922, Ross Sterling, 1922, Chas. F. Wheeler, 1923. In the February 1917 meeting, the Chairman, T. E. Tomlinson, nominated Sam J. McFarland to be the President of the Board and he was elected[3]. He was from a pioneer Texas and Disciple family of Ladonia and had come to a position of leadership in the church and in the banking circles of Dallas. Through a trying period, he led the Board until 1927, and he really did lead. It was his custom to come to Fort Worth the day before the meeting and go over the details with the several committees and administrators. He came, too, with constructive plans. The financial campaigns of this period were largely shaped up by him and one of them was directed by him. Another leader of great importance was H. M. Durrett, who gave up his business in Fort Worth to become Business Manager of T. C. U. in 1913 and served until his health failed in 1921.

[2]Minutes, 2-22-17, pp. 408, 409; 9-19-16.
[3]Minutes, 2-22-17, p. 405.

The University Christian Church enjoyed a period of expansion at this time, in the pastorate of Walter P. Jennings with his lovely family. It had been customary to use a professor or a visiting minister as preacher, for the Sunday services in the Chapel. In place and personnel, this seemed to both teachers and students too much like another college occasion. The day before the election of President Waits, the Board received a request from the faculty "relative to establishing a University Church near the campus[4]," and a motion prevailed to ask the State Board of Missions to help support a pastor. By the next September Mr. Jennings was on the campus as the pastor, his salary being provided, $800 by the T. C. U. Board, $600 by the Missions Board and the balance of the $2,000 by the church members. The presence and leadership of the pastor for the next five years was a blessing to the campus and to the community. For a while, also, a church house seemed assured. Pastor Jennings had his heart set on this objective. He found a site of five lots on the southeast corner of Forest Park Boulevard (later University Drive) and Gibson Street (later Cantey) which five professors bought by borrowed money for $1,500. Just about the time a united campaign was set up to include the money for the church house, A. C. Parker, a prominent preacher who was temporarily an oil millionaire, agreed to provide the church house. He pledged $90,000 and gave a mortgage on a Dallas business house to secure it. Then after the receipts of the United Campaign had been spent on a Gymnasium, Mr. Parker, along with many others, lost his fortune. Pastor Jennings, disappointed, resigned and moved to Texarkana. The lots were purchased by T. C. U. in 1925 to enlarge the campus and the dream of a church house was postponed, to be realized later in 1933.

The life of the campus was rigorously affected by the War of 1917-18. The Service Flag showed 145 stars, three of them gold stars. Classes in German continued to be offered but were not taken. The "flu" epidemic of 1918 hit the campus as it did elsewhere generally. The flag pole was knocked down into the form of the letter S by an airplane with an exhibitionist pilot who headed into the parapet on the north side of Main building and fell unhurt on the honeysuckle arbor.[5]

Several seniors went to Leon Springs Training Camp for Of-

[4]Minutes, 9-19-16, p. 376.
[5]*Skiff*, 1-4-18, 3-15-18, 11-11-22.

ficers more than a month before the Spring term was out, and were graduated in absentia.

The War had little effect on finances or enrollment, but it had much on morale. The record of attendance shows a steadiness through 1917-18 and an increase just after that. With the war excitement brought close to the campus by the proximity of the large Camp Bowie, the President recommended in September 1917 that military discipline be considered. This was repeated in February, with a request that a military commandant be secured[6]; it was approved by the Board. The answer was found by an order from the Secretary of War, May 6, 1918, outlining the plan which came to be the Students Army Training Corps, which began operation the next September.

> The Government proposes . . . to take over all institutions which will create units of over 100, over the age of eighteen. The necessary military equipment will, so far as possible be provided . . . . enlistment voluntary . . . . students under eighteen not legally eligible will be encouraged to enlist in the training units.[7]

There were 256 boys enrolled in the S. A. T. C. by September 17 and doubtless more later. Clark Hall was devoted to it completely and some rooms were set up in Brite Building.[8] No change was made in the regular college offerings except the addition of a "War Aims" course, which was mostly European history.

There was no doubt in the minds of the faculty about the value of the S. A. T. C. As a school it was a complete failure. The Lieutenants in charge had had but brief training in military affairs, and were disdainful of the college classes. Orders for drill were shouted down the halls by orderlies without regard to classes in session. How much military drilling was accomplished fortunately was never proved, for the Armistice came in less than two months and by December 19, the S. A. T. C. was mustered out. There was nothing inherent in the plan, perhaps, to make it fail. The days were full of confusion, the faculty were willing to subordinate themselves to the military, out of loyalty, and the officers were new. It was a part of the unpreparedness.

[6]Minutes, 9-18-17, p. 426; 3-3-18, p. 450.
[7]Minutes, President's Report, 6-4-16, p. 465.
[8]Minutes, 9-17-18, p. 471; 9-5-18, p. 469.

The boys who went into the service and crossed the seas into actual warfare came back in various attitudes of mind. Most of them were restless, requiring some time to get settled. There can be no doubt that the war left attitudes that made it hard on discipline. Instead of teaching men to submit to authority, the war experience gave some of them a spirit of independence and challenge. This spirit came to a hasty climax at the opening of the fall semester of 1919. The older men among the Varsity athletes took it on themselves to inaugurate a regime of exceedingly severe hazing. The President, having found the ring leaders without doubt, called in the Captain of the football team, from the practice field, in his togs, and suspended him and five others on the spot. Some had not completed registration and were not allowed to do so. Very strong pressure by the students was put on the administration to relent. "The football season was ruined!—T. C. U. was ruined!" The hazees were subservient to their tormenters. The hazers were defiant. The Editor of The *Skiff*, Morrow Boynton, wrote a very courteous editorial plea for reinstatement arguing, "no one was hurt and all were equally guilty." The Trustees met in special sessions and stood by the Administrative officers.[9]

The students organized a boycott. The boys threatened to leave school in a body if the suspensions were not withdrawn or mitigated. They began to pile their trunks up in front of Clark Hall as a sign they were leaving. The pile was some seven rows high and thirty or more feet long, in orderly fashion. The Business Manager, Mr. Durrett, announced that the truck would haul all trunks to the depots free of charge, and the hauling would start at six P. M.; any boy who did not want his trunk moved must take it back to his room. Several boys phoned home to see if the folks would back them up in leaving school, and found the answer was "No." These few slipped their trunks inside and by noon the next day all the trunks were back indoors. Some of the boys announced that they would transfer to other Texas colleges, but honorable dismissal was denied them. After a case had been filed in the District Court to enjoin President Waits, he agreed to issue the transcripts, with a statement of the facts in the case. But the other college presidents were having similar trouble, and declined to accept the transfers. Several of them congratulated the T. C. U. President. Thus ended the strike.

[9]*Skiff*, 9-30-19.

This episode of the super-hazing and the student strike left a spirit among the boys that seemed to require rigid control. For several years a policy of discipline was exercised in the dormitories which the students characterized as bordering on "policing." Other after-effects of the war were obvious to the experienced observer. The general spirit of disillusionment which marked the attitudes of the American people in general, after the war, found expression in the campus life. This was manifest in the so-called "bull-sessions," in the class and platform discussions, and doubtless in some degree of apathy toward church attendance. There was even a rumor that an "atheistic society" had been formed on the T. C. U. campus. This rumor was investigated and it was discovered that a group—hardly an organization—of men and women of the city was meeting weekly in various homes, downtown. It was a company of the discontented, disjointed and disillusioned, without aim or purpose. Its only connection with T. C. U. was that one student was active in its discussions and occasionally others dropped in. Gradually, the meetings lapsed. This psychology of disillusionment, it has been observed, went like a wave over all college campuses. It was most evident during the years from 1925 to 1927.

An experiment was made in student government. In 1914, pressure was brought by some of the students for what they called the "Honor System."[10] A system was adopted, the jurisdiction of the students being limited, at their request, to matters of "cheating and stealing." The examinations were left without faculty supervision; each student was expected to report to the Student Council all cheating which he saw. It was not long until the attitude "I'll refrain but I will not report others" took the value out of the plan and it was abandoned, students and faculty agreeing.[11]

A new health program was inaugurated in 1918, on the recommendation of Dr. S. A. Woodward, a loyal friend and a superior physician, who then became the College Physician. By this plan each dormitory student paid $7.50 a semester and received the services of the physician and of a resident nurse.[12]

There was a desire to give some notable award to the students of outstanding scholarship. Naturally the preferred medium

[10]*Skiff*, 3-27-14.
[11]*Skiff*, 9-3-14, 10-2-14, 9-18-23.
[12]Minutes, 3-12-18, 5-29-18, p. 459; *Skiff*, 12-19-19.

was to have a local chapter of the Phi Beta Kappa. Indeed, an official representative of that honored Scholarship group made a visit to the T. C. U. campus about this time. An administrative officer remarked to him that the conservative character of Phi Beta Kappa was well understood and appreciated, whereupon the official declared that the Society had become much more liberal, that it had recently voted to add to its list an additional college in the Southwest every four years. "What do you consider the Southwest?" he was asked. His reply was, "Everything south and west of Washington, D. C." Considering the extent of this territory, it was thought best not to wait. A number of colleges of Texas met and organized the Scholarship Society of Texas, which was soon changed to the Scholarship Society of the South, and later to Alpha Chi. Its purpose, of course, was to give recognition to the superior scholarship of students in this region. Dean H. Y. Benedict, later President of the University of Texas, deserves great credit for the time and encouragement he gave to this move, as does Dean A. H. Nolle of Southwest Texas State Teachers College, who served as Secretary.

The early '20's brought to the campus as large a group of celebrities as any period, it would seem. Among these were Dr. Chas. A. Ellwood, sociologist; Dr. Edgar J. Banks, Orientalist; Charles Rand Kennedy, playwright; Will D. Upshaw, prohibitionist; Sir Basil Thompson of Scotland Yard; Mother Ross, missionary inspirationist; Wm. Jennings Bryan (announced to speak on "Evolution" but speaking more on politics); Paderewski, pianist; Vachel Lindsay, (who spent a week or more visiting around); Robert Frost, poet; and Stockton Axson. The latter delivered a series of lectures each year for several years, and was catalogued as a Visiting Professor.[13]

During the thirteen years from the arrival in Fort Worth to the Jubilee Celebration in 1923, there was a constant struggle to meet current expenses and to avoid the accumulation of a dangerous deficit. The old indebtedness of about $32,190 in addition to the cost of moving, was cleared by the money from the fire insurance and the sale of the Waco property. This sale, ratified March 20, 1912, brought $38,000. Thus the start in Fort Worth was made on a clean slate: no debts, but no endowment.[14]

---

[13]*Skiff* in loco.
[14]Minutes, 1910, pp. 225, 232, 253; 2-12, p. 283; 3-20-12, p. 285.

The $200,000 bonus offered by Fort Worth was expected to erect the new plant. But $35,000 of this was in the form of city lots, and the city fell short by $25,000 of raising its share. This left a deficit of $60,000, plus some more later from the building of Clark Hall. A review at a later date revealed that the total shortage on the buildings was $75,000.[15] There was no deficit left from the Medical College venture because the Trustees had guarded against that from the first. The responsibility for this College was carried by a Holding Board, which was, in practice, supported by the contributions of the doctors.[16]

Inevitably there was a deficit on current upkeep, the more especially in view of the newness of the plant, the necessity for buying new equipment, and the adjustments due to the move. The Business Manager warned in November 1910 that the current deficit was $3,000; by February 1911, it was $7,000 and by June, $10,000.[17]

To provide for these accumulations, a loan was made from the Mercantile Trust Company, of St. Louis, for $75,000 in January, 1912.[18] Due dates on the installments came faster than the inflow of funds to meet them. A frequent feature of the Trustees' meetings was the endorsing of paper to make temporary loans. One time W. M. Williams, the Field Secretary, resorted to an appeal directly to the Trustees for individual cash contributions to meet a particular payment, and $1,300 was raised.[19] A note for $25,000 to the National City Bank was once signed by twelve Trustees, and later the Board voted to give them a lien on the campus property, in order to protect their own credit.[20]

By one plan or another a financial agent was employed to solicit funds. Chalmers McPherson, Endowment Secretary, who insisted always on concentrating on endowment, rather than current funds, resigned September, 1911.[21] At one time J. T. McKissick was offered the position of Field Agent, but the arrangement was never consummated.[22] The most fruitful field solicitation by a regular Agent was by Dr. Clifford Weaver,

[15]Minutes, 5-31-21, p. 605. The President's Report.
[16]Minutes, 6-4-18, p. 468.
[17]Minutes, 11-10, p. 231; 2-11, p. 249; 6-11, p. 263.
[18]Minutes, 1-3-12, p. 277.
[19]Minutes, 2-10-14, p. 342.
[20]Minutes, 2-9-15, p. 377.
[21]Minutes, 9-19, p. 274.
[22]Minutes, 4-7-15, p. 363.

who began work in the summer of 1915 and continued until February 1919. In his last year, he raised $19,000 by personal solicitation. His good work was recognized by conferring on him the title of Chancellor.[23] This income was sorely missed after he returned to the pastorate, as Business Manager Durrett reported.[24] John W. Kerns was called as Financial Agent in the summer of 1919, just as he was leaving the pastorate at Austin. But the work of solicitation was uncongenial to him, and he soon withdrew.[25]

In addition to the need for current income and the accumulated debts, there was the urgent necessity for larger gifts to provide expansion of the plant and permanent endowment. To meet this need, there were, within the thirteen year period, five major financial "drives": the Clark Hall campaign, 1912-1914; the Men and Millions Movement, 1914-1918; the Local Fort Worth campaign, of 1916; the United Campaign in 1919; and finally the Indebtedness Campaign in 1922-23.

The call for the building of a boy's dormitory to be named Clark Hall, in honor of the whole Clark family, was made first at the State Convention at the Magnolia Avenue Church in 1911. The dedication of the Main building was a part of that program. W. M. Williams was called in February 1912, from the pastorate of, the church at Belton, to conduct a personal solicitation, from town to town. In this he was joined, for short periods, by several of the faculty.[26] This task was fairly well completed and he left for the Bonham pastorate in March 1914.[27]

The Men and Millions Movement was a national affair, headed by that genius for generalship, Abe Cory, aiming to undergird all of the enterprises of the Disciples of Christ, and to lift them to a new level of support. It encountered the War, soon after starting, yet it succeeded. The first public meeting of the Movement was held in Texas, at the State Convention at Gainesville, and Texas had an active share in the labor and in the receipts.[28] The solicitation was done by teams consisting of the administrators of the general agencies of the church and

[23]Minutes, 9-14-15, p. 366; 3-29-18, p. 464; 6-4-18, p. 464; 2-11-19, p. 474.
[24]Minutes, 9-28-20, p. 529.
[25]Minutes, 6-3-19, p. 496.
[26]Minutes, 2-14-12, p. 277 c.
[27]Minutes, 3-3-14, p. 346; Skiff, 4-3-14.
[28]Skiff, 11-28-13.

selected pastors, all under the direction of the leaders. President Waits spent much of his time in 1917 in the field.[29]

The most productive gift of this campaign, designated to T. C. U. was made by H. W. Stark of Gainesville, for $25,000, on which he paid six per cent interest for years, until he paid it out by deeding some farm land in Grayson County. A pledge of $100,000 was made by Mrs. Ida Van Zandt Jarvis, nearly all designated to T. C. U. This was paid by deeding a block of land in North Fort Worth, which was evaluated at the amount of the pledge. There were back taxes, and some other claims against it, so that when it was finally sold in 1943, the net return was $798.50.[30]

The amount paid to T. C. U. out of the Men and Millions Movement, aside from the Stark and Jarvis gifts, was $22,600.[31] The greater blessing that came from this Movement was psychological as much as financial; it broke the minds of the brethren into a new attitude toward giving. They began to give in larger sums.

The third financial campaign, the Fort Worth local drive, came almost before President Waits had had time to take a look into his office as the new President. This drive, for which Senator R. K. Hanger served as chairman, was directed by a professional firm. The general attitude of downtown Fort Worth seemed to be that it was the responsibility of the Christian Church people to do most of the giving. The aim was $150,000; the result was about $60,000.

In 1917 a campaign was advocated which never materialized. On the suggestion of the President of the Trustees, S. J. McFarland, the attempt was made to have the three colleges, Carr-Burdette, Midland and T. C. U. join in a campaign under the direction of the newly organized Board of Education for Texas Disciples.[32] The emergency needs of the two junior colleges were so stressing they would not wait for a joint campaign.

The fourth "Drive" was one of the largest and most fruitful campaigns ever put over by Texas Disciples. It was proposed by the T. C. U. Board in February 1919, ratified by the State Convention in Paris in April, and completed the following fall and winter.[33] The aims were: for T. C. U. $190,000; for Carr-

[29]Minutes, 3-12-18, p. 447.
[30]Minutes, 2-44.
[31]Minutes, 5-29-18, p. 447.
[32]Minutes, 1917, p. 431.
[33]Minutes, 9-29-19, p. 500.

Burdette $25,000; Midland College $25,000; Texas Christian Missionary Society $75,000, Juliette Fowler Homes, $25,000— Total of $350,000. Sam J. McFarland was the Chairman of the Executive Committees, and indeed the active manager and presiding genius of the movement. There were no paid executives or solicitors. The canvassers were volunteers from the institutions involved, and many ministers. The expenses were surprisingly light and the returns very gratifying.

The ambition of the Trustees at first had been to raise $250,000, designated: for a church, $75,000, a gymnasium, $70,000, a library, $30,000, and a girls' dormitory, $75,000.[34] But on going into the United Campaign these figures were cut to: church $60,000, library, $30,000,, balance for housing students to be adjusted.[35] The campaign succeeded, but building costs, after the close of the war, sky-rocketed so that only one building could be squeezed out of the funds collected. By a peculiar quirk of fortune that building turned out to be the gymnasium, and not the first choice—the church. For it was assumed that the church was cared for by the Parker gift, as told in the story in the earlier pages of this chapter. The gymnasium was completed (in 1921) at a cost of $150,000; yet the collections were such that a $25,000 deficit was left.[36]

Meanwhile the Endowment Fund had received a pledge of $100,000 from Andrew Sherley. This enabled the President to report to the Southern Association that the required goal of $300,000 in endowment had been attained. This was a genuine help toward the acceptance of T. C. U. by the Association.

Another encouraging interlude was the immediate help of the General Education Board. President Waits reported that application had been made to that Board for a gift of $300,000 and an allowance of $25,000 a year for three years to increase salaries of teachers. The petition bore fruit two years later in the grant of $8,000 a year for two years, designated to the single purpose of increased salaries.[37] This was a statesman-like provision of the wise Board to preserve college faculties at a time when living costs had risen enormously beyond the power of colleges to make adjustments. This relief probably encouraged

[34]Minutes, 6-3-19, p. 497.
[35]Minutes, 9-23-19, p. 505.
[36]Minutes, 2-21, p. 532.
[37]Minutes, 2-4-21, p. 583. President's Report.

the Trustees to withdraw a resolution already passed, to borrow $150,000.[38]

But still the debt persisted. There was one more campaign due, the fifth, and it was bravely tackled. This situation was presented frankly in the President's report of May 1921.[39]

It is sufficient to say that we have reached our limit and our backs are against the wall . . . The entire indebtedness of this university including the $75,000 which was left over from the original building enterprise, plus the amount of money which has been spent for real estate, plus the accumulated deficits of ten years plus the $50,000 deficit which will be turned over to us from the gymnasium, aggregates in the neighborhood of $200,000.[40]

As on many an occasion before, it was moved to float a loan rather than face a drive. It was voted to borrow $150,000 from the Mississippi Valley Trust Co.[41] but the board rescinded this action the following month.[42]

In the midst of the discussion of many plans for meeting the financial crisis during the Board meeting of February 14, 1922, President Waits made the bold suggestion, that

T. C. U. not only secure the $67,500 needed to meet our present emergency, but that we plan by June 1, 1923 to raise sufficient money to pay all our indebtedness, get one thousand students in the College of Arts and Sciences, one hundred and fifty in the Brite College of the Bible—plan to celebrate the culmination of this program in a big centennial—celebrating our Fiftieth Anniversary at the June Commencement, 1923 at which time honorary degrees would be conferred on deserving individuals.

Andrew Sherley moved that the plan be accepted with the exception that the Endowment aim be one million instead of a half million dollars.[43] At this same meeting, a large number of ministers were called in conference to rally the brethren of the Churches to the support of the plans.

Inasmuch as the Business Manager's report, a little later, showed the indebtedness to be $300,000 and the Southern Asso-

[38]Minutes, 9-27-21.
[39]Minutes, 5-21, p. 605, President's Report.
[40]Minutes, p. 605.
[41]Minutes, 8-15-21, p. 621.
[42]Minutes, 9-29-21, p. 631; 2-14-22, p. 681.
[43]Minutes, 2-14-22, p. 684-685 and 9-23-27.

ciation was about to require $500,000 of endowment, rather than the $300,000 already reported, the Campaign was assuming large responsibility. It was obvious that such a sum could not be raised without some large individual gifts to start it off. The spark plug for such a start was found in the person of Harry Rogers, who had recently moved to San Antonio from Tulsa, where he and his brothers had prospered generously in the oil and banking business. He had a background of deep devotion to the church, and an attitude toward giving to its enterprises in larger figures than the average business man. It was in his office, in San Antonio, on Friday the thirteenth of October 1922, that the action was taken that gave assurance of success to the campaign. His pledge of $25,000 brought forth responses of the same amount from Dave Reed, and from his brother Malcom; Van Zandt Jarvis and President Waits promised to see that an equal amount would come from Fort Worth citizens. Later Mike Thomas of Dallas gave $25,000 in response to the same challenge. Dave Reed and Ross Sterling gave $100,000 each before they were through.[44]

Ross Sterling was an addition to the group of unusual value. He was the originator and developer of the Humble Oil Co. along with his brothers and sister, and an active leader in the South End Christian Church in Houston. He was at this time in the flush of success, resolving that when he became sixty years of age he would retire, and travel. The sequel, which may as well be mentioned here, shows that instead of retiring he went into politics, became Governor of Texas for one term, and while he was absorbed in serving his State, in the midst of the depression in the early thirties, lost his fortune, and had to start over again. He did so, bravely, and still serves as a trustee of the University.

At the first Trustees' meeting he attended after this break in his affairs, he remarked in effect: "It does my soul good to see here in T. C. U. the good that is being done with the money I gave it. In fact the only money I have left is what I gave away."

With this excellent start, with the valuable help of some of the ministers, and the patient persistence of President Waits (especially to make good that $50,000 pledge of Fort Worth), as well as many another over the state, the campaign came to a glorious success. At the Trustees' meeting in June, 1923, the

[44]*Skiff*, 10-17-23; 10-24-22.

172

report showed "Notes Rec'vd $247,305, Pledges unsigned $66,165, Cash received $13,041, Total, $326,305."

During the five years after the close of the World War I, and while the financial campaigns were being pushed with vigor, there was creeping into the consciousness of the people the fact that the old School was getting to be about fifty years of age "1873-1923" began to ring in their minds and to stir their imaginations. President Waits brought this idea to the attention of the Board of Trustees in May 1921, as told above, and proposed the debt campaign as a worthy preparation for the celebration of the Jubilee Year.

The City of Fort Worth also at this time was celebrating its Jubilee year. Such a bringing out of four gallon hats, boots, spurs, and even saddles and horses on the streets made "Cowtown" almost fulfill the expectations of the Easterners who drop in to get a first hand view of the "wild and woolly west." A more substantial feature of the celebration by the municipality was the tide of street paving. The Mayor of the city at the time was a member of the T. C. U. Faculty, Professor E. R. Cockrell. He led in the movement to incorporate several outlying sections into the city, including all of the T. C. U. Hill that was not already in, built the Municipal Golf Course just beyond and abutting the campus, and paved the boulevard from the city to the campus, then known as Forest Park Boulevard. This particular street, by the way, was torn up during the celebration of the Jubilee in June 1923, and caused no little inconvenience, but no regrets.

In this paving program T. C. U. was obliged to join. There was much paving to be done in the streets about the campus. R. L. Rogers, a neighbor and a real estate man, along with others, including Dr. R. M. Green, proposed to the Trustees that they sell some of the vacant lots which they owned on the hill and use $7,300 of the proceeds to help pay the University's assessment for the paving. It required an additional appropriation of $2,500 to cover the cost. Dr. Green and Mr. Rogers took the responsibility for selling the lots. This plan was carried out.[45]

A feature that added to the architectural and the sentimental aspect of the celebration was the erection at this time of the Memorial Arch. This was the Class Gift of the Class of 1923

[45]Minutes, 6-4-23.

promoted by Edwin A. Elliott, a member of that class and then Dean of Men, himself a veteran of the War. He had gone in as a private and had come out as a Chaplain, on the petition of his regiment. The funds for the Arch were raised by the contributions of many friends outside of the class. It was "dedicated to the men and women who served humanity in the World War of 1917-1918," with special mention of the three whose lives were lost in the war, Milus Little Jr. of Lampasas, Herndon (Dick) Hardwicke of Aquila, and Aubrey Cooper. The Arch was located in front of the Main Building at the street entrance, and promptly became the traditional place for meeting friends.

Another consummation of hopes that gave zest to the celebration of 1923 was the admission of T. C. U. to the Association of Colleges and Secondary Schools of the Southern States, in December, 1922. This was a distinguished body, organized in 1895 as a means of consultation among the colleges, and of contact with the secondary schools. It has gradually grown into the recognized body for accrediting the colleges and schools of the Southern region. In its early period, admission to membership was largely by invitation. A letter addressed to the T. C. U. faculty came in about 1914 suggesting that the school consider membership in the Association. The faculty, realizing that T. C. U. was a charter member of the Association of Texas Colleges, (organized in 1912) and that most of its transfers of students were with Texas colleges, decided that it would not be of value to belong to the Southern Association, and they so graciously replied to the letter.

By 1920, however, when a new Dean came into office, the outlook was broader. There was ambition to win a recognized place among the colleges of America. Interchange and travel were on the increase. T. C. U. graduates were going to Eastern Universities for graduate work. T. C. U. should be known among the top educators of the nation. So application was made to the Southern Association for recognition. In order to make the proper connections, and to meet the right personalities, President Waits and Dean Hall both attended the Annual Meeting of the Association at Chattanooga in December 1920, taking along with them Professor W. M. Winton. He was a Vanderbilt graduate and a friend well known to the chief executive of Vanderbilt, Chancellor Kirkland, who was one of the founders and the leading spirit of the Association. It was discovered, by this visit, that a college was expected to sit on the door step and learn humility for a few years before it could expect recognition. Also it was required that a half a million dollars of endowment must be shown and that must be net above debts.

Seriously were the standards of the Association taken as the expression of the best thought of the educators, and the policies of the University were adapted to them. Diligently the reports were sent in each year, and gladly the inspectors were received. They were Dr. W. J. Battle of the University of Texas, and Principal Wm. James of the Ball High School, Galveston, two very gracious scholars and gentlemen. All of T. C. U. rejoiced on the announcement at the meeting of the Association in 1922 that their school was recognized.[46] T. C. U. thus became the sixth institution of higher education in Texas to obtain this recognition.[47]

The faculty and Administration have all along been appreciative of these Associations which, although much criticised for being subject to too many rules and red tape, have nevertheless made rich and necessary contributions to the elevation of educational standards. How much better for the schools to regulate themselves, voluntarily, in cooperation, than to have regimentation by authority of the political state, as is the rule in Europe. Incidentally, the Dean of T. C. U. began about this time a service as Chairman of the Committee on Standards of the Association of Texas Colleges, which continued for thirteen years, the longest on record.[48] As the author of these lines he delights to utilize this opportunity to testify to the high character of the men and women who represent the colleges in these Associations, on the platform and behind the scenes, especially the latter. To work with them is to know them, and to know them is to have renewed confidence in the educational program of America.

the Southern Association, the presence of the graceful Arch, the stream of publicity that was pouring out, and the plans for the gathering of old friends, all conspired to work up the feelings of expectancy for the Jubilee to a high pitch. The prospect for a record-breaking attendance was heightened by the fact that the Texas Christian Convention was to meet in Fort Worth at the First Christian Church downtown several days before the Pageant.

[46]*Skiff*, 12-12-22.
[47]These were University of Texas, 1901; Rice and Baylor, 1914; Southwestern, 1915; S. M. U., 1921; T. C. U., 1922.
[48]*Skiff*, 12-12-22.

The excitement rose to a new high when a circus tent began to raise its huge form on the campus. This was prepared to house the day sessions of the Pageant, from sun and rain. But the rain came first. And wind with it, the night before the big program was to come off. And down came the big tent. Out came the hot sun, and in its blaze was held the program of each morning.

The regular Commencement was built into the series of Jubilee programs. For the first time the big out-of-door platform erected in front of the Honeysuckle Arbor was used for this purpose, and with it began the tradition of the out-of-door Commencement. The high light of the graduating exercises was the conferring of nine honorary degrees, the first ever conferred by T. C. U. and the last for the next decade. Those thus honored were: S. G. Inman, L. D. Anderson, R. H. Miller, H. O. Pritchard, A. D. Harmon, Hugh McLellan, Col. Louis Wortham, Major K. M. Van Zandt and Randolph Clark.[49]

The awarding of the Doctor of Laws degree to Randolph Clark was, naturally, full of deep sentiment; it was also highly dramatic. For "Mr. Randolph" had been under treatment for blindness; this was his first appearance after a critical operation. An octogenarian and feeble, with the bandages still over his eyes, he was led on the platform, amid thundering applause, the noble representative of the founders of the institution which had won its way into the hearts of so many thousands, and was now happily celebrating its fiftieth anniversary.

But the Grand Event of the Golden Jubilee was the Pageant, "These Fifty Years," which was staged on the out-of-door platform, at ten o'clock in the bright summer morning of June 5, 1923. The Pageant was wholly indigenous, the work of students and faculty both in its composition and its performance. Professor Rebecca Smith, the brilliant and versatile Professor of English, later the Head of the Department, was its chief promoter, author and editor of the Pageant. She had this word to say of the text:

The poetry of the pageant is the work of several authors, and therefore uneven in meter and style. While it is not so lofty or so great as its theme deserves, it represents the devotion and the ideals of the students and faculty of 1923 for their alma mater.

[49]Catalog, 1925, p. 209. There a misprint names "Mrs." S. G. Inman instead of "Mr." as it should have been.

The thirty-six page pamphlet containing the text of the pageant reveals this quotation and also that it was

contributed by the English Department of T. C. U. to the Golden Jubilee Celebration, June 5, 1923; presented to the public with Mrs. H. D. Guelick, Pageant Director, Miss Charlotte Owsley, in charge of costumes and Dr. H. D. Guelick in charge of music.[50]

Some of the characters represented were Addison Clark, by Thos. E. Dudney; Randolph Clark, by J. Lindley Wood; Tommy Clark, by John Stevenson; the Spirit of Add-Ran by Sybil Black; Panhandle Farmer by J. Erwin Montgomery; and Cattle Man, Nimmo Goldston. There were forty persons in all, besides a group representing students in general.

There were five parts in addition to the Prologue, that having been composed by Miss Smith. The others were written by the following: "Founding of Add-Ran" by Ray M. Camp; "May Day at Thorp's Spring," by Miss Smith; "Waco Days" by Miss Mabel Major and Miss Eula Burton Phares; "Interlude" by Claude Wingo; and "The Golden Jubilee" by Helen Lock.

The Pageant was thoughtfully composed, well delivered, and successfully rendered. It expressed vividly the ideals that had stirred the founders, and helped to fix them in the hearts of the generation then in action. May they be revived again and again through the years.

The sonnet, composed by Professor Rebecca Smith was put into the mouth of Addison Clark as a finale.

You stand four-square across the rolling plain—
No shadowed ancient towers, but modern halls
With yellow sunshine glaring on brick walls
Laid bare to sun and wind and driving rain.
Erected to make learning serviceable and cheap.
Your blocks of buildings, unromantic piles,
Gaze out across the prairies miles on miles
To vast horizons with an endless sweep.
Your daughters are of good and ample height;
Your sons are rough shouldered, raucous-voiced,
With tang of cattle camp, and derrick hoist
Whose eyes accustomed to far distant sight
Search through old learning for the Present Truth—
The unprobated heritage of Youth."

[50]The Pamphlet Program is on file in the T. C. U. Library.

# ✤ XVII ✤

# The Cattle Frontier Yields Dividends

*The Story of the Burnett Trust*

MRS. MARY COUTS BURNETT—DR. CHARLES H. HARRIS

T HE SUMMER AND AUTUMN FOLLOWING the brilliant celebration of the Jubilee Year in June 1923 was a kind of soft afterglow of Indian Summer. Never before had there been such ease of mind for those who carried the responsibility, never such rosy hopes among the supporters and friends. The celebration, with its attendant publicity, was of sufficient size to challenge the attention of the Fort Worth public and to induce at least a vague consciousness that among its prideful possessions, along with the old stand-bys, the packing houses and the nascent oil booms, was this institution of higher culture, which had won recognition for itself, and therefore prestige for the city.

This general good feeling had solid ground in some substantial facts. The indebtedness campaign had secured pledges to pay off all of the debts, as soon as the collections were in. The books showed half a million dollars of endowment, although much of it was as yet unproductive. On the basis of this good showing, T. C. U., the previous December, had been admitted as a member of the Southern Association of Colleges and Secondary Schools, which put it in a class with only five other Texas institutions of higher learning. The faculty salaries were being supplemented by the grant of $8,000 a year from the General Education Board. This same wise and far-seeing Board had given a finishing touch to the elation of the Jubilee by a letter dated May 25, 1923, promising a gift of $166,667 on condition of T. C. U.'s raising additional endowment of $333,333 to make a total of $500,000 new funds, and showing a clear balance sheet, without any indebtedness.

There was not a cloud in the sky. The possibility of shrinkage in the pledges to the indebtedness campaign was not large, the hopes were high for raising the $333,333. It was high noon!!

But this group of obscure Westerners were to discover, as the Apostle Paul had done of old, that there could shine a light that is brighter than the noon-day sun. It fell upon them with suddenness, without solicitation, save by prayers in general, and without warning. It came on December 2, 1923—the announcement that Mrs. Mary Couts Burnett had arranged to devote her entire fortune to Texas Christian University!

The story of the unfolding of this wonderful news is worth recording. A telephone call that morning brought an invitation to President Waits to join in a conference at 9 A. M. in the home of Mrs. Burnett, on Summit Avenue. He mentioned the call to two of his associates and departed, curious. There he found, besides Mrs. Burnett, her attorney, William J. Slay, and the President of T. C. U. Trustees, Van Zandt Jarvis. Through the fog of legal language, as the attorney read the document of Trust, the good President perceived, in general, that Mrs. Burnett was giving, through a Trust, her entire estate to T. C. U. The details he studied out later. Only one decision he had to make on that occasion, besides agreeing to accept the offer. Provision was made for $150,000, to be used to erect one building as a tangible memorial to the donor. On the spot he chose a Library, and was abetted in his choice by Mr. Jarvis. The formalities were over—but not the excitement.

The next steps are attested by the author as an eye witness. The good President returned to his office, called in the Dean from next door, and carefully closed the door, so carefully that he almost seemed to have locked it. Then he began a dance. Yes, really a dance, a solo dance! Now the reverend President was not designed, either by experience or anatomy, for dancing, and the tight little office he then occupied (later the Modern Language office) gave entirely too modest a space for an exhibition, cramped, as it was by furniture and bookcases. But dance he did, first on one leg and then on the other, for what seemed a quarter of an hour, although the one witness is willing to admit it might have been shorter. It certainly was not very artistic prancing, but it was expressive of some pent-up emotion of a pleasant nature. After the terpsichorean outlet of emotion had worked sufficiently, the words began to flow, giving the Dean the story of the interview of the morning. It looked like three million dollars of endowment for T. C. U.; at that time it might as well have been ten millions.

179

That afternoon was spent by the administrative officers mapping out the proper psychology in breaking the news to the public. Copy was prepared for release to the newspapers, but first the announcement should be made to the school people themselves, at the General Assembly the next day. Before the assembled and unsuspecting student body and the usual sprinkling of teachers, the President began, as usual, his "chapel talk." Now the good President was famous for the beauty of his phraseology and the prolificity of his poetical quotation, but not for rushing to the termination of a speech. So when those who were "in the know" heard him start in on some of the phraseology of the paragraphs of his recent speeches of the financial campaign, they thought the phonographic needle had gotten caught on the wrong record, and it would have to be completed before he could come to the point of the hour. But, surprisingly, suddenly the needle jumped; boldly and abruptly he announced that T. C. U. had fallen heir to three million dollars. The audience was caught off balance. It is suspected that some were giving more attention to books or partners than to the address of the moment. One of those pauses that feels like a minute ensued before the applause began. Then it thundered uproariously. The President ended his part by saying, "The Dean will tell you the rest of the story." And so the Dean did. And so the news broke. The Dean got even with his superior for this imposition at a later public occasion by telling on him: "We have found out how to induce President Waits to make a short speech; just give T. C. U. three million dollars."

The clipping bureau service proved that the news went to the ends of the earth, and often swelled as it traveled. The amount was reported variously as from two to ten millions. Many was the news editor who sought a College Blue Book to find what and where was that little college down in the cattle country. One enterprising St. Louis paper sent a feature writer to report, on the ground. He posed this question, first to the President: "The Trust refers to the school as 'Liberal' and as admitting all students without regard to creed, etc. Does this mean it is a 'modernistic' school?" "Most assuredly not," said the President. "Then it is fundamentalist?" "No," insisted the President. He then tackled the Dean with the same queries and the added one: "It must be either modernist or fundamentalist." Whereupon the Dean assured him that he had some lessons yet to learn, that T. C. U. was neither, but was just plain Christian, and would not be tagged.

The document by which the gift was made was a Deed of Trust conveying all of Mrs. Burnett's property to a Board of Trustees of five members, to be operated by them and their successors until twenty years after the death of the last one of the original five; then it was to go in fee simple to T. C. U. The five were Dr. Charles H. Harris; Mrs. Ollie Burnett, divorced wife of Tom Burnett, the son of Burk Burnett by a former wife; John Sweatt, a banker of Mexia, Texas, who had married a kinswoman of Mrs. Burnett; Mrs. Ella Bardin, the secretary of Mrs. Burnett; and William Slay, the attorney. Mrs. Burnett was to serve during her life time as Chairman. As long as she lived, one-fourth of the income from the estate was to go to T. C. U.; after her death, all of it. The Trustees were to have full power in handling the estate, including the payment of salaries to themselves and the attorney. There was provision for $12,000 for the endowment of the Dixon Colored Orphanage at Gilmer, Texas. This was paid in liquid assets early in the process.[1]

At the February meeting of the Board, Mrs. Burnett was present to receive the expressions of appreciation of the T. C. U. Trustees. A decorated hand-engraved scroll was presented to her, with appropriate remarks by Harry Rogers. Copies of this scroll were made and given to each member of the Board and one was hung in the Library.[2]

How did Mrs. Burnett come to choose T. C. U. as her beneficiary? This was a question on the lips of many. She was not a member of the same church communion, the Christian Church. She had had no children to attend T. C. U. She was not on terms of acquaintanceship with any of the personnel of the institution. She had never been solicited. The very clever and frank Methodist, Rev. H. D. Knickerbocker, remarked, in all good humor, yet with a wistful flavor in his speech, "Why, that was Methodist money; her old father was a good Methodist."

As a matter of fact, she was a member of the Protestant Episcopal Church, and had made an offer to its girls' school, St. Mary's, in Dallas, on condition that it be moved to Fort Worth. Doubtless she was unaware of its history and condition at the time. It was a pet project of Bishop A. C. Garrett, an unusually gifted and gracious personality, a genuine pioneer, and

[1]Minutes, 2-9-24, p. 819 records a full copy of the Deed of Trust.
[2]Minutes, 2-9-24.

widely beloved. He had made it a small select girls' junior college, and had nursed it so that it was very much of a one-man school. Now he was in his dotage, and so was the school. Such girls' colleges were going out, gradually. This one closed a few years later, on the death of the good bishop.

That she should decide to leave her money for some cultural institution rather than to any of her kin or to any of the Burnett family, is easy to understand, in view of her relationship with them, as told in a later paragraph. She was, besides, a woman of refinement, with a genuine interest in culture, with a natural interest in education, and a decided loyalty to her home town.

Several facts would make the idea of supporting T. C. U. quite congenial to her. There was the memory of her childhood that her father, Col. J. R. Couts, a banker at Weatherford, Texas, had been a generous admirer of Addison Clark, pioneer President of Add-Ran, the progenitor of T. C. U., and that he had contributed money to the school at Thorp Spring. Mrs. Burnett could well remember the high standing of the Clarks in the eyes of the pioneer public.

At the very time when she was thinking through her plans came the publicity of the Jubilee celebration, to remind her of these early associations and to strengthen her confidence in the institution. She made a definite investigation and learned that it was "a non-sectarian institution, open to all alike, to those of any faith or creed, and alike to rich and poor," as was expressed in the Deed of Trust.

She was no doubt influenced by her advisers, Dr. Harris and Mr. Slay. Slay appeared before the T. C. U. Trustees on at least two occasions, and in both instances made it quite clear that all of his counsel to Mrs. Burnett had been in favor of her selecting T. C. U. as her beneficiary.[3] It is much more likely that Dr. Charles H. Harris was her most trusted confidant, and that he had more to do with influencing her to select T. C. U. He was her physician. She called on him in her most critical hour, when she was trying to get her portion of the estate, at her husband's death. This story was told April 20, 1941, by Dr. Harris himself, to the author of these lines while he was in the Harris Memorial Methodist Hospital, convalescent from a nephrectomy. Dr. Harris' story in part is paraphrased as follows:

[3]Minutes, 3-3-25, and 2-9-39.

182

Mr. Burk Burnett's body was not cold before Mrs. Burnett called on me in my office. She put the pointed question to me, "Dr. Harris do you think I'm crazy?" "No, I certainly do not," I replied. "I think you are one of the most intelligent women I know." "Would you be willing to go into Court and swear to that?" She wanted, of course, to try to get out from under the court sentence that she was insane, which Burk Burnett had passed on her when they didn't get along. Well, I knew she did have some hallucinations that he was trying to kill her and that this would be hard to fight in court. So I said, 'I'd be willing to testify in court for you, but my advice would be for another plan.' On her request for this plan, I suggested that she get several affidavits, including mine, and present them to the Court and avoid a public trial. Of course she would have to get a good lawyer to handle it for her. She asked me to recommend a lawyer. I thought about Walter Morris, a good lawyer who had grown up out in her part of the state, Weatherford and Granbury. She asked me to call him up. I called up the firm he was with at the time, Slay, Simon and Smith. Bill Slay answered and said Morris would be out of town for many months ahead but he would be glad to attend to any business I might have. So I advised him to call on Mrs. Burnett. He did and that's the way he came into this case.

Dr. Harris also stated that Mrs. Burnett almost gave the property to Bishop Garrett of the Episcopal Church for his girls' school, St. Mary's, in Dallas, and he tried to keep her from it. He stated specifically that he recommended that she give it to T. C. U. Dr. Harris said he suggested the plan of putting the property in a Trust, but was not responsible for the details as they were worked out. He felt himself to be the closest to Mrs. Burnett, as her physician for years. He did not claim that he was the one who decided for her in favor of T. C. U., but he certainly encouraged her to do so.

One can scarcely appreciate the actions and attitudes of Mrs. Burnett without knowing something of the background of her experience. Also Dr. Harris' reference to her "hallucinations" calls for explanation. So let us look briefly into the family complications through which this good woman had been passing.

Burk Burnett in his youth was a typical cow-man, with the habits, limitations and attitudes common to the men of the rough frontier. He was a successful stock raiser and a bold trader. He lived through the period when cattle raising was a money-making business; he prospered, accumulated much land, and because oil was discovered on it, came to be in the millionaire class. His interests did not lie in the direction of colleges and churches, and he declined to contribute to T. C. U. when called on in a campaign. One gift he made to a church was the pipe organ in the First Christian Church of Fort Worth. This was in memory of his father and mother, who, according to the bronze tablet in the church, were members of that communion. He donated to the city of Fort Worth the block of land which became Burnett Park. When it was announced that a portion of this tract was about to be purchased as a site for a new First Presbyterian church, Mr. Burnett revealed that it had been his purpose to buy it and make it a memorial, on account of some sentimental connection in the years agone. He did buy it and gave it to the city as "a place where the mothers could take their children to play." This phrase, used in his dedication, prevented the use of the tract as a location for the City Library, when that question arose about 1938.

Mr. Burnett had a son by his first wife, Tom Burnett, who married Ollie Lake Burnett, a woman of culture and excellent personality and character, who was later divorced. Their daughter, Anne Burnett, grew up to be the favorite of the elder Mr. Burnett, and was named in his will as the chief beneficiary.

There were indications that Mrs. Mary Couts Burnett did not fit well into the home of the "rough and ready" cow-man. Tension developed. She became fearful for her life. He claimed her fear to be "hallucinations," took advantage of it, went to court and had her adjudged insane. He provided for her a private home in Weatherford, where she was confined as legally insane.

Dr. Harris, as stated, regarded her as "one of the most intelligent women I know." She gave evidence of this intelligence by escaping, on the day of his death, and returning to her home in Fort Worth. The mourners, on their return from the cemetery, found her there, in charge. And there she stayed. Wisely, she followed the counsel of her physician, Dr. Harris, secured affidavits, and freed herself from the charge of insanity. Naturally she sued to break his will, which had left nearly everything to the granddaughter, Anne. The records show that practically every one of the wills of the large cattle estates of Fort Worth has been broken in court. This one was broken, and she received her wife's half. The other half was put in charge of a board of trustees, to be administered for the other heirs.

Mrs. Burnett also displayed her intelligence by her attempt to circumvent the usual history of broken wills. She determined to place her property where she wanted it to go, while she was still living, and avoid a suit over her bequests. Out of this determination came her plan for the Board of Trust to administer her estate in favor of Texas Christian University.

She had no children who might put in any counter claims, but she had four sisters. One of these was deceased but her children and husband were living. Realizing the danger of their claims, she offered to give each one twenty-five thousand dollars in cash if they would sign a waiver of interest in her estate. They declined. Their motive became obvious when, on her death, within hours of her passing, they filed a suit in the Weatherford court attacking the legality of the Deed of Trust. This threw the Trust immediately into receivership. The sisters had employed three of the strongest firms of attorneys in Fort Worth. The Trust immediately employed three other firms. The T. C. U. Attorney joined them in the defense.

It was obviously a case for compromise. The sisters had no claim in equity, but they had some conditions in their favor. The record of Mrs. Burnett's legal insanity was ground for argument and prejudice. The fact that the case was filed in their home town might win them favor against a corporation. The verdicts of juries were known to be undependable and capricious. Even if the sisters should lose, they would be able to drag the case out for years, while attorneys' fees mounted. Meanwhile, the Trust being in receivership, the school would be deprived of income.

Under these conditions, the attorneys negotiated a settlement out of court, to which the Trust and the University gave approval. According to this settlement, the Trust paid each of the four sisters $150,000, paid the three lawyer firms the total of $253,000, and T. C. U. paid its attorney $25,000 extra. Mr. Slay had previously received $75,000 "in the original separation of the Burnett estate."[4] Thus, before the Trust was released from receivership, it had forfeited nearly a million dollars—$928,000 besides the $25,000 paid by T. C. U. To pay this in cash, the Trust had to borrow money and to skim the cream of the liquid assets.

[4]Minutes, 2-18-25, 5-18-25, and 3-3-25.

Quite promptly the plans for erecting the Memorial Library were begun. A committee was appointed on December 17, 1923.[5] It was completed sufficiently for Mrs. Burnett to drive by and see it before her death in December 1924. The T. C. U. Trustees voted to pay the extra $3,000 that it cost above the $150,000 allowance.[6] In March 1925, a formal dedication ceremony was held.

The Trust began operations promptly, paying to T. C. U. one-fourth of the income of the estate during the year of Mrs. Burnett's life. The interim of receivership was not so long, considering its gravity. A payment of $30,000 is reported on March 3, 1925, and another of $47,000 on June 2 following.[7] The Burnett Trustees, under the provisions of the Trust, voted to pay each of the four members $2,000 a year and to Chairman Slay, $6,000 and 5 per cent of all oil lease money, as a retainer for handling the estate. Later it appeared that the firm of Slay and Simon was employed as attorneys for the Trust in addition to the Chairmanship of Mr. Slay.

The books of the Trust were kept by Mrs. Ella Bardin, one of the Trustees, until her death. She was always cordial and helpful in all relationships. This was the attitude of all the Trustees toward T. C. U. Mrs. Ollie Burnett was gracious, and always careful that everything was handled with business conservativeness. Dr. Harris was cordial and deeply interested in the welfare of the school, and also conservative. Mr. Sweatt followed Mr. Slay in whatever action he favored. Mr. Slay himself expressed always almost a boyish enthusiasm for T. C. U. and all of its welfare, being ever the most ready to grant favors for it. No favors were needed for the first several years. The income amounted to more than $100,000 a year. It was restricted to use in paying teachers' salaries, student scholarships, and loans. It was used for that, while the general income from student fees and other revenue was used for paying off debts. For the news of the receipt of the Burnett gift had greatly reduced the paying of pledges that had been made for the liquidation of the indebtedness.[8]

The first favor asked of the Trust can hardly be called a favor. It was simply T. C. U. borrowing from itself, and was a loan

[5]Minutes, 12-17-23.
[6]Minutes. 3-3-25.
[7]Minutes, 3-3-25, and 6-2-25.
[8]Minutes, 6-3-23, and 6-2-25.

by the Trust with good security. The 150 acres lying immediately west of the original campus was about to be plotted and put on the market as city lots. Obviously, they would be needed as campus in later years, and, if not purchased now, would cost vastly more later on. So the Burnett Trust made a good loan, taking this land and a number of scattered lots as security. The T. C. U. Trustees authorized the borrowing of $80,000 on February 9, 1928, and $96,933.33 on September 8, 1930.[9]

Inasmuch as the need of the University was steady, and the income of the Trust was fluctuating, arrangement was made to fix an annual appropriation and pay it in monthly installments, charging it to "advances," then crediting the account with the net income at the end of the fiscal year. With the decline of business conditions through the late twenties and early thirties, the income was greatly reduced. One year the audit showed the income of the Trust to be in the red for about $9,000. Thus the advances, though also reduced, ran ahead of the income, so that T. C. U. became in debt to the Trust.

At the lowest point of the depression, when faculty salaries had to be thrice cut, to a net of 43 per cent, the Trust granted a loan of $70,000, taking a mortgage on all of the rest of T. C. U. property, including the Library land, but omitting the fifty acres of the original campus.[10] In order to lift the faculty salaries out of the ditch of the 43 per cent reduction, the Trust was asked, in March 1934, to grant an additional $10,000 a year, so that salaries could be raised 10 per cent.[11] The following year the Trust agreed to put up $12,000 extra, provided the T. C. U. Trustees would set aside an equal amount, so that salaries could be raised 20 per cent. These extra appropriations were charged as advances, to be returned at such time as the income should overtake the regular appropriations. These advances did not come out of the corpus of the estate. They came from the income from oil and gas sales. The Trust had ruled that all income from lease sales should count as income, but that sale of the oil or gas itself, being not replaceable, should be interpreted as part of the corpus and the amount so received should be placed back in the corpus. This point was clarified by the Texas Legislature in about 1940, as will be explained later.[12]

[9]Minutes, 2-9-28, 9-8-30, and 2-10-27.
[10]Minutes, 2-9-33.
[11]Minutes, 3-29-34.
[12]See p. 199.

In 1939 a bill was introduced into the Texas Senate, by Senator Clint Small, which provided for the limitation of the amount of gas that could be produced and sold. The Senator was the attorney for a Company that would profit from the bill, as he frankly admitted. The Trust had developed the field and the market for it, and now it was to be restricted in the amount to be produced, to the benefit of the other producers nearby. Mr. Slay appeared before the T. C. U. Board at its February meeting, showing some maps which had been prepared by Dr. Gayle Scott, Professor of Geology in the University, and asked for the University to appeal to its friends over the state to petition the Legislature against the passage of the bill. The bill was defeated.[13]

The Trust issued annually an official audit, and furnished a copy to the T. C. U. authorities. In a few instances notation was made of loans to persons of doubtful security, in some cases to persons related to the Chairman of the Trust. But beyond this the affairs seemed to be operating fairly, as viewed from the outside. The audit did not undertake to make evaluations of securities. On the inside, things were not so satisfactory. Early in 1940 it was learned that Mrs. Ollie Burnett, in protest against the way the Chairman of the Trust was operating, resigned as a Trustee. Dr. Harris also, privately, was expressing extreme concern, and was intimating to several T. C. U. officials that the T. C. U. Trustees should take action. In the early summer of 1940 Dr. Harris became seriously ill. As a physician, he knew that his life was in danger. He called in a lawyer friend, Mark McMahon, and confided in him that things were unsatisfactory within the Trust, that he, Dr. Harris, could not be content to die without starting something to correct the abuses that were going on. He engaged Mr. McMahon to do some investigating.

The ways of investigating attorneys are perhaps professional secrets. But the records of the T. C. U. Trustees and the actions of the State Courts are open material. A few items may be drawn from these.

After the investigation had revealed sufficient ground for action, and after careful scrutiny of the situation by the new President of the T. C. U. Trustees,[14] R. H. Foster, a meeting of the Executive Committee of T. C. U. was called on July 30, 1940.

[13]Minutes, February, 1940.
[14]Van Zandt Jarvis had died in April.

Here George Thompson was employed to be associated with R. M. Rowland as attorneys, authorized to enter suit at once to displace the two Trustees of the Burnett Trust, Mr. Slay and Mr. Sweatt. These attorneys, together with Mr. McMahon, called on Mr. Slay, presented him with enough of the facts which they had in hand to induce him to act seriously. He asked for a delay of two days so his partner, Mr. Simon, could return from Boston, promising to take no steps until then.

How much and what evidence was presented to Mr. Slay and to Mr. Simon is not known. But enough was revealed to induce Mr. Slay and Mr. Sweatt (who did not appear at the meeting, but was represented by Mr. Slay) to sign their resignation as Trustees, effective September 1, and irrevocable. Meanwhile a meeting of the Trustees of the Burnett Trust was held and the two vacancies in the number were filled by the election of E. E. Bewley and Charles Roesser. Also, Dr. Harris was elected Chairman of the Trust to succeed Mr. Slay. The two new members, with Dr. Harris, were designated as the executive Committee in charge. When the resignations became effective in September, two other good friends of T. C. U. were elected to fill the vacancies: Mark McMahon and Will K. Stripling.

Thus was the transition made in the control of the Trust, without resort to court, and with the least possible criticism of the offending parties. It is needless to comment upon the feeling of relief and gratitude on the part of the T. C. U. Trustees and friends to have the operation of the Trust in the hands of proven friends. But at what cost did this come!

The new Board of Trust felt under obligation, as Trustees, to recover as much as possible, so they dutifully entered civil suit to recover the sum of about $500,000 allegedly lost to the Trust by the mismanagement of the two Trustees. It was a jury case and the evidence was so full of technicalities that it was confusing to any jury. The judge therefore took the case out of the hands of the jury and rendered a verdict in favor of the Trust. It was appealed, and on April 25, 1945 the Supreme Court of Texas handed down its decision in the case which

> whittled down judgments awarded by the trial court, which amounted to $397,261.56 against Slay and Simon, $405,110.43 against Proctor, and $115,868.41 against Longmire. The

total judgment of $567,492.54 against Sweatt's estate was left undisturbed, since contest was offered.[15]

Sweatt had committed suicide, soon after the charges were preferred. Issues involving $141,975.54 were sent back to the 17th District Court for a new trial.

The new Board of the Burnett Trust immediately got to work clarifying the status of the estate. The first action taken by them was to vote that they would receive no remuneration or honorarium for themselves. This was an action long advocated by Dr. Harris, new Chairman of the Trust. They ratified and executed the action already taken by the previous members, of loaning to T. C. U. $300,000 for the erection of a new Girls' Dormitory. They raised the question of the income from the sale of gas and oil, which had been heretofore classified as belonging to the corpus. While they were studying this question, the Texas Legislature passed a bill (S. B. 251) on the subject. It provided that the trustees of any corporation were required to place twenty-seven per cent of such income into the corpus, and that they were free to place the remainder in either corpus or income.

Conferences were held with the T. C. U. administrators and Trustees to see how the needs of the University and its longtime interests would best be served. The plan worked out, and put into operation finally, was a most satisfactory and happy one. The regular income from sale of minerals, $100,000, should be set aside as permanent endowment, that is, turned into the corpus. The remainder of this inflow from sales should be credited against the accumulated indebtedness to the Trust by T. C. U., until that was all cleaned up. Some of this had already been eliminated through an interpretation of the new Board. The old Board had charged some of the losses on loans directly against the income to T. C. U. The new Board charged these losses against the conduct of the business. If the earnings of the Trust continue as at present, the "advances" will all be cleared within about seven years, and within ten years an additional million dollars will be added to the productive endowment.

The prize witticism concerning the Burnett gift was written by Dr. J. Frank Dobie, the ranch boss of "Texas Folk-lore," in a

---

[15]Fort Worth Star-Telegram morning, April 27, 1945. The same article says, "New Trial Ordered Involves $141,975 in Burnett Judgment."

MRS. MARY COUTS BURNETT

A view of the Mary Couts Burnett Memorial Library with the
Memorial Sunken Garden, centering in the Lily Pond.

EDWARD McSHANE WAITS
President, 1916-41.

SOME OTHER TRUSTEES
*Below ;* Presentation of Trophy to Dutch Meyer, by Amon Carter, on
the football field, November 5, 1940. Others from left: Roy Tomlinson,
President of the Alumni, Dean Hall, Milton Daniel, Ki Aldrich, Meyer,
Carter, I. B. Hale, President Waits.

SAM J. McFARLAND,
T. C. U. Trustee, 1917–;
President 1917-27. 30 years.

VAN ZANDT JARVIS,
T. C. U. Trustee, 1902-40 ;
President, 1927-40 ; B. C. B.
Trustee. 1927-40. 39 years.

R. HOUSTON FOSTER
T. C. U. Trustee, 1932-41 ; President, 1940-41 ; B. C. B. Trustee,
1926-41. 15 years

L. D. ANDERSON.
B. C. B. Trustee, 1914– ; T. C. U.
Trustee, 1922– ; President 1941–.
33 years.

The Second Four Presidents of the Trustees.
For more details consult the Appendix.

*Saturday Evening Post* article on the "Heraldry of the Range." After recording the story that had gone the rounds, that Burk Burnett had got his start as a ranch owner by winning a complete ranch in a poker game, and that his brand, 6666, was selected because he had drawn a hand of four sixes, Mr. Dobie dryly remarks that "this is probably the best poker hand that a Christian Institution ever drew."[16] In view of Mr. Burnett's reputed boast that no college would ever get any of his money, the theologically inclined professors might figure out that this was a case in which Providence had "made the wrath of man to praise Him."

There were many cattle fortunes in Fort Worth. For Fort Worth from the early days was "Cow-town." There the men shipped their herds, and there the women came to do their shopping. There, too, came the families to have a gay time at the Southwestern Exposition and Fat Stock Show, while the men inspected the exhibits of fine strains of cattle, and bought bulls to improve their herds. It was to Fort Worth that the wealthy cowman looked as a place to retire and enjoy his fortune. Out of the many cattle fortunes that retired to Fort Worth, it was naturally a part of fate that one of them (why only one?) should fall to the earliest surviving college of the Texas Cattle Frontier. Truly, the primacy of old Add-Ran as the college of the Cattle Frontier was now bearing dividends.

---

[16]*Saturday Evening Post*, December 20, 1930, Vol. 203, No. 25.

# &#x223D; XVIII &#x221E;

## The Seven Fat Years 1924-1930

T HE BAROMETER OF COLLEGE PROSPERITY goes up and down along with the prosperity of the community. To the general wave of affluence that swept over America in the middle and the late twenties, T. C. U. had the added impetus of the Jubilee celebration, with its successfully completed financial campaigns, climaxed by the marvelous acquisition of the Burnett Estate. Thus was brought on a period of easement, expansion, and excitement which, compared with any and all previous periods, can well be nominated "The Seven Years of Plenty."

The thousand mark in the annual enrollment was passed for the first time in 1923-24, being 1024. It gradually increased through the next five years: 1924-25, 1186; 1925-26, 1330; 1926-27, 1412; 1927-28, 1528; 1928-29, 1687; 1929-30, 1334. The staff of teachers was increased during this period by 133 per cent, the provision for student scholarships was greatly enlarged, the instrumentation for publicity put on a new basis, faculty salaries reached the maximum; even athletics, for the first time in history, went to the black side of the ledger, and the first Southwest Conference championship was won by the Horned Frog football team! A touch of elegance was added by the occupancy of the new library on February 27, 1925, thus permitting more spacious quarters for executive offices in the Main Building.

The Trustees were rushed into the expansion of the campus grounds by the crowding of city building, which came on like a fever with the new paving of University Drive and many other streets on the Hill.[1] Efforts were being made by commercial firms to acquire the choice locations for business houses adjacent to the campus, and now that the paving reached all the way, the Hill began to be popular as a residential section. Impetus to this trend was given by the decision of the Fair-

---

[1] *Skiff*, 12-5-22.

mount Land Company to put on the market for the first time its choice group of blocks lying east of the Drive, north of Cantey and south of Park Hill Drive. These, so far, had been utilized as commons for the grazing of the neighborhood cows. The tract north of Park Hill Drive was occupied by Bobo's Dairy, and was at a later period opened up as the elite Park Hill. The Fairmount Land Company had been the leader in promoting the real estate deal that brought about the location of T. C. U. in Fort Worth. It now came into the realization of its profits for its venturesome faith.

The city growth was sweeping in around the campus. Unless the adjacent vacant spaces were at once pre-empted, it would soon be impractical ever to expand. To some extent, this problem had been anticipated. The Cassell property, the first three lots, with house, on the north side of Lowden beginning on the Drive, named for a veteran Fort Worth Trustee, (John L. Cassell), had been purchased years before, in order to prevent a move to build a store thereon. The several blocks lying between the Drive and Lubbock Street, between Lowden and Bowie, known as the Library location, had been purchased in 1916.[2] This was at the far-sighted instance of the good neighbor, Dr. Green, who urged the Trustees to buy it up for future expansion, and offered it for $15,000 on time at a low rate of interest.

The first move, in 1924, to enlarge the campus was the purchase of many lots on the east side of the Drive, in order to control all of the frontage. On the north side of Lowden, the property was purchased as far down the street as six lots, including the large home of Mrs. Joe Camp, which was named Sterling House, for Ross Sterling, who had put up $50,000 for the general purpose of this expansion. On the south side of Princeton Street, the home of Dean W. B. Parks was bought and named Reed Cottage, after Dave Reed, who had likewise donated $50,000 for the same purpose. The next two vacant lots were purchased, and the next one, on which the brick cottage sits, was donated by Dr. Green to the University on the annuity plan, the University paying $75 a month until his estate should come into the possession of T. C. U. It was provided in his will that after the life interest of Miss Lucy Smith, his wife's sister (all of this east side was the original home of the Smith family), all of his property would go to T. C. U. This will in-

[2]Minutes, 12-27-16, p. 38.

clude his new home, a two-story brick, on the northeast corner of Princeton Street and University Drive. The next two lots eastward were purchased. Dr. Green died July 30, 1930.[3]

This left only the south side of Cantey street to be obtained, in order to finish out the entire frontage on the east side of the Boulevard. On that corner five lots were owned by the University Christian Church, bought for the site of the new church that was to have been built in 1922, as related in Chapter XVI. The Trustees took over the notes that had been made to the bank for the $1,500 which had been borrowed for the church by five of the professors, and renewed the promise that when the Church was ready to build, they would donate a lot.

They were called upon to fulfill this promise sooner than expected and earlier than the church building was ready. For the Church decided that the northwest corner of Cantey and University Drive was the one and only satisfactory site for the church house. The plot was owned by Professor E. R. Cockrell, who had by that time become President of William Woods College Fulton, Missouri, and had the home place for sale. In the summer of 1925, it was learned that these lots were about to be sold, and that the architect's plans were already drawn for a block of business houses to be built thereon. The presence of business houses in this particular spot was so undesirable that the Executive Committee, at a special meeting, authorized the purchase of this property. Mr. Cockrell was paid $12,500 for the two lots 100 x 125 feet and Mrs. Keith $4,500 for the 50 x 100 foot lot in the rear. The Cockrell home was used for a girls' dormitory for two sessions, then, in 1928, moved diagonally across the street. The Keith house was moved at the same time to 2932 Lowden.[4]

The success of the Fairmount Land Company in its sale of home sites, and that of Mr. Wilkes and Dr. Green in theirs, evidently encouraged the owners of the land west of the original campus to attempt to market their lots. When the Trustees learned that this land was plotted and was about to be marketed, and when they thought of the many colleges in the older states that had cramped campuses, they hastened to purchase all of the land west, to and including the site of the Stadium. For this purpose, they borrowed the sum of $80,000 from the Burnett

[3]Minutes, 9-19-30.
[4]Minutes, 6-2-25; 9-18-25; 9-20-28, and 2-19-24.

Trust and later, an additional sum of $96,953.33, giving a mortgage on the land for security.[5]

In this extensive purchasing of additional land, care was observed to avoid piling up an indebtedness on the University itself. The promise of a donation from the General Education Board hinged on a clear balance sheet. The land was purchased by a separate corporation known as the "University Corporation," entailing none of the University property budget. It was able to carry itself because of the value of the land purchased, and the capitalization from the two gifts of $50,000 each by Dave Reed and Ross Sterling. After its purposes[6] were accomplished, the University Corporation was dissolved, in 1933.[7]

In June, 1927 the President reported, "We will need $50,000 to liquidate the indebtedness and meet the conditions of the General Education Board's offer." That Board had agreed to accept the Burnett gift as fulfilling the condition of the $500,000 endowment; it awaited the evidence of the clearance of all debts. This evidently was accomplished by using the general incomes to pay the debts, while the Burnett income was used for salaries. The final report was sent to the General Education Board in September 1927, and the check for $166,667 was received soon after.[8]

The receipt of this contribution made the Endowment Fund appear of more importance than heretofore, and stirred the Trustees to a fresh sense of responsibility for handling it. It was already kept in a separate fund in the bank. Now they passed a resolution that "all checks signed by this (Endowment) Committee shall be signed by the Chairman and countersigned by the Secretary-Treasurer, and the Committee shall report monthly to the meetings of the Executive Committee."[9]

T. C. U. had long desired to lift the level of preparation of the faculty, as indicated by advanced degrees. Now was her opportunity. When the Burnett gift was being talked of early after its receipt, one faculty member with an M. A. frankly remarked, "This means that I will never be the head of the department, for it is too late for me to get a Ph. D." Another department head resigned because he did not have and could not, so late in

[5]Minutes, 2-9-28; 11-20-30.
[6]Minutes, 2-9-24.
[7]Minutes, 2-9-33, p. 1557.
[8]Minutes, 9-23-27; 11-19-27.
[9]Minutes, 11-19-27.

life, secure a Doctor's degree and he knew that the Department would now require it. In this period when the competition for Ph. D's was strong, and vacancies had to be filled promptly, it is quite remarkable that out of the 35 added, 22 remained until the present or until their death; seven were temporary appointments, and six were dropped during the depression.

One of those "dropped" brought first brush with the American Association of University Professors. Having served only two years, and having no permanent contract, he had no case. The prestige of the Association was somewhat lowered by its backing of him.

For some time the demand for graduate work for the Master's degree had been increasing. Now was the opportunity to answer this demand. Accordingly, in 1926, Dr. John Lord was appointed as the Dean of the Graduate School, in addition to his duties as Head of the Department of Government. He was a most excellent and popular instructor, holding the respect of the students and of his fellow teachers as a scholar and a colleague. The spirit of conservatism was still pursued, however, the offerings being confined to such departments as were approved by the committee on graduate work under the Dean.[10]

The year 1928 proved to be a landmark in the progress of T. C. U. up the hill of recognition and prestige. During that year the institution received notice that it had been placed on the Approved List of the Association of American Universities. Ever since its admission to membership in the Southern Association, T. C. U. had had its eye on this highest of all recognitions available through American rating associations. It was a rather high ambition, since only four institutions in Texas at that time held it, and two of these were members of the Association. The membership is confined to Universities that give the earned Doctor's degree. The approved list consists of those colleges which, after careful inspection, prove to be capable of preparing students for graduate work sufficiently well, and whose graduates through the years have kept up the standard, as shown by their records.

Progress was made that same year in the matter of prestige within the Southern Association. The Association leaders were, of course, of the Old South, rather conservative, and in all the thirty-three years it had never occurred to them to go west of the Mississippi for the annual session. Indeed, when a bold

[10]Minutes, 1-5-26.

Texas Dean, representing the Texas delegation, in 1926, presented a formal invitation to hold the next session in Texas, the gentlemen were almost incredulous. They received and filed the invitation as a matter of courtesy. But the following year conditions were more favorable. The meeting was in Jacksonville, Florida in a hotel room on the second floor, where the speakers' voices were drowned by the noise of the street. Moreover, an ingratiating politician, in his welcome address, did the usual thing of boring the busy crowd with overpraise of his state. Following this, the speaker inviting them to Texas promised that, if they would come to Fort Worth (agreed upon by the Texas group) he would promise them a meeting place fourteen stories above the street, and reported that the mayor of Fort Worth was tongue-tied, stuttered, and hated making speeches. They came to Fort Worth, visited T. C. U. and went away with a feeling of friendship and confidence. Incidentally the Dean of T. C. U. was elected a few years afterward as a Vice-President of the Southern Association.

It was in the year 1928 that the first contact was made with another highly respected association, the American Association of University Women, whose object was to elevate the recognition of women in the colleges of America. At the February meeting of the Trustees in that year, a committee of Alumnae appeared, requesting that certain steps be taken to qualify T. C. U. for recognition by that association. Three steps were pointed out as essential: to have a Dean of Women with a college degree, a woman member of the Board of Trustees, and a woman on the faculty with a Doctor's degree.

It was pointed out to the women (and later to the Association) that T. C. U. had from its founding been favorable to the recognition of women on a plane with men, that it was originally chartered as "The Add-Ran Male and Female College" at a time when co-educational schools were scarce and unpopular. The Trustees promptly fell in with the proposals by electing Mrs. Ida Van Zandt Jarvis a member of the Board, and announcing that plans were already prepared for adding a Ph. D. woman to the faculty. On the third point they reasoned that the present Dean of Women, Mrs. Sadie T. Beckham, possessed in superior degree, all the qualities needed in such a position, and they would be unwilling to exchange her tested and proved qualities for one depending on a degree. Sometime later, it was arranged that an Assistant Dean of Women with a Master's degree would make the matter satisfactory, so Miss Lide Spraggins, an assistant professor in English with a Master's degree, was elected Assistant Dean of Women and given an office in the Main Building. Thus, in 1930, T. C. U. was approved by the A. A. U. W. and everybody was happy.

If there was any tendency toward overenthusiastic expenditures these days, encouraged by the increased income, there were also plenty of brakes to stop the trend. The definite policy was agreed upon, and reiterated each time the budget was presented, that the program should not be built upon the expectation of a steady continuance of the large income from the Trust. The news of the great gift had directly affected the collections of the pledges on the Debt Campaign.[11] The flow of contributions from the churches on Education Day and through the annual budgets almost ceased, except from three or four churches. This was so marked that, when the two junior colleges of the Church in Texas put on a crusade for funds in 1925, T. C. U. announced that it would withdraw for the time any solicitations from the churches.[12]

When the Burnett money came to T. C. U. in 1924, the friends of the junior colleges easily fell into the attitude that T. C. U. had no further need. Some raised the cry that T. C. U. would doubtless be lost to the control of the Church, as Vanderbilt had been lost by the Methodists. All of this talk came to open discussion at the Abilene Convention of the churches in June 1925 in a resolution to require all the trustees to be members of the Christian Church, and to be elected by the Convention. The discussion was lengthy and rather warm at times. The calmer minds prevailed, and an Educational Commission was appointed to study the facts in the case and bring a recommendation to the Convention a year later. This Commission discovered that T. C. U. was the only school of the Texas Brotherhood that had all its trustees members of the Christian Church. It recommended that at least 75 per cent of each college Board be such members. It also recommended that the Trustees, after their election by the Board, be ratified by the Convention. This action was taken by the Convention, and each college incorporated this provision in its by-laws.

This Commission also recommended that a Permanent Educational Board be set up to coordinate the work of the colleges

[11]Minutes, 6-2-25.
[12]Minutes, 8-6-25.

that appealed to the Churches. The Board was set up and given these powers: (1) To initiate and conduct surveys, (2) to initiate plans for any new schools if needed, (3) to investigate the plans for any proposed new school and approve or veto them, subject to the Convention, and (4) to continue to work out a coordinated program for the colleges.[13]

This Board of Education consisted of some twenty members, including the executives of each of the three schools, some trustees, and friends of each. They met at each Convention and between, endeavored to integrate the financial calls upon the churches and drives in general. The needs of the junior colleges, however, were so insistent that they, especially Randolph College, were unwilling to admit any practical restrictions. Finally, at the convention in Breckenridge in 1929, the Board of Education was formally abolished.[14]

The emphasis of appeal for financial support was for a while shifted from the churches and small individual gifts to possible donors in larger sums. The example set by Mrs. Burnett surely would encourage others! Accordingly, on the suggestion of S. J. McFarland, President of the Board of Trustees, Henry Bowden was employed as a special solicitor for large gifts, and was dignified with the title of Vice-President. Mr. Bowden had grown up as a Y. M. C. A. secretary, had been very useful as an employed executive in the Men and Millions Campaign, and was devoted to the Brotherhood and all of its program. He possessed a genial, expansive personality, capable of impressing favorably men of large affairs. He worked diligently and devotedly, but, as in each previous attempt to reach givers of big sums, the effort was without tangible results. He resigned as of January 1, 1929, and accepted the position as Executive Secretary of the Fort Worth Community Chest, in which he served until his death in 1940.[15]

One expression of expanded program was the launching of an illustrated monthly periodical, called "The Interpreter," as a means of contacting the ex-students and supporters in general. It was printed on enameled paper, richly adorned with photoengravings, and, thanks to the editorship of the brilliant pro-

---

[13]The Commission was composed of Will H. Evans, Dave Reed, Chalmers McPherson, Patrick Henry, and Colby D. Hall. The full text of the report is on file in the T. C. U. Library. The data herein is checked with it. See also Minutes 4-27-27, p. 1145.
[14]Minutes, 3-14-29.
[15]Minutes, 6-27-26; 8-6-28.

fessor of philosophy, E. W. McDiarmid, was sprightly, entertaining and wisely balanced. It was, undoubtedly, at the very top of college publicity literature. One dramatic "scoop" was the printing of a photo-engraving of the $166,667 check from the General Education Board.[16] It was initiated November 1926 and continued through Vol. V. No. 1, May 1931. In 1930 it was reported that as many as 8,000 copies were circulated.[17]

The allowance in the budget for student scholarships was generously increased. This included scholarships for students playing in the University Band, and a few for athletes, as permitted under the regulations of the Southwest Conference. Ten scholarships were announced available to any student graduating from a junior college in the upper third of the class, and showing proper recommendations. Not all of the ten were ever taken in any year; usually the student required a job in addition, to pay a major portion of the expenses.

The policy of caution was exercised somewhat in the matter of salary raises. In several instances teachers were nearly lost to other institutions by larger offers. It was considered by the administration as an evidence of the solid condition of the institution that no one was actually tolled away by this route.[18]

Changes in the Board of Trustees were few during this seven-year period. In 1923, Charles Wheeler of Fort Worth was added, bringing in a man of valuable financial judgment. He served as Chairman of the Finance Committee for several years, always having his reports and suggestions ready. W. Steve Cooke of Fort Worth came on the Board in 1926,[19] recognized generally in the city as one of the very substantial, conservative, dependable citizens, a leader in Masonic circles and in the First Christian Church.[20] E. E. Bewley gave valuable counsel out of his busy life from 1930 to 1941, when he became a Trustee for the Burnett Estate instead. Rev. H. C. Garrison, 1927, and B. S. Walker, 1924, served the last several years of their lives.

Another alumnus and ex-teacher, Milton Daniel, added great strength to the Board by coming on it in 1928, serving continuously since then. Lewis Ackers of Abilene, T. C. U. Ex., was elected in 1929. He came from one of the old West Texas families which had supported the school through the years,

[16]November-December, 1927, p. 16.
[17]Minutes, 2-13-30. A complete file is in the T. C. U. Library.
[18]Minutes, 1-5-26.
[19]Minutes, 2-13-23.
[20]Minutes, 1-5-26.

and added conservativeness and substantiability to the board.[21] The addition of the first woman to the Board has been mentioned. Mrs. Jarvis had been connected with the affairs of the institution longer than any one living, and had perhaps been more influential in making decisions than many a Board member.[22] One faithful member, who worked and contributed, but talked little, was S. P. Bush of Allen, who resigned in 1930 and died not long after.[23]

At the meeting of the Trustees in February 1928, Sam J. McFarland resigned as Chairman of the Board, because of his business situation. He had devoted a large amount of time to the T. C. U. affairs, as already told. His banking business was based in a large measure on land values, which at this time were going down. As President of the large Security National Bank in Dallas, and of several small-town banks, he found himself in a strait betwixt two problems, whether to go out and save his country banks or stay with the Security to pull it through. He chose the latter to protect the depositors, and saved them from loss. But in doing so he lost heavily in his smaller banks, and closed them out. He later moved to Lubbock, established a real estate and insurance business, became a leader in the church there as he had always been, and lived a happy and useful career. He still serves as a Trustee, living in retirement in Dallas.

This break in the business conditions was a signal, though unobserved, of the general break that came in 1929. The conditions did not affect the affairs of T. C. U. at once. But by 1930 the signs multiplied, bringing to an end the seven years of plenty, ushering in the years of depression.

It can well be said that the years of plenty went out in a blaze of glory, for it was in February 1930 that the contract was signed for the erection of the new Stadium that was to bring fun, and fame, and finances to T. C. U.[24]

[21]Minutes, 2-14-29.
[22]Minutes, 2-9-28.
[23]Minutes, 2-19-30.
[24]This story is told in Chapter XXI on Athletics. 2-13-20.

# ~ XIX ~

# Through the Depression Years Together
# 1930-1940

URING THE SPRING in which the depression was touched off
by the break in the New York stock market, affairs at
T. C. U. had an air of prosperity. In February 1929,
President Waits recommended plans "to build an Auditorium
and Fine Arts Building, a Commons for boarding students, a
Science Building and an additional dormitory,"[1] the tuition fee
was raised from $75 to $100 a semester, board from $6 to $7
a week, teachers' salaries were at their highest (full professors, $4,000), and in the following December, fired by the first
Southwest Conference Football Championship by the Horned
Frogs, the business men of the city, under the leadership of
Amon Carter, initiated the drive for the new $350,000 Stadi-
um.[2] The President's Report in February, 1930 recognized the
depression conditions for the first time. The Business Manager
reported that $20,000 had been borrowed to make the payroll,
and by the following June he advised that some of the lots
from the campus be sold to supply funds. The income from the
Burnett Trust began a steady decline.

The first move toward a salary reduction, dreaded by both
Trustees and teachers, was initiated by the faculty. President
Waits called a conference of the employees two weeks prior to
the opening of the fall term 1931 and explained to them the
state of finances, whereupon the group voted voluntarily to donate 10 per cent of their salaries for the ensuing session. This
generous gesture was received by the Board with relief, deep
appreciation, a vote of thanks and a suggestion that later on a
sum of $30,000 be set aside as a Faculty Endowment Fund in
appreciation of the faculty of 1930-32.[3] One more college year,
and the conditions were worse. The final pay-roll of the session,

[1]Minutes, 2-14-29.
[2]Minutes, 12-11-29; 2-12-30; 2-13-30.
[3]Minutes, 9-18-31, p. 1480.

June 1932, was passed up until October (the first delay in payment of salaries for several decades), and the faculty was notified that beginning in September the salaries would be further reduced by 15 per cent.[4] Hardly had the employees received that delayed payment on October 1 when they received, also, notice that another salary cut of 25 per cent would become effective with the November pay-roll. This made a net reduction of 43 per cent. This continued until 1934-35, when the salaries began to creep upward again.[5] The Board, meanwhile, found it necessary to borrow $70,000 from the Burnett Trust to meet accumulated current bills.[6]

The cut of 43 per cent raised a serious problem with the teachers in the lower brackets, especially in the summer term when salaries were three-fourths of the regular scale. So the teachers devised a "pool plan" by which all teachers received equal salaries for the summer. Detailed regulations safeguarded any abuses and competition. A class must have at least five students asking for it and the pool was divided by the number of classes rather than by the number of pupils. It worked as a practical plan and developed a splendid spirit of fellowship in the group.

Three of the trustees, in order to simplify their personal business situation and to protect their credit, found it necessary, with the consent of the Board, to pay off their notes, which they had made as contributions, by the deeding of land to the University. Dave Reed deeded 7,463 acres in La Salle County for his note of $50,000. H. W. Stark deeded a farm in Grayson County for his note of $25,000 which he had made through the Men and Millions Movement in 1914. Both of these men had been paying to the University annual interest on these notes, which had been a very helpful income. Andrew Sherley also deeded a number of farms in Grayson and Collin Counties to cover his pledge of $100,000. These farms were received and have been operated by the use of renters. The Stark farm produced a small oil well which has brought in a little income.

It was in the midst of these disturbing financial worries that a change in the Business Management occurred. On the resignation of Butler S. Smiser, L. C. (Pete) Wright, B. A. 1910, since 1923 Director of Athletics, was elected as Business Manager,

[4]Minutes, 5-30-32; 2-9-33.
[5]Minutes, 2-9-33.
[6]This was in November 1932. Minutes, 2-9-33.

207

L. A. Dunagan became cashier, and the handling of the business was put in charge of the Administrative Committee. Inasmuch as the number of teachers had been increased quite a bit in the late '20's, it was inevitable that under the financial stringency and the consequent reduced student enrollment, there should be some dismissals of teachers. So following the spring meeting of the Trustees in 1933 notice was given to a number of teachers that their contracts (which were for one college year at a time) would not be renewed for the next session, beginning seven months away. This list included some who were quite desirable as permanent members; it was grievous to leave these out, but it seemed necessary.

These dismissals, a by-product of the depression, caused two of the most painful and regrettable episodes in the faculty-administration relations of all the years. The first of these was a suit by four of the teachers for the recovery of the portion of their salaries withheld by the 15 and the 25 per cent reductions. The T. C. U. attorney advised that they had no case in law, and counseled against a compromise out of court. One case was brought to trial and the Court found for the University; the other three cases were dropped.[7]

The second distasteful episode was a brush with the American Association of University Professors, much more serious, extensive and unpleasant than a former one in 1929 over the failure to reelect a teacher who had proved to be below standard after two years trial. One of the dismissed teachers (in 1933) who had been on the faculty only two years, persuaded the Association to send an examining committee to the campus, and gave them much data he had prepared against the University. The Committee was shown every courtesy, given a room for their meeting and supplied with all information requested. They preferred no charges and gave no opportunity for any rebuttal testimony. Their report which came several months later, in mimeographed form, was composed largely of unproved opinions of the one disgruntled professor, much of it in his own language. The official report of the Association, published in the A. A. U. P. magazine the following December, was a much milder document, having passed through the hands of the cautious attorney. Nevertheless it adjudged T. C. U. as a place undesirable for any of the A. A. U. P. members to be employed.

[7]Minutes, 9-22-33. The four were W. C. Smith, Arthur R. Curry, H. D. Guelich, and Mrs. Connie Brockett, according to the Court records.

There was a revealing aftermath. The mimeographed copy of the A. A. U. P. Committee's report was marked "Confidential" and the letter of transmissal gave assurance that it was available only for the institution and not for distribution. How surprising, therefore, when word began to come in from many friends throughout the state that they had received copies of it through the mail. Of course it was readily discovered that these copies had been mimeographed and mailed by the disgruntled professor who led the whole affair. This breach of faith was reported to the officers of the Association, but without any effect. The administration regretted exceedingly that the matter had been handled so unwisely by the officers in charge.

The aims of the A. A. U. P. were known to be good. In common with several other national associations of educators, it has a good provision for the protection of the teachers in the matter of tenure and academic freedom. This standard provides that an institution shall give permanent tenure to teachers with the rank of Associate Professor or Professor, after two or three years of temporary tenure, or else drop them entirely. T. C. U. had grown up as a small school with close personal relationships between administration and faculty and had felt no need for such a definite policy, but had practiced equity in the matter. Now that the question had arisen, President Waits recommended to the Trustees that they adopt a definite policy in harmony with these generally recognized standards. These were worked out by the skillful hand of R. Houston Foster, who studied the provisions of other universities, and presented them "to bring T. C. U. in line with the practices of the best colleges and universities in the land." The document was so well prepared, the experience of other universities so clearly cited and the prestige of Mr. Foster was so high with the Board that the standards were adopted with but little discussion as amendments to the By-Laws.[8] This was done in June 1933, but the list of permanent tenure teachers was not finally approved until March 1935.[9]

The need for some arrangement for the retirement of teachers was brought to attention by the permanent disability of Professor G. W. Dunlavey and the gradual decline in health of Professor C. H. Roberts as well as the awareness that others were approaching the age of declining strength. A Group Insurance

[8]Minutes, 6-5-33.
[9]Minutes, 2-7-35; 3-1-35.

plan was inaugurated in 1927, by which each employee who desired, paid $1.20 a month, the school paying the balance, the estate of the insured receiving a $2,000 death benefit. Later a voluntary hospitalization plan had been added at standard rates. But no provision had been made for old age income. It had been assumed that each person would make his own insurance arrangements. But the trend in the insurance world was steadily toward a provision for retirement insurance and that by groups. The Carnegie Foundation had performed a valuable experiment by placing fifty million dollars in a fund to be paid out in retirement benefits to retired professors in certain selected colleges, neither the college nor the teacher contributing to the fund. After a few years its basic error became apparent: even so great a sum would sometime become exhausted if there were no provision for replenishment. So the Teachers Insurance and Annuity Association was organized, the overhead endowed and the funds provided by contribution by the college and the teacher, on an actuarial basis. Each of the older, larger church bodies established Pension Funds and many states, including Texas, set up such a system for public school teachers. The Disciples of Christ, after a long and careful study established the "Pension Fund of the Disciples of Christ" available for all its ministers and college employees, beginning operation January 1, 1931.

The Disciples Pension Fund provided for a retirement income amounting to one-half the average salary through the years of service for the teacher, one-half of that amount for the widow, $100 a year for each minor child besides $1,000 death benefit and a permanent disability feature. For this the employee would pay five per cent of his salary and the institution an amount equal to five and one-half per cent. The plan embodied the principles that had been proved successful in the insurance world. It was (1) contributory, enabling the employee to maintain an interest and a self respect; it was (2) permanent, not being discontinuable at the will of the institution, for the employee had a vested interest; it was (3) sound actuarily, being based on standard mortality tables and constantly checked by expert actuaries; it was (4) safe, because the risk was carried by a corporation whose sole business it was; the risk was spread over a large number and was inspected by legal authority; and (5) its benefits were thoughtfully adapted to the circumstances of teachers.

The President and the Dean, having carefully studied the field, recommended the adoption of the Disciples Pension Fund by T. C. U. The Board hesitated on three grounds: it would cost something like $6,500 a year to start it; the provision for the older members, who would not have time to accumulate benefits, would cost even more if it could be arranged; and third, the majority of the members of the Board (at first) were opposed to any form of retirement insurance for teachers. Some of them frankly regarded it as a charity—even the word dole was used. The administration argued that it was good business and a help to efficiency. A Board Committee was appointed and reported June 1936 approving the Disciples Plan.[10] But the mind of the Board was not unanimous, so delays ensued. The faculty attitude was sought (twice) and found to be favorable. The attitude of the Board gradually swung favorably and in February 1940 it was voted to make provision in the 1940-41 budget for the Disciples Plan Pension Fund. But at the June meeting the war clouds were over Europe. The Finance Committee pointed to these and asked that the decision to begin the operation of the Plan be postponed until October and at that time, by the same influence, it was postponed indefinitely.[11]

By 1943 the financial strain was eased and President Sadler (President Waits having retired in 1941) brought up the matter again. This time the point of providing for those already growing old in service was cared for. The Committee worked out a plan, presented it in February 1944, it was adopted without discussion and it began operation at once.[12] This plan provides, in general, that "any and all workers in the University" who shall have been employed in full-time service for at least fifteen years shall receive, after retirement, annually, "twenty-five per cent of the salary received for the five years preceding retirement" and "one-half of one per cent of the average salary for each year of service in excess of fifteen" provided in no case one receive more than $1,200 per annum. The age of retirement is to be any time after sixty-five at the discretion of the Board, except for those who are sixty or more on November 1, 1943; for them it is seventy. By this plan the employee contributes nothing and has no claim until he had served fifteen years. The

[10]Minutes, 6-1-36.
[11]Minutes, 6-1-36; 9-18-36; 2-4-37; 6-3-40.
[12]This Committee was Dr. L. D. Anderson, Lewis Ackers, Dan D. Rogers, Dr. Harry Knowles, Dean Raymond A. Smith.

Board is not bound "in any amount in excess of the actual available income for the upkeep and maintenance of the Institution." A fixed sum was set aside and invested to provide the annual payments of the pensions of those already retired. It is quite practicable to add to this plan, later on, the features of contribution, mutual dependability and actuarial assurance, which are considered as of great importance.

During the depression years the Alumni and Ex-student Association took on new life. Ever since the attempt to have a full-time Office Secretary, Miss Beth Coombs in 1925-27, when the records had been brought down to date, the chief activities were the Home Comings and the highly commendable programs of the Fort Worth and Dallas Ex-Students Clubs of the women. The series of presidents during the 30's was especially fruitful in leadership. In 1940-41 a full time Alumni Secretary was kept in the field by the University, Kenneth Hay (B. A. '37, B. D. '39), who stirred up local Clubs in a dozen cities, raised quite a bit of money and secured many students. But no successor was provided when he returned to the pastorate.[13] During the Fort Worth Building Campaign of 1946 much work was done by the Campaign office force in bringing this Alumni list down to date. Following that, Noel Keith (B. A. '38, B. D. '40), Special Assistant to the President for Public Relations, has greatly improved this list and promoted the contacts.

The climb out of the valley of the depression began creepingly in 1934-35 by the raising of salaries ten per cent. This was made possible by an advance of the Burnett Trust of $10,000 on condition that the University appropriate a like sum. President Waits "tramped the streets of Fort Worth" to solicit and secure the sum required, and thereby won the eternal gratitude of the teachers. The following year this process was repeated. After that the salaries were raised gradually until by 1943 they were back at about the 1930 level.[14] The summer term pool plan was abandoned in 1939. Obviously the depression was about over when the solid and conservative Business Manager, L. C. (Pete) Wright reported in June, 1940:

We are in good condition financially . . . if we will continue to keep our expenses well within our income as we have for the last three or four years, we will be able to look forward with confidence in making out of the school what it should

[13] Minutes, 4-11-39.
[14] Minutes, 3-29-34; 2-7-35; 3-1-35.

be instead of spending all our time trying to find some way to barely exist and keep going.[15]

The tug between the conservatives and the liberals is an ever-present phenomenon in society. Men engaged in the day by day conduct of business, with investments involved, are naturally conservatives, defending the status quo. Scholars, who measure from history and dig into the philosophy of things, are more ready to question the present and propose the new. Which one turns out to be right, only the future can reveal.

Now the strain between these two viewpoints was especially strong in the period under review. It could not be expected that T. C. U. would be free from conflict of ideas between some professors and some trustees. This strain became noticeable in the case of Dr. E. A. Elliott, who was highly esteemed as a sincere, Christian gentleman, a valued alumnus of the University, as Dean of Men, and then the Head of the Economics Department. He was full of zeal for the cause of labor and the underprivileged in general. This attitude sounded like socialism to the conservative businessmen whose ears were keen to catch any echo of "Bolshevism." The problem was solved in this case by Dr. Elliott's decision to accept a position with the Government. After a while in some other branch, he became Regional Director of the National Labor Relations Board for the Southwest district.

A similar attitude developed toward Dr. W. J. Hammond, Head of the Department of History, who was liberal in his economic thought. His special devotion was toward poor and oppressed groups of people, and he gathered evidence of much going on in the city of Fort Worth which he believed the city government could and should correct. In 1937 a group of local politicians started a campaign against the group of substantial business men who made up the City Council. They saw in this college professor a good man to head their ticket; they put him up, and elected him, then chose him as the mayor. The general business interests of the city were against him; some people used the fact to talk against T. C. U. and assume that the support of the good people of Fort Worth would be withdrawn from the school.

Some of the trustees frankly wanted to get rid of the Professor, but they were loath to offend the principal of academic freedom. Several conferences were held with him, by the Presi-

[15]Minutes, 6-3-40, p. 1907.

213

dent and by the Executive Committee, with the final result that he declared that he had accomplished the results he had desired as mayor and was planning to resign from that office. He stated it in these terms on one occasion:

A year ago I was involved in a campaign for Mayor, which terminated successfully. I have now succeeded in nearly all of my aims . . . It is unfortunate that a social scientist must apologize for his success, since the world is in need of social guidance and reconstruction . . . Teaching is my profession and T. C. U. is my life.[16]

The aftermath of this case was that Dr. Hammond retired from the city office and, for the most part, from city politics. The Board passed a Resolution that "When any member of the faculty shall accept appointment to or become a candidate for any public office whatsoever, his position as such faculty member shall become automatically vacated." This, of course, was based on the experience with two teachers who had served as mayor, and caused some embarrassing situations.[17]

The development of the Evening College is an illustration of the fact that institutions are sometimes pushed into new enterprises by the facts, rather than by the bold venture of faith. For several years evening classes had been provided for the public school teachers, who were under pressure to advance their degrees faster than the summer terms would provide. This plan was slowed down by the fact that the Teachers Colleges offered classes in Fort Worth at the rate of five dollars per semester hour, whereas the T. C. U. rate was much higher. As a concession to the teachers, the lower rate was adopted by T. C. U. and the attendance increased.

Evening classes in the field of business were announced in 1923, at the time of the organization of the School of Business, but this project did not succeed, because the effort was too timid, both in advertising and in faculty supply.

Then, in February 1936, the administrative officers recommended that a definite unit of the University be organized, to be known as the Evening College, to offer classes in several departments, and to be well advertised. The one feature emphasized was that it was to have a director who would spend much time in promoting the idea in the city. This sounded

[16]Minutes, 2-16-38.
[17]Minutes, 9-23-38.

expensive to the careful, if not wary, Trustees. Another vision of the schoolmen, perhaps! The Dean made a proposal which they accepted: "Give us the privilege of losing two thousand dollars (omitting charge for overhead) on the venture the first year, to try it out." This sounded like a good investment, so they agreed. The sequel showed that the two thousand was on the credit side rather than the debit. So the venture proceeded.

At first the teaching was done by the regular faculty members, as an extra chore with extra pay, just as the other colleges and the public schools were operating their evening classes. The rate of pay was only half as much as the regular salary, i. e., a sixth class at 10 per cent extra salary. Abuses of good standards under this plan were easy and well known, so it was changed. Since then, an evening class is treated just as a day class in the teacher's load. About half the evening classes are taught by persons outside of the fulltime faculty, people who are specialists in their fields.

The merchants and professional men in the city manifested valuable cooperation and appreciation of the Evening College. Some large firms paid the tuition or portions of it, to induce their employees to keep on studying.[18] An advisory committee was set up by having each of the clubs, commercial, educational, and business, to appoint a representative. These proved very helpful.

It was under the leadership of Dr. A. L. Boeck, Head of the School of Business, that the Evening College grew rapidly, while he served as director. After he resigned in 1942 to go with the O.P.A., and a year's interim, Dr. Cortell Holsapple was made Dean of the Evening College in the new setup of six Deans for the University. About this time the load was increased by the development of classes under contract with the Government for the Engineering, Science, Management, War Training Division of the U. S. Office of Education. This work, which had been handled by the Dean of the University, was placed under the Evening College.[19]

The temptation to overindulgence in the granting of Honorary Degrees is one hard to resist by a small, struggling college that is in need of friends. T.C.U. can hold her head high in this matter; she has acted with restraint and discretion. The first time the subject was mentioned, with any suggestion of use,

[18]Carl Wollner, President of Panther Oil and Grease Company, was an outstanding example of this practice.

215

was in the Report of President Waits in 1917. Then it was not urged.[20] As a part of the celebration of the Jubilee Year in 1923, on the proposal of President Waits, approved by the Faculty and Trustees, nine Honorary Degrees were conferred. This was recognized as a high occasion, and the event was not taken as a precedent. Just at this time the University had been admitted to the Southern College Association, and was desirous of building its prestige within that influential body and through it, in the college world, as a solid, substantial institution, with the best of standards voluntarily practiced. The Dean was especially insistent on this policy and felt that it were safer to refrain from granting any such degrees, until the prestige was increased.

The first exception to this policy was in 1931, when some of the students of Dr. Clinton Lockhart petitioned the Trustees to confer on the good Doctor the honorary degree of Doctor of Literature. Of course he had an earned Ph. D. and several honorary doctorates, and was in no need of recognition. But he was seventy-three years of age, and might not be able to teach much longer (he really taught for twelve years more). It may be confessed now that the young men also had in mind the scheme of raising a neat sum of a hundred thousand dollars to endow a Chair to be named in honor of the good doctor and the degree would touch off that effort. It was the depression, perhaps (that was in 1931), that blocked that laudable enterprise.

By 1935 it was considered that the prestige of T.C.U. was sufficiently established that degrees could be granted in moderation, and in good taste. So a committee of the faculty laid out a policy that not more than three a year should be granted. The faculty at once raised that to five, as a maximum. The maximum is not often used. The idea was to restrict the basis of the grant to recognition of some educational or scholarly achievement of merit. Later on there was a strong feeling that men

[19]The Evening College enrollment record is:

|  |  | Fall | Spring |
|---|---|---|---|
| 1937-38 |  | 320 | 296 |
| 1938-39 |  | 375 | 293 |
| 1939-40 |  | 358 | 254 |
| 1940-41 |  | 296 | 243 |
| 1941-42 |  | 282 | 265 |
| 1942-43 |  | 170 | 280 |
| 1943-44 | Net Year | 875 |  |
| 1944-45 |  | 525 | 500 |
| 1945-46 | Net Year | 1.141 |  |
| 1946-47 |  |  |  |

[20]Minutes, 2-22-17, p. 413.

216

who had rendered the institution large service deserved a like recognition in terms which the school had in its power to give. So it was agreed that members of the Board of Trustees would be eligible for recognition. The oldest man on the Board was first selected, T. E. Tomlinson, then eighty-five, who had served as President of the Board through the days of the move.[21] This was followed in 1943 with Dan D. Rogers, in 1944 by Dave S. Reed, in 1945 by Milton Daniel, and in 1947 by Ed Landreth. Universal commendation was given to these actions in consideration of the high and long continued personal services of these good men to the University.[22]

Just as everybody had become accustomed to think of the depression as past, hearts were saddened by an unusual number of deaths in the leadership. A professor beloved by all, E. W. McDiarmid, Head of the Department of Philosophy, passed quietly to his rest on September 5, 1937, after having lain all summer on his bed awaiting his end. For years he had kept to himself his battle against the white plague, to which he now succumbed. This was the explanation of his deliberate movements which he often explained by saying, "A man should never move so fast that a thought cannot overtake him." In addition to his brilliant professorship, he had served as chairman of the Athletic Council and as President of the Southwest Conference as well as the T. C. U. representative for years. Everywhere he contributed a spirit of good fellowship and good will.[23]

In April 1940 came the news that Van Zandt Jarvis, President of the T. C. U. Board of Trustees, had been found dead in his automobile while working at his farm. His mother, Mrs. Ida Van Zandt Jarvis, had passed away three years before[24] at the age of ninety-one. Thus closed the cycle of fifty-one years of service to the institution by this pioneer family. The father had come on the Board in 1889 as its first President under church control, resigned in 1899, but continued his interest in the Fort Worth days. It was he who (only advisory member then) made the motion on November 13, 1913 that the Trustees "enter heartily into the Men and Millions Movement."[25] His son came

[21]1909-1917.
[22]Minutes, 2-17-38.
[23]Minutes, 9-17-37.
[24]May 31, 1937.
[25]The *Skiff*, 11-28-13, records that Major Jarvis made a chapel talk in December "in a vigorous voice that gave evidence of the training of the pioneer days when he rode the pack saddle and spoke in the open air."

into the Board membership in 1902. The mother encouraged her husband always, advised the officials often, served as a visiting matron for awhile and became the first woman trustee (1931-37).

On the passing of Van Zandt Jarvis, L. C. Brite took great delight in nominating as his successor for the Presidency of the Board, R. Houston Foster, who had graduated from T. C. U. in 1904, had become an active member of the Board in 1923, and had won the confidence of all as a skilled and consecrated leader. His wife, also, Bess Coffman Foster (B.A. 1905), was active along with him in T. C. U. affairs and in church leadership where he was an elder and a Sunday School teacher in the First Christian Church of Fort Worth. He was ill at the time of election as President of the Board, served with vigor and great effectiveness, but died a year later, June 19, 1941. An oil portrait was provided by Ed Landreth and Milton Daniel and hung in the parlor of Foster Hall, which was named as a memorial to him.

Three months later, L. C. Brite died, after an appendectomy at eighty years of age (September 4, 1941). Deep was the feeling of sorrow at his passing. His influence had been felt in deeds rather than words. His faithful attendance despite difficulties, his words of wisdom, few but weighty, his shrewd selection of leaders, all were more highly valued even than his financial gifts. Fortunately his good wife was fully in sympathy with his lofty aims, and was familiar with his business and the school affairs. Promptly she was selected as his successor on the Board, where she has shown real ability.

Time marches on! The calendar clicks even when men try to ignore it. The good President of the University, Dr. E. M. Waits, rejoicing in the completion of a quarter of a century of service and still alert, was reluctant to admit that the advance of years had slackened his pace. Yet, as executive, he was aware of the provision for automatic retirement at the age of seventy; so after a heart-to-heart talk with Mr. Foster, the Board President, he proposed to the Trustees in his Report of February 1941 that he be permitted to become "Ambassador of Good Will" and that the executive responsibilities be passed on to younger shoulders.[26]

The affection of the teachers, ex-students and friends for the good President was expressed by a testimonial dinner and the provision for an oil portrait which was hung in the Mary Couts

[26]Minutes, 2-20-41.

Memorial Library with appropriate ceremonies.[27] The ornate hand-engraved Scroll hanging on the wall of his study at home certifies that he was the Honoree of the Exchange Club at the Golden Deeds Banquet, as the outstanding citizen of Fort Worth for the year 1939. The record of his accomplishments as President of the University appears throughout these pages.

These twenty-five years of golden service were made to shine more brightly and to operate more smoothly by the presence at his side of his talented daughter, Mary Beth Waits Scott, who served throughout these years as his "Lady" in social affairs and in friendly contacts. How graciously she filled this exacting role was evinced by her charm on the many social occasions, including the annual President's reception (often in the library) and the Senior Lawn Party (at the home). With talents similar to her literary-minded father's she made a place of her own as a witty, entertaining speaker, especially popular with the student groups.

The days of the emeritus President have proven not to be idle days. Until a decided break in his health in 1946, he continued the task which he had initiated, that of contacting during the autumn months the businessmen of the city for support of the Building Program. Brite College of the Bible utilized his obvious proficiency in English Literature by inviting him to teach a course on "The Use of non-Biblical Literature in Preaching." As his greatest joy has always been his friends, so his greatest service these later days is that of greeting the former students and other friends, keeping warm the loyalties to himself and to the school to which he has devoted the best strength of his life.

Before the coming of the new President, Dr. M. E. Sadler, in September 1941, the worries of the depression were left in the past, but new and tragic concern fell on all hearts: the war clouds were gathering over Europe and threatening to engulf the world.

---

[27]Minutes, 10-28-41.

## ❧ XX ❧

# The Silver Anniversary of Brite College of The Bible
# 1914-1939

E DUCATION FOR THE MINISTRY in this institution began as classes in Bible, emerged in 1895 as a Department under the name of The College of the Bible, and became incorporated in 1914 as the Brite College of the Bible, as told in Chapter X. During all of those years and until 1939 this College carried the responsibility of supervising the education of the ministerial students, both graduate and undergraduate, teaching their classes in religion, and jointly with the University, of providing classes in Bible for all undergraduate students. In 1939 Brite College of the Bible became a professional school for the ministry on a graduate level, or in popular speech, a theological seminary. The process of this development can best be interpreted by tracing the patterns of ministerial education through which the Disciples have passed, which are, on the whole the same as those experienced by the other communions which won the frontier for the church, the Methodists, Baptists, and Cumberland Presbyterians.

The Disciples of Christ (or Christian Churches or Churches of Christ) is a Movement born on the frontier of America and quite characteristic of it, so much so that a recent history of the Movement is entitled "Religion Follows the Frontier."[1] It has been characterized by competent scholars as "the one large denomination which is of native origin."[2] Naturally, being of the frontier, the ministers among the Disciples, were characteristically men of "little book learning." Most of them made their living at farming (the one universal occupation on the frontier), or teaching. A few practiced medicine or dentistry. Their ser-

[1]W. E. Garrison, Religion Follows the Frontier.
[2]For example, Robert Hastings Nichols, in "Church History," September, 1942, pp. 181 ff.

220

mons came from two sources: the Bible, and the sermons they heard. Under frontier conditions, schools could not have been organized fast enough to provide the number of preachers required for such rapid growth.

This unschooled ministry was not to the liking of the leaders of the Movement. The four ministers who are usually recognized as the prime founders, were all university- and seminary-trained men. They were Thomas Campbell, Alexander Campbell, Barton W. Stone, and Walter Scott, all from a Presbyterian background where the respect for an educated ministry was most deep-seated. Many of the leaders in the earliest days were of this well-educated type.

Moreover, the nature of the plea of the Disciples called for an intellectual type of preaching. The Movement was a reaction against the extreme reliance on feeling in religion, and a plea for a more intellectual foundation for faith. Thus its natural inheritance was favorable to a well educated ministry. It was the necessities of the frontier conditions described above, that led to the widespread use of the unschooled parson. As the "little red school house," so often sentimentalized and so little desired, has given way to the modern magnificent public school systems, so the exhorting type of preacher gradually yielded to the well-schooled minister.

Three types of ministerial training have appeared among the scholars of the Disciples of Christ; the one merges into the other through the years. The first was set by Alexander Campbell in Bethany College, of which he was the founder in 1841. He gave much thought to the problems of education in his day; his voice was frequently heard in lectures to educational assemblies. He was a leader in the struggle to free the public school, in its infancy, from the control of the Catholic Church. It was in this controversy, indeed, that he encountered Archbishop Purcell, in the famous debate in Cincinnati in 1837.

His pattern for the education of the Christian ministry which he embodied in the curriculum of Bethany College was a four-year course in the Liberal Arts, leading to the standard Bachelor's degree, stressing history, literature, and (unusual for the times) the physical sciences. It included also a thorough mastery of the Bible text, history, and literature. But there was no theological seminary to follow. And there were no courses on "systematic theology." This was taboo, because of Mr. Campbell's belief that the stressing of human creeds and theological specu-

221

lations had been a large contributing cause of the divisions in the churches. He, therefore, eschewed theological terminology and insisted on speaking Bible truths in Bible terms. He desired preachers schooled in the Liberal Arts, including the Bible.

Thus, early in the great migration westward, while Texas was still a republic and before the California gold rush, a stream of liberally educated ministers began to go out from Bethany across the West, to lead among the Christian Churches in this Reformation Movement. But these college graduates were in the minority; the unschooled still prevailed.

The second type of ministerial training school grew up at Lexington, Kentucky, in the College of the Bible, beginning in 1865 under President Robert Graham and President John W. McGarvey. Kentucky University, with the background of traditions of the older Transylvania University from the previous century, was inclined to stress a very broad and quite liberal type of education. The American "cult of reason" was strongly influential in the school.[3] The Bible, some of the brethren felt, was being neglected. So in 1865 they organized, separately, the College of the Bible, which has ever since been affiliated with the University, but under separate management.

In this spirit of protest, the College offered an undergraduate ministerial curriculum, a course consisting mostly of the study of the Bible itself, with some philosophy added, but lacking in the broad spread of the liberal education which Campbell had espoused. No degrees were given: an English Bible diploma was granted to the student completing the fixed three-year course; a Classical Diploma, to one who presented also the B.A. degree from the University, including Greek. The Lexington training stressed the practical preparation for the minister's task, especially evangelism, whereas the Bethany type stressed the basic and broad education, with the Bible interwoven.

Add-Ran College started out with the Bethany type. The Bible was taught as a part of a Liberal Arts curriculum, by Addison Clark himself. Addison and Randolph had been schooled under Charles Carlton, a graduate of Bethany. J. B. Sweeney, who came in 1895, being a graduate under the Clarks and also McGarvey, mingled the two types, stressing the teaching of the Bible more than Campbell but requiring the Liberal Arts curriculum and degree more than McGarvey. This combined type

[3]The story of this is told in Liberal Kentucky by L. H. Sonne.

was continued under President Zollars, as told in a previous chapter.

In 1906 came Clinton Lockhart as President, and Dean of the Bible College, with a Diploma from the College of the Bible at Lexington, two degrees—a Bachelor's and a Master's—from Kentucky University, and, in addition, a B.D. and a Ph.D. from Yale University.[4] Naturally, though not a Bethany man, he favored the Bethany type. He believed, like Alexander Campbell, in the broadly educated minister of culture. He added what his generation was just beginning to appreciate but could not afford, a professional training, in addition to the general cultural degree. So he began offering the B.D. degree. Within four years, four such degrees had been granted.

The ideal of Dr. Lockhart, therefore, reached back to the standard of the older settled churches. But the time was not ripe for this level of education on the cattle frontier. In fact, it had not been reached by any Disciple college. The study of Dr. Riley B. Montgomery made in 1931[5] shows that the educational level of the ministry among this pioneer people was definitely lower than this. Their churches were not demanding, or even expecting, graduate degrees of their preachers. The expectation of the students was not up to this level. To raise it so, was a responsibility of the faculty and administration of the University. The following sections tell the story of how this responsibility was carried out.

How this typically frontier expectancy of little schooling prevailed in the group of students in T. C. U. is clear from the figures. The total number of students for the ministry from 1910 to 1926 was 85. More than half of these (61.25 per cent) came without graduating from high school, and half of this latter group quit college before graduation. Of the 33 who entered college on high school diplomas, only three failed to graduate. This low level of education had its effect in a lack of permanency in the ministry. Of the 52 who entered college without high school graduation 25 per cent dropped out of the ministry; of the 33 others, only 6 per cent. It had its effect on the expectation for education by the entire group. The most of the men were married and mature, pressed for time and finances. They felt fortunate if they were able to persist to one degree. Their

---

[4] For a fuller account of his education see Chapter XII.
[5] R. B. Montgomery, Education of the Ministry of the Disciples of Christ, Bethany Press, 1931.

average pulled down the expectation of the entire group. Only four men in that sixteen year period pulled against the current sufficiently to achieve a B.D. degree.

During this period the tendency was to enroll first for the English Bible Diploma Course. This was seldom awarded, however, for the more fortunate ones persisted to a degree, and the others dropped out before receiving even the diploma. The effort of the faculty was, therefore, to give the best preparation practicable, within the four year college course.

The sights were raised somewhat in the early twenties, by offering the Master's in Religion. Six of these had been conferred by 1925. Then it was observed that one year's work for a Master's was more attractive than two years' for another Bachelor's degree, the Bachelor of Divinity. So the Master's was withdrawn and emphasis placed on the two year B.D. Three of these were taken by 1930. Then the tide turned. The B.D. aim had taken hold. Three were awarded in 1931 and from then on, one or two or three annually. It was a company of stalwart, outstanding young men who, during the 1930's, stood together for high scholarship and developed the expectation of the student group to persist to the B.D. degree. There were thirteen of them in eight years.[6]

This expectation had been established just in the nick of time. For it was in 1938 that the American Association of Theological Schools announced for the first time a list of "accredited" theological seminaries. "Surely Brite College of the Bible should be on such a list," was the thought of the faculty and of the students. Another circumstance that made it propitious to undertake such an aim was the fact that the College was now about to have a birthday, its twenty-fifth. What better birthday present than accreditation in the distinguished national body, the American Association of Theological Schools!

The faculty readily agreed; the Trustees voted to approve; but there were still some lions in the way. According to the standards, four teachers must be set aside to devote their time exclusively to the graduate classes. Could we afford to deprive the undergraduates of such teachers as Dr. Lockhart and Dr. Morro? Also, three full years of study beyond the B.A. degree, without the usual year of overlapping that had been permitted, would be required. Would the students, who had just recently raised their sights to undertake the two years of

---

[6]The complete list of graduates will be found in the Brite College catalogs.

study, be willing to add another year? The faculty broached the question to the students, and received hearty support. The Trustees readily approved. So, as a part of the celebration of the Silver Anniversary, it was announced that, after August 1940, the B.D. degree would require three years beyond the B.A., and that beginning September 1939, a standard Bachelor's degree would be required for entrance.

The effect of this announcement was most gratifying. The enrollment in the graduate school (from then on frequently referred to as the "Seminary") increased about three-fold. Two of the former students who had completed all of the requirements for the degree except the thesis, began work immediately on the thesis, in order to qualify, and did so just in time for the graduation in August 1940. Several of the men who were entitled to take the two-year course chose to stay for the third year. The 1940 graduating class numbered six, the largest yet. The enrollment (graduate students only) for 1944-45 was 45, for 1945-46, 51.

Meanwhile, preparations for meeting the requirements for acceptance into the Association, proceeded. Dean Hall and Dr. Morro attended the meeting of the Association in Lexington, Kentucky, June 1940, made personal contacts with the leaders, and had occasion to have some of them visit the campus to get acquainted at first hand with the faculty and plant. At the Lexington meeting Brite College was accepted into membership. But membership was different from accreditation. The standards had to be in operation for several years before accreditation could be allowed, and the third year requirement had been added only with the 1939-40 class. By December 1941, however, the accreditation was announced, much to the gratification of all students and faculty and friends.

Brite College was the second seminary of the Disciples to be accredited, the College of the Bible at Lexington having been on the first list published in 1938. The third school to be accredited was the School of Religion of Butler University in 1945.

One fruitage of this achievement came in 1943 in the selection of Brite College to train the Navy V-12 Chaplains. Only accredited seminaries were eligible, and the College of the Bible at Lexington had no Navy training unit close enough by to supervise the Chaplain unit. The relations with the Navy were at all times cordial, simple and satisfactory. There was no effort made to control the content of teaching; there was no appreciable financial profit or loss. The total number of students served was seven.[7] This story of the raising of the level of ministerial training has been considered of sufficient importance to give it first place in this chapter on the life of Brite College of the Bible. With this perspective before us, let us now turn back and follow the details of the story of the personnel and problems of these years.

The chartering of Brite College of the Bible in June 1914 was the culmination of long preparation and struggle as told in Chapter X. After G. A. Llewellyn had first opened the mind of Mr. Brite "to the possibilities of good to be done through educating preachers,"[8] President Kershner followed by showing the need for an endowment and a building. In 1911 Mr. Brite gave $25,000 for the endowment of a Chair of English Bible and, in 1914, pledged $35,000 to erect a building.[9] The trustees met June 7, 1914, adopted the charter, made plans for the building, and elected the faculty. Classes were started in the Main Building, since the new building was not ready for dedication until the following February.[10]

On the occasion of the dedication, February 9, 1915, the speakers were Dr. Carey E. Morgan, pastor of the Vine Street Church, Nashville, and President of the A. C. M. S., and John W. Kerns of Austin. The dedicatory prayer was offered by Dr. Harry D. Smith, then pastor of the Central Christian Church, Dallas.

The building was designed under the direction of President Kershner, modeled after the College of the Bible at Lexington, where he had been a student. It had three stories, with four recitation rooms each on the first two floors, with two offices between. Two of the rooms on the second floor were thrown together to make the Library, but these were separated later in 1926 when the Library was joined with that of the University. The third floor was given half to the Chapel, seating 200 (later the McPherson Memorial Lecture Room), and half to two large "Society Rooms." One of these has since been converted into

[7]They were Charles Malotte and Coleman Raley, who received their degrees and Chaplain's Commissions in October, 1945; Wm. J. Hall, who, after one semester, was disqualified on account of eye deficiency; A. W. Robertson who withdrew November, 1945, and George Matthews, March, 1946; and Jim Fairbrook who qualified just in time to get in the winter trimester of 1945-46.
[8]Supra Chapter X.
[9] Minutes, 6-6-14.
[10]Minutes, B. C. B. Trustees, 6-7-14; 12-8-14; *Skiff*, 1-29-15.

L. C. BRITE,
B. C. B. Trustee, 1914-41 ;
President, 1925-41 ;
T. C. U. Trustee, 1912-41. 29 years.

MRS. L. C. BRITE,
Trustee, B. C. B. and T.C.U.
1914-

MILLARD PATTERSON.
Trustee, B. C. B., 1914-20.

JOHN W. KERNS,
Trustee, B. C. B., 1914-42.
28 years.

A GROUP OF BRITE COLLEGE STALWARTS.
For more details consult the Appendix.

University Christian Church

The second of Ten Quadruplexes erected as Homes for Married
Ministerial Students

Main
Building
in 1919.

The Arch, 1923.

Campus Looking North, 1919.

Some Early Campus Views. *Below* : Looking South, 1916.

Goode Hall and Clark Hall.

*Below :* Foster Hall.

the Morro Memorial Chapel. The estimated cost of the building was $34,000, for which Mr. Brite gave his check. The cost exceeded the amount by $7,000, for which the Trustees gave notes.[11] One of these notes for $3,500 was paid by Mr. Brite, the other out of current income.

Mr. Brite's investment of $62,500 was not made because he had that much to spare, or to use as deduction on income tax, or to satisfy his conscience. It was given because he believed in the purpose of the College. That is shown in his extreme care to see that the right kind of teaching should prevail. He had a faith which he wanted propagated; he tried to set up safeguards to see that no other teachings would ever be presented. He was therefore very careful in the selection of the groups that would control: the Trustees and the Faculty; he exercised caution in a third safeguard: the Charter.

The nine trustees were indeed select men, full of integrity, faith, and devotion to the church. Three of them were preachers, and the preachers usually constituted the Committee on selection of the faculty. Dr. L. D. Anderson, Pastor of the First Christian Church, Fort Worth, substantial then as he ever after proved to be, was the first, and so far, the only Secretary. John W. Kerns, then pastor at Austin, later Waco, was a Hiram graduate, a powerful Gospel preacher, evangelistic, sensibly conservative, with a sweet spirit, and universally trusted. In his later years, broken in health and retired in Austin, he would respond to the Board meeting call, "I am physically unable to attend, but if you really need me, wire me and I'll be there." He remained a member until his death September 1, 1942. Eugene Holmes was a former Add-Ran student, a graduate of the College of the Bible at Lexington, the son-in-law of the old pioneer of Collin County, R. C. Horn. He died in 1926 and later his sister, Mrs. Mary Jane Thomas of San Angelo, gave $8,500 on the annuity plan to endow a scholarship in his name. One of these Trustees was a distinguished physician, Dr. Bacon Saunders, an elder in the First Christian Church of Fort Worth, the founder of the Fort Worth Medical College[12] and a disciple of "Uncle Charlie" Carlton of Bonham. He was made President of the Board and so served until his death in 1926. C. W. Gibson, Waxahachie, one of the leading members of the T. C. U. Board, was another, who served until his death in 1919. Van Zandt Jarvis of the

[11]Minutes, B. C. B., 4-18-15.
[12]Supra Chapter XV.

First Christian Church, Fort Worth, a ranchman, a trustee of T. C. U., later the president of its Board, served until his death in 1940. James Harrison, another T. C. U. Trustee, served until his death in 1937, not only as a member of the Board, but also as trustee and treasurer for its Endowment Fund. His business was loaning money; he handled the funds for the College, without cost to the institution, and did a magnificent job of it, for which the Board often resolved its gratitude. Millard Patterson of El Paso, an elder of the church there and a successful attorney, was selected especially by L. C. Brite. It was he who drew up the Charter, and "Brother" Brite often remarked that the charter was "water tight," because it was drawn by "one of the best lawyers in Texas." Mr. Patterson left a legacy of some $60,000 to Brite College at his death, December 16, 1934. Finally there was Mr. Brite himself who served faithfully, attended regularly, and was elected as President of the Trustees in 1926.

Every member served as long as he lived, except Mr. Patterson, who retired and moved to California in 1921. The successors were: A. C. Parker, in 1919; Andrew Sherley, 1921; R. H. Foster and H. C. Garrison, 1926; Thurman Morgan (B.D. 1936), 1935; George Cuthrell, 1936; Judge Tom Beauchamp, 1938; Lewis Ackers, 1940; Elmer D. Henson (B.D. 1940), 1942; and Mrs. L. C. Brite, succeeding her husband who died September 4, 1941. Douglas Tomlinson of Fort Worth succeeded R. H. Foster, who died June 9, 1941. In 1945 George Cuthrell moved from the state and resigned. His place was filled by Granville Walker (B.D. 1937). On the resignation of Thurman Morgan due to physical disability, W. Oliver Harrison (B.D. 1935) was added to the Board.

The issuance of the first catalog, an artistic document containing a copy of the charter, revealed the selection of the first faculty. Three already on the T. C. U. faculty were included: President Kershner; Dr. Clinton Lockhart, Professor of Old Testament; and Colby D. Hall, Professor of English Bible. The fourth member, a favorite of the Brites, and soon to be a favorite of the students, was Chalmers McPherson. His preparation was his long pastoral and evangelistic experience. For years he had been recognized as a leader in the general organized work of the Brotherhood, had served a long pastorate at Waxahachie, and as Endowment Secretary for T. C. U. Now, at sixty-four years of age, in vigorous health, he began his teaching career. His department was "New Testament Christianity." His courses in "Acts," "The Gospels," "Doctrines and

Practices," etc., grounded the students in the elements of the Gospel, and provided practical preaching material. "Brother Mac" devoted his life in love and zeal to his "boys and girls," giving them spirit as well as lessons. He stirred interest by offering prizes, for which his friends gave funds. Returning from a vacation trip in September 1927, he was found to be toxic from bladder trouble; he had declined to have a physician. It was too late to save him. He passed peacefully to rest at the age of seventy-seven.

Dr. Clinton Lockhart, devoted scholar and delightful personality, continued his good work as teacher of Old Testament. Part of his time was taken during 1916-1920 to serve as Dean of the University. This type of administrative work, however, was not congenial to him. As Professor Winton remarked, "His best friend would not claim that he was cut out for a bookkeeper."[13]

The first expansion in the faculty came in the field of Religious Education. On the suggestion and example of Dr. L. D. Anderson and by the energetic work of S. W. Hutton in collecting the pledges, the amount $28,402.72 was raised from the Church Schools of the Texas churches as an endowment for the Chair of Religious Education.[14]

The professor chosen for this new Chair was Frank E. Billington, from the pastorate at Ellensburg, Washington, whose sweet Christian spirit blessed the campus the remainder of his career. For one year, 1922-23, he spent a leave of absence in graduate work in Boston University. In 1927-28 he yielded the Chair to H. L. Pickerell while he took the Chair of Christian Ministries. Mr. Pickerell established a reputation as a thorough, scientific teacher whose courses were attracting numbers of non-ministerial students for lay leadership, until the depression required the diminishing of the faculty, and he transferred to the University of Michigan.

Following the Jubilee Celebration in 1923 and the receipt by T. C. U. of the Burnett gift the year following, the spirit of Brite College arose to larger plans. The Dean urged the expansion of graduate offerings.[15] An invitation was extended to

---

[13]More concerning Dr. Lockhart will be found in Chapters X and XII.
[14]B. C. B., Minutes, 2-18-29.
[15]B. C. B., Minutes, 2-17-26.

Dr. Walter Athearn to join the faculty.[16] Arrangements were made with Dr. Charles Reign Scoville, while he was conducting a meeting at the University, to spend half the session on the campus teaching and inspiring evangelism, although the plan was never operated.[17]

To succeed "Brother McPherson" whose death occurred in September 1927, one of the most distinguished scholars ever produced by the Disciples was called, Dr. W. C. Morro, a product of the Lexington school, with B.D. from Yale and his Ph.D. from Harvard. He had served as Dean of the College of the Bible at Lexington, then taught at Butler and the College of Missions in Indianapolis. He began his teaching in Brite College in September, 1927, having been loaned for a year to the University of Michigan Bible Chair.

During 1931-33 Professor E. C. Cameron served as Assistant Professor of Old Testament, in preparation to succeed Dr. Lockhart, who was nearing the time for retirement. He came at the time of the depression, was restless, asked for a leave of absence for further study, and before returning accepted a place on the faculty of Butler University.

It was during the period of depression when the faculty had to be limited, that Dr. L. D. Anderson graciously agreed to carry a part of the teaching load without remuneration. Since then, with but small pay, he has taught a course in Homiletics. This has been a great blessing, coming as it does out of his rich experience as pastor of a great church.

The finances of Brite College of the Bible from the first have been indefinitely intermingled with those of T. C. U. This was quite natural and logical, inasmuch as the teaching loads were also intermingled. The scope of responsibility of the College was, in general, the ministerial students, all of whom were enrolled in the University, and most of whom were intermingled with other students in classes. During most of the years there were very few graduate students. Moreover, the teachers taught non-ministerial students in large numbers as well. Hence, through most of the years, two of the professors were paid by Brite College, the others by T. C. U. For a few years the matriculation fee was collected by the College, then all the funds paid by students went through the T. C. U. office.

[16]B. C. B., Minutes, 2-19-24.
[17]B. C. B., Minutes, 9-23-25.

This intermingling was further effected by the arrangement for soliciting funds from the churches. At its meeting in February 1916, the Trustees of Brite College authorized a "quiet campaign" for funds, in addition to the call on the Church Schools for gifts to endow the Chair of Religious Education.[18] But the June meeting following postponed that campaign, out of deference to the "State Educational Campaign" being then conducted by T. C. U.[19] The following February a Committee reported to the T. C. U. Board concerning the plans for endowing the College.[20] By February 1920 a policy was definitely fixed. C. W. Gibson introduced a resolution to the effect that all appeals to the churches be made in common by T. C. U. and Brite College, and that no rival calls be made. Realizing that the call of Brite College for ministerial training had a warm appeal to the churches, it was agreed that whatever funds were needed by the College would be furnished out of the T. C. U. treasury.[21] In addition, it was agreed that the gifts for endowment for T. C. U. would be shared with Brite College. At this same meeting, President Waits agreed that one-fourth of the amounts received from the Men and Millions Movement should be allocated to Brite College.[22] This principle was recognized later when Andrew Sherley made a pledge of $100,000 with the specification that Brite College was to share in the funds. Indeed the money had been promised through "Brother" McPherson, then a professor in the College. As the Endowment Campaign got under way, the Brite Board appointed two of its members to represent it in the Campaign.[23]

On this understanding, the relationship between the two treasuries continued successfully and happily through the years. An item was placed each year in the T. C. U. budget for "Brite College Advances." As the work of Brite College became distinctly a graduate school a more specific division of funds was needed. So in January, 1947, it was agreed that one-fifth of the offerings from the churches and one-half the income from Living Endowment would go to Brite College. Through the early years of Brite College, until the interest on the Bible School Chair endowment began to come in, the only other income was the $1,500

[18]B. C. B., Minutes, 2-4-16.
[19]B. C. B., Minutes, 6-8-16.
[20]B. C. B., Minutes, 2-8-17.
[21]B. C. B., Minutes, 3-12-20.
[22]B. C. B., Minutes, 4-5-20.
[23]B. C. B., Minutes, 6-9-20.

check from L. C. Brite which came promptly every year. This was the interest at 6 per cent on his $25,000 gift to endow a "Chair of English Bible." James Harrison, one of the Trustees, who handled the investment of the endowment funds, was getting 8 per cent on the Bible School endowment on hand. He observed that the note of Mr. Brite was past due. The other Trustees and the Administration thought that so long as the $1,500 interest came in so steadily there was no need to collect the principal. But Mr. Harrison, as Trustee for the Endowment Fund, wrote Mr. Brite that he could get 8 per cent if he would pay the principal. So a check came in promptly for the $25,000. This incident was humorously recited by Mr. Brite himself in 1923 before a huge crowd at the Texas Hotel, on the occasion of the banquet as a part of the Jubilee celebration. Mr. Brite was called on for a speech. Being a taciturn cattle man, he was hesitant. But he arose, faced the crowd, and brought down the house by the shortest speech of the occasion: "You thank me for giving money to T. C. U. That's not much. It's easy to give money to T. C. U. All you have to do is sign a note. They'll collect it."

A bequest from D. D. Boyle, one of the preachers, came to Brite College in the form of a section of land in Webb County, Texas. It was in the midst of the huge ranch of the Callaghan Land and Cattle Co., from whom he had purchased and to whom it was sold, to the net profit of Brite College of $3,101.27.

A loan fund to students seems to be, in the public mind, the most popular form of helping them. Back in 1897-99 the State Convention aroused quite a bit of enthusiasm to establish a Ministerial Loan Fund, and collected several hundred dollars. It was handled, not by the school but by a committee, chiefly by Sam Hamilton, who was responsible for raising the money. The records are not available to show how much was loaned and how much returned. It has already been told how President Zollars specialized in a Loan Fund. D. G. McFadin, then a prosperous farmer and land man at Austin, formed a corporation known as the McFadin Ministerial Loan Fund, into which several men put funds or notes. These included, in addition to Mr. McFadin, Dave Reed, Malcolm Reed, T. E. Alexander. The funds were handled by E. H. Yeiser, an attorney at Austin and an elder in the Central Church there. These funds were loaned with conservatism, and became the means of seeing many a lad through his college years. On the removal of Mr. McFadin and

Mr. Alexander to Dallas, the Board was reorganized; Kenneth Hay and later Harrell Rea, was made Treasurer. Two other loan funds handled by the Brite College office are by Shelby N. Strange (of Temple), $5,000; Mr. and Mrs. E. F. Gates (of Amarillo), $1,000; Mr. and Mrs. George A. Ray (of Pettus), $5,000.*

Several facts have been learned in the administration of these funds: it is better for the student to earn than to borrow, so long as possible; it is difficult to repay a large loan on a preacher's small salary; the borrower who begins to repay soon is more sure to pay out; a devoted friend can assist the student best by giving to the endowment of the school, thus reducing the cost to the student.

The key to the problem of educating ministers is a low living cost for the students. This is often sought by the club boarding plan. Such a scheme was operated by Dean Sweeney at old Add-Ran. The first year at Waco, an abandoned street car barn was rented and divided up into barracks, where the boys "batched." The next year the Wortham House put the responsibility on the contractor "Brother Wortham," who fed and housed the boys at $11 a month. In Fort Worth, Goode Hall, home for Ministerial students, gave room rent at one dollar per week and provided a basement in which the students could operate a Boarding Club. The weekly rates began about 1912 at $1.75, but, due to the rising costs, crept up to $5 a week. At that point the business manager of T. C. U., figuring the subsidies provided (utilities and rent) and the fact that bulk in the University Dining Room made for lesser costs, proposed to board the group at $5 a week, which was one dollar less than the regular rate. So, in 1919 the Boarding Club was abandoned.[24]

Goode Hall had plenty of room for all of the ministerial students, single and married. So a company of men and women gathered there, including some children. Still there were vacant rooms. In Clark Hall, for boys, there was a shortage of room. The real situation that brought about the change, however, was the petition of the ministerial students themselves, that they be no longer separated from the other boys. They wanted

[24]Minutes, 2-11-19, p. 488.
*Mrs. Ray is a daughter of the late Clint Haggard of Plano, a Texas pioneer who was a steady supporter of ministerial education. One of the progenitors of this family, Rice Haggard, proposed the name "Christian Church" as the designation for the Reformation Movement. He did this first in Virginia to the O'Kelly group, then later to the Barton W. Stone group, in Kentucky.

to mingle as boys with boys, and avoid the breach between the regulars and the preachers. So it was agreed that Goode Hall should be used for upper classmen, Clark Hall for underclassmen; the ministerial boys should be placed among the others, but should receive a reduced rate on the room rent to carry out the purpose of Goode Hall. This was a welcome change all around. The problem of the married students was not solved for several years.

The plan of erecting Quadruplex Apartment Homes for the married ministerial students is one of the most brilliant ideas yet. Patrick Henry is a business man of shrewd practical sense, not hampered by the rules and conservatism of the usual business men. He saw the vacant lots owned by T. C. U. and knew that money could be borrowed and houses built. So he proposed to the Dean the scheme of borrowing the money at 5 per cent, building efficiency apartments and renting them at a low rate to married ministerial students. Between the two adventuresome minds the details were worked out. The Brite College Board readily approved the plan, but the lots were owned by T. C. U. The real problem was to secure the consent of the T. C. U. Executive Committee. These were business men who did not believe in rental residence property as an investment. They were looking at it from the investment viewpoint; the administration saw in it the opportunity to serve the purposes of the school. By repeated arguments and mutual faith, the consent was finally secured by a faint margin.[25]

The first plan for borrowing the money was to sell bonds to friends, offering 5 per cent. But an ad in the *Christian Courier* really got the result. Two Christian women answered the ad. Mrs. M. J. Barker and her sister Miss Georgia Jones of Pritchett, Texas, loaned about $3,500. This was paid off in a few years, and the money was borrowed from the surplus in the Strange Loan Fund.[26]

The first Quadruplex, a frame building costing $6,000, was erected in the summer of 1936. Each apartment rented at $15 a month, furnished. Its success was so obvious that the second was welcomed in 1938. It cost about $8,000, a brick veneer, renting for $17 an apartment. The money was borrowed mostly from the Permanent Fund of the Texas Christian Mis-

[25]T. C. U., Minutes, 2-8-34, p. 1614; B. C. B., Minutes, 2-8-34.
[26]B. C. B., Minutes, 2-6-36.

sionary Society, but this was paid off after several years by a gift of Mrs. Brite of $5,000 to the Endowment Fund, to be loaned temporarily for this purpose. The third followed two years later, 1940, at a cost of $8,000, borrowed, partly, from the Permanent Loan Fund established by Mr. and Mrs. G. A. Ray of Pettus, Texas.

While this apartment enterprise was really a Brite College enterprise, the business had to be done through T. C. U. because the title to the lots was in T. C. U.'s name. In 1942, the six lots (facing Greene Street) were sold to Brite College for $3,000, and Mrs. Lee Bivins of Amarillo, very graciously donated that sum to pay for them. Beginning with the session of 1943-44, Reed Cottage was turned into a quadruplex and was occupied by four ministerial couples. In 1945 the pressure for Apartments became so strong that a fifth Quadruplex was constructed. The added costs required that the rental price be increased to $20 a month. With the returning of the War Veterans in 1946, despite increasing costs and scarcity of materials, five more quadruplexes were built (completed in February 1947), thus making a total of 40 apartments besides Reed House.

This plan for providing homes for married students has proved to be of such benefit that other schools have been inspired to follow the example. Brite College has shared the idea, even the blue prints with some of them.

The growing strength and prestige of Brite College of the Bible, without a doubt, had much to do with the revival in recent years of the annual Ministers' meetings of the Disciples of Texas. Beginning in the 1890's, the brethren had assembled each winter for a "Lectureship," bringing annually a Guest Lecturer. Such notables were listed as J. W. McGarvey, Burris Jenkins, D. R. Dungan. Most of the speeches were made by the local brethren.[27] This was financed by a one dollar fee. About 1913 the project began to drag, and finally, in 1916, was abandoned. Brite College tried to revive it on the basis of a school, with regular courses taught by the professors, and the one Visiting Lecturer. The first attempt was in 1919. Dr. S. Parks Cadman was brought at a cost of about $750. Aside from a score of ministers who were employees of the Texas Christian Missionary Society (expenses paid), who combined a Conference with the Lectureship, only two other ministers came. This

[27]For a complete list see J. W. Holsapple, *Autobiography of an Octogenarian.*

was so disappointing and so expensive that the attempt was dropped. It was revived again in 1933 under the proddings and leadership of Perry Gresham, the pastor of the University Christian Church, who served as the chairman of the program committee. It was financed by a $1.25 fee and it succeeded splendidly. A list of brilliant speakers came year after year.

In 1943 the McFadin Ministerial Loan Fund, on the initiative of Kenneth Hay, made a pledge to pay $300 a year out of the interest on its investments for the Ministers' Institute. This was named the McFadin Lectureship. The following year the East Dallas Christian Church promised $600 a year for the Lectureship Fund, to be managed by T. C. U. The Trustees therefore named it the Wells Lectureship, in honor of the pastor of that great church. Thus the initiative of Brite College eventuated in the permanent establishment of this annual feature which is known as Ministers' Week.

The placing of student pastors with the churches is a vital function in a ministerial school of the Disciples, whose policy admits of the plan of learning to preach by preaching. This responsibility was carried by the Dean until he took on the extra load of Deanship of the University. For several years then, A. B. McReynolds, a recent graduate, served as Brite College evangelist in the field on the support, largely, of Russell Hill of San Antonio. Mr. McReynolds, of decided evangelistic temperament, spent two months in the fall placing ministerial students with student-pastorates. This was very fruitful, especially the mission meetings; the time allowed for placing the students was not sufficient for the requirements. Professor Billington did the work for a while, then in 1934 the best plan of all was gradually developed. Patrick Henry, State Secretary of Texas Missions, found the ministerial students the best means at hand for reviving and shepherding the small churches. It was genuine mission work, and helpful to the students. The College appointed Dr. Henry as Student Counsellor, and pays the Missionary Society $400 a year for his services.

When the Mary Couts Burnett Memorial Library was acquired by the University in 1924, the Brite College Library was coalesced with it, as a matter of economy and efficiency. One large room was designated for the stacks of the field of Religion. The library became the beneficiary of the libraries of several deceased ministers, including Chalmers McPherson, M. M. Davis, J. J. Cramer, J. W. Lowber, and others. This naturally collected many books by Disciples writers, and on the Movement of the Disciples. This led to the idea of setting aside a room for the housing of such literature. The Librarian, Mrs. Bertie Mothershead, applied her enthusiastic disposition to the idea, encouraged it and largely executed it. The collection was begun in 1927, the room set aside in 1935. It has achieved its desire of having one of two or three most nearly complete collections in existence. In 1944 a gift of $300 was received for the Disciples Collection from Mrs. Mary G. Siros in memory of her son, Ernest, who was lost in the war.

The J. W. and Maggie Lowber Collection came in 1939 as a bequest of Dr. Lowber and a gift of his wife, Maggie Pleasant Lowber. The complete collection of this noted scholar was moved into the room assigned to it, and formal dedication was held in February, 1940. A legacy is provided to keep adding books to the Lowber Rooms.

Many of the brightest and best features of the life of the College cannot be transmitted to paper. There is, for instance, the spirit of foreign missions that burned brightly during the decade of the 20's, resulting in the sending to the foreign field of about a score of men and women, besides the preparation of others who were not sent because of the retrenchment of the program just at the time. It was this cutting down of the missionary program that caused the decline of interest in foreign missions on the campus.

There are, too, the student organizations. The Timothy Club was the original. The students voted to simplify and shorten the name; so they changed it to the "Brite College of the Bible Ministerial Association"! The Homiletic Guild, started at the suggestion of Perry Gresham, became a luncheon club for discussion of preachers' problems. The Timothy Club became the undergraduate organization for practice of preaching, the Homiletic Guild the graduate club. The Association includes all. The Retreat held twice annually takes all of the men off the campus for a day and night for fellowship and discussion.

The weekly chapel meetings have been always sources of much inspiration. Out of the student interest arose the effort to build a worship chapel of their own, and it was done, largely with the money they raised. Then came the desire to have an organ of their own. By the same process the money was raised to purchase this, inspired and led by Dr. W. C. Morro, for whom, after his death, the chapel was named. He was insistent on se-

241

curing an organ with genuine pipes. A Wickes Organ of real pipes was purchased and installed just a few months before his death.

In addition to the growing number of friends and alumni and the increasing gifts from churches, some of the recent individual donations are: as annuities, Mrs. Mary Jane Thomas of San Angelo in memory of her brother, Eugene Holmes, $8,500, and Mrs. Sadie Beckham, Dean of Women, emeritus, $10,000; on endowment an additional $65,000 from Mrs. L. C. Brite; in bonds $1,100 from Dr. J. L. Holloway of Dallas.

Following the gratifying progress of 1939-40, there came a series of changes in personnel and disasters by death that shook the hearts of all. One definite loss had been sustained on February 27, 1937 in the death of James Harrison, who had served so efficiently and unselfishly as Trustee for the Endowment Funds. In June 19, 1941, came the sudden death of R. H. Foster, an alumnus of T. C. U., a distinguished attorney and great Christian leader and lay teacher, who had been a member of the Board of T. C. U. and B. C. B. for years, and was at the time President of the T. C. U. Board. On September 4 following came the shocking news of the death of L. C. Brite,[28] the chief benefactor of the College, in whose heart the welfare of the institution was so deeply imbedded.[29] On September 1, 1942, John W. Kerns, one of the original Trustees, very faithful and beloved, went to his long home. Soon after, the brave, scholarly professor, Dr. Morro, devoted as he was to his garden and expert in plant life, while digging in his garden one Saturday afternoon, fell over with a cerebral hemorrhage and passed away, March 24, 1943. The retirement of Dr. Clinton Lockhart was long due. So unusual was his physical and mental vigor that he had been retained each year, but now he had attained the age of eighty-five, and retirement was due him, though not at all sought or perhaps even welcomed by him. A great occasion of appreciation was extended to him and his gracious lady during the Ministers' Institute in February 1944. He taught his last classes in the summer of 1943. Pages could be written in praise of these two great scholars who had made such rich contribution to the lives of the students and the brotherhood.

Institutions are larger than men. And even the ripening of the lives of the greatest saints and scholars cannot halt the

[28]See Chapter XXI.
[29]Ibid.

242

progress of the institution that is rooted in the life of a devoted host like a Brotherhood of Christians. New personalities arise to carry on the work. Granville Walker had been prepared to succeed Dr. Morro, or to head the undergraduate Bible Department, as he preferred. But when the pulpit of the University Christian Church, across from the campus, became vacant, and Mr. Walker was in Yale on leave of absence, he was called to that pulpit, and accepted. The College, realizing his superb and unique ability as a pulpiteer, did not protest. Dr. Fred West, just receiving his Ph.D. from Yale, was elected to the place as Head of the undergraduate Bible and allowed time to teach one course in Brite College. D. Ray Lindley meanwhile had completed his work at Yale and came to assume the Chair of Christian Ministries and Religious Education. The place of Dr. Morro was filled by changing Dr. Roosa from Old Testament, where he had been assisting Dr. Lockhart, to become Professor of New Testament. Dr. Cecil F. Cheverton was called to be the Professor of Old Testament, after a long career as Professor and President of Chapman College in California. He proved to be such an unusually effective teacher of the Bible, that with the session of 1947-48 he was shared with the undergraduate Department of Religion, as its Head. Another product of Brite College joined the faculty in 1945. W. A. Welsh, marked for scholarship when he was a student, became Associate Professor of New Testament.

During the session 1946-47, Dr. W. L. Reed made such a favorable impression for scholarship, effective teaching and cultured personality that he was made Professor of Old Testament, beginning in the fall of 1947.

In the fall of 1943, Dean Hall returned to full time duties as Dean of Brite College. He was that in 1920 when he was called by the T. C. U. Board to become also Dean of the University. He agreed, with the understanding that after a few years he could return to build up Brite College. That "few years" stretched out to twenty-three. So in September 1943 he moved his office from Main to Brite and immediately began some improvements that had been delayed by the absence of an executive at that end of the campus. After four years at this welcome task he looked about him and discovered several enterprises completed. Full standing as a theological seminary had been achieved, and the students generally had the expectancy of securing the B.D. degree. The campus problems of World War II were past and many of the boys were back in class again, with

243

a goodly number of new ones; the enrollment had passed the fifty mark. Two of the alumni of Brite College were now well settled on the faculty, having proved to be of permanent caliber. The apartment project, now eleven years old, with all of its complications of planning, contracting and financing (always with the efficient and indispensable aid of Patrick Henry) was completed. The financial support, thanks to the churches and the leadership of President Sadler, was greatly strengthened; an "Intensive Effort for Ministerial Training in T. C. U." in the autumn had been productive, and in the last days of 1946 plans were matured for the enriching of the program of Living Endowment. It looked like a good time to pass some responsibilities on to younger men. He also realized that he was now of retirement age and that he had often avowed that executive work was for a younger man. So on January 2, 1947 he requested the Trustees to relieve him of the office of Dean and allow him to become only Professor of Church History. He was very happy to have his former pupil and associate as teacher, D. Ray Lindley, assume the responsibilities as Dean, on July 1st following. He held and will continue to hold the faith that the new generation will build on the foundations a better structure and that Brite College of the Bible will continue to enjoy the confidence of the Brotherhood as a wide-awake, forward-looking, open-minded, substantially conservative school of the prophets, true to the spirit of the Disciple Movement and even more, true to the message of the Christian Gospel.

## ➣ XXI ➢

# The Trail of the Fighting Frogs
# 1897-1945

T HE STORY OF ATHLETIC ACTIVITY IN T. C. U. naturally falls into four periods. The pioneer stage lasted until about 1902. It is the tale as of an awkward youth, abounding in restless, untutored energy, restricted by lack of equipment and experience, restrained by the absence of an appreciative public and resisted by the semi-frontier outlook of the earnest and serious-minded trustees.

The second period, covering the latter half of the "Waco years," 1902-10, was one of rough and tumble, intercollegiate contests, with little regulation and less finance. It provided the experience out of which was constructed the later regulations, the first embodiment of them being the Texas Intercollegiate Athletic Association in 1909. This period ended for T. C. U. in a blaze of glory just before the move to Fort Worth.

The third period was more slow and sober, replete with troubles and disappointments, affording more toil and tears than gain or glory. It was a transplanted school, sinking its roots into new soil with all the athletic advantages against it, from 1910 until it entered the Southwest Athletic Conference in 1922.

The days of greatest achievement and adventure, excitement and glory came in the fourth period from 1922 on. The younger generation, and the generation that once was young and now is adult, would be unforgiving if this story of athletic activity in T. C. U. did not rank a chapter of its own.

In view of the frontier attitude[1] toward play, the recreational activities at Thorp Spring can scarcely be classified under the title of "athletics." Both baseball and football were played there, but mostly of the "sand-lot" variety; certainly it was not intercollegiate. Van Zandt Jarvis often enthused over his own football experiences before his graduation in 1895. The last

[1]See Chapter VI.

245

issue of the *Collegian* published on the old campus, December 1895, reported that "the football and baseball clubs are becoming very expert and are accumulating a great deal of lung power."[2]

The only organized sport, and doubtless the most popular one, was Military Drill, in harmony with the tradition of all Southern colleges for men, following the Civil War. "A very fine Company of thirty members with Springfield rifles" was reported in 1894, with an application to the War Department for the detail of an officer to organize a regular Military School for the following session."[3] In 1893 Col. T. M. Scott (popularly known as Captain Scott) came on the Board of Trustees, and being semi-retired, lived near the campus for a while, both at Thorp Spring and at Waco. Being a graduate of Texas A. & M. College he became the inspiration of the military drill, which flourished so long as he was there.

So let us consider the Thorp Spring days as a preliminary, and the early Waco days, 1895-1902, as the first period. It was during these Waco years that intercollegiate athletics developed, and in true West Texas style. For just as the cactus, the mesquite, the horned frog, the mustang pony and the longhorn cattle prospered through droughty seasons that killed out less hardy life, so football and baseball came to life at Add-Ran during the "seven lean years," persisted despite the thwarting elements, and sent living roots so deep into tradition as to explain something of the flourishing plant in the later generations.

Texas University was the only other college in the state playing football at this time (1895); however, in 1893, Austin College at Sherman and Texas University had organized teams to play various town teams. In 1894, Texas Agricultural and Mechanical College organized a team, and on October 20, 1894, the first intercollegiate football game in Texas was played between Texas University and Texas A. & M. However, in 1895 all other colleges but Texas had disbanded their football teams.[4]

Obviously, in this feature, as well as others, Add-Ran was among the pioneers. And, as a pioneer, it had much timber-cutting and brush-clearing to do before a clear trail was blazed.

The first tall tree in the way was the venerable President. Venerable, they felt him to be, for, although only fifty-three

[2]*Collegian*, December, 1895.
[3]Catalog, 1894, p. 22.
[4]Paul Ridings, The History of Football in Texas Christian University, p. 2, quoting as a source Theron J. Fouts, History and Influence of Football in Texas Colleges and Universities, S. M. U., 1927, Chapter II.

years old, he belonged to a generation which grew serious early; and he was of the sterner type. Addison Clark was a true son of the frontier, where every man was strong and every lick had to count, where it was a sin to waste bread and almost as bad to waste time. The old catalogs glitter with his warnings against idleness. He himself, physically most hardy, could wield an axe with the best, and could out-walk anyone. Often he walked the three miles to town in preference to a ride. It is said that he took a plunge in the old swimming hole in Stroud's Creek every morning—believe it or not—winter as well as summer. Those who knew him could believe it. But athletic as he was, he got his strength by work and not by play; he expected others to get it the same way. He thought more of the boy who would clear a field with a hoe than one who could clear a fence with a high jump. That was the pioneer in him. Football and baseball didn't appeal to him. Either was a waste of time. So it looked bad for those who began to aspire for a football team.

But Mr. Addison had a son whom he adored. "Little Addie" was just back from Michigan, bitten by the Football bug. He weighed not much more than a hundred pounds and was bookish; but he was spunky, and he followed out his thinking at any cost. A. C. Easley, lover of all sports, and expert in the military drill, also came to be enthusiastic over football. These two "profs" lined up the boys on Thanksgiving Day, 1896, in two squads the "black stockings" and the "brown stockings"—that was the extent of the uniform—and had them kick off for a football game about which the boys knew nothing. The score was four to four.[5] It was a delightful shin-kicking affair with little rules and no skill, but it began an era. Gradually, the old President, viewing the game through the eyes of his beloved son, melted from opposition into enthusiasm, and football had won a start in Add-Ran.

That first season, beginning (not ending) with Thanksgiving, saw three match games: Toby's Business College, Waco, 8 to 6 in Add-Ran's favor, December 7; Houston's Heavyweights, December 19, lost by 22 to 0, and a tie with the same team a little later in the month.[6]

With a season completed, the students inspired and the President won over, they would seem to be out of the woods. But they soon discovered that they were just beginning to run

---

[5] *Collegian,* Volume II, September, 1896, p. 7; December, p. 93.
[6] *Collegian,* Volume II, January, 1897, pp. 131, 132, March, 1897, p. 201.

the gauntlet with the Board of Trustees. And a long run it turned out to be before football was officially free. These were men also of pioneer background, with little sensing of student attitudes and a larger sense of responsibility to the Brotherhood and to financial concern.

That "southwest corner of the campus" of which the athletic association had "secured control" was "leased from the Board under a contract approved January 5, 1897."[7] Thus it is evident that to the Trustees, athletics was an outsider, not a part of the educational program. At the next meeting President Clark felt the need of arguing for athletics in his report to the Trustees:

In order to cultivate intercollegiate fellowship, and arouse among our young men a proper university spirit and pride, we have invited and accepted invitations from the A. & M. College and from the State University ball teams and also exchanged visits with the Houston football team. All these games we are sure were helpful in many ways to our young men and to our University. It is proper to say that on each of these visits a teacher accompanied the young men and that they went at such times as did not interfere with the duties of either pupils or teachers. These athletic sports, as you know, are encouraged and provided for by all our best and oldest colleges and universities. We are a little tardy in the progressive movement but flatter ourselves that we have made encouraging advancement this session.[8]

Good evidence that the grand old man was thoroughly converted and even trying now to convert others! But with the Trustees, he was not a very successful evangelist. The next day they voted "not to allow the students of this school to engage in games of ball outside the city of Waco and additions thereto, and that they confine all athletic sports to this territory."[9] They voted "to approve the requiring of athletic exercises as a part of the University courses,"[10] but evidently were afraid of the out-of-town trips.

The athletically-minded students and faculty had faith in the good dispositions of the Trustees, however, for they proceeded that summer to make plans with a football season definitely on the program. On September 6, 1897, an Athletic Association was

[7]Minutes, January 5, 1897.
[8]Minutes, 6-1-97.
[9]Minutes, 6-2-97.
[10]Minutes, 6-2-97.

organized[11] with teeth and sinews, which the one a year before did not have. This time there was a manager who could date games and raise money. He was W. O. Stephens, a mature student, a lawyer turned preacher. This combination may have whetted his financial abilities, for, under his management, enough money was raised to secure a coach. There was no provision in the University budget for a coach, surely not for any athletic jobs or scholarships, and no prospects for gate receipts of adequate size. Neither were there restrictions against any method of financing these things. Naturally the coach's salary absorbed all the available donations. So it came to pass that, while out-of-town games were still under the ban, the money was raised, the coach employed, and the coach arrived on October 1.[12] If no out-of-town games were to be played, much ammunition would be wasted, for Baylor was the only team in the town. But it was not wasted. The Trustees relented on October 12, with permission "to play four games out of town with other college teams," and the first game was played with a Dallas team (not a college) October 23.

This gain for athletic permission was "by a neck" only. The vote of 5 to 4, followed by an attempt to instruct that "either Addison Clark or J. B. Sweeney should always accompany the team," lost by the same 4 to 5. There must have been much heat engendered, for these were the only votes on which the names of the ayes and noes are recorded in the minutes.

That the coaching was no child's play is witnessed by the list of training rules laid down by Coach Joe Y. Fields.

"1. Abstain from all intoxicants, also coffee and tobacco.
2. Go to bed at ten.
3. Eat no sweets or pastry.
4. Indulge in no kinds of dissipation."[13]

That first season recorded a very worthy set-up:

| Add-Ran 6 | Dallas University 0 |
| Add-Ran 10 | Texas University 16 |
| Add-Ran 30 | A. & M. 6 |
| Add-Ran 32 | Fort Worth University 0[14] |

[11]Horned Frog, 1898.
[12]Horned Frog, 1898.
[13]*Collegian*, Volume III, 1897, p. 22.
[14]Ridings, History of Football in T. C. U., p. 4, citing T. C. U. Department of Journalism Athletic Files, 1897.

It was during this session of 1897-98 that the title "Horned Frog" was selected to indicate T. C. U. activities. The first Annual was issued that spring under the title, and continued steadily to be used. The application of "Horned Frogs" to the football team did not take hold so readily or remain so continuously, but it was adopted in 1897-98, according to an account by Archie Wood:

In 1897 we decided to give the team a name and select school colors and there being two literary societies in the college, the Walton and the Add-Ran, two were appointed from each society to make the selection. Miss Bessie Reed of Rockdale and Claude McClellan of Coleman were selected from the Add-Ran and Miss Birdie Reed from Bertram and myself were selected from the Walton, and from the committee came the name Horned Frog and the colors, purple and white.

The Horned Frog name came about because there were so many of these creatures on the site of the old school at Waco and the colors were chosen as a matter of preference, and we thought the combination beautiful.[15]

Since that was the first season of intercollegiate football, it deserves space for a summary as found in the first annual, the Horned Frog of 1897-98.

We organized early and there can be no doubt that, for the greater part, the material which presented itself seemed poor and the outlook seemed anything but encouraging: Financial matters were in a bad shape and subscriptions were small and scarce. Nevertheless it was determined to secure as good a coach as possible and to make the best of what we had. Fortunately our coach gave eminent satisfaction, and the material developed remarkably. Truly the team made phenomenal progress. It, in a few weeks, jumped from obscurity into enviable notoriety. In our second game we accomplished what no other college team in Texas had ever done—we scored against the State University. And it may be added parenthetically, not only did we score, which was a virtual victory, but we played them to a stand-still throughout the game. When time was

[15]From a letter written to L. C. Wright, on December 9, 1938, by Archie F. Wood, of Athens, Texas, who was a student at Add-Ran at the time, and played on the first football team. Letter on file in the T. C. U. Library.
Another version is told of the selection of the colors. The 1896 class reports that the purple and white was selected during the spring of 1896 by a committee of Julia Easley Robertson, Jim Campbell and one other. It is most likely that the colors were selected in 1896 and the Horned Frog in 1897.

called and the game was over, we had turned an unsympathetic majority into a crowd of enthusiastic admirers. We left the field that evening with a score of 16 to 10 against us, proud of our effort, and determined, ere the season closed, to demonstrate to the Texas public that we might justly claim their administration and support . . . A.&M. . . . was no match for us, and 30 to 6 is the lasting memorial of their misfortune. Fort Worth University 32 to 0, making the splendid record of 78 points against our opponent's 22.[16]

The names of that first team of 1897, from its pictures in the Annual of that year can be accurately reconstructed. They are:

Claude McClellan, R. E., Capt. (Coleman); R. Earle Sparks (Waco) R. T.; C. I. Alexander, R. G.; Sam Rutledge, C.; W. G. Carnahan, L. G. (Dallas); Guy L. Green, L. T. (Coleman); Frank Pruett, L. E. (Waco); C. W. Herring, Q. B. (McLennan Co.); J. V. McClintic, R. H. B. (Groesbeck); M. R. Sharp, L. H. B. (Davilla); Jeff R. Sypert, F. B. (Holland). Substitutes: S. S. Glasscock (San Gabriel); R. Holt; G. A. Foote; H. E. Field.

Thanks to that same precious No. 1 Horned Frog, we know that a track team and tennis team operated in that school year of 1897-98.

The fall of 1898 started off with bright hopes, James Morrison as the new coach, W. O. Stephens still manager, Jeff Sypert, captain (J. R. Sypert, M.D., Oak Cliff), and a special favor from the administration as follows: "The football boys are grateful to the management for the table set apart for them where they are allowed to eat with their suits on after regular practice."[17] Thanks to the Administration, but none to the Trustees, for their September meeting voted "to allow no students to leave the city to engage in any match game of ball of any kind."[18] This was met by a petition the next day from the team, approved "by the male members of the faculty," to reconsider the ban and to allow four match games out of the city. This petition was lost by a vote of 2 to 4. How the season was saved in the face of this action does not appear in the records. Something must have happened between the lines, for season there was, most assuredly. The famous game at Midland on Thanksgiving Day was, that year, played in the snow. Even the second team was able to match a game at Taylor, against a local team. To that the writer of these lines can testify personally. He was captain of the second team, and remembers, and could right now sketch

[16]Horned Frog, 1898.
[17]*Collegian*, Volume III, October, 1898, p. 25.
[18]Minutes, 9-7-98.

some of the plays that won that game in which he (125 pounds) played Fullback and Guy Inman (110 pounds) played Quarter. Unfortunately the names of the other nine men are not recorded. Nine? Yes. There were no substitutes.

The only action by the Trustees concerning the season they had not sanctioned, was a promise by President Clark made in the December 20 meeting that he would hereafter "prohibit the playing of match games outside of Waco in conformity to the resolutions previously adopted by the trustees."[19] The dampening of the Trustees must have overcome the rooting of the students, for the season's record looked like this:

| | |
|---|---|
| Add-Ran 0 | Texas University 16 |
| Add-Ran 41 | Toby 0 |
| Add-Ran 0 | Texas 29 |
| Add-Ran 0 | Fort Worth University 0 |
| Add-Ran 0 | A. & M. 15[20] |

It was during this season that the preacher students came heavily into football. They claimed that they could gather from the entire squad enough preachers to beat any other collection of players. Among this number, in addition to those already named, were J. N. Wooten, J. J. Ray.

On the Board thus far, there had been a preacher voting on each side of the question. In the fall of 1899, a new preacher was added to the Board, Chalmers McPherson, and he was friendly to athletics. So a motion was passed authorizing football and baseball that year. But it was still restricted to the campuses of Baylor and Add-Ran, and the menacing clause was added, "this shall be considered as final for this school year—no further concession, or deviations."[21] They stuck to that, too.

The next spring, when they received a petition to have the baseball games in a park in the city, not on a campus, they denied the petition on the grounds that the students had previously agreed to ask no more concessions for this season.[22] "All of this opposition resulted in only one game's being played in 1899, a scoreless tie with Baylor, and no games were played in 1900."[23] "Jim McClintic, whose father was on the Board of

[19]Minutes, 12-20-98, p. 126.
[20]*Collegian*, November and December, 1898, pp. 18, 27.
[21]Minutes, p. 148.
[22]Minutes, 3-12-01, p. 150.
[23]Ridings, op. cit., p. 6, referring to Fouts, Appendix.

Trustees, was captain of the 1899 team and C. I. Alexander was captain in 1900."[24]

In their zealous restrictions on athletic games, the Trustees had an eye to the sentiment of the brotherhood throughout the state. T. E. Shirley, Chairman of the Board at the time, wrote in a letter to S. M. Hamilton, Secretary, in August, 1899: "No competitive games with teams on college grounds; match games only between Add-Ran teams. That is what the brotherhood demands."[25]

This weather eye to the brotherhood is corroborated also by an authentic story from Midland, Texas, where the team played a game with a local team in the snow on Thanksgiving Day, 1898. Its best friends admitted that it was a rough game, and that the conduct of the boys was not the best. One wealthy cattleman, who could probably endure steer dogging but couldn't take football, made a proposition to one of the trustees: 'I tell you what I'll do: I'll give the college two thousand dollars, on condition they never play another game of football as long as the college lives!' If only they had taken him up! How much later trouble they would have saved. For instance, all the trouble of counting up fifty thousand dollars gate at a single game in the thirties!

Was it a calm consideration of the educational benefits of athletics that won the Trustees and the brotherhood over, or was it the sheer enthusiasm of the game? Who knows? In a few cases the answer was clear. There was the case of Trustee G. V. McClintic from Groesbeck, who had all but forbidden his son Jim, one of the stars, to play the rough game. The father came to a game down in the old Padgitt's Park, against the University of Texas. He sat doggedly on the topmost seat in the grandstand, grimly determined not to enjoy the rough stuff. As the game progressed, the father slipped down a row or two, then another and another, until long before the second half, he was on the front row yelling like a Comanche Indian. Jim was knocked cold that day and didn't recover until an hour after the game was finished, but the father was so soundly converted that

[24]Department of Journalism Athletic Files of T. C. U. cited by Ridings, op. cit.
[25]Minutes, 8-11-99, p. 137.

this did not phase him. It was football that went to glory; Jim survived and went to Congress.[26]

Jim tells the following story about one of his teammates by the name of Edwin Bull, whom he encountered on the streets of Waco in the fall of 1898 and enticed into Add-Ran:

I immediately took him over to see Morrison our coach who asked him a few questions concerning football. Evidently he did not know any more about the game than he did about the solar system. Anyhow, I detected a gleam of satisfaction in Morrison's eyes as he looked his big frame over. We had him enrolled in Professor Easley's business school before one could say "Jack-Rabbit" as he agreed to play with us boys in the gentle game we pictured to him as a fine manly sport.

The next afternoon, I saw that he was rigged out in football togs as we assembled on the field for daily practice. Coach Morrison briefly explained to the Cowboy some of the rudiments of the game, the art of tackling and carrying the ball and finally the Cowboy was given the ball and told to run down the field to experience his first tackle. A young player by the name of Foote with a good running start made a lunge tackling him low and the cowboy landed on his head with a thump and the ball went spinning from his arms. I never saw such a disgusted look on a human and when he got up, he said, "To hell with this kind of a game—I'm through with this foolishness."

We talked him out of quitting and it wasn't long before he learned how to protect himself and really made the team an excellent Guard. Finally came the time for the big Annual contest with the State University at Austin, Texas. This was the Cowboy's first game away from the College, and we were assigned to the same room at the hotel. When we were dressing for the game, I got the surprise of my life when I saw him take from his grip a pistol and place same under his belt just before he started to pull on his top shirt. I gave out a yell, and said what on earth are you going to do with that gun? He seemed surprised at my attitude and calmly replied that he always wore his pistol when away from home and among strangers. I told him he would lose same in the first scrimmage, but he replied that he had been carrying a pistol for years, and had never lost it in any

[26]This was James V. McClintic, the first Congressman from the 7th District, Oklahoma, serving 1915-1935: then Executive Assistant to the Governor of Oklahoma, (1936-1940), Special Federal Governmental Offices of Washington, D. C., retiring in 1945.

tussle he had ever had. Finally, I convinced him that this was to be a friendly contest, and above all things we didn't want to hurt anyone. With a good deal of reluctance he put the pistol back in his grip and we went on to the game.

The second period for athletics opened in 1902 on a rather thin background. In the three previous seasons only three games of football had been played, all with Baylor. In 1899, it had been a scoreless tie, in 1901, two crushing defeats.[27] There was no coach after 1898 until 1904, and only an Acting President after 1899 until President E. V. Zollars came in 1902.

The new President was not a fan, but he encouraged every move that would make the school popular with the students and the public. The complexion of the Board of Trustees had changed. In that year appeared in the membership two alumni, representing the views of the younger generation. Van Zandt Jarvis, 1895, son of the former Board Chairman, J. J. Jarvis, born the same year as Add-Ran, and now twenty-nine years old, was among those who had endured the first rough and tumble football on the old campus at Thorp Spring. J. J. Hart, (B.A. 1897, M.A., 1898) had shared the students' enthusiasm under the first coach in 1896, and had doubtless absorbed athletic interest while a law student in the University of Texas, where he received his LL.B. in 1899. G. V. McClintic, who had been won by his son's playing, also was still on the Board. Public interest, too, had grown toward, rather than against the sport. This balance of power made it possible for the *Skiff* Editor in September, 1902 to write "We expressed the hope, in the last issue, that the matter of athletics would be left in the hands of the faculty. That now is a reality. To play on the team your class average must be 80% which all our team will easily make." If the editor was optimistic, the faculty was wise. For they put their finger on the one point which, more than any other, served to curb excesses and abuses of inter-collegiate athletics in the later organized years.

The 1904 team under C. E. Cronk, the first coach for five years, won the first victory for six years. Then the investment began to pay. The next year under E. J. Hyde as coach, the first full season schedule was played, and the encouraging percentage of .500 was attained. Coach Hyde was one of those personalities, like a number of the teachers, who proved to be

[27]Ridings, *History of Football in T. C. U.*, p. 6.

larger than the small school realized at the time. He had been trained under Michigan's famous Yost. In October, 1905, Yost visited the T. C. U. campus and, incognito, watched the squad drilling. To the student manager, Doug Shirley, he casually remarked: "Do you know the difference between my ability to coach and Hyde's?" "No, what is it?" "There is none," said Yost, and walked off while the flabbergasted manager was inquiring "Who was that man?" Mr. Hyde in the later years accumulated a good estate and donated several years of service to raising an endowment for his alma mater, Michigan.

In 1908 came another coach to keep the tradition of efficient, gentlemanly coaches, J. R. Langley, another product of Michigan, who continued through three seasons. The 1907 team, captained by L. C. (Pete) Wright, lost only two games and that of 1908 won second place in the state.

This season was also outstanding because of the presence of T. C. U.'s first all-state men. They were: Captain Manley Thomas, end; L. C. Wright, tackle; John Pyburn, Guard; Noah C. (Cy) Perkins, quarterback.[28]

Other history-making names appear in the picture of the 1909 team for which L. C. (Pete) Wright served once more as captain and Thurman (Hoss) Allen was manager. Manager in those days meant manager, for there was no employed faculty manager. On this team were Grantland (Grits) Anderson, Bill Massie, Paul Tyson, Charles Ashmore, and others. One name outstanding was "Blue" Rattan, who since has earned high rank of General in the U. S. Army. He returned in 1913 and served as Captain. The General always stops by the campus when he can. For the first time appears Milton Daniel, who later became Coach, Law Professor, and Trustee in T. C. U. These years produced as brilliant, spirited and successful sport as in any period of the history of the institution unrivalled by any unless it be the glories of the 30's.

Increasing interest in football at this time created a need for better organization than the loose ones that had been used in the first fifteen years of college football in Texas; therefore, in May, 1909, delegates from A. & M., Austin, Baylor, Southwestern, Texas, Trinity, and T. C. U. met in Waco and formed the Texas Intercollegiate Athletic

[28]Ridings, citing J. R. Langley; *Skiff*, December 9, 1908.

Association with Professor O. W. Long of T. C. U. as president.[29]

The spirit of youth ran high at this time. Intercollegiate rivalry was keen, unbridled, and sometimes bitter. There was something of the boisterousness of adolescence about it. This news items from the *Skiff* records one of the worst samples:

Thanksgiving Game with Baylor, 1908. At the half the score stood 8 to 6 for T. C. U.

Fouts (Baylor Quarter) appeared in Blue stockings (T.C.U. color) and at first a grey jersey (Baylor). Immediately after the kick-off, however, he rushed to the sidelines, tore off the grey jersey, revealing one of blue immediately underneath. With the addition of (T. C. U.) headgear, he had a deception that even his own teammates could hardly penetrate. Captain Gannt and Coach Mills were appealed to; both smilingly refused to have the garments removed.[30]

Such a scheme as wearing the opponents uniform caused bitterness that was hard to down. That and many a fist fight at the close of the game made history which stirs more regrets than pride. T. C. U. had its share of the pugnacious type to start the fight. Sportsmanship has grown a long way since that day.

The Captains for these years deserve honor: J. V. McClintic, '99; C. I. Alexander, '00; Tom Reed, '01; Homer Rowe, '02; H. H. Watson, '03; A. J. Muse, '04; Howell G. Knight, '05; Bonner Frizzell, '06; L. C. Wright, '07 and '09; Manley Thomas, '08; Bill Massie, '10.

Football was not the only sport in those days. Basketball appears in the *Skiff* notices in 1908 and in the Horned Frog. Even the Girls' Basketball showed some activity in 1907, but it was not flourishing. Track flourished all along as much as a sport can without the enthusiasm of crowds.

Military Drill continued through the session of 1903-04, at which time there was published an imposing list of officers and prizes. The Major was Homer Rowe; Captains Douglas Shirley, Clovis Moore and B. W. Procter. There were sponsors too, including Miss Pauline Shirley (Mrs. Elster Haile) and Miss Willena Hanneford (Mrs. Douglas Shirley). The authority in charge was Col. A. C. Easley of the Texas National Guard. It is significant that the following year when he withdrew from the faculty to go into business, the Military Department not long

[29]Ridings, p. 9, citing Fouts, op. cit., Ch. III.

afterward disappeared.[31] In 1905-06, Douglas Shirley had become the Major with Alonzo Ashmore and Hardy Grissom as Captains. The latter was one of the famous quarterbacks.[32]

Football was not even the king of sports, in those days. It is difficult for us of the '40's to conceive of the superior place which baseball held on the college campus in the early years of the century. And when baseball was on top, T. C. U. was on top. That is history.

One of the best, if not the best records ever made by any team in the state was made by the T. C. U. baseball team that year (1905). We played eleven association games and lost only one . . . T. C. U. wins the championship with Captain Ben Moulden, Shirley Graves, Bert Bloor, Carpenter, Franklin Kinnard, Walter Bush, Joe Clark, Tom Gallagher and L. C. Procter . . . In baseball, T. C. U. has held the championship for four years.[33]

The notables who went into professional baseball were many in that period and much later. In 1905-06, it was Louis Drucke who started the procession by going to the New York National League Team. His brother, Oscar, was in the Oklahoma League.[34] Much of the credit goes to that fine gentleman, clean sport, and master player, Ellis Hardy, a Waco boy whom T. C. U. was fortunate to have as coach.

Much more than athletic records came out of this spirit-stirring period of sport as it arose through a loose-joined intercollegiate arrangement into a well-organized and thoughtfully controlled educational and business enterprise, involving mass psychology of the general public on an astonishing scale. Its story is not comprehended without recognizing the careers of men, who, as boys, developed under its vigorous motivations. This includes the managers, student leaders, as well as players on the field. But for the intense interest and loyalty as a yell leader and manager, it is doubtful if Dan D. Rogers in later years could have had so much of sustained leadership and persistent support of athletics and of the University as a whole, as he has manifested in his remarkable record as a public leader. And his every move has been for the highest type of clean business

[30]*Skiff*, November, 1908.
[31]Catalog, 1904, p. 148.
[32]Horned Frog, 1905.
[33]*Skiff*, May 27, 1905.
[34]*Skiff*, July 26, 1910.

and clean sportsmanship, exceeded by no one individual. For this phase of his career alone, he fully deserved the LL.D. conferred on him in 1942. The roots of high ethics and loyal sportsmanship were laid deep. And so it was in the lives of many others.

In this era a genuine hero was made. "Cy" Perkins was one of those rare, small men of football, whose gritty spirit made him a great player despite a small body. He had a natural brain for a quarterback, the love and respect of every player and every student. His early and untimely death fixed him in mind as a sort of heroic figure, an ideal for those who knew him. In a later generation when another "Cy" (Leland) came along into football fame in T. C. U., also a blond and also a swift runner, it brought many a heart-twinge to the old grads of the leaner years of 1905-10 as they thought of their beloved "Cy" of precious memory.[35]

The first dozen years in Fort Worth, constituting the third period in athletics, proved to be a sort of anticlimax. There was enough steam in the student group, the traditions of the glorious past burned brightly, the Trustees were now converted to support athletics, the faculty was enthusiastic in its loyalty, and the efforts to build a strong program were persistent. But the prevailing conditions made a successful career in athletics in T. C. U. at that time an impossibility, as the perspective of these later years reveal. There had not been time to whet the appetite of the Fort Worth public for games, and there was no strong local rival, such as Baylor, on which to do the whetting. There was no stadium to attract or to hold the crowd; only bleachers. Financially, college athletics was still accounted on the debit side of the ledger, if it was even recognized by the ledger. The largest crowd ever assembled on the old bleachers (which were on the spot where the Library now stands), was 4,000, well remembered because it was so unusual.

The other members of the T. I. A. A. had distinct advantage over T. C. U. Baylor was long established in Waco; the two big State schools had large and growing alumni groups; baseball, in which T. C. U. excelled, was declining as a college sport and Texas University was gaining that strangle hold on this sport which it held through the years of the coaching of Billy Disch. In spite of these untoward conditions, T. C. U., during

---

[35]Noah C. Perkins graduated in 1909, died in 1910. His brilliant sister, Mercy Perkins, finished in 1908, and became Mrs. Murray Ramsay of Austin.

this period from 1910 to 1922, turned out some very famous players and leaders, and made a record of which all may well be proud.

These were the days of adolescence in athletic standards, marked by earnest efforts to maintain levels which were not yet accepted by the public, or absorbed by the students. The spirit of good sportsmanship, so essential to the operation of rules, although strong in many individuals, was inclined to break down under the pressure and excitement of competition. It was under this sort of psychology that there came to T. C. U. its most embarrassing moment and the most disheartening blow of all its athletic history: T. C. U. was debarred by the T. I. A. A. from participation in intercollegiate athletics for the season of 1913-14, as a penalty for alleged infraction of rules in the football season of 1912.

The case caused a great sensation in the public, stirred deep feelings on the campus and heated discussions in the Council of the Association. Let it be said first of all that the outcome proved clearly that the T. C. U. faculty and management were innocent of any wrong or complicity, that the guilt was confined to the coach (who was dismissed) and to two or three students who put over a smooth trick. Many of the records of the episode are available, including the minutes of the T. C. U. Committee of investigation. From these and the first-hand knowledge of the author, who was a member of that Committee, the following story is related. Names of the students involved are omitted; their later record proved them to be honorable gentlemen.

The storm broke when the T. I. A. A. at its December meeting in 1912 suspended two T. C. U. football players, and held in suspense action against the University itself. The T. C. U. faculty, conscious of its good intentions, set about to ferret out the facts. The faculty representative, Professor C. I. Alexander, was well known to be a man of the highest honor and responsibility, clearly beyond the suspicion of any conniving with wrong. When the facts were cleared it was found that two brothers had, that fall, transferred from a university in another state, where one of them had played the previous season on the football team. The other one had not played. The player registered on the T. C. U. eligibility form under the name of his non-player brother. The deception was not caught by the faculty representative, but it was discovered by a rival fan from a published picture of the team of the former school.

The second offending student was in the same picture. He had registered in T. C. U. as an ineligible, under the transfer rule, having to wait a year to become eligible. It was charged that he had played in one certain game. The coach, under questioning, admitted that, in a pinch, short of substitutes, he had played this man about five minutes. The faculty members were surprised at this, all the more because the coach had appeared at a faculty meeting prior to a trip (in his football togs, coming from off the field), asking that he be recognized as the faculty representative for that trip, to save space for substitutes, giving his assurance as a gentleman that he would observe every precaution that any teacher would. The administration, on learning of the Coach's betrayal of trust, dismissed him, and barred the two students from athletic participation.

Professor Alexander went to the spring meeting of the Association at Brownwood believing that the Association would confirm the debarments and dismiss the case. But complications arose. The students themselves, the guilty ones and their friends, believing that the two were essential to the success of the team next fall, were ambitious to get the boys reinstated. The faculty declined to have any part in any such effort. But one member of the faculty, out of the goodness of his heart, yielded to the persuasions of the boys, took it upon himself to go to the Brownwood meeting and make a plea for their reinstatement. This action had a disastrous effect. It gave color to the feeling that the faculty of T. C. U. had not recognized the guilt of its students, and was not supporting the standards. Professor Alexander, the official representative, declared the contrary, gave evidence of the true actions of the faculty, and insisted that the appearance of the professor was on his own, entirely. But the chase was hot. The desire for a cleaning up was intense. The pressure was strong. T. C. U. was suspended for the year and the coach permanently debarred from serving a school in the Association.

The sentiment of T. C. U. was that the two students and the coach got what they deserved, but that the institution itself was quite unfairly treated, that it had been made the goat in an effort to reform. There were rumors of infractions by other schools and some of them proved to be well founded. In one notable case a player was proved to be a full-fledged "ringer"; yet the school was let off with an apology. This was not at all soothing to the feelings of the T. C. U. supporters. But they bowed their heads, took the decisions as good sports, and proceeded to prepare for the 1914 season.

The prime moving spirit in this case of T. C. U.'s penalizing was Dr. C. C. Gumm, President of the T. I. A. A., a professor in the faculty of Polytechnic College. At the time of his election to the presidency of the Association he had declared that his policy would be to "clean up athletics." He had a Ph.D. degree, which was not so common in those days, and was a person of some dignity and determination.

After this episode, he was not at all popular on the T. C. U. campus. It was, therefore quite an unwelcome announcement, in the fall of 1915, that Dr. Gumm was to join the T. C. U. faculty. That fall Polytechnic was closed, theoretically merged into the new S. M. U. But there was to be a gap of two years before the faculty could be taken into S. M. U. and President Kershner very graciously took three of the teachers into the T. C. U. staff. One of these was Dr. Gumm. The climax of the tense situation came when Dr. Gumm made a talk in chapel that autumn on "Clean Athletics."[36] It was a mark of great restraint that he was listened to with respect. This was possible because the T. C. U. folk generally speaking were cultured people, some of the former students were gone, and Dr. Gumm was a very gracious, capable, sincere person.

Of course the dampening of spirits by reason of the suspension was heavy but only temporary. Optimistic leaders were found on the faculty. Patrick Henry, then Principal of the College of Business, was made Athletic Director and had some definite plans.[37] Fred Cahoon became the "Coach," by which title he was popularly called for many a year, for he continued as Assistant Coach for Football and Baseball and took charge in the other off-season of 1919. It was his enterprise, by the way, which built the bandstand on the front campus, in honor of Professor W. T. Hamner. The two were from the same home town, Temple, and good pals. It was a good idea and a big one, despite the fact that the band soon outgrew the stand.[38]

The move which boosted the spirits and the prospects of the football team, however, was the coming in 1916 of Milton Daniel as Coach, and Director of Athletics. Daniel was a McLennan County boy who followed T. C. U. to Fort Worth, graduated in

[36]*Skiff*, November 14, 1913.
[37]*Skiff*, January 9 and 18, 1913; February 20, 1914.
[38]*Skiff*, July 7, 1916.

The Football Team, 1897, the first to play intercollegiate. *Top row, from left :*
Seth Glasscock, RE ; Jeff R. Sypert, FB ; W. O. Stephens, Mgr.
*Second row :* Claude McClellan, RE, Capt. ; C. I. Alexander, RG ; Sam Rutledge,
C. ; W. G. Carnahan, LG ; Guy L. Green, LT,
*Third row :* R. Holt, Sub ; C. W. Herring, QB ; Frank Pruett, LE.
*Bottom row :* M. R. (Rag) Sharp, LHB ; Jim V. McClintic, RHB ; Earl E. Sparks, RE.
*Other subs :* G. A. Foote, H. E. Field, Guy Inman, Colby Hall, Jim Ray.

FIRST FOOTBALL TEAM
THE FIRST CHAMPION BASEBALL TEAM.
"State Champions for 1904" (From 1905 Horned Frog).
*Manager :* Homer Rowe
*Back row :* Left, Walter Bush, Steffins (?), "Slim" Harris, Nelle (?), Joe Clark,
Leslie Procter.
*Bottom row :* Gano Carpenter, Tom Goodson, Tom Gallagher, Ben Moulden.

W. O. STEPHENS,
First Athletic Manager,
1897-98.

DAN D. ROGERS,
T. C. U. Trustee, 1915- ;
Chairman, Athletic Com.
Total, 32 years.

MILTON DANIEL,
T. C. U. Trustee, 1928- ;
Coach, Professor,
1915-18. Total, 19 years.

C. I. ALEXANDER,
Chairman,
Atheletic Com., Faculty.
1912-19 ; Professor,
1910-19.

E. W. McDIARMID,
Chairman, Athletic
Com., Faculty, et al ;
Prof., 1918-39.
Total, 21 years.

GAYLE SCOTT,
Chairman, Faculty,
Athletic Com., 1939-,
et al ; Professor, 1926-.
Total, 27 years.

J. WILLARD RIDINGS,
Publicity Director ;
Professor, 1927-.
Total, 20 years.

LEO R. (Dutch) MEYER,
Coach 1924-. Total, 24 years.

FRANCIS SHMIDT,
Coach, 1929-33.

E.J. HYDE,
Coach 1905-08

SOME LEADERS IN ATHLETICS
(For more details see appendix)

RAYMOND (Rags)
MATTHEWS,
All American End,
1927.

JOHHNY VAUGHT,
All American Guard,
1932.

DARREL LESTER,
All American Center,
1935.

SAM BAUGH,
All American Quarter,
1935.

CHARLIE
KI ALDRICH,
All American Center,
1937-1938.

DAVID O'BRIEN,
All American Quarter,
1937.

L. B. HALE,
All American Tackle,
1937.

DERREL PALMER,
All American Center,
1943.

EIGHT ALL ALL-AMERICANS.

*Below :* "The Number One Team of the Nation," 1938.
No. 10, Johnny Hall ; 51, Connie Sparks ; 8, Davie O'brien ; 36, Earl Clark ; 25,
Durwood Horner ; 18, Allie White ; 38, Bud Taylor ; 48, Ki Aldrich ; 24, Forest Kline ;
22, I. B. Hale ; 30, Don Looney.

BEN MOULDEN,
Baseball, 1904.

LOUIS DRUCKE,
Baseball Pitcher, 1909.

CHESTER "Boob"
FOWLER, Baseball.

PETE DONOHUE,
Baseball Pitcher.

"BUSTER" BRANNON.
Basketball.

"DOC" SUMNER,
Basketball.

CY LELAND,
Track and Football.

MARSHALL BALDWIN,
Baseball

Some Stars from Baseball, Basketball and Track.

*Below:* THE STADIUM FILLED.

1912, returned in 1916 with his law degree from the University of Texas to become a Professor in the T. C. U. Law School, and Coach. It was under his leadership that the old troublesome tradition of class rushes and the April Fool "help yourself" holiday was broken up. He organized a Field Day on April first, set up many interesting contests between classes and groups, entertained the whole campus, and absorbed the overflowing energies of the students made restless by the coming spring. He made a most valuable contribution in personality, in character, and in, sportsmanship, foreshadowing his later leadership as an outstanding citizen in Breckenridge, as a trustee, well deserving the honor of the LL.D. degree conferred on him at the 1945 Commencement.

Heroes in football developed in these days too. All State men were: 1915, Captain Bryant Ware, and "Blue" Rattan (returned after his career in 1910) and John P. Cox; 1917, Bryan Miller (team was second in the Conference); 1918, Captain Bryan Miller, Will Hill Acker; 1920 (State Champions) Captain A. S. Douglas, Leo (Dutch) Meyer, Will Acker, Pete Fulcher; 1921, Blair Cherry, Melvin Bishop, Chester Fowler. Other prominent names during these years are: Howard Vaughn, Ralph Martin, Abe Greines, "Heine" Prinzing, Harold Sharpe, Jesse Martin, Scottie Rutherford, not to overlook the girl yell leader, Cobby de Stivers.[39]

About the last word spoken in this period was a message in the *Skiff* from a fan pleading that the Horned Frog was too pacific a beast to represent so ferocious a team; that the name should be changed. The reply was that a name comes to mean what you make it mean. The later history proved the editor right.[40]

During all of these years, baseball continued to have a warm place in the hearts of the students, although it drew smaller crowds than in former years. Popular was the name of Marshall ("Fuzzy") Baldwin, "who in 1910 was made Captain and Manager of the only undefeated college baseball team in Texas. He was selected as Coach for the 1911 baseball team."[41]

[39]The figures and names throughout this chapter up to 1934 are largely summarized from "The History of Football in T. C. U." a manuscript in the Library, being a Freshman Theme written by Paul Overton Ridings, who was mascot for the championship team of 1929, son of the Head of the Publicity Department of T. C. U.
[40]*Skiff*, January 28, 1922.
[41]Horned Frog, 1912, p. 161.

The professional baseball coach "Kid" Nance was engaged, and fitted in beautifully. Some names became famous on the campus and over the state: Reub Berry, Charles "Snake" Bassler, Howard Vaughn, "Hop" Tom Hopkins, Jim McKowan, as well as "Blue" Rattan. At least two from this period became famous nationally: Chester "Boob" Fowler had a long successful career with the Cincinnati Reds, and "Pete" Donohue was one of the outstanding pitchers with the National League.

The fourth period of athletic history, beginning with 1923, proved to be one of achievement, victories and great glory. Football came of age in T. C. U. in 1923 upon its admission to the Southwest Conference,[42] the employment of Madison Bell as Head Coach, Leo Meyer as Freshman Coach, L. C. Wright as Athletic Manager, and the honor of winning second place in the conference in its first year of membership. During the next twenty-two seasons it won four Conference Championships, whereas one-seventh of the times would be only three and one-seventh.

Its second season, 1924, also made a record: the cellar. It was quite outstanding, too, for it proved to be the first and last time the team has ever occupied that lowly place. The high spot of the 1925 series was the defeat of A. & M., the champions that year. It was our first time to defeat the Farmers in twenty-eight years; it was accomplished by a famous field goal from the toe of Johnny Washmon. Johnny was elected captain of the 1926 team, which tied Texas for third place. Harry Taylor was a brilliant safety man and quarter during this time.

The first nation-wide recognition was won in 1927 when Raymond "Rags" Matthews, rugged end, was chosen to play in the New Years' East-West Classic at San Francisco, and was mentioned on a few All-American teams. The captain that year was Jake Williams, who in later years became a player and a coach in professional football.

The season 1929 was one of great climaxes. Material and men had been accumulating for a good season, when the coach, "Matty" Bell was taken away suddenly and unceremoniously by A. & M. Gloom prevailed, but grit won. The Arkansas coach, Francis Schmidt, was employed, Raymond "Bear" Wolf who had just graduated, was selected as Assistant Coach, and with

---

[42]The Southwest Conference had been organized in 1914; T. C. U. was admitted December, 1922.

the leadership of "Mike" Brumbelow as Captain and Howard Grubbs as Quarter, and using the material trained by "Dutch" Meyer as Freshman Coach, the Conference Championship was won for the first time. Every game of the season was won, except the final with S. M. U., which was a tie. This was one of those games long remembered, how after the tie was cinched by the toe of Harlos Green and the fans yelled for a bold attack for another touchdown, Schmidt held the team to a tight defensive to the end, insuring a tie and the championship.

This 1929 game was notable, also, for being the last one played in the short-lived, steel-structured stadium known as Clark Field, erected in 1924 east of the Library. Its chief promoter had been Dan Rogers, alumnus and trustee, who was destined to play a major part in athletics in the state and nation in the later years. The money was borrowed, rapidly repaid out of the receipts, during the six years of its use, then the steel sold to a high school. This stadium was completely filled only once—that game just referred to, in 1929. But the championship fired the imagination of the Fort Worth fans. They were sure the time had arrived for a Big-Time Stadium. The idea was encouraged by the fact that in the new land recently purchased, lying west of the old campus, lay a valley which seemed designed by nature for a sunken stadium. Amon Carter got behind the move which assured it of success. The Trustees were careful to safeguard the interests of the University by seeing that the papers were drawn so that the property or the income of the school would not be entailed by the loan on the stadium.

The T. C. U. Stadium Association was incorporated, leasing the ground from the University Corporation (a subsidiary of the T. C. U. corporation), sold $150,000 first mortgage ten-year bonds at 6 per cent to the banks, then $200,000 second mortgage bonds to friends, bearing interest at 6 per cent after the first five years. The University contracted to conduct the athletic games, to retain full control over the operations, to pay 25 per cent of the gross receipts of home games, and 25 per cent of the net receipts of games away from home into the bank each season to cover the interest and sinking fund. To the original capital of $350,000, the University had to provide an additional $50,000 for fencing, gravelling, grading and such improvements.

The outcome of this financial venture—which may be here anticipated while the picture is before us—was far more successful than anyone could have dreamed at this time. Each year the interest and installments on the first mortgage bonds were paid. When the five years were up and interest on the second mortgages was to begin, no one requested it. In 1939 a letter was sent to each of the holders of the second mortgage bonds offering three choices: either donate the bond, or accept a new first mortgage bond in its place, provided the interest to date be waived, or receive cash for the face value, waiving all interest. Nearly everyone accepted the third alternative, rejoicing to receive back an investment which had been regarded generally as a donation.

The new stadium has not yet been named. It was built after the pattern of the Ohio State stadium. The base pillars are strong enough to support a balcony later if needed. The west side runs up sixty-one rows (one more than the S. M. U. stadium!). The east side runs only twenty, but has base enough for sixty-one and a balcony. The seating capacity at present is approximately 20,000, with movable bleachers available for expansion.*

It was dedicated on October 1, 1930 by a 40 to 0 victory over Arkansas, from which school the new coach, Francis Schmidt had just transferred, succeeding Matty Bell, who had gone to Texas A. & M. Whereby hangs a remarkable tale of coaches illustrating the adage that "truth is stranger than fiction." In 1925 T. C. U. beat A. & M. for the first time in twenty-eight years, then kept it up rather steadily. This was too much for the Farmers with their several thousand men against T. C. U.'s less than 500. "It must be the T. C. U. coach," they reasoned. So they enticed Bell from T. C. U. by a higher salary. Yet the winning streak of the little school continued: so A. & M. fired Bell—literally fired him. S. M. U. needed an assistant coach to Ray Morrison that year, so with the recommendation of T. C. U., Bell was engaged by S. M. U. Within a year Morrison was called to Vanderbilt, and Bell inherited the head coaching job and also a well prepared championship team, won the Conference championship and was voted the Outstanding Coach nationally. The uniqueness of this experience was recognized by an article in the *Saturday Evening Post*.

The last game of the 1930 season is memorable for Red Oliver's famous field-length return of the initial kick-off on the S. M. U. field that was muddy and the rain still falling. Red Oliver was fast, but not too quick at following signals. This play was prepared for his fleet foot, the blocking all laid out; he

*In 1947 the East side was enlarged raising the capacity by 6,000.

ran down the lane prepared for him, made the touchdown; the rain prevented any others. So the game was won on the first down.

The 1931 basket ball team won the championship under Schmidt, who was a specialist in this game. 1931 produced two All-Conference football men: Madison "Pap" Pruitt, and Johnny Vaught; the brilliant play of the latter at guard earned him all-American mention.

The second Conference championship was earned in 1932, T. C. U. beating every team it played except L. S. U., which it tied. Johnny Vaught won All-American place as guard, and the team was rated as fifth in the nation. Seven men were on the All-Conference team: Madison Pruitt, Ben Boswell, Johnny Vaught, Foster Howell, Lon Evans, J. W. Townsend and Blanard Spearmen. The spirits of the campus and the town were highly elated.

The limelight continued in 1933. Ben Boswell was selected to play in the All-Star Century of Progress game in Chicago; Charley Casper made the longest return of a kick-off in the nation, 105 yards, and led the conference in individual scoring. The all-conference winners were: Johnny Kitchen, Bud Taylor and Charley Casper; Jack Graves was Captain.

Intersectional football was begun by T. C. U. in 1934 (the year that Meyer became Head Coach) by defeating Loyola and Santa Clara. Darrel Lester, Center, made All-American. All-conference men were: Vic Montgomery, Darrell Lester, Judy Truelson, Willie Walls, Tilly Manton, and Walter Roach. The season of 1935, though missing the championship, was such a climactic one that everyone felt there could not follow a greater. The team was rated by Williamson's chart as the No. 1 Team of the Nation. All-American: L. D. "Little Dutch" Meyer, Tracy Kellow, Darrell Lester and Sam Baugh.

"The greatest game that every was" is the characterization given by many to the S. M. U.-T. C. U. game of 1935. The 20,000-capacity stadium that day held over 34,000 people. The top sportswriters from the nation were present. One of them wrote, "The game was played in the glorious golden sunshine that is advertised only by California and experienced only in Texas." They were calling it the Rose Bowl preview, for the winner would be invited to the Rose Bowl. The winning play by S. M. U. will never be forgotten by any who saw it. S. M. U. stopped on the T. C. U. 37 yard line, on fourth down called punt

271

formation—but didn't punt. They passed, instead. T. C. U. was caught by the surprise.

S. M. U.'s fleet Quarter, Bobby Wilson, ran down the field, got behind the T. C. U. safety man, caught the surprise pass and ran it for a touchdown. After that Sam Baugh, then a junior, went into a wonderful streak of passing, but the T. C. U. receivers were nervous and let the ball slip through their fingers. Jimmy Lawrence, "the most determined halfback who ever wore a Frog unie" (a Pop Boone expression), and Dutch Cline were carried out as casualties and Rex Clark got a broken leg.

"As most of you know, T. C. U. out-first-downed the Mustangs 25 to 17, outpassed them with 16 completions to S. M. U.'s 4, outgained 345 yards to 317, and out-kicked them, with an average of 48 yards compared to the Methodists' 41 yard average."[43] S. M. U. won, went to the Rose Bowl, and lost that game; T. C. U. went to the Sugar Bowl and, in a heavy rain, won the game by a baseball score of 3-2. The two was a safety by Baugh. The three was a 26-yard field goal by Tilly Manton. "The season gave T. C. U. more publicity than any amount of money could buy." And it made Sam Baugh the top passer of the nation, which he proved again and again in professional football in the later years.

When Sam Baugh finished his amateur football eligibility with the 1936 season, the great passing of the Horned Frogs was supposed to have ended. "Little Davey" O'Brien, to be sure, was "a promising passer, but too slight to become a great player." "Oh yeah," thought the crowd when they saw two heavy opponents rush him viciously in the open field, as if to end him there; both men were left lying on the ground, Davey came bouncing up with the ball in his arms. "Tough"! By the close of the 1938 season he had attained a fame that equaled Baugh's and won more trophies than any man had ever won, as the star of the T. C. U. Championship Team of 1938 and the No. 1 team of the nation with a record of 1.000.[44]

Regarded as the greatest passer in intercollegiate play and one of the best all-around performers on an Ameri-

---

[43]Loren McMullen in the Fort Worth Star-Telegram 11-20-45.
[44]Here is a summary of O'Brien's passing record:

| | Completions | Yds. | TD | Percentage |
|------|------------|------|-----|------------|
| 1936 | 21 | 252 | 2 | .525 |
| 1937 | 96 | 947 | 3 | .405 |
| 1938 | 110 | 1733 | 20 | .567 |

can gridiron, O'Brien was a unanimous choice for the mythical 'all' teams. He made the all-American elevens released by N. E. A., Life Magazine, Paramount, United Press, Associated Press, Eddie Dooley, New York Sun, International News Service, Collyer's Eye, Grantland Rice, All-American Board, Williamson's Ratings, and Kate Smith.[45]

The list of awards is so unusual and remarkable that it is surely worth recording. Those of national scope were: the Robert W. Maxwell Trophy, the Douglas Fairbanks Trophy, the Williamson Award, Christy Walsh's All-American Board gold football, the Detroit Yacht Club, the Walter Camp Trophy, and perhaps the greatest of all—the Heisman Trophy (won by 519 out of a possible 550 points). Southwestern recognition was expressed in the Houston Post Trophy (shared with Ki Aldrich) a gold football from the Sugar Bowl, a diamond-studded football from T. C. U., the coveted Dan D Rogers Trophy (the one he appreciated most), besides several plaques, blankets and sweaters. The occasion of the awarding of the Heisman Trophy was a highlight. It was a grand occasion in New York City, where he was accompanied by his teammates Ki Aldrich and I. B. Hale, his mother, Ella Keith O'Brien, and his uncle Boyd Keith, who, from his childhood had been his mentor, inspirer and counsellor. A very unusual honor was given Davy in the action of the Board of Trustees of T. C. U. in voting that the numeral 8 which he wore should be withdrawn from further use, and reserved for his record.[46]

Remarkable: throughout all this parade of honors, Davey remained unspoiled.

O'Brien was raised in the East Dallas Christian Church. He never indulged in drinking intoxicants, or in cursing or even in smoking. A beer company used a picture of him to advertise their product, intimating that he drank the beer. He sued for damages, and although he lost the suit on a technicality he let the world know where he stood.

"Little Davey" and "Big I. B. Hale," his pal, joined the F. B. I., in which there is no publicity.

[45]Horned Frog, 1939, p. 172.
[46]Minutes, 6-6-39.

"Champions do not repeat." The Teams of 1940, 1941 and 1942 could not rival the record of their famous predecessors. But they made creditable records and produced some notable players. Among these were: Dean Bagley, Wilbur Nix, Drummond Slover, Van Hall, Beecher Montgomery, Dee and Don Ezell, Don Looney and Clyde Flowers. The latter was Captain of the teams of 1943 and 1944, a 4F because of the loss of one eye.

Obviously, war conditions broke down the high quality of all college athletics. The coaches enlisted, mostly in the Naval Physical Education program. Only two were left, both of them beyond military age. The bulk of the football boys enlisted in the Marines. The Southwest Conference voted to permit the playing of Freshmen on the regular teams. The teams of 1942, 1943 and 1944 consisted of Freshmen, 4F's and boys under eighteen. Each team felt its inadequacy for contest, but it found the opponents under the same handicaps.

Under these circumstances the 1944 Horned Frogs surprised themselves and everyone else by winning the Conference championship. This automatically elected them to represent the Conference in the New Year's Day Cotton Bowl game. There they lost to Oklahoma A. & M. The 1945 team, with the help of several service veterans and the outstanding playing of several extra good men, made a record of .500 in the Conference.

The T. C. U. Horned Frogs, representing the school with the smallest student body in the Conference, have nevertheless, made the best record of any team of the Conference, over the long period. The following story, written by that reliable and energetic compiler of accurate statistics, J. Willard Ridings, head of the T. C. U. News Service, was spread by the press in general in 1944.

Fort Worth, Tex.—Football champions come and go annually, but Texas Christian University rolls along as the all-time champion of the Southwest Conference.

T. C. U. played its first year in the conference in 1923, and in the 22 completed seasons since has earned the best percentage of any school in the circuit.

Coach Dutch Meyer took the reins at Frogland with the opening of the 1934 season, and during his 11-year reign has likewise produced the best record in the conference.

T. C. U.'s Cotton Bowl encounter January 1 with Oklahoma A. & M. will be the fifth bowl appearance of a Meyer-coached eleven. His Horned Frogs defeated L. S. U. 3 to 2 in the 1936 Sugar Bowl; inaugurated the Cotton Bowl in 1937 with a 16 to 6 victory over Marquette; won from Carnegie Tech, 15 to 7, in the 1939 Sugar Bowl; and lost to the University of Georgia, 26 to 40, in the 1942 Orange Bowl.

During Meyer's 11-year regime, the Frogs have won the title twice, finished in second place four times, third once, fourth once, fifth twice, and sixth once.

The Southwest Conference standings for the 11-year period, 1934-44, inclusive:

| School | W. | L. | T. | Pct. |
|---|---|---|---|---|
| T. C. U. | 36 | 23 | 5 | .601 |
| A. & M. | 33 | 25 | 6 | .576 |
| S. M. U. | 33 | 28 | 3 | .539 |
| Texas | 32 | 30 | 2 | .516 |
| Rice | 31 | 29 | 4 | .516 |
| Baylor | 21 | 29 | 4 | .426 |
| Arkansas | 19 | 41 | 4 | .314 |

The conference standings for the 22-year period during which T. C. U. has been a member—1923-44, inclusive:

| School | W. | L. | T. | Pct. |
|---|---|---|---|---|
| T. C. U. | 68 | 40 | 12 | .617 |
| S. M. U. | 65 | 42 | 15 | .594 |
| Texas | 62 | 49 | 8 | .555 |
| A. & M. | 53 | 51 | 14 | .508 |
| Baylor | 43 | 55 | 13 | .446 |
| Arkansas | 42 | 64 | 6 | .402 |
| Rice | 45 | 69 | 5 | .390 |

What are the elements that have made this record possible? Certainly it was not what the critics usually surmise: easement on grades, commercialism or importation of players. There has not been any list of foreign names on the roster. During the thirties several Slavic names appeared on the campus, such as Zlatkovitch and Zeloski; but not a one of these was an athlete. All of the players were Texas boys, many of them from old T. C. U. families. O'Brien was pointed to T. C. U. from his childhood, as was I. B. Hale. Baugh came from Sweetwater. Grubbs was not a football player in high school, came to T. C. U. for science. These are fair samples. Some boys may have been allured by the speeches of "Dutch" Meyer at their high school banquets, and after the banquets, but it was probably the record of his coaching and the success of the coaches he turned out that persuaded them, rather than any inducements promised. Those were standard.

His policy has always been open. If a boy says, "I have such and such an offer from another school," his reply is "Boy, that's good, you'd better take it." For years the T. C. U. athlete was given a job to pay all expenses except about a hundred dollars a session. This was the limit under the Conference rules for T. C. U. with its $100 a semester tuition fee. The boys paid the $100 then, or later. Even Sam Baugh, whose prowess brought to T. C. U. much fame and some finance, came in, two years after graduation, and paid down his $400 with a smile and an expression of gratitude. Later the Conference, under the prodding of Professor McDiarmid equalized the opportunity among the member schools by allowing them to give a job and scholarship to pay all expenses—but no more. T. C. U. refrained from giving scholarships to athletes until the Conference made it regular. Then it was confined carefully to those who made a C average.

To the query often made, "How do you manage to get such good passers at T. C. U.?" the answer often is "We raise 'em." And there is something to that reply. The coaching is of high caliber, as the record of the high school coaches trained at T. C. U. reveals. The spirit of unity among the players and student body helps.

Not only do "we raise" players; "we raise" coaches also. The bulk of the coaching staff are T. C. U. graduates. After Schmidt went to Ohio State in 1934 and Meyer was promoted to Head Coach, the entire staff was of T. C. U. products. Meyer graduated in 1922 and after playing professional baseball in the summer and coaching Poly High in 1922-23, served as T. C. U. Freshman Coach from 1923 until he was promoted to Head Coach. That has something to tell about the quality of training the boys received. He taught fundamentals. Raymond "Bear" Wolf, from Jack County, B. A. '28, was line coach until he went to North Carolina U. as Head Coach. Howard Grubbs, B. S. '30, M. S. '31, major in Geology, was Athletic Manager and Assistant Coach and Scout after 1934 until the Navy call came. Lester "Brum" Brumbelow, witty Irishman, B. A. '31, was line coach until he enlisted in the Navy. Mack "Poss" Clark, B. A. '29, was Track Coach and assistant manager until the Army lured him. Walter Roach (B.S. '37) was Assistant Coach until his Navy enlistment. Othel (Abe) Martin (B.E. '32) joined the staff in 1944 and Clyde Flowers (B.A. '46) in 1946, keeping up the tradition. Such men, pals all, men of high character, imbued with the ideals of their alma mater, comrades with the administrative officers (including the business Manager L. C. "Pete" Wright, Captain two years, B.A. '09) have made for a spirit of camaraderie that is unusual. That spirit has been passed on to the players. Trainer Smith joined in this family spirit, alternately scolding and petting the boys to whom he was always devoted. The annual banquets at the Fort Worth Club have contributed much to this spirit. Herbert ("Hub") R. McQuillan, secured in 1941 as Basketball Coach, has fitted into this T. C. U. group splendidly and has made an excellent record, serving also as Scout and Assistant in Football. All of the coaches who went into Service returned in time to help in the 1945 season except Howard Grubbs, who returned later. Brumbelow in the spring of 1946 received a rousing appreciation dinner on the occasion of his retirement to go into business.

One factor that contributed richly to the T. C. U. spirit was the personality of E. W. McDiarmid, Professor of Philosophy, Tennis Coach and Chairman of the Athletic Council. For years he represented T. C. U. in the Southwest Conference and for several years served as its president gaining the respect and admiration of his fellows on the Council. His quiet, philosophical spirit and his unhesitating maintenance of fair play helped to build the desirable attitude in the entire group.

If the quality and quantity of the publicity has any contribution to make to the spirit of a team, surely the Horned Frogs owe some of their success to the "demon for statistics," as J. Willard Ridings is dubbed by his good friends, the Sportswriters. Knowing the players and the coaches intimately and gathering facts about them from the day of their arrival on the campus, he precedes the team by several days to every away-from-home game, where he supplies the local writers with all of the facts and figures they can use. His skill in writing and his friendly personality win the confidence and friendship of the newsmen, and gain him entrance to their columns. He is the hard-working Head of the Department of Journalism and of Publicity for the University.

If the name "T. C. U." is familiar to the multitudes from Maine to California, it is so, doubtless, by reason of the fame of the Horned Frog football team. This fact has given much concern to the administrative officers. After all, its mission is as an educational institution, and they believe it is fully worthy as such. In their public addresses, they often insist that "there are other great features in T. C. U. besides football." Those who come from the outside and feel the life of the institution, soon discover that the emphasis on athletics is quite normal, and that the educational and cultural phases are not neglected. One of these has written his impressions. Dr. C. F. Cheverton, a longtime college president and professor came in 1943 to join the T. C. U. faculty, as Professor of Old Testament. He is not himself athletic, and has only an average interest in sport. His impression will serve as a fair estimate of the situation.

Before coming as a teacher to Texas Christian University I had often heard of the wonderful football teams that the institution had developed. This, together with the fact that I had read almost nothing about the purpose of the school, had made me suspicious that its chief interest was to be found in the development of winning athletics teams, and the advantage that such teams could bring to their Alma Mater.

Imagine my surprise, after coming to the campus, to find that the consuming passion of the leaders of this great institution was not the production of outstanding physical giants but the development of scholarly, efficient, Christian men and women.

The evidence of such purpose is not entirely in the headlines of promotion material. It has come to me quietly and unostentatiously from behind the scenes of college life and administration.

He then enumerates six specific facts, easily observed in the life of the campus, to substantiate his conclusion. In this judgment is found one of the glories of athletics in T. C. U. The other is discovered in the careers of these athletes as men in life, clean, capable, honorable and serviceable.

At the conclusion of this chapter on athletics, the author assumes the privilege of two personal observations. One is a testimony. In the span of a half century through which he has known intimately the faculty members of T. C. U. he has known but one teacher who was definitely opposed to athletics. A few have been luke-warm in support—very few—almost all have been ardent fans. They have admired and encouraged "the boys" on the teams. On one occasion when the football team was being honored at a civic club luncheon, President Waits was called on to present Sammy Baugh, at the height of his popularity. The good president with facetious modesty did it this way: "That I, a mere college president, should present the great Baugh! Rather should I be quiet and quote: 'When the eagles are abroad, let the swallows take to cover.'"

The other word is an apology. It is offered to any athlete whose name has not been mentioned in this story. For many of them deserve praise for whom room could not be found. Perhaps the author is dreaming: "Tomorrow, I am just sure to meet face to face, the very man whose omission will make my face red."

ADD-RAN FACULTY 1901-02

Seated, from left: H. E. Luck, Frank Marshall,—?—, Col. A. C. Easley, J. B. Eskridge, E. C. Snow, —?—, Dura Brokaw Cockrell, E. R. Cockrell; seated in door: —?—, Mrs. E. C. Snow, Mamie Schafer, A. F. Armstrong, Martha K. Miller, —?—. Three on left and man on right standing —?—.

# The Evolution of the Curriculum and the Faculty

THE CHAPTER WILL TRACE THE TRENDS away from the pattern of the classic education as found, naturally, in the Add-Ran days, ever with an eye to the currents in American education of which T. C. U. is a part and to which it has done its due share of contributing.

The Preparatory Department was a very prominent part of the typical college at the turn of the century, and the most prominent fact about it was its complete disappearance within the first third of the century. Its frequent title, "The Academy," bore something of the aura of the ancient classic Greece and was the title often used for college in a previous generation. Its importance in T. C. U. may be seen in the fact that until 1910 its enrollment was larger than that of the College of Arts and Sciences, and constituted more than a third of the total.[1] The cause of its rapid decline was the steady increase in quantity and quality of the high schools, climaxed by the Texas statute which provided that any student of high school age whose district did not provide a high school might attend one near-by by having his scholastic appropriation transferred. The influence of the college associations hastened it also by requiring the rigid separation of the preparatory school from the college, and encouraging the elimination of the former. T. C. U. reached this stage of progress in 1921, one year before admission into the Southern Association. This sharp distinction brought to attention the admission requirements into college. The Carnegie units, now so familiar, appeared in the T. C. U. catalog for the first time in 1909. Then, full admission required 14 units, con-

---

[1]The percentage which each division had of the whole attendance is shown:

|  | 03-04 | 04-05 | 12-13 | 18-19 | 20-21 |
|---|---|---|---|---|---|
| College of Arts and Sciences | 21 | 24 | 50 | 74 | 70 |
| College of Fine Arts and Bible | 44 | 33 | 30 | 14 | 13 |
| Preparatory Department | 35 | 43 | 20 | 12 | 17 |

ditional, 12½. By 1918 14½ were required and the announcement made that "After June 1, 1919, 15 units will be required," and there would be no conditional entrance.

The leading teacher in the Academy from 1902-1907 was W. T. Hamner, that beloved bachelor who taught English and gave his time and heart to the supervision of the boys in the dormitory. He served first from 1897 through 1900, then again 1902 until 1907. After that he became instructor in English in the College, still in charge of the boys. Along with him in 1904-1906 was Lee Clark, eldest son of Randolph Clark. He taught History and was Principal of the Academy. His loyalty to the old school was always hearty, but his large family required a larger income than the school could afford him. Professor Charles H. Roberts served as the very efficient principal of the Academy and teacher of history from 1910 until its close in 1921, when he was promoted to the headship of the Department of History in the College.

In the Add-Ran days all sciences were taught by one professor, "the grand old man of science," W. B. Parks, who continued as the Head of Chemistry and Physics until he retired in 1916.* From this one department have branched out Biology and Geology in 1904 and Physics in 1919, each one enlarging its staff until by 1945 there were fourteen teachers of the sciences three in Chemistry, five in Biology and Geology and three in Physics, besides four part-time instructors, and many laboratory assistants.

After Professor Parks' resignation in 1916, Professor John R. McClung succeeded him for three years. Then came the permanent teacher of Chemistry, F. Woodall Hogan, on whom poliomyelitis had set its mark—in vain. His keen brain was the keener, and his self-reliant spirit was ever obvious in the skill with which he manipulated his crutches and his withered, steel-encased legs, rejecting any thought of assistance. When the Burnett money was received and the plans were made for graduate work, a teacher with a Ph.D. degree was added, the head of the department, Dr. J. L. Whitman.[2] Dr. Whitman was a man of quiet demeanor, an active church man, highly efficient as a scientist, with wider interests of culture. He enjoyed good music, sang in the church choir, and counseled all of his majors to take a course in public speaking.

*A. F. Armstrong headed the Sciences 1901-05.
[2]1928-45, d. 11-30-45.

The first of the sciences to branch off to its own department was Biology in 1904, when Professor J. F. Anderson was called as vice-president and professor of Biology. He was a popular, friendly teacher, inspiring young men with a love for the science. His time was occupied as Business Manager so much that he could offer only elementary courses and relied more than he liked on assistants. After Miss Willie Birge served one year, 1912-13, there came, in 1913, a modest appearing young man who really put Biology and Geology on the map in T. C. U., and put T. C. U. on the map in the world of those sciences. Will M. Winton, with a Master's degree and much work on his doctor's degree at Rice Institute, became so absorbed in his creative work of surveying North Texas for the basic Geology maps, that he never took time off to complete his doctorate, but by his printed researches he won the recognition as a Fellow in the American Academy of Science, which he prized more than the degree. These surveys were published by the Bureau of Economic Geology of the State of Texas in conjunction with the University of Texas, and became the foundation of the geological work that lay back of much of the petroleum development in north and west Texas. Professor Winton's rating in the world of science was discovered one time when a Fort Worth citizen wrote to Harvard University for some technical information on Texas geology. The Harvard geologists replied: "Why write us? Your neighbor Professor W. M. Winton knows all about it. Ask him."

His wife, Hortense Winton, without any college degree, has worked by his side as curator of the Geological Museum and instructor in Biology and Botany, mothered the boys who aspired, and has added much worth to the Department.

If a teacher may be measured by the quantity and quality of scholarly careers he inspires, Professor Winton's measurement will be truly large. The carefulness of the plans in preparing young scientists is illustrated in the case of Gayle Scott, the first one of the group. He received his B.S. in 1917, just in time to enter the Army and serve as an officer (for which he received some medals of distinction). After the war he completed his master's degree in 1920, taught awhile, then went to the University of Grenoble, France. This University was chosen because the world's greatest specialist in cretaceous geology was there, and cretaceous is characteristic of the Texas formations. He received his Dr. es Sc. in 1925, returned, and has had, besides his career as professor on the faculty, distinguished service in the National Geological Society as editor of its magazine. Seven others of these Ph.D's returned to the T. C. U. faculty.[3]

Physics, so long subjoined to Chemistry, was given more attention by Professor Norris in 1919-1921, but it was not until 1924 that it got its real opportunity for full growth. That year came Professor Newton Gaines, with a sentiment in his soul also for art and Southwest folk-lore, who has devoted his time and zeal untiringly to building up Physics in T. C. U. With diligence and dogged determination he has collected apparatus, buying to the limit of the budget, securing more second-hand and remaking it, until the laboratory has become quite extensive. By 1928, Physics was a separate department, offering a major. By 1931, Professor Gaines had attained his Doctor's degree. In 1941, came Dr. Joseph Morgan, a specialist in Electronics, just in time to be of great usefulness in training for the war and war industries. For inasmuch as this was "a physicist's war," this department was called upon heavily for teaching during the war period. This department is to be credited with the production of several scholars in the field, who went on to the doctor's degree and careers in science. Dr. Gaines, despite this heavy load of teaching, has produced as a scientist, having worked out a suggestion into practical application on the use of super-sonic sound waves in the treatment of bacteria, in connection with Dr. Leslie Chambers of the Biology Department.

Naturally these departments all have made a contribution to the training of physicians through the premedical courses. In order to keep the standard high a rule was adopted that no student would be recommended to a medical college unless he had made as high as B in Biology and C in Chemistry. A combination course for the premedic was announced in 1918. Two years in T. C. U., prescribed, and an M. D. degree would entitle the student to the B.S. degree from T. C. U. In 1921 this was changed to three years in T. C. U. and one year of the medical course.

---

[3]The following are eighteen, with the University where they earned the Ph. D.: J. Shirley Sweeney (Hopkins, also M. D.), Carl R. Doering (Hopkins), Gayle Scott (Grenoble), Ivan Alexander (Princeton), Walter More-man (Kansas), Samuel E. Hill (Princeton), Ben H. Hill (Michigan), Leslie Chambers (Princeton), Willis G. Hewatt (Stanford), Jerome Smiser (Princeton), Leo Hendricks (Texas), John Forsythe (Princeton), Frank E. Lozo (Princeton), Frank Council (Army Grad. Medical School, also Gorgas Medal), Clyde Arnspiger (Columbia), John Sandidge (Hopkins), Lloyd Arnold (D. Sc. in a Chicago School), David Nichol (Stanford).

The student was always urged, by catalog and conferences, to complete the bachelor's degree before entering medical college, and this became the prevailing pattern until the wartime.

A definite contribution to the raising of the level of preparation in the field of medicine was made in 1939 by the inauguration of a degree course in Medical Technology under the leadership of Dr. J. J. Andujar, and in conjunction with the Harris Memorial Methodist Hospital, where he is director of laboratories. Three years in the Liberal Arts College and twelve months in the Technological School at the Hospital earned a B.S. degree. This was done in harmony with the standards of the National Association of Medical Technologists. T. C. U. is one of the early schools to adopt this plan. The W. K. Kellogg Foundation has recognized its worth by providing several scholarships for the students. A similar plan was adopted in 1939 for the profession of nursing. In 1946 Dr. Charles H. Harris announced an endowment for the Harris School of Nursing as a part of Texas Christian University, providing a five year curriculum in the University and the School of Nursing combined, leading to both the R.N. and B.S.

That a college is a part of the whole world and must use the common language is illustrated by the history of the Bachelor of Science degree in T. C. U. The departments of the Natural Sciences took some pride in making the degree a worthy one, requiring one year, each, of the four sciences, and mathematics, and two years of one modern language, besides a major and minor in each of two sciences. This degree called Bachelor of Science really signified preparation in the field of science. But other colleges, especially the teachers colleges, were awarding a Bachelor of Science degree to a host of students with majors in the subject of Education, with very little science, and no foreign language. It was generally rated as a much easier degree. The public was coming to think of a B.S. as a major in Education or some other semi-professional field. The B.S. thereby lost its prestige. So in 1935, it was announced:[4]

Before, the B.S. had been reserved for majors in the natural sciences, which it is maintained, is the more consistent term. The practice of using the B.S. for the semi-professional major, however, is so general, that the institution is constrained to adopt it for the sake of clarity. Majors in science will receive the B.A.

[4]T. C. U. Catalog, 1935, p. 20.

Mathematics, an integral part of the old classic curriculum, held its own during the period of the expansion of the sciences. The advanced courses were taken largely by science students, while the enrollment bulked large in the freshman year, for that much was required for the B.A. or the B.S. degree. It was around this point of requiring Mathematics for a degree that a faculty battle swirled for several years. It came to a head in a compromise in 1927-28: three semester hours instead of six were required. This was unsatisfactory; the student got enough to be worried and not enough to be much benefited. Another compromise was tried during two sessions, 1930-32: six hours were required, but substitutes were accepted from Greek or Latin, or Logic, or an additional year of Physics or Chemistry. The effect of this was the sudden swelling of the enrollment in Logic, and the recognition by the faculty that this make-shift plan had no reason on which to stand; it was abandoned, and Mathematics was made optional for the B.A. degree. The result was fewer puzzled, misfit students, and more happy mathematics teachers. The classes drew the interested and somewhat capable students, only, and were more successful. When the stress was put on mathematics by the demands of war training, the classes were overflowing.

The course content of freshman Mathematics was rearranged in 1932 better to adapt it to the needs of the several objectives of the students. A course in Mathematical Analysis was offered for those who were to major in the sciences, and a separate course, with problems in the field of finance, was arranged for majors in commerce and the social sciences. This nice arrangement was somewhat confused during the stress of war training, but only temporarily.

The personnel of the Mathematics faculty has been a steady, capable one through the years. When E. C. Snow retired in 1908, he was succeeded by a son of old Add-Ran, C. I. Alexander (known in the athletics as "Big Alex," for he was a stubborn guard) who made "Math." clear and attractive for a decade, until his all-too-early death in 1919. "Dependable" should have been his middle name: he was the soul of honor, inspiring confidence always. After an interim under A. J. Hargett (1920-27), assisted by E. R. Tucker (1920-32), who was also Registrar after 1924, there came the present head, Charles R. Sherer, under whose leadership the department has maintained its steady place, and has expanded in staff and in influence. Professor Sherer has been of unusual value on the faculty in administrative capacity, especially in personnel work and as a leader in the Student Christian Association. During the year 1945-46 he was used by the Army in the Army University in Biarritz, France. Miss Elizabeth Shelburne, after her outstanding service at Carr Burdette College,[5] returned to T. C. U. in 1929 on the Mathematics staff, where she has been a dependable factor ever since. Even after becoming Dean of Women in 1937, she has usually carried at least one section of teaching.

An experiment in Engineering education was undertaken by this Department in 1937, offering the first two years only. Many parents pleaded for it, on the grounds "my son is a born engineer, he's always taking his toys to pieces to see how they are made." After trying it for two years its was found that the majority of those boys lost interest in engineering when it came to measuring the "toys" by strict mathematics. Only two out of the first class of twenty went on to an engineering school. Professor L. W. Ramsey, who taught these classes, was called back in 1940 to establish elementary engineering classes (two years only) again, under the stress of the war program.

The social sciences have matched the physical sciences in their increase in enrollment and spread of subjects. Out of the single Department of "History and Political (or Social) Sciences" as it was in 1900, have issued four separate departments, Government, History, Economics and Sociology, each offering a major, and a long list of courses, together using nine full-time teachers, besides several part-time instructors. This process of expansion has developed under the continuous leadership of two strong personalities through forty-six years, and one of them is still active. Egbert R. Cockrell, fresh from graduation at Drake University, came in 1899 as the Head of History and Political Sciences, continuing on the faculty until 1921, with two periods off for study.[6] One of these was 1903-06, when the subjects were taught by Professor Walter Lee Ross. The other was a year's leave (1911-12), which he spent in England. In 1914, History branched off into a separate Department, taught by a younger man, M. M. Knight, but still under the supervision of Professor Cockrell.

The other personality of leadership in the social sciences was Dr. John Lord, who joined the faculty in 1920 as Professor of

[5] See Chapter XXV.
[6] For a summary of his career see Chapter XV, last page.

286

Spanish, for he had served as a missionary in the Philippines, being compelled to return on account of his wife's heart condition. He had prepared himself, however, in the field of Government, so when Professor Cockrell resigned in 1921 to become the Mayor of the City of Fort Worth, Dr. Lord was appointed as Head of the department.

A few courses in Economics, Government and Sociology had been offered all along in the combined Department, but in 1920 a separate Department of Economics and Sociology was begun, and continued for several years, taught by a succession of teachers, but all the while under the general chairmanship of Dr. Lord. Meanwhile, he was raising up younger men to take over a portion of the work. Among these was Edwin A. Elliott, who had interrupted his college career for a term of service in World War I, had returned and served as Dean of Men, while yet a student, and had graduated in 1923. He became Assistant Professor of Economics in 1924, and the Head of the Department of Economics in 1930, having in the meantime secured his Ph.D. degree from the University of Texas. Having enthusiastically espoused the cause of Labor, he resigned in 1934 to go into Government service, becoming later the Regional Director of the National Labor Relations Board. The Economics Department continues in strength under its Head, Dr. Herbert R. Mundhenke. It serves also the School of Business.

Sociology was made a separate department in 1929, but failed to find a continuous Head until the coming of Dr. Austin Porterfield in 1937. He is a minister, a Ph.D. from Duke University, and interprets sociology from a constructive Christian point of view. He is therefore free from the overemphasis on materialism that characterizes so many sociologists.

Under Dr. Porterfield's leadership, this department has offered numerous courses in applied sociology and social service work, often taught in the Evening College by specialists who are engaged in the professional work in the city. This has included several from the United States Hospital in Fort Worth.

Meanwhile, History, after being taught as a Department by a series of younger men, found its genuine leader in 1920 when Professor Charles H. Roberts was promoted from the place of principal of the Academy to Head of the History Department. He was a painstaking, methodical scholar, full of historical data, demanding much work of his students and inspiring the better ones to a love of history. He was somewhat of a pioneer. He prepared and taught courses in Latin American History, the second to be offered in Texas colleges, the University of Texas being the first. He initiated courses in the Near East and the Far East, as early as 1920, long before most people had sensed the growing importance of these regions. He literally wore himself out by his steady application to study, and died in 1933. He, too, had raised up younger men to succeed him. W. J. Hammond, another veteran of World War I, returned in a daze, finally found himself through the love of the study of History, under Professor Roberts, followed up his graduate degrees, and became an instructor and finally in 1934 the Head of the Department. Another devoted pupil of Professor Roberts was Allen True, who also attained the doctorate and became an Associate Professor of History, making a very attractive teacher until the O.P.A. called him into war service in 1943.

These two young professors, discovering along with some of their associates and the students, that the required freshman course in European History was too much of a repetition of the high school course in the same field, devised, by several years of trial and study, an orientation course in Social Science, which has become a standard, required freshmen course. It is a survey, building a background for all of the social sciences. It is now taught by Mrs. Mirth Sherer and Professor Ralph Garrett and others. This Orientation course was the expression of a general trend among the alert colleges.

While the world was still shocked at the revelation of the terrible power of the atomic bomb, a senator is reported to have made a plea on the floor of the Senate for a "moratorium on modern skill until our consciences can catch up." Perhaps the rapidly expanding social sciences might have helped in this dilemma, if they had followed less slavishly the technique of the physical sciences, and had given more consideration to the spiritual nature of mankind. To charge the social science field with such a responsibility might require the inclusion of ethics and religion within its scope. Texas Christian University has endeavored to discharge its responsibility as a Christian institution, among other means, by building the teaching of religion, especially the Bible, into the pattern of education it offers. With varying details, practically one course out of twenty has been required in Bible or religion. The aim has been to give the student a survey of the history contained in the Bible, and to interpret the great ethical principles of the Christian religion without sectarian bias.

There has been very little objection on the part of any student to taking these courses. Even those who enter them unwillingly or with little enthusiasm most often find them attractive after a little while. Up to about 1916, the requirement was usually applied in the junior or senior year, hence the classes were small. Then some of the classes were graded to the sophomore level, and even the freshman, and the student was expected to take it in those years. The classes became very large. In 1927-29, while three hours of Mathematics was the requirement, making a half year course, Bible was put in as the other half of the year, and the enrollment included practically every freshman.

In addition to these Bible classes required of every student, there was the extensive offering of Bible courses for the ministerial students, available as electives by others. The presence on the faculty of scholars of much merit for the advanced ministerial students gave the usual student the benefit of outstanding teachers in this field. Through the years, this group included such scholars as President Zollars, G. A. Llewellyn, Dr. Clinton Lockhart, President Frederick D. Kershner, Colby D. Hall, F. E. Billington, C. McPherson, H. L. Pickerill, S. W. Hutton, W. C. Morro,[7] and in the later years a group of younger scholars for shorter periods. Later these classes have been taught by Professor Clarence A. Burch, a returned missionary from China; Dr. Fred West, '44-'46; Dr. W. L. Reed, and several teaching fellows. Beginning with the session of 1947-48 Dr. C. F. Cheverton is the Head of this Department of Religion, having proved to have unusual ability in the art of presenting the Bible clearly and popularly.

A notable change has occurred in the educational world in the matter of acceptance of credits in Bible in transfer. In the early years of the century it was not uncommon for such credits to be declined, by state universities, especially. More lately, it is a rare occurrence that any Bible credit is questioned. The change has come about by at least two influences. Most of the colleges which teach the Bible in courses have been careful to make them non-partisan and scholarly. T. C. U. has always held this ideal up, and backed it by the fact of having teachers of genuine scholarship. The other influence is the development of "Bible Chairs" on the campuses of state universities. The Disciples of Christ can take some satisfaction in having pioneered in this field. The first several of such Chairs were promoted and supported by

[7]A fuller account of the Bible teaching is given in Chapter XX.

their missionary society, known as the Christian Woman's Board of Missions. These were established in the State Universities of Michigan (1893), Kansas (1901), Texas (1904), and Virginia (1906). The one in Texas was especially influential. Dr. Frank L. Jewett began teaching there in 1905 and retired in 1946. His work was on a scholarly basis, was recognized for credit, and was followed by the establishment of a Chair by about a dozen of the large religious bodies. Dr. Jewett was succeeded by a T. C. U. graduate, Dr. Paul Wassenich.

With the picture in mind of the one Science Department developing into four, and a like process for the Social Sciences, in addition to the growing stress on the semi-professional curricula, which will follow, there need be no further explanation of the decline of enrollment and interest in the classical languages and literatures. And decline there was. Professor James B. Eskridge. joined the faculty in 1898 as the Head of the Department of Latin and Greek, and resigned in 1912 as Professor of Latin. His classes became smaller and smaller. For two years his successor, his former pupil, Colby D. Hall, served as the Head of the Latin Department with classes in three years of Latin (one student even majored in it). This was a temporary arrangement; he had come with the understanding that he would teach only Bible after two years. After 1914, the teaching of Latin fell to one of the instructors in English, at first Miss Eula Burton Phares (Mrs. Charles Mohle), then to Mrs. Artemisia Bryson. These ladies were eager Latin scholars, but the classes did not materialize. The last Latin class taught was about 1916.

Greek remained in the active list by reason of the ministerial students. Dr. Clinton Lockhart through the years has stood out as a classic linguist, taking great delight in giving his time to even one student who would follow him in one or more of the rare Semitic tongues, in addition to the Greek.[8]

From this story, it becomes quite obvious that the classic languages and literature, rather than being neglected, were pushed out of the curriculum by the swelling intrusion of multiplying fields in the physical and social sciences. An effort is being made in 1945 by President Sadler, who is himself an excellent Latin scholar, to revive the study of Latin and classic Greek by having a classic professor on the faculty. There were classes in both fields in 1945-47.

[8]For more details see Chapter XX.

With the decline of the classic languages came the rise of the modern. At first it was German, made popular in the years 1906-09 by the attractive teacher Orie W. Long, who organized a Deutsche Verein and had the girls and boys garbling the "Deutsch" all about the campus. French was not so popular but was coming. Spanish had not yet hit its stride. Mrs. M. L. Sargeant, in Fort Worth in 1910-17, a native German, was a skillful teacher, and made German popular again. World War I put a stop to that. German was available without intermission, despite prejudices, but for about three years no one chose it. Then the sciences began to require and advise it. It picked up, but only for the first two years of the language.

German was seldom taught in the Texas high schools, French in a very few, but practically every one of them offered Spanish. The proximity to Mexico, also, and the familiarity of many students from the border with the Spanish tongue, all conspired to make it the most popular choice. Miss Eula Lee Carter, having lived in Cuba and having taught in the Fort Worth high schools, came on the faculty in 1924, and still teaching, has manifested an unusual devotion to Spanish and has built up the attendance in the department.

French grew in popularity despite the circumstances. Science majors were advised, English majors were encouraged, to take it, and many lovers of literature were attracted to it. Dr. Josiah H. Combs came in 1927 as Head of the Modern Language Department.* He had lived in France for some years, had married a charming French wife, had edited several French texts, thus bringing prestige to the department. Several instructors and assistant professors have taught French from time to time. The latest one, Bita May Hall, with her unusually high scholastic record and a year of study in the University of Toulouse, France, has added attractiveness to the study of French. On the request of Professor Sammis and Dean McCorkle, she has taught a course for music students, in the pronunciation and interpretation of foreign phrases used in music.

The coming of the new Dean of the Add-Ran College of Arts and Sciences in 1943 brought attractiveness to the Department of Foreign Languages, for Dean Jerome Moore (B.A. '23, M.A. '27) had majored in Spanish for his doctorate in the University of Pennsylvania (Ph.D. '37) and had been serving as the Head of Spanish in Texas State College for Women. He has estab-

*Dr. Combs resigned in Sept. 1947.

lished connections with leaders in Mexico and other Latin-American states and has arranged some exchange scholarships with those countries.

The expanding influence of World War II can be observed in the increased offering of Spanish (especially in the Evening College, for conversational Spanish), the offering of a course in Russian, and in 1946 a course in Portuguese. The latter is taught by Dr. Eunice Gates (1946-), who lived in Brazil for a number of years. The teachers in Modern Languages are alert to welcome the freshened interest in the foreign tongues that will increase with our new "One World."

Do the newer semi-professional degrees and majors represent an improvement or a retrogression in education? This is a question much debated within and without the college faculties. No doubt a much broader cultural education will be developed in the future and be utilized profitably by those who are apt for it. But it is believed that the rise of these so-called semi-professional degrees marks thus far a definite elevation of the training for the professional careers. Let us look into the details of the story as it has unfolded in T. C. U. in the first half of the century, and see the facts in the case. This study applies especially to the fields of Pedagogy, Fine Arts and Business.

The teaching profession received more of the graduates of Add-Ran, perhaps, than any other calling, yet the first effort to teach the science of Pedagogy was "The Normal College" in 1904, which, as its name implies, stressed the reviewing of the subjects to be taught in the public schools. It was quite in harmony with this view of teacher-training that the faculty of the "Normal College" was exactly the same as that of the Preparatory Department. These were W. T. Hamner, for English, Lee Clark, for History, and A. C. Elliott, the Principal, the latter serving just one year. Education became a department of the Add-Ran College of Arts and Sciences in 1909, and it was announced that "the A.B. diploma with a prescribed course in the Department of Education entitles the holder to a Permanent State Certificate." The first head of this department was John W. Kinsey, B.A., of the Add-Ran class of 1900, an experienced public school administrator, who took pride in the new field of teaching, and built it up with much energy. Mrs. Kinsey taught mathematics in the Academy. Together, they were devoted to the school, where they continued to teach until 1915.

A definite scientific basis was attained in 1915 by the transferring of Professor W. H. Batson from the chair of Philosophy and

Psychology to that of Education. He was well on his way to the Ph.D. degree in the University of Michigan, a capable scholar and a serious student of pedagogy. Education under him was reckoned as a "hard" subject. After two years Professor E. C. Wilson, a devotee of G. Stanley Hall's psychology, served as the Head from 1917-19. Then came the leader, Raymond A. Smith, who put the department on a permanent basis. Coming in 1920 from the presidency of Atlantic Christian College at Wilson, North Carolina, a good teacher, an omnivorous reader, a lover of books and a friend of people, he has devoted himself and his library to the joyous task of raising up teachers for Texas schools, and still continues. Through the years 1928-1935, he was assisted by Professor Franklin G. Jones, one of the old time Add-Ran products, in person and in spirit, who served as Professor of Secondary Education. Other good helpers served shorter terms, Professor Burl A. Crouch, versatile, cheery, and practical, serving since 1928. Dr. Sandy A. Wall (B.A. '35, M.A. '37, Ph.D., U. of Texas '44) came on the faculty in 1944.

The Department was recognized in the catalog as the "School of Education" in 1924, having three teachers devoted to it exclusively and a dozen other departments giving courses that counted toward certification. In 1943, the title was changed from Professor to Dean Smith. The advancing requirements for certification of public school teachers pressed them into summer terms and evening classes. Out of this came the nucleus for the Evening College, and the large portion of candidates for the Master's degrees.

Prior to the erection of the Gymnasium in 1921, physical training, required of the girls in the dormitories, was directed at times by an assistant in Oratory; the boys got what they could by organized play under the encouragement of the busy coaches. As soon as the Gymnasium became available, classes were started in Physical Training required of all freshmen and sophomores, boys and girls, three hours a week, for the general purpose of health and exercise. This work was directed, usually, by advanced students under the general supervision of the Director of Athletics, until degree teachers were employed and credit courses were initiated. For the women, this was in 1926 with the coming of Mrs. Helen Walker Murphy (1926-45), and for the men, Walter Knox in 1929 (1929-34), followed by Tom Prouse in 1934 (1934-). In addition to the three hours a week by all underclassmen, without credit, the credit courses have been used to train leaders of Physical Education for the public schools. During the war days, Mr. Prouse did valiant service in the exacting Physical Training program required by the Navy. In 1946 another T. C. U. graduate, Miss Kitty Wingo, succeeded Mrs. Murphy, who retired. A degree of Bachelor of Science in Physical Education has been granted to many young men and young women who have served in this new field with distinction. The coaches have had an important part in this teaching program. The program has had much to do with raising the standard of coaches from the brawn to the brain measurement. What a change from the frontier days when play was rated as a waste of time!

So this is what these semi-professional degrees in Education have accomplished: in 1908, a review of high school subjects for an examination (for elementary teachers as well); within thirty years a four-year college curriculum, including the technique of teaching differentiated for the elementary and secondary, with a goodly number taking also the Master's degree. This is gain! This is progress! There are higher levels to be attained, to be sure, but credit should be allowed for the contribution of this period, whatever the weaknesses and deficiencies yet to be cured.

The field of training for business has witnessed an even more striking and rapid rise in the level of preparation. The old "C. O. B." (College of Business), one of the most popular, populous and successful departments, under the aegis of A. C. Easley, was little more than a business college with the added cultural contacts of the college campus, and the opportunity to elect some college subjects on the side. This pattern continued, under J. A. Dacus (1905-19, intermittently, J. J. Hart (1908-10), Patrick Henry (1914-15), H. L. Barber (1917-18)—he later served in the Business Office. Then in 1921 a two year curriculum was announced in Business Administration, with the suggestion that, by two additional years elsewhere, a degree of Bachelor of Business Administration could be earned. It was further announced that "Arrangements are completed for a full Department of Business Administration to begin September, 1922." Begin it did, under the inspiring leadership of J. W. Ballard, and progress it did, answering the demand for the training of the business man on a level to that of the professional man. When Mr. Ballard was lured into Government service in 1935, he was succeeded by Dr. A. L. Boeck (1935-43), thus bringing into the teaching of Business a teacher with a doctor's degree. This precedent was followed, on Dr. Boeck's release for Government service with the O. P. A., by securing a practical business man who had acquired his doctor's degree in Commerce at the University of Texas, Dr. Ellis M. Sowell (1944-).

The old "C. O. B." course, with or without high school graduation, required one year of practical subjects, bookkeeping, stenography, typing, etc., all with commendable thoroughness, but all technical and elementary. The new curriculum requires graduation from high school as a base, has the same spread of "required subjects" as the B.A. degree, except for foreign language, affords majors and minors in Economics, Finance, Accounting, Management, or Secretarial Science, demands four years of residence, and grants the degree of Bachelor of Science in Commerce. This is progress! The day may come when the business man will get a broad cultural education; today he is getting a much broader one than his fathers received.

Into the field of Fine Arts, also, the semi-professional degree has entered. A study of the changes made in the teaching therein is very illuminating; the effects of the changes are quite noteworthy. A general characteristic of the teaching of the Fine Arts during the nineteenth century was that they were taught in women's schools and were taboo in men's colleges. Gradually they crept into the curriculum of the pioneering, co-education colleges such as Add-Ran, but always as "specials." The curricula were rigidly separate; no credit was given toward the degree; only a Diploma was awarded.[9] This attitude of holding the arts outside the regular curriculum prevailed throughout the first two decades of the twentieth century. Most of the students in the arts were taught by private teachers, in their home towns; only those of unusual promise (or wealth) went away from home to study music. And they were girls; it required a deal of determination for a boy to specialize in music. The teachers were prepared, for the most part, in the Conservatory style, with emphasis on skill in performance, with little attention given to theory, and almost no time given to general cultural subjects. Rarely did the teachers of the Fine Arts on College faculties have college degrees. The first in T. C. U. were in 1923. They were H. D. Guelich, B.A., B.M., Professor of Piano and Director, and Bernice Carleton, B.M., Violin. All of the teaching then was done by private lessons, charging separate tuition for each subject; even theory was taught in this fashion. In the teaching, skill of

[9]See Chapter VI.

performance was emphasized; theory was usually touched rather lightly.

It is obvious, therefore, that the tardiness of recognition of music for credit was due to more than mere tradition and had some justification. Musicians were not trained in a college pattern. There was no standard by which a course in music could be measured and thereby compared or transferred. The teachers were too generously inclined in their grading; most of them never used any letter below B. This by itself put them in a separate category, in the minds of competing students. Such was the force of all of these influences combined that the colleges in general were slow to admit the Fine Arts to the same category as the Liberal Arts. The University of Texas, for instance, declined to offer any course in Music or Art, or even to accept credits in transfer in these subjects, until in the 1930's.[10]

In T. C. U. the first gesture toward crediting music was in 1910 when it became possible for a student to accumulate up to 15 term hours (10 semester hours) of credit toward the B.A. degree. This was available only to those who achieved graduation. By 1920 this amount had been raised to 20 term hours. In 1922, the student who had gained the Diploma in Music was invited to continue for the B.A. degree by the statement that "a student completing the above (the Diploma requirements) will have from 87 to 117 (term) hours toward a degree, depending on the choice of electives."[11] The Bachelor of Music degree was offered in 1924, for a four year curriculum, providing that 18 of the 33 electives be chosen from the College of Arts and Sciences. If the student chose his electives properly, he could complete both the B.A. and the B.M. in five college years. The B.M. was withdrawn in 1932, because of complications at the time, and the B.A. with a major in Music was offered instead. The Bachelor of Music was classified by the Southern Association as a professional degree. The faculty was convinced that four years was too short a time to train a high school graduate into a professional musician. The American Association of Schools of Music required, for the B.M., 90 semester hours of music, allowing only 30 in other fields. The faculty was unwilling to grant a Bachelor's degree with only 30 hours (one college year), of general cultural

[10]The School of Fine Arts of the University of Texas was established by Act of the Legislature in May, 1937—U. of T. Catalog 1944, p. 12.
[11]The degree then required 180 term hours; the plan was changed in 1925 to semester hours, requiring 120.

subjects; moreover, the American Association of University Women declined to recognize any Bachelor's degree that did not show as much as 60 hours in non-professional subjects, and every woman wanted to be eligible for the A. A. U. W. The administration planned later to offer a B.M. which would require 90 hours of music and 60 hours of literary, a total of five college years. But the public was not yet ready for this.

The music offerings, in 1946, spread to five majors: the Bachelor of Arts with a major in Music, Church Music, or Music Education, or a Bachelor of Music or of Music Education. The faculty of 26 teachers includes three from the Arts and Sciences who teach one or two classes in music. Of the 23 who teach fully in music or speech, three have (earned) doctor's degrees, two have master's. Ten of them are without college degrees; all of these teach applied music and are notable artists. All subjects, except applied music, are taught in classes at the regular tuition rates; extra tuition is charged only for work which requires a teacher's time with an individual student. Stress is laid on the foundational musicianship studies. Courses are clearly defined as to content, and are standardized so they can be transferred.

Thus has the old pattern of music education been altered. Surely there is much gain. It has been accomplished by the leadership and venturesomeness of the church colleges and the teachers colleges, through mutual helpfulness in cooperation through the various music associations. Perhaps the professional degree should include more cultural subjects. Maybe a general cultural degree such as the B.A. should be required as a basis, as in Medicine, Law, and the Ministry. That goal may be reached at some future time. Whatever improvement may be achieved in the future of education in Fine Arts, it is doubtful if the next third of a century will be able to match the progress of the one just past.

A survey of the list of teachers of Music through the Period 1902-45 reveals that the list is long and their terms were short. The average term of a Director, up to 1922, for instance, was two years; since then it has been more nearly ten years. The list of directors is: W. B. Schimmelpfennig, 1901-03; Alexander Findley, 1903-04; Harold Techau, 1905-06; Harriet Frances Smith, 1906-08 (also piano 1904-08); Fred Wimberly, 1908-10; Arthur Johnson, 1910-12; Carl Beutel, 1912-15; Helen Fouts Cahoon, 1915-18 (also Voice, 1913-20; 29-38; Carroll C. Mc-

Kee, 1918-22; H. D. Guelich, 1922-33; Claude Sammis, 1933-42,[12] (also Violin, 1925-42); T. Smith McCorkle, 1942-. The tenure of the teachers is longer than that of the Directors, except for the last two Directors. In the 43 years there have been 34 teachers of Piano, averaging about 4 years each. Violin teachers have averaged about 5½ and Voice teachers about 5 years. The changes in methods of training and teaching described in the preceding paragraphs evidently have produced a more settled status for the faculty. For, of the present music teachers, one has been on for 15 years, two for 12 years, and four for 8 years. The others with shorter terms have been added recently under the expansion program, and are continuing. A new policy, encouraging to long terms, was adopted in 1938. It was that of utilizing, as members of the Fine Arts faculty, teachers in Fort Worth who have, also, students of their own who are not of college grade. Any student of theirs who desires college credit and who is eligible for college grade work, must enroll in T. C. U., and the teacher gets the regular commission. This policy was worked out (in conference with Dean Hall) by Claude Sammis, the Director. He had come as a teacher of Violin, added Theory and finally became Director, having proved to be an artist of unusual skill and a diplomat of wide influence. He contributed much to the spirit of harmony among the local musicians through the Music Associations, developing the attitude of fellow professionals rather than rivals. The policy is continued and expanded under his successor, Dean McCorkle, and is working splendidly.

In addition to those already mentioned above and in other chapters, the following names will stir fond memories in the hearts of students: Mr. and Mrs. W. C. Hunter, Violin and Voice respectively, (1906-10); Mr. and Mrs. Carl Doering, both Piano (1917-20); Paul Klingstedt, Voice (1925-30). There came in 1913 a couple whose lives built themselves deep in the heart of the institution's life. Fred Cahoon not only taught violin and played it with great skill, but he also came to the rescue of football and served as Coach for several seasons, and coached Tennis regularly.[13] Helen Fouts Cahoon brought distinction to the Voice Department by her beautiful coloratura soprano voice and her scintillating personality. They both left in 1920, but Mrs. Cahoon returned in 1929 after a period of teaching in Chi-

[12]Terminated by his death, August, 1942.
[13]See Capter XXI for this story.

W. M. WINTON,
34 years.

MRS. W. M. WINTON,
31 years.

MABEL MAJOR,
28 Years.

F. WOODALL
HOGAN,
27 years.

L. L. DEES,
27 years.

REBECCA SMITH
LEE, 26 years.

MRS. GEORGIA
HARRIS, 25 years.

MRS. BERTIE
MOTHERSHEAD,
24 years.

S. P. ZIEGLER,
24 years.

F. E. BILLINGTON,
23 years.

W. J. HAMMOND,
23 years

TEMISIA BRYSON,
23 years.

Some Faculty Members; in the order of their length of service. See also,
Appendix VI, with full list.
(for details see Appendix VI.)

| | | | |
|---|---|---|---|
| NEWTON GAINES, 23 years. | EULA LEE CARTER, 23 years. | L. D. FALLIS, 23 years. | BONNIE M. ENLOW, 23 years. |

| | | | |
|---|---|---|---|
| L. A. DUNAGAN, 23 years. | DURA BROKAW COCKRELL, 22 years. | C. H. ROBERTS, 21 years. | JOSIAH H.COMBS, 20 years. |

| | | | |
|---|---|---|---|
| HAZEL TUCKER WOODWARD, 20 years. | J. L. WHITMAN, 1928-45. | CLAUDE SAMMIS, 1925-42. | WALTER E. BRYSON, 1917-22. |

Other Faculty Members; in continued order of their length of service; but see complete list in Appendix VI.

| JOHN LORD, Professor, Dean, Graduate School. Total, 27 years. | RAYMOND A. SMITH, Professor, Dean, School of Education. Total, 27 years | CORTEL K. HOLSAPPLE, Professor, Dean, Evening College. 8 years. | T. SMITH McCORKLE, Professor, Dean, Fine Arts. |

| ELLIS M. SOWELL, Professor, Dean, School of Business. | JEROME MOORE, Professor, Dean, Arts and Sciences. | SADIE T. BECKHAM, Dean of Women 19 years ; the second woman Trustee, 1928-. | ELIZABETH SHELBURNE, Professor, Dean of Women, Total, 18 years. |

| S. W. HUTTON, Professor, Registrar. Total, 18 years. | E. R. TUCKER, Professor, Registrar, 1920-32. Total 12 years. | LUCY HARRIS, Dean School of Nursing. 1947-. | D. RAY LINDLEY, Dean Brite College. 1947-. |

SEVERAL DEANS AND REGISTRARS.
(For details see Appendix VI.)

—Jarvis Hall.

—Brite Building.

cago. She returned with added prestige and that personality which marked her as a superior leader. She left of her own accord in 1938 to go to New York, where she prospers as a coach of Broadway singers and others.

The teaching of Painting and Drawing has followed much the same pattern as music with reference to the preparation of teachers and the awarding of diplomas or degrees. A venture was made in 1933 by offering the B.A. degree with a major in Art. It is believed that T. C. U. is the second college in the South to announce such an offering, Sophie Newcomb being the first. In the matter of the tenure of teachers, however, Art has made quite a different record, in fact quite a remarkable record. For, through a period of 47 years, the Department of Art has had only two heads, and the second is still serving. The one, Mrs. Dura Brokaw Cockrell, came in 1899, the bride of the new Professor of Social Sciences, and continued through 1923, except for two periods off for study, 1903-07, and 1911-12.[14] Since that time the work has been led by Samuel P. Ziegler, who had served a previous term as Professor of Cello and Theory (1917-20) and who, meanwhile, had, in spare time, earned the B.A. degree. These long terms speak eloquently of the high quality of work done and the balance of the program. Both of these have proved themselves by their work to be successful teachers and artists. The Brushes, a student organization, has kept the spirit alert and interesting, and the number of distinguished artists that have come out of this inspiring group is impressive. Among those who have served as assistants through the years are Miss Kate Jackson (1907-11), and Miss Sue Darter.

The art of teaching speech went through metamorphoses during this period, not only in the titles it wore, (Elocution, Oratory, Spoken Word, Public Speaking, Speech, and finally (?) Speech-Drama), but also in its change from private teaching to class work, and from special tuition to a part in the general tuition, somewhat after the pattern of Music, Theory and Art. A line of strong personalities headed this Department through all the years, the outstanding ones being Olive Leaman McClintic (Johnson) (1901-07), followed by Clyde Batsell Reeves Broad-

[14]Mrs. Cockrell prepared a manuscript on the History of Religious Art which was most excellent but was not practical commercially because of the large outlay required for the pictures involved. She returned to T. C. U. as House Mother for Sterling House 1940-42. Her personality contributed much to the spirit of friendship, loyalty and culture through the years.

head) (1907-13), Leila Long Powell (1913-19), and finally Lew D. Fallis (1925-), assisted by Katherine Moore Norton (1928-45). Professional preparation for Journalism was inaugurated in T. C. U. in 1928 with the offering, not of the degree of Bachelor of Journalism but rather the Bachelor of Arts with a major in Journalism. Inasmuch as it requires at least 66 semester hours in general subjects (including 15 hours in the social sciences, Government, Economics and History), and limits credits in Journalism to a maximum of 41, it can scarcely be charged with being too heavily vocational.

A young man came to the Dean in the late 1930's to enroll for a degree in Journalism, explaining, "When I applied for a job as a reporter on the Big Daily, I was advised to get a college degree, then apply." What a change from the old time policy of breaking in the cub reporters by rough experience only and scoffing at the theoretical college graduate! It chanced that the managing editor of that Big Daily, and several of his neighbors, had already added several T. C. U. graduates to their staffs. Evidently he found them satisfactory. The students achieve much practical experience by working on The *Skiff*; the editor must be a Journalism major. They get much excitement and a lot of experience out of the annual day when they assume the full responsibility of operating an issue of the Fort Worth Press, or the Mineral Wells Index, or other regular newspapers.

This department has been developed by one man, J. Willard Ridings, who grew up in a newspaper office, and was educated for the profession under that pioneer of college teaching of journalism, Walter Williams, founder of the School of Journalism in the University of Missouri. With the help of an assistant and his unusual energy and readiness, he is able to conduct, also, the Publicity Department of T. C. U. This includes the publicity for the Horned Frog football team.

Home Economics, as told elsewhere, was brought into the list of departments at the behest of Mrs. Ida Van Zandt Jarvis, who claimed to have some "old fashioned notions" that every girl should learn to cook and sew. It has never aimed to develop many of the several specialties nor to train professionals, except as teachers of the subject. It offers a major in foods and one in clothing. Many girls elect a few courses in this Department. After short terms of teaching by Mary Lee Moore (1915-17), Vesta Burford (1917-19), Gladys Turner (1919-22), and

Charlotte Owsley (1922-24), there came the efficient, devoted teacher, Bonnie Enlow (1924-), who has kept a steady stream of young women going out into life. She won the approval of many an experienced housekeeper by her teaching of special classes during the war preparations in the early 1940's.

The Department of English, prominent from the first, has held a steady pace of leadership all along. A freshman had tried English 311 for one semester and was begging the Dean to let him register for the spring without that subject which is required of everybody (whether he needs it or not). "Why do you wish to drop English?" asked the Dean. "Well, I don't need no more; I done got enough," was the candid reply. Through the years, that story (a true one), has persuaded (or shamed) many a reluctant freshman into persevering in English language. And the Department of English has carried the burden of modifying the colloquialisms of the novices and endeavoring to drill them into a proper use of their mother tongue. While the classes in Rhetoric have bulked large, the Introduction to Literature, sophomore English, has been required also as a prerequisite for any advanced English. Out of the mass of beginners, the teachers have inspired a goodly number to develop a taste in literature and others to aspire to productive writing. This ambition has been stimulated by the establishment of prizes. The Bryson Prize of $10 for the best poem of the year was established by Professor Walter Bryson in 1921 and has been continued by his wife since his death. The Dallas branch of the T. C. U. Woman's Club started a $75 Poetry Prize, afterward changed to a Creative Writing Scholarship for the best piece, either prose or poetry, by a new student. Creative Writing Day, in the spring, is always a high day on the campus when these awards are presented. Some of the alumni or alumnae who have published books are often present to stimulate interest. So it has come to pass that even boys enthusiastically engage in the writing of poetry and win the acclaim of their fellows.

The English Department has not been so fortunate as others in having a long continuous leadership, but has been blessed with very capable Heads for shorter terms, and a group of dependable, devoted teachers on the staff. Bruce McCully (1902-09, a likeable, scholarly, Christian gentleman, was followed by O. W. Lyon (1911-14); and C. C. Gumm, (1914-17); then by the brilliant poet and inspiring teacher, Walter E. Bryson, whose promise of permanency was shattered by his sudden death in

1922. Mr. Bryson was a New Englander from Transylvania and Harvard, a lover of beauty, an inspiration to the students, a joy as a companion and as a colleague, delightful. During this period there came two young women who have given a continuity to the Department ever since their coming in 1919. Rebecca Smith (1919-45), received her doctor's degree in 1932 and became the Head of the Department after the resignation of Dr. Herbert Hughes, (1925-33). During her absence in the Navy (1943-45), her companion, Mabel Major (1919-), served as Head. These two yoke-fellows developed a vital interest in Southwest Literature, securing a special room in the Library for it, publishing a text in the field and working in the Folklore Society. Miss Smith gained a wide reputation as a speaker on literature, being much in demand. Having a decided strain of patriotism from her Tennessee background, she enlisted enthusiastically in the WAVES in 1943. Along with the announcement that she was mustered out of the WAVES (1945) came the surprise that she was to take a new degree, "Mrs." (Owen Lee). On the very competent staff with them are Mrs. Artemisia Bryson, Miss Loraine Sherley, Dr. Paul Dinkins, Mrs. Alma Bailey, Mrs. Ruth Angell, and William P. Baker. In 1946 Dr. W. B. Gates became the Head of the Department. Miss Mary Elizabeth Waits was drafted in the Department of English in 1925, over the head of her father, · the President. She made good in her own right as a teacher and scholar, served until her marriage to Dr. Gayle Scott in 1927.

In the early years, Philosophy and Psychology had been taught by the President, Addison Clark, under the then prevailing titles of Mental and Moral science, with ethics in the form of Evidences of Christianity. This same pattern was continued under President Zollars through 1906. With the arrival of Ellsworth E. Faris in 1908 came a fresh breeze of more modern patterns of thinking. In fact, it was almost too modern. He taught, also, some classes in Bible. He presented the views of modern scholarship in both fields with the evangelistic fervor of a new convert, without sufficient regard to the mental background of his pupils. The result was an unsettling of the faith of some of the students and opposition by some of the brethren. Professor Faris proved his keenness and ability most completely; he went to Chicago University, took his doctor's degree and a few years later became the head of the Department of Sociology there, a world-renowned scholar in the field. After an interim by the professorship of W. H. Batson (1913-15), and C. A. Exley, there came another scholar of first grade dimensions to the Chair of Philosophy. T. V. Smith, having taught English for one year, was transferred to the Chair of Philosophy, which he invigorated with scintillating and inspiring leadership. He stimulated the minds of his pupils immensely. He, too, went to Chicago and developed a unique place for himself as a leader of thought in the Philosophy Department.

The longest term and most constructive in this field was that of Professor E. W. McDiarmid, who came in 1919, modestly, quietly, led the students into a love for philosophy and set them an example of a true philosopher by his practical and Christian way of living. As told elsewhere,[15] he exercised the human side of life abundantly; though frail in health, he served as Chairman of the Athletic Council, lived with the athletes, loved them and lured them into some sound philosophy of life. On his passing in September, 1939, one of his pupils filled in temporarily, while serving as pastor of the University Christian Church. Perry Gresham carried on his spirit splendidly. Then came Dr. Cortell Holsapple from the University of Texas English faculty. He has devoted a goodly share of his time to executive work as director of wartime classes, and later as Dean of the Evening College.

Psychology, through all these years, was a part of the combined department. Mrs. E. R. Tucker, a pupil of Professor McDiarmid, became his assistant, then his successor so far as psychology was concerned. She became Mrs. E. C. Woodward in 1942 and continues to teach Psychology. In 1944, Dr. T. F. Richardson, Director of Personnel, became the Head of the separate Department of Psychology.

The scholastic rating of the faculty, as measured by degrees, has kept pace with the growth of the institution and the rising standards in the educational world. The master's degree is expected of every regular teacher, except a few beginning instructors, temporarily, some of the coaches and teachers of applied music. The growth in the number and percentage of doctor's degrees is significant. Counting the entire faculty of all of the colleges, except the Evening College (which uses several part-time teachers), the number of doctor's degrees at several periods and their percentages are: in 1923, 3, or 10 per cent of the faculty; in 1933, 13, or 25 per cent; 1943, 23, or 25.5 per cent; 1945, 27, being 29 per cent; 1946, 34, or 29 per cent. In addi-

[15]Chapter XXI.

tion there are five professors who have professional degrees, such as B.D. The policy of the Administration is to encourage leaves of absence for the purpose of pursuing the higher degrees. On the faculty at present there are eight teachers who have completed their doctor's degrees while on leave and five who are at present on leave. Several of these are on scholarships which were encouraged by the Administration.

The Library has made commendable progress toward the goal of all University libraries—to become the center of all departments. In the Waco days, under Librarians Mrs. M. B. Gibbons (1904-06) and Mrs. E. C. Boynton (1906-08) and by the encouragement of the presidents and teachers, the books, although limited in number, were used extensively. After the complete destruction of the library accumulations in the fire of 1910, the work of rebuilding was slow. A Library Committee (headed at first by E. E. Faris) was diligent in soliciting donations of books. The money budget was limited. Miss Nell Andrew, self-taught and self-reliant, was enthusiastic about adding volumes and was especially apt in collecting and preserving old records.

When the Main Building was designed in Fort Worth the Library was assigned to the two northeast rooms on the main floor, with the small room between (used for the office of the Dean of Women later). The space actually occupied was the southeast quarter of the main floor, where it suffered growing pains until the new Mary Couts Burnett Memorial Building was dedicated February 27, 1925. Just at that time Miss Nell Andrew resigned and a Librarian with professional training was secured in the person of Arthur R. Curry (1926-33), a graduate of the University of Illinois. Mrs. Bertie Mothershead, a lover of books and of people, had been called in as an assistant in 1923, where her energy and devotion enabled her to master the library science and her thoughtfulness for the needs of the students and teachers won their loyalty. In 1927 she was made Assistant Librarian. Under her leadership the Library has grown, the staff has increased to eight full time employees besides a score or more of student assistants, and the annual appropriations have increased; for books to about $7,000, and periodicals $3,500. The number of volumes exceeds 100,000 including some 30,000 Government documents. It has been for years a Government Depository. Four rooms have been designated for special collections: The Southwest Literature Room, the Disciples Room,[16]

[16]See Chapter XX.

the J. W. and Maggie Lowber Room (housing his library), and the Dr. and Mrs. Goodal Wooten collection of rare and valuable editions. In order to strengthen the sources for graduate study the North Texas Regional Union Library was formed in 1941 with the cooperating schools North Texas State College, Texas State College for Women, Southern Methodist University and Texas Christian University. Also affiliated with it are the Southwestern Baptist Theological Seminary and the two Public Libraries of Dallas and Fort Worth.

This chapter on educational trends, already too lengthy, albeit woefully scanty of the personnel of the faculty, will be brought to a climax by the story of the development of Personnel Guidance in T. C. U., a field of growing importance and value in the college world. "Credits for quality" had been recognized since 1916, by a point system. At a faculty council in 1928, Dean Colby D. Hall presented a paper proposing a plan for checking up on the basic skills of students about the time of the sophomore year, in order to be assured that these were mastered (even those lacking from high school experience), before the student came too near to time of graduation. This suggestion developed into what was named the Pre-Junior Achievement Test, which began operation in 1929-30.[17]

This plan had the effect of making both teachers and students conscious of the need for watching for these skills and developing them. It set some students to working on them instead of going on into the junior year without them. It was an attempt to do what the famous Chicago Junior College Level plan undertook to do; and it was announced before the Chicago plan. The chief weakness of the plan as here used was that each department made out the test questions in its field; some of them used only the usual content questions; most of them were inexpert in the difficult art of evolving the right type of question. When the nationwide Sophomore Testing Plan was announced in 1932,

---

[17]Its idea was thus expressed: "There is need of shifting the emphasis away from 'credits' to accomplishment, of measuring the student's merit in terms of achievement, skills, culture, mental attitudes and masteries he may show at the end of a period, rather than merely in terms of courses passed, hours in class and sum of credits. The features of the plan: each student, before being admitted to the Junior year must prove by tests . . . a satisfactory mastery of the fundamental tool courses of his education, specifically." (Then follows a list, which included, personal demeanor, neatness, politeness and physical training). "The sources of information for judging were to be: Freshman entrance tests, reports from instructors on personnel, preliminary tests near the Freshman year's end and finally the achievement tests at the close of the Sophomore year."

the T. C. U. faculty adopted its questions for their system, and gradually substituted that test for the pre-junior test. The scores of the students were passed on to the teachers; personal counseling was done on the basis of them; many students were deeply impressed by the results and utilized them for good. The better students took them more seriously than the poor students, who needed them more. This nationwide sophomore test was used until about 1940, at which time the personnel office had developed a series of testings that covered a wider scope.

An office measurement was set up in 1939, having Dr. J. H. Dougherty as Director of Testing and Otto Nielsen as Director of Personnel, making available for students and teachers a list of standard tests as desired, and the counseling of the Directors to guide their use. A further advanced step in guidance was made in 1943 with the coming of Dr. Thomas F. Richardson, who had specialized in personnel psychology on his Ph.D. in New York University, and had a zeal for the work. He became the Head of the Department of Psychology, was given an office with helpers, and has organized a fully equipped system of testing and guidance. This field of recent development is therefore well on the way in T. C. U. at this time. It is being utilized for the benefit of the veterans of the war as they endeavor to pick up the broken threads of their educational careers.

# ᴄᴏ XXIII ᴄᴏ

# T. C. U. In World War II

WORLD WAR II WAS UNIQUE in the extent to which it used the facilities of colleges in its program. It was obviously a technician's war; and the colleges are the seeding ground of technology. Training was on a vaster scale than in any preceding conflict, thorough training, skilled, precise, and rapid training. Hence, college teachers were called upon as never before. Immense plants had to be available for hundreds of thousands of men and women where they could study, teach, and live, and all of this in a hurry. So the plants of colleges, being already available, were utilized. All of these features combined to bring the war training programs abundantly to the college campus.

And it was a new kind of training. Military drill was at a minimum, technical skill at a maximum. All of the old drama was present: the volunteering, at first, then the drafting, the broken plans, the excitement and the deep concern—all of this and schooling too. It was genuine schooling with well-wrought curricula, serious students and skilled teachers. For war, this was something new under the sun.

The story of this episode on the T. C. U. campus must be largely a plain recording of facts; it is too close for any interpreting. This proximity may make the record seem commonplace to those who have participated, but for the sake of the future, the record should be made while the facts are fresh.

The rumblings of war in Europe and its outbreak in September, 1939, were observed with anxiety and studied with interest by the teachers and students in many a class in T. C. U. By June, 1940, the threat of the war situation was vivid enough to persuade the Trustees to postpone the inauguration of a pension plan for the employees, which had been worked out and author-

311

ized. In October, they delayed it indefinitely under the apprehension of financial strain of prospective war.

It was this same month of June, 1940, that the first war training activity was inaugurated on the campus. The University contracted with Civil Aeronautics Authority (to whom the Government had assigned the task), to teach the ground and flying training to a series of groups of prospective pilots. It was called Civilian Pilot Training, "civilian" because our country was not then at war. The name was changed in December, 1941, to War Training Service. The flying part of the training was sublet by contract to the Aircraft Sales Company, whose president was Les Bowman. The first quota was 20 boys for the elementary class and 10 for the secondary, but the number was gradually raised. At first the prerequisite was 60 hours of college credit, but that, too, was relaxed; any lad whose testing promised that he would make a good flyer was admitted. The classes, called Physics 23 and Physics 33, were for college credit, taught by regular teachers (until some extras had to be added) and, at the beginning, were composed of regular college students, who took these as a part of their regular college load. Later, however, the course was speeded up and occupied the students' entire time, sometimes without college credit. This group of pilots, whose training began 18 months before the United States was in the war, was ready to be in the first line of defense when the war came in December, 1941. This W. T. S. program continued until August, 1944. By that time, the Army and Navy had developed their own extensive and intensive training programs.

The second war training activity included several groups of officers training for pilots or instructors. It began with the Special Flight Instructors Program (AV-P), which was an experimental effort by the Navy to utilize as instructors a number of ensigns who were slightly over age or under physical requirements to make combat pilots. There were only six such units in the U. S. A., the one at T. C. U. being the first. Jarvis Hall became available for their occupancy because the newly completed Foster Hall was just then occupied by the girls. Their classes were exclusively for them, and were in technical subjects; the teachers were provided by the University, most of them being in addition to the regular staff; the flying was taught by the Air Craft Sales Company; the students were transported back and forth in buses which T. C. U. purchased for the purpose. These students were under military discipline under the direction of the Commanding Officer. The program, begun in the summer of 1942, was closed in January, 1944.

Among the other units occupying Jarvis Hall were the Enlisted Reserve Corps, some Army, some Navy, and a group of men of the Marine Corps, training for pilots. There was also later a group of V-5 men, mostly sophomore students, training for pilot service. It was conducted much like the AV-P, the students being in special classes and transported to the flying fields in special buses. This program began September, 1943, and closed in August, 1944.

The fourth training program was of a different type. Its purpose was to train workers for the war industries which were rapidly increasing in Fort Worth. This program, too, was prudently started before the U. S. A. was in the war. It had begun in 1940 as the Engineer Defense Training program using Engineering Schools to give up-training for workers in war plants. When it was expanded, in July, 1941, to become the Engineer, Science, Management Defense Training (changed in July, 1941, to the E. S. M. War Training) to include classes in Physics, Chemistry, and Business Administration, T. C. U. came into the program. The classes were free of tuition charges, open to any who could qualify, gave no college credit, and were composed of persons who were employed, hence were held mostly at night. The list of subjects grew constantly, as the needs arose. Radio Fundamentals, Advanced Radio, Personnel Management, Accounting, Office Management, and such subjects were offered. The regular faculty was used, but several special teachers had to be called in also.

The four schools in the state which had engineering colleges, the University of Texas, A. & M. College, S. M. U., and Texas Tech, had E. S. M. W. T. classes in Fort Worth. A local organization was formed under the general regional chairmanship of the Dean of the Engineering School of the University of Texas, W. R. Woolrich. The members of the Fort Worth committee were: Dean W. T. Adams, Texas Tech, Chairman; Dean Flath of S. M. U.; Professor H. W. Barlow, A. & M.; Professor Reed Granbury, Texas University; Dean Colby D. Hall of T. C. U.; and later Dean Campbell of Simmons; and Dean Cortell Holsapple of T. C. U. A full-time local coordinator was engaged, General L. R. Gignialette (ex-Commandant of Kemper). An extensive program was carried on. Some of the classes of the out-of-town colleges were held in T. C. U. classrooms. A. & M. and Texas U. rented buildings downtown for theirs, and each had a full-time director living in Fort Worth. The local war plants and businesses of many kinds looked to these classes for up-grading their employees, and providing technicians for the hurry-up job they had on hand. This program, begun in July, 1941, was dissolved by the government June 30, 1945.

The fifth program of War Training was the most conspicuous of all, the Navy V-12, which began July 1, 1943 and closed October 25, 1945. During this time, the "ship's company," consisting of about four commissioned officers, several helpers and a number of naval trainees, varying from the original quota, 242, to about 122, occupied Clark Hall and added color to the entire campus. The Commanding Officer was Lt. (jg) George C. Decker, later Lt. (jg) Carl M. Schmidt; Assistant C. O., Lt. (jg) B. C. Watts; Medical Officer, Lt. Commander J. E. Ross, M.D.

The purpose of the V-12 program was to train officers for the Navy. The officer who presented the plan to the group of boys, when inviting them to enlist, stated it something like this: "The plan of the Navy for preparing its officers is to give them, normally, in the Annapolis Academy, a thorough, cultural education, plus the technical preparation to fit them for any of the several types of service, such as Deck Officer, Supply Officer, etc.; this accelerated V-12 program will provide the cultural education through the regular college course while the technical portion will be limited for each indivdual to one line of duty, instead of all of them. All of the traditions of the Navy will be kept in your training." This was the spirit which actuated the widespread speeded-up program. Some of the classes, such as Naval History, Engineering Drawing, and Celestial Navigation, were made up of Navy men only. The most of their classes were taken along with the regular college students. Their curriculum was largely prescribed, a few electives being allowed. The group included Supply Officers (who majored in Business Administration), Pre-Medical, Pre-Dental, and Pre-Theological; but the bulk of them took the Deck Officer curriculum. Five undergraduates and six graduate students were Pre-Chaplains. These men entered freely into the social and student life of the campus, engaged in athletics, glee clubs, and held office. One, David Hibbard, was president of the student body for the Summer-Fall, 1945. This same lad was awarded, on a special occasion, an Air Medal for distinguished service while he was air gunner in the fleet. Of the total, 750 separate individuals from first to last, 150 had seen previous combat experience in the fleet. Their one separation from the civilian students was in the Dining Room, which had a section marked off for the Navy; this was because their food bill had to be kept separate. There was never any friction between the civilian and Naval groups.

The records made by these students in the midshipmen's schools after leaving T. C. U. were a source of pride on the part of the teachers and administrators. Their average grades were high; several made distinguished records. As many as 150 of them got into combat before the war closed, several of them at Iwo Jima. At the graduating exercises on October 25, 1945, when the Navy V-12 was leaving, the Commanding Officer, Lt. Schmidt, prescribed to the University an Award of Appreciation from Secretary of the Navy Forrestal. He also presented the commissions as Lieutenants (jg) to the two graduating chaplains, Charles Malotte and Coleman Raley. Altogether, the Navy V-12 program was a complete success, and a satisfying service.

The financial arrangement with the Government was different for each of these five plans of training. For the Civil Pilot Training (later called the War Training Program), the University received a stipulated sum per class hour for each student for instructors, and furnishing the teachers, either the regular faculty or extras, the students providing their own board. This arrangement made possible a fair amount of profit.

The AV-P teaching was handled on the same basis for instruction; each student paid out of his maintenance allowance for his board and room in Jarvis Hall, at a maximum of $50 per month. The V-5 program was on a basis similar to the AV-P. In both cases the Navy provided supervision of the men.

In all three of these cases, the University entered into a joint contract to provide the training, the flying portion by the Air Craft Sales Co., and a smaller portion to the Singleton Flying Field and the Ritchie Flying Service. Fort Worth became a famous flying center when the Headquarters of the National Army Flying Training Command was moved out of crowded Washington, D. C., to Fort Worth, and put up in the Texas & Pacific office building.

In the case of the E. S. M. W. T. the Government was careful to see that the opportunity for any margin of profit to the University was guarded. Each separate class with its full budget

315

had to be approved in advance, although the recommendation of the local committee was usually approved.

The Government paid T. C. U. for the service of the teacher, at the rate of so much per hour of class time, the rate varying according to the rank of the teacher. It was always enough to reimburse the University. Then, there was a payment also for the upkeep (janitor, and utilities, no rent) of the class rooms, and a percentage for overhead administration.

The contract for the conduct of the Navy V-12 program was based on the principle that the University should be paid just what it cost and no more. For Clark Hall, in addition to the maintenance and up-keep, a use-charge was paid on the basis of four per cent annually on the book valuation of the building, which, practically, amounted to about $350 per month. The feeding was paid for on actual cost basis. Separate accounting was kept on the food, the help, and the overhead, although all went through the same warehouse and kitchen. The instruction was on the same cost principle. The proportion of Navy men in each class had to be reported each month; the University received that portion of the teachers' salary. Brite College of the Bible, with its six chaplain students was on a different basis, being a graduate school. The students were permitted to live outside if they were married, and they received the regular University rate for board and room. The Navy paid their tuition.

The excessive accounting required by this cost plan entailed the employment of an extra accountant for the Mess Hall, several days a month of a professional accounting firm, and the part time of at least two professors (Winton and Sherer) in addition to many an extra hour by the Business, Dean and Registrars' offices. Such of this as could be counted was paid for by the Navy. Despite the initial impression of an over-dose of red tape, the plan worked well, the relations were cordial and the era ended with good feeling and a sense of having rendered a service to the Government, in time of emergency. Most assuredly the Government was wise in utilizing the plants' facilities and faculties of the schools of America already in operation rather than setting up special Army and Navy schools. And the expense was thereby greatly lightened.

Even before the war ended a sixth relationship with the Government became active. The Veterans' Administration of the U. S. Government, under the authority of the so-called "G. I. Bill

of Rights," pays the tuition, fees, and books, plus $50 a month for
a single veteran, or $75 a month for a married veteran. In Jan-
uary 1946 this was raised to $65 and $90. This is much simpler
accounting, a point that was quite welcome. Veterans, under this
plan, began to come in during 1944-45, the number constantly
increasing. These students have fitted into the school life quite
normally, with no unusual complications. The number had increased, by the fall of 1945, so that the Veterans' Administration
felt justified in placing a representative on the campus with an
office in the building to counsel incoming veterans. In the spring
trimester, 1946, the number grew to be over 900. A limit had to be
placed on the fall semester enrollment.

The entire faculty and administration entered into the extra
work required by the abnormal war situation with commendable
heartiness. Some of them were assigned special responsibilities
in working out these new features. The initiation of the C. P. T.
and E. S. M. W. T. fell upon the Dean of the University, assisted
by Dr. Boeck for the latter and Dr. Morgan for the radio courses.
By January, 1941, the details of the C. P. T. required a definite
portion of one man's time, so Dr. C. K. Holsapple was appointed to
guide the C. P. T. work and later was made military coordinator
for the campus. In 1943, the E. S. M. W. T. work was put under
his charge also, being so closely related to the Evening College of
which he had just been made Dean. His work has been thorough
and helpful, and his connections with the national offices quite
wide and influential.

The extra responsibility for the Navy V-12 program, besides
what the Naval personnel provided, was cared for by Professor W.
M. Winton for the general records, Professor C. R. Sherer for the
curriculum advising, and personnel dictor Dr. T. F. Richardson
for general counseling.

The campus life of T. C. U. went through the metamorphoses
of the war feeling very much as the public did. A panorama of
events that expressed and enhanced the war fever may be stated as follows. June 1940, boys enrolling in classes of the Civil
Pilot Training in the Physics Department, and going out daily to take flying lessons. June 1941, defense training classes
swarming on the campus in the evening, the Radio Fundamentals courses attracting some of the regular students. September
1941, an appeal in The *Skiff* by Dr. Holsapple for boys to enlist
in the C. P. T.; December 18, 1941 a "Policy for the War" announced by the faculty. This policy, which later was expressed

in a rule was "to grant degrees to seniors who lack only a fraction of a semester when called by draft, and to give full credit to any student who is called out by draft, for any course in which he has completed as much as half a semester." January 19, 1942, the practice blackout in Fort Worth. March, 1942, Cleland Early, former popular editor of The *Skiff*, a Lieutenant in the Marines, spent a week on the campus, enlisting recruits; he got many athletes and others. September 1942, Jarvis Hall goes to the Navy; Foster Hall opened. This made a deep impression, including those neat gray uniforms of the Ensigns. October 1942, a joint presentation of the Army, Navy, Marines, and Coast Guards to all the boys assembled in the Amphitheater, to end the rivalry in recruiting and give each branch an even break; volunteering was still allowed and T. C. U.'s quota for the Reserves was announced. January 1943, a Red Cross bandage-making room opened in Brite 104, some girls showing up in Motor Corps uniform. January 8, 1943, all girls required to take a strenuous physical training program while the boys started the military drill under Dr. Scott, a veteran of World War I, who was appointed Liaison Officer. April 30, 1943, a service flag presented in Chapel, 683 blue stars, 13 gold stars. May 5, 1943, the Army Institute Test given to 50 students for eligibility for the Reserves. January 1943, much confusion among the boys about enlisting, whether, and in what. July 1, 1943, the Navy V-12 program starts, the Navy takes over Clark Hall, civilian boys go to Goode and Sterling; white uniforms all over the campus create a new psychology; dining room divided, Navy and Civilian. November 1943, a Memorial Service in the University Christian Church for sixteen war casualties; sobered hearts.

Then came the cessation of volunteering, the leaving of boy after boy in response to the call of the Selective Service, the settling down to a steady devotion to the War Service, hearty response to the call for buying war bonds, trips to entertain soldier camps, and constant anxiety and prayers for the boys in danger. The period when thoughts were most diverted from studies in the fall of 1942 and spring of 1943 when the boys were distracted about volunteering. After the Selective Service got to working, there was more steadiness.

A roster of all students and former students who enlisted in the Service has been kept in the Registrar's office, totaling 1324, although inevitably incomplete. The chaplains numbered 59. Three memorial services, November 5, 1943, January 19, 1945, and February 10, 1946, were observed for those who made the supreme sacrifice. This list of 59 honored names, although it is probably incomplete, is here given for permanent record.

Balaban, Robert E. (1940-43), Caldwell Kansas, Lieut. U. S. Army. Killed in action in Germany, Nov. 20, 1944.

Baugh, Jim Ted (1941-43), Tampa, Fla., Lieut. Marine Corps. Killed in action on Iwo Jima Feb. 24, 1945.

Blanke, Arwin H., Jr. (1934), Fort Worth. Killed in accident while in training.

Byars, Edmond O., Jr. (1940), Fort Worth, Lieut. (jg) Naval Air Corps. Killed Aug. 1, 1945, in Pacific Area.

Carpenter, Sam Ed (1942-43), Knox City, Pfc. U. S. Marines. Killed on Iwo Jima March 15, 1945.

Carswell, Horace S., Jr. (1935-39), B. S., Fort Worth, Major U. S. Army Air Corps. Killed in plane crash, China, Oct. 26, 1944.

Cason, John Byron (1936-41), B. S. Com., '41, Fort Worth, Aviation Cadet. Killed in plane crash into a power line.

Chesser, Wm. Thomas (1931-34, 1937-40), Fort Worth, Lieut. U. S. Army Air Corps. Killed Aug. 16, 1942, in plane crash.

Cobb, Edward Everett, Jr. (1935-38), Dallas, Major, U. S. Army Air Corps. Killed in plane crash at Reno, Nev., Feb. 12, 1943.

Cowin, Douglas (1942-43), Ann Arbor, Mich., U. S. Marine Corps. Killed July 29, 1946.

Cyrus, John V. (1939-42), Fort Worth, First Lieut. U. S. Army Air Corps. Killed over Belgium Jan. 2, 1945.

Day, Lemuel E. (1918-20, B. A. '24), Major U. S. Medical Corps. Served also in World War I. Died in action, Buna, Dec. 23, 1942.

Finkin, John Adam (1937-38), Fort Worth, U. S. Army Air Corps Pilot. Killed in service Dec. 30, 1941, Hamilton Field, California.

Flournoy, James Monroe, Jr. (1942), Cisco, U. S. Army Air Corps. Killed in plane crash in Mexico June 14, 1944.

Fry, Jack Curtis (1937-41), Fort Worth, U. S. Army Air Corps. Killed June 14, 1941.

Gilbert, Harold (1944-45), Fort Worth, Pfc. Killed in action Dec. 26, 1944.

Haden, Mansel Richard (1939-42), Galveston, S/1c (RdM) USC GR. Went down on the U. S. S. Jackson, Sept. 14, 1944.

Harrison, Ernest H., Jr. (1940), Fort Worth, U. S. Navy. Went down on the U. S. S. Argonaut Feb. 6, 1943, in battle of Coral Sea.

Hill, George Holman (1937-41, B. A.' 41), Fort Worth, Captain U. S. Army Air Corps. Died in service in Alaska Area.

Hinton, J. W. (1928-32), B. Ed. '32, Eagle Lake, Col. U. S. Army Air Corps. Killed Dec. 10, 1941, in the East Indies.

Hockett, Luther H. L. (Summer, 1942), Dallas, Flight Officer, U. S. Army Air Corps. Killed May 2, 1944, Maxston Army Air Base, N. C.

Hooper, Preston L. (1938), Fort Worth. Killed in Normandy invasion, 1945.

Johnson, Charles C., III (1935-37), Fort Worth, Captain, U. S. Army Air Corps. Killed in plane crash, Tonopah, Nev., February, 1943.

Jordan, Elmer H., Jr. (1937-41), Fort Worth, Lieut. U. S. Army Air Corps. Killed in action March, 1943.

Kysar, Herbert Allen (1937-41, B. S. Com.), Fort Worth, Lieut. Army Air Corps. Killed on bombing mission over Mediterranean, July 9, 1942.

Lindsey, Herbert Wayne (Summer, 1942), Fort Worth, Flight Officer, glider pilot. Killed behind the lines in France, June 7, 1944.

Lissner, Philip David (1939-40), Eagle Pass, Lieut. U. S. Army Air Corps. Killed in action Nov. 28, 1942, buried Port Moresby, Australia.

Lowe, Willis E. (1936-38, B. S. Com.), Fort Worth, Lieut. U. S. Army Air Corps, Navy Ferry Service. Killed in plane crash May 27, 1944. Cal.

Lynch, Jack Oglesby (1938-42, B. S. Com.), Fort Worth, Ensign, U. S. Navy. Went down on U. S. S. Helena, Kula Gulf, July 6, 1943.

Malmberg, George C. (1933-35), Fort Worth, Lieut. U. S. Naval Air Corps. Killed in accident, Pacific Area, July, 1943.

Matthews, William Prenton (1936-41, B. S. Posthumously, '42), Floydada, Lieut. U. S. Army Air Corps. Killed, plane crash, Ore., May 5, 1942.

McComb, Harold E. (1940-43), Fort Worth, Lieut. U. S. Army Air Corps. Killed in action over Europe, Feb. 6, 1945.

McGraw, John J. (1938-40), Fort Worth, Lieut. U. S. Army Air Corps. Killed in action in raid over Rumania.

McKinney, Murray Charlton (1937-41, B. S. Com.), Sulphur Springs, Lieut. Navy Air Corps. Killed in action, South Pacific, July 7, 1943.

McElroy, William Harold (1942-43), Fort Worth, U. S. Marine Corps. Killed (no definite information regarding date).

McRoberts, Floyd M. (1937-41), Fort Worth, Lieut. Royal Canadian Air Force. Killed in bomber mission over Germany Dec. 6, 1944.

Mecaskey, James (1938-41), Panhandle, Lieut. U. S. Army Air Corps, bomber pilot, Egypt. Killed in action Oct. 24, 1942.

Montgomery, Garland (1937-39), Fort Worth, Lieut. U. S. Army Air Corps. Killed June 20, 1943, on Trans-Atlantic flight.

Mood, John Leavell (1938), Fort Worth, First Lieut. U. S. Army Air Corps. Killed June 5, 1943.

Nichol, Jim (1935-40, B. S. Com.), Fort Worth, Lieut. U. S. Army Air Corps. Lost on Army transport Sept. 7, 1944, Philippine Area.

Oster, Ellison (1942-43), Fort Worth, Pfc. U. S. Army Infantry. Killed in action, Germany, April 3, 1945.

Phillips, Edward Winston (1939-41), Fort Worth, Sgt. U. S. Army Air Corps. Killed in action over Germany May 14, 1943.

Pridemore, Walter Ralph (1933-37, B. A. '37), Fort Worth, Lieut. U. S. Army Air Corps. Killed in crash in Tennessee.

Ragland, Robert Allen (1937-39, B. A.), Homer, La., Lieut. U. S. Army Air Corps. Killed Dec. 24, 1944, on B-29 mission in China.

Ramsey, Bill (1939-42), Breckenridge, Lieut. Marine Air Corps. Killed in raid over Rabaul.

Rawlings, Weldon (Summer, 1940), Fort Worth, Lieut. U. S. Army Air Corps. Killed Nov. 5, 1943, over France.

Reineke, George B. (1940-42), Fort Worth, Navigator Army Air Corps. Killed June 14, 1944.

Roberts, James Peck (1937-40), Clinton, Ky., Lieut. U. S. Army Air Corps. Killed in airplane accident, West Indies, Oct. 1, 1942.

Sikes, Jack Day (1939-41), Eastland, Lieut. U. S. Army Air Corps. Killed in plane crash while instructing.

Smith, John Burgess (1941-43), Fort Worth, U. S. Marine Corps. Killed April 2, 1945, in battle of Okinawa.

Smith, Kelton Leroy (1940-41), Fort Worth, Aviation Cadet, U. S. Marine Corps. Killed in collision of planes Altus, Okla.

Strube, William Ernest (1932-36, B. A.), Fort Worth, Lieut. Navy and Marine Corps, Medical. Killed in action in the Pacific.

Talley, Louie Homer (1938-40), Weatherford, Lieut. U. S. Army Air Corps. Killed in bomber crash near Hastings, Mich., August 14, 1942.

Tomlinson, Douglas, Jr. (1936-42), Fort Worth, Lieut. U. S. Army Air Corps. Killed in action over Politz, Germany, June 20, 1944.

Townes, Rollie, Jr. (1942-43), Fort Worth, Sgt. U. S. Army. Killed in action in Germany March 29, 1945.

White, Douglas Hayden (1940), Fort Worth, Lieut. Army Air Corps. Killed on bombing mission over Germany, Aug. 14, 1945.

320

White, Floyd Earl, Jr. (1935-40, B. S. P. Ed.), Plano, Lieut. U. S. Army Air Corps.
Killed in action Oct. 24, 1944, in France.

Williams, Wiley C., Jr. (1942-43), Moran, Pfc. U. S. Army Air Corps. Killed in
plane crash Miami, May 5, 1944.

Yarborough, Woodrow, Pythian Home, Weatherford, U. S. Army Air Corps.
Killed in action.

The following faculty members were called into various services, about half of
them returning to T. C. U. after the war:

Baker, William P., Coast Guard; Blair, Arthur Witt, Aviation Instructor; Boeck,
A. L., O. P. A.; Braddy, Haldeen, Aviation Instructor; Bowman, B. H., Army; Brum-
below, Lester (Mike), Physical Education (Navy); Clark, Mack, Army; Cummings,
Nettie Jo, Interpreter; Grubbs, William Howard, Physical Education (Navy); Hen-
ry, Robert G., Army Air Corps; Hewitt, W. J., U. of Puerto Rico; Jones, H. J., Army;
Maceo, J. R., Chaplain; Mixson, Keith, Army; Oliver, Clifton Jr., Army; Roach,
Walter, Physical Education (Navy); Sherer, Charles R., Army School at Biarritz;
Smith, Rebecca W., WAVES; Street, James Clark, Army Specialist; True, C. Allen,
O. P. A.

A Typical T. C. U. Band, 1935-36

# ◌ XXIV ◌

# The New Era of Expansion
# 1939-47

M. E. SADLER      ED LANDRETH

THIS STORY IS COMING TO ITS CLOSE in the sixth year of the presidency of Dr. McGruder Ellis Sadler, on the eve of the celebration of the seventy-fifth anniversary of the birth of Texas Christian University, in the midst of the agonies of postwar reconstruction and marked by the high fever of building expansion. The events of this final short period are too close to be related in more than summary fashion; their interpretation will be made by some later historian.

President M. E. Sadler, like Joseph Addison Clark, was born in the Tarheel State, where he graduated from Atlantic Christian College in 1919. His later education was obtained in Vanderbilt (M. A. '21), University of Chicago ('21-'22), Yale (B. D. '25, Ph.D. '29), with an Honorary LL.D. from T. C. U. in 1941.[1] His major volume *Japan* was based on his researches for a year in that country under the auspices of the Rockefeller Institute of Social and Religious Research. After serving as Dean of Lynchburg College he spent several years as district, then national Director in the field of Religious Education for the Disciples of Christ. After the death of his brother Lee Sadler, outstanding minister, he accepted the pastorate of the Central Christian Church in Austin, Texas, where he gained an intimate acquaintance with the workings of the University of Texas and with the personnel of the faculty. He also won the esteem of the ministry of the Disciples in Texas, which was a strong factor in his selection for the presidency of T. C. U. The report of the committee nominating him in April 1941, prepared by Dr. L. D. Anderson, is a classic statement of what the president of a Christian University should be, and presented him as fulfilling these qualifications.

---

[1]This was voted for him prior to his election as President.

Perhaps it is enough to say that he seems to be attaining the standards set forth in that noble document.[2]

The new president was quickly plunged into the details of negotiations with the U. S. Navy in arranging for and conducting the various forms of cooperation with it, as told in Chapter XXIII. His major policy at first was to augment the current income of the University in order to increase the faculty salaries and expand the equipment. This was done through two channels, church offerings and Living Endowment. He called J. Erwin Montgomery from the pastorate at Longview to be Assistant to the President especially charged with contacting students and cultivating the support of the churches. Abetted by the prosperity of the time, the result was a large increase in the offerings from the churches, and of student enrollment. The genial personality of Mr. Montgomery is responsible for more than money; it is a positive force for friendship to the school.

The Living Endowment plan was to secure annual gifts from individuals in amounts of $100 to $1,000, somewhat on the order of the Community Chest pattern, the funds to be used for current income, becoming the equivalent of interest on endowment. This plan was substantially undergirded through the year 1944 by the gift of $10,000 from an anonymous donor to cover the expenses of the campaign. The Assistant to the President in charge of this effort for the year 1944 was Bayne Driskill, who later accepted the pastorate of the Magnolia Avenue Christian Church in Fort Worth. He was succeeded in the work by Paul Campbell, who came from the pastorate in Weatherford, in January 1945. The yield of this fund the first year was about $50,000. The same anonymous donor renewed his support for 1947 in the amount of $25,000, and the Dean-elect of Brite College of the Bible, D. Ray Lindley, was added to the staff as general director.

After two years of service the new President readjusted the executive organization of the University to fit the expanding growth. Prior to this date there was one "Dean of the University" through whom each department head and each director of the school operated. Beginning September 1943 each school or college has its own Dean who reports directly to the President. The former Cabinet, made up of all of the department heads, is now displaced by the Dean's Council consisting of the seven (later eight) Deans with the President as the chairman. This readjustment was in harmony with a long standing request of

[2]For a copy of this statement see Minutes, 4-19-41.

Dean Hall who had served as the Dean of the University for twenty-three years, and of the Trustees of Brite College of the Bible, who desired the full time of their Dean.

In this new arrangement the status of Dr. John Lord was little changed. He had been Dean of the Graduate School since its inauguration in 1926. Dean Raymond A. Smith was simply promoted from Director of the School of Education to Dean. Dr. T. Smith McCorkle, who had come in 1942 with the doctor's degree in Music from the University of Texas, to become the Director of the School of Fine Arts became the Dean thereof. Another Dean, Dr. Cortell Holsapple, had earned his place as Dean of the Evening College by his assiduity in the management of the affairs that dealt with the flying schools, the Navy and the E. S. M. W. T., in which he had showed his executive capacities. The other two Deans were drafted from the outside. Dean Jerome Moore who took over the arduous duties of administering the central school of the University, the Add-Ran College of Arts and Sciences, is an alumnus of T. C. U. (B. A. '25, M. A. '27), After receiving his Ph.D. in Spanish from the University of Pennsylvania ('37), he served as Professor of Spanish in Texas State College for Women. As a student in T. C. U. he had held many offices, won many scholarships and had revealed his ability to dispatch much work in short order. Being an ordained minister, a proven scholar and a well balanced diplomat, he has fitted into the exacting responsibilities successfully. It required a year to locate a man to fit as Dean of the School of Business. He was found in the person of Dr. Ellis M. Sowell, a devoted churchman, with a record as a successful teacher of a men's Sunday School class at Nacogdoches, his former home, with practical experience as a business man and a teacher and a scholar with a Ph.D. degree in Business from the University of Texas. He is putting this School on a high plane of efficiency and scholarship. With the founding of the Harris School of Nursing, beginning February 1, 1947 the eighth Dean was added in the person of Dean Lucy Harris, who is engaged in developing this new school on sound educational basis for a broad training of nurses with an educational preparation in Liberal Arts and in the profession of nursing.

The Building Expansion Program was well under way when President Sadler came into office, having been started under the leadership of President Waits, to whom, along with the Fort Worth Committee of Laymen the new president deferred in the leadership in this matter for several years, while he was concentrating on increasing the current income. As the restrictions of the depression years had begun to relax in the late 1930's plans were discussed for new buildings, and with the rising tide of prosperity those plans constantly expanded. President Waits recommended in 1939 a Million Dollar program of building. After the problem had been studied by a committee of the Trustees, a one and one-half million dollar program was adopted, with the policy of fitting the campus for an attendance of 2500 students and no more. A small college with a thorough equipment and emphasis on personal attention was the ideal. All that was lacking to get it started was the person to be the sparkplug for raising the money. The very man proved to be at hand in the person of Ed Landreth, an oil producer, a Methodist, and one who had attained the reputation of being able to elicit money from Fort Worth citizens in large sums and leaving them happy about it. He was always energetic in any cause for the good of the community. Besides, in this case, he was a business partner of R. Houston Foster and very fond of him. After Mr. Foster's death in 1941 the devotion of Mr. Landreth to the T. C. U. enterprise took on the flavor of urgent crusade.

In September 1939 the erection of a Science building and a girls' dormitory was authorized, and the Committee on Building Program was enlarged to include several prominent Fort Worth men.[3] The following May a Student Union building was agreed upon. As a part of the program and much to its encouragement the Board arranged to borrow from the Burnett Trust $300,000 to build the new girls' dormitory, to be repaid out of its earnings. By September 1941 Mr. Landreth was able to report pledges of $284,000 and the promise of $100,000 on condition of raising an additional $200,000 beyond the $300,000 borrowed for the new dormitory. The building program took on enthusiastic reality when the walls of the new girls' dormitory began to go up in the fall of 1941 and the building was completed in the spring of 1942 in time for occupancy for the fall semester. It was designed to be the best dormitory in Texas and was actually the newest, for the priorities were secured just before all such building became impossible. It was named Foster Hall in honor of R. Houston Foster, President of the Trustees, who had died in June 1941

[3]Minutes, 9-22-39.

The war interfered with the building plans, but did not completely stop the financial efforts. One notable and dramatic example of this fact was a meeting of donors of larger amounts which had been called to meet on December 8, 1941. The questions was "shall this campaign be recessed or pushed, in view of the threats of war?" The day before the meeting the great tragedy of Pearl Harbor had occurred; a pall of discouragement hung over the discussions. After all the blue speeches had been made, man after man declared his readiness to proceed. The agreement was that the pledges should be collected, more of them secured, and all money deposited with the Treasurer, Ed Winton, to be held in a distinct fund until conditions would permit building to proceed.

On each December following, the same policy was pursued. "At the conclusion of the War, the plans were brought out, dusted off and given top priority." In November 1945 more comprehensive plans were recommended by the Building Program Committee and adopted by the Board of Trustees.[4] The goal was $5,500,000[5] of which three of the items were announced

[4]The composition of the committee was: Honorary Chairman, Amon Carter; Chairman, Charles Roesser; Co-Chairman, E. E. Bewley, E. A. Landreth and Marshall Fuller; Secretary, Y. Q. McCammon; Treasurer, Ed Winton. Other members, F. J. Adams, Clay J. Berry, Lionel W. Bevan, T. J. Brown, Floyd L. Carmichall, J. Marvin Leonard, Herman Gartner, R. E. Harding, Dr. Charles H. Harris, Ben E. Keith, Galen H. McKinney, William Monnig, Dan A. Levy, Arch H. Rowan, Dr. M. E. Sadler, W. L. Stewart, W. K. Stripling, J. B. Thomas, Dr. E. M. Waits.

[5]The Building Program Plans called for the completion of the following construction projects before 1950:

| | |
|---|---:|
| 1. New Dormitory for Women, Foster Hall (completed) | $ 300,000 |
| 2. New Dormitory for Women, improved duplicate of Foster Hall | 475,000 |
| 3. New Dormitory for Men | 325,000 |
| 4. New Utility Shop, Warehouse, Garage, Servants House | 75,000 |
| 5. Goode Hall, rehabilitated | 110,000 |
| 6. New Fine Arts Building | 1,000,000 |
| 7. Jarvis Hall Rehabilitated into classrooms | 150,000 |
| 8. Clark Hall, Rehabilitated 175,000 | |
| 9. Student Union and Administration Building, Rehabilitated | 250,000 |
| 10. New Science Building | 850,000 |
| 11. New Field House, seating capacity 6,000 | 700,000 |
| 12. Mary Couts Burnett Library Enlargement and Rehabilitation | 200,000 |
| 13. Gymnasium, Rehabilitated for Women | 25,000 |
| 14. New Dormintory for Men | 300,000 |
| 15. Brite Hall, Rehabilitated | 25,000 |
| 16. Beautification of Campus | 290,000 |
| 17. Stadium Enlargement to 25,000 seating capacity | 250,000 |
| Total Cost of Building Program | $5,500,000 |

As shown in *Gifts*, p. 30.

as already "provided": by the Burnett Trust, as a loan, $1,400,000 for two dormitories; by the Stadium Association $250,000 for the enlargement; by an unnamed friend $850,000 for the Science building. The balance of the program, $3,000,000, was set to be the goal of "an intensive financial campaign" scheduled for May and June 1946 among the Fort Worth citizens. The campaign utilized the professional services of the Wells Organization and the volunteer assistance of hundreds of Fort Worth citizens in a series of dinners for stimulation of it. Leading and soliciting was the dynamic personality of Co-Chairman Ed Landreth, despite his impaired health condition which had forced him to retire from active business. The Campaign received a great boost early in its progress by a gift of $200,000 from Tom J. Brown, which was in addition to his previous one of $100,000. By midsummer the goal had been practically reached, but the cost of construction had so mounted that an additional million dollars was added to the goal.

Meanwhile, the beautification of the Stadium grounds proceeded during the autumn, reserving the additional seating until building costs were lower.* The two dormitories, one for men and one for women, began construction, to be ready for occupancy in September 1947. The funds for the great building program are accumulating in the bank, ready for construction when building conditions warrant.

Following World War II the United States Government made one of the wisest and most generous provisions for its veterans ever devised: $65 a month for single men, $90 for married men, plus school supplies, while enrolled in any approved school. The result was an immediate and surprising, even embarrassing increase in enrollment in all colleges, girls as well as boys. Barracks were secured from Camp Barkeley to house 250 additional boys in the spring of 1946, and other barracks from Camp Bowie to be used as classrooms by the fall of 1947. The fortieth apartment for married ministerial students was completed in time for the spring of 1947.

Under this plan the stream of veterans began to flow in the spring of 1946. The enrollment of 1945-46 was 3703, against

*During the summer of 1947 the Stadium was enlarged by 6,000 and the whole campus was graded extensively.

327

the 2633 of the previous year. That of 1946-47 was about 4200.[6]

What does this indicate as to the future size of the T. C. U. student body? Some light may be thrown on the matter by a study of the experience after World War I. The year the U. S. A. entered the World War I (1916-17) the enrollment was 589; the first year after the war (1918-19) it was 805, an increase of 37 per cent. Within seven years it had increased by 67 per cent, surpassing the thousand mark in 1923-24.[7] The percentage of increase following World War II is naturally larger, because of the government subsidy. But the fact of the sustained and permanent increase after the previous war should indicate that the recent swell in enrollment, though it may recede somewhat, will not subside to the former figures.

And now we are ready for the Diamond Jubilee of Texas Christian University, to be celebrated from January to June 1948. How far we have come since the beginning of the "college of the cattle frontier"! From the small stone house on the top of a hill overlooking a sparsely settled country side to a thriving city of nearly half a million and a campus soon to have buildings costing nearly ten millions of dollars. From the financial support of small fees and family sacrifices to the backing of an endowment of practically five million dollars, and an annual budget of two million dollars. From a one-teacher school at the beginning, to a faculty of more than 200 and students counted by the thousands, coming day and night. What changes! One thing remains the same: the ideals, the purposes, the philosophy. It is the educated Christian man and woman making Christian homes who are the hope of the world after these three intervening wars, just as the Clarks envisioned them as the hope of rebuilding the New South in the early seventies.

It has come to be a common saying that there are no more frontiers. So far as new land in the U. S. A. is concerned that is true. Such new terms as "airplane, atomic bomb, United Nations" have dispelled the old frontier concepts and are fast making this truly one world. But there are frontiers to be explored in science, in social sciences, in politics and in religion that challenge the coming generations as boldly as the old frontiers of the

---

[6]These figures are obtained by counting each student once within the twelve month period. The limit of 2,500 set by the Trustees in 1939 intended, doubtless, the number of day students at any one time.

[7]A complete list of annual enrollments is in the Appendix.

untamed forests. To conquer these it will require a different type of hardihood, that of brains, technic, scientific knowledge, diplomacy. But the same basic character of personality is required as was demanded of those who conquered the cattle frontier, courage, venturesomeness, faith. To this end the Texas Christian University of the new world frontier is dedicated.

### LEGEND

Shallow prairies, rolling onward
To the utmost edge of night,
Meeting with the blue horizon
In a line of yellow light.

'Twas the domain of the Tehas,
Guarded with courage bow;
Heritage from sire to grandson,
Kept intact from every foe.

On a hill above the river
At the threshold of the plain
Lived a chieftain, sage and hoary,
Lived and died—but not in vain.

For he blessed the land he guarded
Left his sons this dying will;
"Let my plains be free and fruitful;
Post a lookout on my hill."

Ancient Tehas, thou wert building
Better far than thou couldst see;
For on the hill that crowns the river
Stands the look-out strong and free.
And your plains were ever fruitful,

Free to freeborn men to till,
Nursing on their ample bosoms
Sons and daughters on the hill.

Behold the lookout on the hill top,
Beacon light of shining truth—
T. C. U. thine Alma Mater,
Guardian of the Tehas youth.

—By Rebecca Smith Lee, being the Prologue to the Golden Jubilee Pageant, 1923. Published in the 1923 Horned Frog, and in "These Fifty Years."

# ∾ XXV ∾

# Related Colleges

SEVEN JUNIOR COLLEGES have operated in Texas at various times, under the same auspices, more or less, as T. C. U., have completed their terms of service and passed out of existence. The histories of two of these have been printed in the biographies of their founders. It is altogether unlikely that the stories of the other five will ever be published. Why not, therefore, add a chapter to give a brief summary of the careers of these seven.[1]

Before concluding the chapter, it may be well to refer to six other schools that are more distantly related.

### CARLTON COLLEGE 1865-1916

Inasmuch as The Life and Influence of Charles Carlton records rather completely the story of Carlton College, and is available, the present story will be confined in a large measure to a condensed summary of the data presented in that book.[2]

Carlton College was distinctly a one-man college. Charles Carlton, English born (1821), spent eight years of his boyhood on the high seas, not much of it in school. Good fortune led him to Bethany College, where he received, under Alexander Campbell and his faculty, a thorough education and a zeal for the plea of the Christian Church, as taught by the Reformers of the Nineteenth Century.

After traveling, preaching, and teaching in Kentucky, Missouri, and Arkansas, then in Collin County and in Dallas, Texas, Mr. Carlton settled in Kentucky-Town near Bonham and established a local school in 1865, which soon grew into a boarding school, using all the available boarding space in the community. In 1867 he was invited to move to Bonham; there he established Bonham Seminary, a coeducational school. In 1881 its name was changed to Carlton College and in 1887 it became a girls' school.

---

[1]The reader will please understand that these stories are quite condensed and that the documentation is necessarily limited.
[2]Kenneth Hay, The Life and Influence of Charles Carlton, published privately, and available through the office of the Texas Christian Missionary Society, 2909 Lubbock Street, Fort Worth, Texas.

After the death of Charles Carlton in February, 1902, his son, Charles T. Carlton, who had been vice-president since his graduation from Bethany in 1875, became the president. The days were coming when girls' colleges, especially in small communities, were having a hard time. The attendance was decidedly reduced. The other college of similar status in Sherman twenty miles away, Carr-Burdette, was without a Head at the time, so in 1913 the two schools were combined and settled in the Carr-Burdette property in Sherman and operated for three years under the name Carr-Carlton College. The shock of World War I was too much for the school. The Carltons moved back to Bonham in 1916 and the school under the Carlton name was no more.

Several personalities made indelible marks in the life of Carlton College. One was J. B. Rosecrans, known affectionately as "Brother Rosie," who came to Texas as Sunday School Evangelist from 1884-1888, then taught Bible and Philosophy in Carlton until 1915. He had a cheerful, optimistic nature, full of sunshine and music, beloved by all. The two daughters of President Carlton were lovely, cultured personalities. Miss Grace taught Art, and Miss Sallie Joe was the head of the music teaching. After the school was closed they continued to live in the old home, large and rambling as it was, and to teach private pupils. They were always devoted to the church, delightful in personality and revelling in the memories of their many girls of the yesterdays of Carlton College. Miss Sally Joe expressed their sentiment in these words, after the school had closed:

> The work of Carlton College is finished, but we trust its influence will be felt through all time, as those educated in this hallowed spot live up to the ideals implanted by their earnest Christian teachers.

The title of Mr. Hay's book is well chosen, *The Life and Influence of Charles Carlton*, for few men have exerted such a deeply abiding influence on their communities as did he. The whole community of Bonham, especially, was marked by the influence of his character and teaching.[3]

### CARR-BURDETTE

The beginnings, struggles, and ideals of Carr-Burdette College are recorded in the volume, The Story of a Life by J. Breck-

[3]Mr. Carlton was the teacher of Addison and Randolph Clark, see Chapter II.

enridge Ellis,[4] which is a biography of Mrs. O. A. Carr, the founder, who was President of the college until her death in October, 1908. This book published a sufficient record of the school until that date, for it was definitely a projection of her ideals and the work of her hands, along with that of her husband.

Her education was that of the typical "female seminary" of that day, with its emphasis on English Literature, French conversation, the "accomplishments," music and art, ladylike conduct, and the social graces, with a sort of subdued recognition of the expectation that the young lady would some day be the mother of a household. She had a consuming passion to establish and head a college for young women that would carry on this cultural tradition. She also had the energy to work, and a will to bend things her way.

With the background of the "Blue Grass Region" of Kentucky and a wealthy home, she was somewhat of an aristocrat in bearing, ornate in dress, with an air of dignity. She was too serious and in dead earnest to be impressive socially. She was a good persuader. She persuaded the merchants of St. Louis and other cities to donate furniture for the school, and the people to buy lots in Sherman to aid in erecting the building.

O. A. Carr, her husband, was a Christian minister, serious, self-effacing, awkward socially, rather heavy as a speaker, and a genuinely sincere, noble, Christian gentleman. He was valuable in the school because he was such a versatile scholar, able in teaching philosophy, religion, history, and the languages.

Carr-Burdette College opened September, 1894, in Sherman, the "Athens of Texas," in the one beautiful building which housed the girls, the faculty and all the classrooms. Art was taught by Mrs. Carr herself. The parlor was arranged very attractively with displays of paintings and statuary. She wanted a small select school for girls, and she got it. The girls expected the Head Woman to be a little bit odd, and they got what they expected. She was different.

For fourteen years Mrs. Carr reigned happily. On her death in October 1908, Mr. Carr carried on as President until he died in 1913.

The school had been generally advertised as the "property of the Christian Church of Texas." During the lifetime of the Carrs, it was well understood that the management was in their

[4]Published by Reynolds-Parker Co., Sherman, Texas, 1910. A copy is in the Library of Texas Christian University.

hands and that the Board of Directors was more or less nominal.[5] But on the death of Mrs. Carr, then of Mr. Carr, the question arose in the minds of the people, which "Christian Church"? For a division had occurred, which was especially prominent in Sherman.

Upon consulting the deed, it was found that the property was deeded to "O. A. Carr and M. F. Carr, as Trustees, for the Christian Church of Sherman, and to be held by the said Christian Churches (note the plural) for the Christian Churches of the State of Texas." Provision was made also that

in case there should hereafter be more than one Christian Church in the City of Sherman, then the Trust herein created shall en(s)ure to all of said churches, equally, the powers herein conferred upon the officers of the said Christian Church, shall be exercised by the officers of all such churches assembled as one body.

It was further provided that on the death of Mr. and Mrs. Carr the directors should continue, and should fill vacancies, and that if the directors should be reduced by death or resignation to less than five, "then the elders and deacons of the Christian Churches, at Sherman, Texas, shall appoint a sufficient number to make the full number of nine thereof, which Board thus created shall have all the powers herein prescribed."[6]

It came to pass that the majority of the Board was of the First Christian Church of Sherman, and they took control at the death of Mr. Carr. It had been generally patronized by this group rather than the "Church of Christ."

The Board consisted of Judge Jesse F. Holt, W. L. Hay, Will H. Evans, W. H. Lucas. All of these were members of the First Christian Church of Sherman. There may have been other members of the Board.

When Mr. Carr died, he had associated with him Professor J. F. Anderson, formerly Business Manager of T. C. U., who continued as President, but, unfortunately, for only a year. For he was killed accidentally by a fall down the elevator shaft in 1914. His son, Grantland Anderson, completed the school year. For three years, 1913-16, the school was operated as Carr-Carlton, the faculty of Carlton College having joined it.

[5]The deed showed that the Carrs appointed the directors.
[6]The quotations in this paragraph are taken from the deed, which is recorded in the Deed Records of Grayson County, Texas, Volume 105, p. 182. A copy of this deed was secured by the courtesy and assistance of Judge Jesse F. Holt and Pastor Robert Badgett of Sherman.

Then the distinguished editor of the *Christian Courier* and widely known minister, Cephas Shelburne, accepted the presidency, and served successfully, but in financial straits, until November, 1924, when he died. His genteel wife carried on as Acting President, and his efficient daughter, Miss Elizabeth, as Dean for several years, most effectively. The *Christian Courier* proposed Will H. Evans, prominent business and church leader of Sherman, as the next President. The Board elected Dr. W. P. King of Louisville, Kentucky.[7]

During this period a major and final effort was made to get a secure financial backing for the College. On October 7, 1926, the formal opening was held in a Dallas hotel of the Joint Junior College Crusade,[8] to include Randolph College and Carr-Burdette College. T. C. U. agreed to refrain from solicitations for a year to give these smaller schools opportunity. In January the report indicated that $135,000 had been raised in pledges and cash,[9] and in May, $342,000.[10] These optimistic reports proved to be disappointing, however. The crusade was carried on by a team from the National Board of Education of the Disciples of Christ, on the technic of the former Men and Millions Campaign, involving a good-sized company of people, with expenses rather high. The expenses outran the cash collections. The Trustees were called upon for advance expense money again and again. They had to borrow this money at the bank. They also had to repay the bank, for the collections never caught up with the expenses. The pledges taken were slow in being paid. This was the tragic ending of the attempts at large campaigns with expensive teams. The enthusiasm of the World War I days was gone, the psychology had changed.[11]

The leaders had done all that human beings could do to carry out the purposes of the institution. Times had changed. The day for the small privately managed girls' college was past. In 1929 the school was closed, the property taken by the loan company. Elizabeth Shelburne became assistant professor of Mathematics in T. C. U., later the Dean of Women. Her mother, Mrs. Cephas Shelburne, served for years as a matron of men, until her death in 1943.

---

[7]*Christian Courier*, 6-19-24; 11-30-24; 7-9-25; 7-25-25.
[8]*Christian Courier*, 10-7-26.
[9]*Christian Courier*, 1-13-27.
[10]*Christian Courier*, 5-5-27.
[11]These facts are attested by the leaders in Sherman.

McGruder Ellis Sadler, President, 1941-

Randolph College (at Lancaster) was started by Randolph Clark as President, and his son-in-law, Robert F. Holloway as Business Manager in 1899, about four years after they had decided not to go with Add-Ran to Waco. The Christian Church was quite strong, locally, at Lancaster; the members had a special love for "Mr. Randolph," and an ambition for a college in their town. They erected two large frame buildings, and raised some money for its support.

However, conditions were not ripe for such a move. The churches over the state were committed to the support of Add-Ran at Waco; Lancaster was in the shadow of the big city of Dallas. Not enough students nor enough money could come out of the little town to support the school. This was discovered after two years of trial. Mr. Randolph accepted the presidency of the newly projected Panhandle Christian College at Hereford, and the Lancaster school closed.

It was not, however, a failure in results. At least three widely known men received their education there. One is A. K. Scott, veteran evangelist and church builder under the Texas Christian Missionary Society, a devoted and capable preacher who could not have accomplished his remarkable work without the training secured at Lancaster. Alexander Campbell Parker, eloquent preacher, received practically all of his schooling here. He mingled business with preaching, and at one time was known as the millionaire preacher, from his success in oil.[12] A distinguished educator, Dr. Elzy D. Jennings, who became Dean and Vice-President of Southern Methodist University in Dallas, a staunch Methodist, attended Lancaster College and received his degree from it. In 1936 Texas Christian University gave a token recognition of the Lancaster School, and honored Dean Jennings by conferring on him the honorary degree of Doctor of Laws.

## HEREFORD 1902-1915

Hereford College and Industrial School opened September 10, 1902, with Randolph Clark as its first President. It soon passed under the control of the Disciples of Christ in the Panhandle who were ambitious to maintain an institution of higher education.

[12]For his later contacts see Chapter XVIII.

In December 1904, a proposition was made to the Board of Trustees of Texas Christian University to assume the indebtedness of the school and manage the college in the name of the Disciples of Christ in Texas. On the recommendation of the Christian Lectureship meeting at Temple, the Board assumed the obligation, and at once took steps to enlarge the scope of the institution.

Jesse B. Haston, pastor of the Christian Church at Hereford, became acting President and held the forces together during the last session.

Until the Charter of Texas Christian University could be amended, a provisional Board of Trustees was chosen, to hold the property in deed of trust, and to arrange for the work of the coming session.

Such is the story of the "Panhandle Christian College" (as the article is headed) in the Catalog of T. C. U. of 1905.[13] The moving spirit in its establishment was T. E. Shirley, President of the Board of Trustees of T. C. U., who, having become a sufferer from asthma, found it necessary to live in the high altitude. Having made his home in Hereford and become a "booster" for that region, he was ambitious for a college in the Panhandle. The Lancaster school having gone down at the time, he was able to persuade Randolph Clark to move to Hereford and head the new school. The establishment of such a college fitted into the dreams of President Zollars, that of having a series of junior colleges, feeding the University. The above quotation reveals that Randolph Clark had resigned from Hereford, doubtless lured by the opportunity to rejoin his brother in the establishment of the Add-Ran Jarvis College at Thorp Spring—and the local pastor had been called on to fill in temporarily. The attempt to commit the T. C. U. Trustees to the support of the Hereford College was hasty and incomplete. The vote of the Lectureship had no validity. The charter was never amended as intended. The majority of the Trustees were definitely of the conviction that the financial responsibility of the one school was all they wanted to carry. President Zollars never did win them on this point. He published nine pages of the "Prospectus of Panhandle Christian College" in the T. C. U. catalog of 1905 with his own name at the head as "President of the University" and Charles Q. Barton as President of the College. On the basis of this announced affiliation, a later president of Hereford Col-

[13]Page 188.

338

lege sued T. C. U. for a balance due on his salary, but he was unable to make out a case. After this experience, the Trustees were more fixed in their determination to avoid any responsibility directly for any other college. This policy is expressed in the catalog of 1910, and others. The several Colleges of the University—Bible, Business, Fine Arts, etc.—are listed, then Hereford and Midland Colleges with this note: "For the sake of convenience and efficiency of administration, the two last named colleges have each more or less independent government than have the others, but, nevertheless, each is correlated to the University."[14] It is listed as an affiliated College as late as 1914-15.

Elster Haile, a graduate of T. C. U. (B. A. '05, M. A. '06), had married the daughter of T. E. Shirley, Miss Pauline. He became President of the College in 1908, but, desiring to continue his graduate work, left for the University of Chicago after two years. The leadership then fell to another notable T. C. U. graduate and a distant kinsman of T. E. Shirley, Douglas A. Shirley, who graduated from T. C. U. in 1904 (B. A.), remained as Registrar and Assistant Treasurer for several years, then joined the faculty of Panhandle College as Head of the Physics Department in 1909. He served as its President for the session of 1910-11, then joined the faculty of the Hereford High School for two years. In 1913 he began his long career with the new West Texas State Teachers College, first as Head of the Physics Department from 1913, then as Associate Dean from 1918, then Registrar since 1923. He has attained a high place of recognition among the Texas colleges.

Douglas Shirley closed the College in 1911, although the T. C. U. catalog listed it as an affiliated college for several years after that. "For the last three years of its existence it was known as Hereford College and was supported by the town and friends in this area and was not restricted to the Christian Church . . . The property where the old school was is now owned by the public school of Hereford.[15]

### JARVIS INSTITUTE, JARVIS COLLEGE, ADD-RAN JARVIS COLLEGE, AT THORP SPRINGS, 1897-1909

When Randolph Clark and his son-in-law, R. F. Holloway decided not to move with the school to Waco in 1895, they soon

[14]Page 18.
[15]From a letter to the author from D. A. Shirley; other information in this paragraph came from the same letter, dated September 30, 1944.

began negotiations with the Trustees to lease the Thorp Spring plant for the operation of a school. This they succeeded in doing, as told in chapter VIII. This same story is told from the Thorp Spring viewpoint in the following language:

Since the first founding of a school here in 1873, by J. A. (Uncle Joe) Clark there has never ceased to be a school at Thorp Spring. It never 'ran down' or 'broke up,' as many have thought, but simply strong inducements effected a change in location.

Jarvis Institute was organized by Prof. Randolph Clark, and had a successful career of two years, when the management could no longer secure the use of the buildings and moved to Lancaster.[16]

This was "Jarvis Institute" which operated from 1897 through 1899, by Randolph Clark under the influence of his aged father (Uncle Joe) who lived until 1901. It is not clear just what was the ownership of the property during these years, but obviously Major Jarvis had some control, since the school bore his name.

But in 1900 the situation cleared and the opening of "Jarvis College" was announced, the property being "owned and controlled by Major J. J. Jarvis of Fort Worth" and the school "managed and controlled by Pres. T. R. Dunlap and his associates in the college work."[16] It continued to draw upon the tradition of the old Add-Ran and to express a kindly attitude toward the University at Waco. "Jarvis College now lives under all the hallowed influences of the great school that moved in 1895, in all its glory, to Waco, where commodious accommodations were offered to the growing institution."[16]

The Faculty of Jarvis College consisted of the President T. R. Dunlap (A. B. and A. M., Eminence, Ky. College 1880) W. S. Dabney (B. S. "from this institution"), C. I. Alexander, (B. A. Add-Ran U., M.A. U. of Tex.) with several teachers in the Special subjects including Mrs. C. I. Alexander in Fine Arts. Major Jarvis was President of the Trustees, and eleven of the thirteen trustees were residents of Thorp Spring. This is the information in the catalog of Jarvis College, announcing for the session of 1903-04, which was evidently the last session under that name and management.

The name Add-Ran Jarvis College came into operation with the session of 1904-05, with Addison Clark as President. Ran-

[16]Jarvis College Catalog, 1903.

340

dolph Clark Vice-President, Lee Clark, Secretary, R. F. Holloway, Business Manager, Joseph L. Clark, Professor of Ancient
Languages, Leoti Sypert Clark (Mrs. Lee Clark) Voice teacher,
Mrs. Ida Nesbit, Primary, (sister of Addison) and other faculty
members. The spirit of this school was avowedly the same as
that of the original Add-Ran. "Add-Ran Jarvis is a lineal de-
scendent of the school of 1873"[17] "It is our aim to build on this
ideal and sacred school site a truly modern university training
school. We desire to correlate our work with that of our best
state universities."[17] The relationship between this school and
Texas Christian University was quite cordial. It was listed as
affiliated with T. C. U. in the catalogs for several years, the
latest such listing being 1908.

This venture was made possible by the love of Major Jarvis
for the Clarks. He agreed to provide the property and a certain
sum of money for operation with the caution that if and when
that sum was exhausted, there would be no more coming from
him.[17] That eventually occurred in 1909 or thereabout, when it
became obvious that even a junior college could not finance itself in a rural location. Addison Clark became pastor of the Mineral Wells church and Randolph a pastor at Comanche. Soon
after, the old plant was purchased by the conservative brethren
who opened Thorp Spring Christian College.

## MIDLAND COLLEGE 1909-1922

Midland, half way between Fort Worth and El Paso, was a
rather wealthy town. Here the families of ranchers for hundreds
of miles around lived so the children could attend the public
schools. Why not have a college also? Land was plentiful. A
group of them chose a hill site, a mile from town, plotted the
tract between in lots to be sold for the endowment of the college.
They induced the T. C. U. Board to appoint a "locating committee" to come out and decide which was the best of several
such sites proposed by different groups. Frank Elkin (B.A. '98),
endeavored to persuade his fellow Trustees of T. C. U. to assume responsibility for the college, as a feeder, but their recent
experience with Hereford made them adamant against the idea.

The first president was Robert L. Marquis (B.A. Add-Ran U.
1901), who served but one year. Then for three years the President was Mr. Henry R. Garrett, a devoted Disciple, who had
come to West Texas for his health.

[17]Add-Ran Jarvis Catalog, 1905. The latter statement of the Major from his son
Van Zandt Jarvis to President Waits and Dean Hall in 1924.

In 1913 was made a wise choice for the presidency. Franklin G. Jones and his wife were both graduates of old Add-Ran at Thorp Spring. He was an ordained minister, had served as a substitute teacher one year at Waco, then had conducted Jones Academy in McKinney for several years. He was held in high esteem by everyone. After four years as president he returned to T. C. U., took his master's degree (1918), then went to Columbia University and took another Master's, and accepted a place as professor on the faculty of the College of Industrial Arts. Later he completed his career as Professor of Secondary Education in T. C. U.[18]

J. T. McKissick (B.A. '96, T. C. U., M.A. '05, Harvard, S. T. B. '06) next became President of Midland College. He was a vigorous evangelist, a gifted mixer among the brethren and was able to collect much money for the school. He started the college career of a number of capable young ministerial students.

The population of the Midland area was sparse, the cattle people were able to send their children away from home to college, so the attendance was discouragingly small. The conditions caused by the War probably put the finishing touches to the situation. The struggle was given up in 1921, the furniture sold to a group of citizens in Cisco; the records were transferred there, and the building was left to the mortgagers, probably lying idle until the oil boom struck in the '30's. Nowadays, some of the old-timers, sitting in their "skyscraper" offices of the prosperous oil city, might be caught musing: "If the College could only have held on until we struck oil, we could have made a go of it."

RANDOLPH COLLEGE AT CISCO 1922-1937

A vacant school property is frequently a temptation to start a college, no matter how clearly the conditions are set against its probable success. And it seems that someone is always available to serve as president. Because there was no support, either in students or funds, and because wisdom indicated that there should be concentration of support on one church college in the state, the effort to build a church college in the small town of Cisco was foredoomed to failure. Seldom has a college struggled with more errors of judgment, mixtures of motives and heroic sacrifice than in the case of the junior college which started out as Cisco Christian College, ran through seven administra-

[18]See Catalogs and *Skiff*, 9-25-13.

tions in fifteen years, and closed in 1937 as Randolph Junior College.

The citizens of Cisco, in 1921, stimulated by a fresh oil boom, urged the local Christian Church people to purchase the furniture and library of the recently closed Midland College, and to open up a new college in the old Britten Training School property. By the autumn of 1922 the first session opened, but during the session of 1923-24 there was no school; the time was spent in the field, working up attendance and support.

Robert F. Holloway was invited by the leaders of the movement to become President. The school was named Randolph College after his father-in-law, in the hope of swinging the influence of the old Clark name in support of the young school. Both of these men first offered their services to the Trustees of Texas Christian University, where their primary loyalty and confidence lay. They proposed that "Holloway could be Business Manager," but T. C. U. had a Business Manager. "Brother Randolph" was invited to make his home at T. C. U., but he could not do so unless his daughter, Mrs. Holloway, could be there also to look after him. So this proposal proved to be not feasible.[19] Mr. Holloway accepted the Presidency of Randolph College and made a conscientious effort to build it up. Mrs. Holloway expressed her judgment against the move, as she testified in later years. In the fall of 1925 Mr. Holloway resigned, and accepted the Superintendency of the Ranger Public Schools, where he served efficiently and established the Ranger (Municipal) Junior College.[20]

During the Holloway administration an incident occurred which proved the loyalty of the old Thorp Spring group to T. C. U. Some of the ex-students of the Thorp Spring era, in their zeal for Randolph College, started a move to organize the Alumni Association of the old Add-Ran, separate from the T. C. U. Alumni Association. A meeting was held, under the chairmanship of J. M. Rieger, at the Cisco encampment grounds on Lake Cisco, August 24, 1924. In the free discussion it became perfectly clear that the group was loyal, first of all, to T. C. U. as the successful continuation of the old school and that they would oppose any attempt to support a separate association. The T. C. U. Association met the situation by providing several Vice-Presidents,

[19]The author was present at these interviews.
[20]*Christian Courier*, 4-23-25.

one for each of the several periods, making the Thorp Spring period the first.[21]

T. T. Roberts, with an English Bible Diploma from the College of the Bible at Lexington, Kentucky, and a good record as a money raiser, served as President for six years, from 1925 through 1931. He increased the attendance and raised some money. Mrs. Lee Bivins of Amarillo pledged $75,000 to build a boys' dormitory. The teachers were poorly paid and became dissatisfied. There was dissatisfaction, too, by some donors.

There was a rumor and a printed announcement that[22] Mr. L. C. Brite had made a donation of $50,000 to Randolph. Some of the men associated with the school at the time maintain that he did so, despite the fact that Mr. Brite told the author that the only contribution he made to Randolph College was the salary of J. T. McKissick as teacher of Bible. After a few years Mr. Brite preferred to have Mr. McKissick as his pastor, so he moved to Marfa. It was during the presidency of T. T. Roberts that the Junior College Crusade was staged, as told in the story of Carr-Burdette. It resulted in raising more expenses than funds.

Joseph Keevil, a good pastor, with no experience in school management except some field work for raising money, and with no college degree, was elected President in June, 1931. But he never served. Unfortunately, he was killed in an auto wreck the next day. Lee Clark, the eldest son of Randolph Clark, then served as President for two years, until the Spring of 1933. John W. Tyndall, who had been serving as Professor of Bible, was made President in May, 1933, worked all summer in preparation, then met with a fatal accident in September before school opened. Mr. Tyndall was a minister of unique personality and of excessive individualistic temperament, charming as a teacher but unstable as a scholar. He had gotten control of a gift from A. D. Milroy of Brenham, a pious and godly man, almost fanatical in his zeal for orthodoxy. With the aid of this fund a brother, David F. Tyndall, was able to keep the school going for two years after the death of John W. Tyndall.

The final effort to perpetuate the school was by the veteran evangelist and school man, J. T. McKissick, who returned, at this time (1935) from his pastorate in Marfa and became Presi-

---

[21]*Christian Courier*, 8-11-24. The author was present at this meeting at Lake Cisco; he suggested the procedure to the T. C. U. Association.
[22]*Christian Courier*, 5-5-27.

dent. The property had long since been taken over by the Temple Trust Company for the mortgage of $75,000. This company had several times endeavored to enlist the interest of the Brotherhood leaders in lifting the mortgage, but the feeling prevailed that the Brotherhood had not been taken into counsel in making the debt, hence should not be responsible for it. President McKissick endeavored, by every device accumulated in his long career, to make the College a permanent institution, but the odds were against him. The accreditation of the Association of Texas Colleges was lost, for lack of equipment, financial stability, and faculty; then that of the State Department of Education. That was the end. He announced the opening of school the next September, 1937. The faculty appeared, but not the students.

E. Buford Isaacks, (B.A. 1914, T. C. U., M.A., University of Texas), served as Dean and Registrar from 1927 through 1936, and during a portion of the time as Business Manager.[23] An impartial after-view may be able to analyze the causes of the passing of these seven junior colleges. The elements were various and intermingled. Some of the schools were individual enterprises, built by and around one personality, and were never developed into institutions, either before or after the passing of the founder. In some cases the motivation was dominated too much by local pride and ambition, which was very good but was not enough to develop the required financial support.

Aside from these local and personal causes, there were conditions that were closing out junior colleges of this type in general. Small colleges in small towns, depending largely on boarding students, will not attract students. If students go away from home, they prefer the larger schools, with more attractive faculties and equipment.

The junior colleges of the early day consisted of four years of high school and two years of college. They supplied the need of students who could not reach a high school near at home. Gradually high schools increased in numbers and availability. Then came the state law providing that any student who did not have a high school nearby could attend any high school in the county, by transferring his state scholastic appropriation to that school. This eliminated the need for the high school department of all colleges. The two years of college left was hardly enough on which to build an institution. The municipal

---

[23]Mr. Isaacks is to be thanked for furnishing some of the data used herein. The records of the institution are not available.

junior colleges fit into the picture because they could simply add to the local high school two years of college and depend on attendance from the local community and county. Taxation also helped out in the problems.

That this picture is accurate is evidenced by the fact that all private junior colleges in Texas, that is, boarding colleges of junior grade, have been closed except those with some endowment. The Baptists, by coordinating the support of the churches through their State Board, have preserved three: Decatur, Wayland, and Marshall, and the latter has recently become a senior college. The Methodists have two, Lon Morris and Weatherford, the latter having the good fortune to possess an endowment of $100,000. The Lutherans have two, Clifton, and Texas Lutheran at Seguin, both small and struggling, supported partly as a place for ministerial training.

And now let us pay our respects to "the six other colleges more or less related" referred to above.

### BAY VIEW COLLEGE

Bay View College was the acme of the one-man college. Thomas Marshall Clark, who was introduced in the chapter[24] on the Thorp Spring period as the artist among the Clarks, left Add-Ran (about 1893) before the move to Waco was even discussed. He seemed to desire a small school for girls in which he could carry out his ideas of culture, which we can be assured were very fine and high. He bought a property in the village of Portland, overlooking Corpus Christi Bay, and there, without asking help from anyone, successfully conducted a small school for girls—Bay View College—for many years. The loss of his wife saddened him; the storm destroyed his plant. He retired, taught music for a while at Canyon, where his only son, Wallace, was Head of the Music Department of West Texas State Teachers College; then languages at Cisco for a few years; then returned to his home at Portland, where he passed away, 1941. Bay View had all of the ideals and flavor of the Clark tradition.

### JARVIS CHRISTIAN COLLEGE 1913-

This excellent College is the expression of the desire for education of their people on the part of the colored Disciples of Christ of Texas. The idea grew up in the heart of Mrs. Mary Alpin, state organizer among the Negro women, and other leaders in that work. The concept was encouraged by the Christian

[24]Chapter VI.

346

Woman's Board of Missions, which believed in education and understood the negro problems.

The dream became a possibility when one of these women of the C. W. B. M., Mrs. Ida Van Zandt Jarvis of Fort Worth, proposed to donate a tract of 465 acres near Hawkins, Texas, for the purpose of establishing a college for Negroes. Mrs. Jarvis was distinctly a Southern woman, who believed in the possibilities and the worthiness of the Negro. She desired to give them opportunity to develop.

The pattern for the school was found in the Southern Christian Institute, already supported by the C. W. B. M. and managed by J. B. Lehman. With his counsel, the school got under way January 13, 1913. A little more than a year later J. N. Erwin was secured as president, a well-educated, cultured, humble, Negro Christian, who knew well how to cultivate the interest of the white people.

The acreage of the property was increased to 847. The buildings were erected by student labor, using lumber from trees on the ground. Later, brick buildings were erected from bricks made on the ground. The work as a high school was accredited by the State Department of Education in 1924, as a junior college in 1928, and as a senior college in 1937. It is a member of the American Association of Colleges.

On the death of President Erwin, P. C. Washington, was called as president. He is continuing to do a splendid job both as a scholar and as an executive.

In order to cultivate more carefully the support of the churches and to have the benefit of their counsel, a Texas Board of white people was organized in 1929. "Two dynamic personalities who have served as president of the Texas Board and whose contributions have been stimulating and dynamic are Boyd Keith and K. V. Lipscomb, both of Dallas." J. L. Lancaster, President of the Texas and Pacific Railroad, was a friend of the school. He served on the Board and designated a station opposite the campus as "Jarvis Station."

The finances have been helped by the discovery of oil in paying quantities on the property. The revenue belongs to the C. W. B. M., or its successor, the United Christian Missionary Society, but enough of it is allocated to care for the needs of the school. The management is wise, well balanced, guided and encouraged by the active, deeply interested white Board.

This institution is a splendid and practical example of the possibilities of a program of lifting the status of the colored people, when the problem is approached with patience, with mutual respect, and in a Christian spirit, on both sides.[25]

## THE COLLEGES OF THE "CHURCHES OF CHRIST"

The unfortunate division of the Christian Churches into "conservatives" and "progressives" became definite about the turn of the twentieth century.[26] Inasmuch as the two groups were originally one, it seems well to mention a list of the colleges of the conservative brethren, also, in this volume. The most extensive writing concerning these schools, so far as is known to the author, is a thesis by W. W. Freeman, A. M., Th.D., presented to Southern Methodist University faculty for his Master of Arts degree in 1933. It includes an extensive story of Abilene Christian College, and fairly complete information concerning the other schools. Much of the data here, though not all of it, is taken from that thesis on permission of the author.[27]

The oldest of these schools was Lockney College at Lockney, Texas, founded in 1894 under the presidency of J. D. Burleson, who was followed by C. H. P. Showalter, then N. L. Clark. The most conservative of them, evidently, was Gunter College, at Gunter, Grayson County, for which N. L. Clark left Lockney in 1903.

The struggle at Gunter was against financial difficulties and ultra-conservative conservatism. As at Lockney, no separate classes were allowed for Bible studies on Sunday, no literature and no women teachers. Later the church undertook, as such, to do the Bible teaching in the school, to avoid supporting an adjunctive institution to the church. Eventually the school was suspended and moved to West Texas. At Littlefield, under the patronage of the anti-class brethren, it lingered in hope for one year, then died.[28]

John R. Freeman, a teacher, later President, in Gunter College at the time it moved to Littlefield came to T. C. U. and earned his B.A. degree in 1915.

[25]The information herein is gleaned from the Catalog of Jarvis Christian College, 1944.
[26]Reference was made to its influence in Add-Ran in Chapter VII.
[27]W. W. Freeman, A History of the Campbell Movement and its Educational System, S. M. U. Library, Unpublished, 1933.
[28]W. W. Freeman's Thesis, p. 610.

The school of this group which started off with the most promise or pretension was the Southwestern University at Denton in about 1905. Its faculty was small but its catalog offered a most extensive curriculum. "A few reports indicate that but for sectional and personal jealousies in Texas, the Denton school might have been a much greater success."[29] In 1906 a Lectureship of the "progressives" was held in Denton, and the fraternizing with them of one of the professors, Dr. H. G. Fleming, led to his dismissal from the faculty and his acceptance of a pastorate with the progressive group.[30]

CleBaRo College was undertaken by A. B. Barrett and C. H. Roberson who had founded Childress Classical Institute at Abilene and had taught a year at Southwestern University in Denton, which had discontinued in the interests of CleBaRo, the new school at Cleburne."[31] It was in existence at least from 1910 through 1916.

Lingleville College was operated for about five years 1905-1909, by D. S. Ligon and others. Sabinal College opened in 1907, with G. H. P. Showalter as President, then W. A. Schultz and Isaac E. Tackett. "The effort at both schools (Lockney and Sabinal) was to avoid worldliness of every sort. It survived several years."

Thorp Spring Christian College served nearly twenty years on the site of the original Add-Ran, at Thorp Spring, beginning in 1910, soon after the Add-Ran Jarvis College closed. It pursued a more liberal policy than the other colleges of this group. It sought and obtained recognition by the Association of Texas Colleges as a standard junior college; also by the State Department of Education. Its Presidents were A. W. Young, 1910-11; R. C. Bell, 1911-15; C. R. Nichol, 1916-18; W. F. Ledlow, 1918-20; A. R. Holton, 1920-27. The last named attended T. C. U. on Saturdays and in summers, and received his M.A. degree in 1920. The Dean there, Batsell Baxter, received his B.A. from T. C. U. in 1916. "As the years passed it became more and more difficult to maintain an institution that could conform to the increasingly higher standards that are being set in the educational programs." The last quotation is from the Prospectus of the "Texas Christian College" at Terrell, 1929, which was an at-

---

[29]*Ibid.*
[30]The author was present at this Lectureship, heard the addresses, and was well acquainted with the later career of Dr. Fleming.
[31]W. W. Freeman's Thesis.

tempt to move the former school to Terrell. Arrangements were made by the city of Terrell to erect some buildings, which were begun but never completed.[32]

Abilene Christian College began in 1906 under the title "Childress Classical Institute," and the presidency of A.B. Barrett, 1906-08. He was followed by H. L. Darden, R. L. Whitesides, and J. F. Cox, 1908-12. Jesse P. Sewell, President 1912-24, was a strong leader, bringing the school to the attention and respect of the educational world, winning recognition for it, in 1919, as a Class A. Senior College. Under President Batsell Baxter (1924-32), the campus was moved in 1929 to a new site east of the city, with seven new buildings. James F. Cox serving as Dean from 1924 and as President from 1932, held the confidence of the educational leaders of Texas, and advanced the school definitely. Among the members of the teaching staff was George Klingman, a son-in-law of Professor I. B. Grubbs, The College of the Bible of Lexington, Kentucky. W. W. Freeman who afterwards earned his Th.D. degree at Southern Baptist Seminary was a professor there, and Henry E. Speck was Registrar. Mr. Hardin of Burkburnett, generous donor to many Baptist institutions in Texas, gave money to A. C. C. to clear most of its indebtedness, in memory of his first wife, who was a member of the Church of Christ.

Abilene Christian College secured the cooperation of most of the brethren of this group, recognized the wisdom of cooperating with the educational system in the state by meeting the generally recognized standards, and became the one successful and surviving Texas college of the Church of Christ.[33]

---

[32]This catalog is on file in T. C. U. Library.
[33]Much of the data is culled from the A. C. C. catalog of June, 1943; and from W. W. Freeman's Thesis.

# Bibliography

## BOOKS

Clark, Joseph L., History of Texas a Land of Promise, D. C. Heath and Co., 1939, 534 pages.

Clark, Randolph, Reminiscences, Biographical and Historical, Publisher, Lee Clark, Wichita Falls, Texas, 1919, 85 pp.

Conger, Roger Norman, High Lights of Waco History, Hill Printing and Stationery Co., Waco., 1945.

Ellis, J. Breckenridge, The Story of a Life, (Mrs. O. A. Carr), Reynolds Parker Co., Sherman, Texas, 1910 (a copy in the T. C. U. Library).

Garrison, W. E., Religion Follows the Frontier, a History of the Disciples of Christ, Harper & Bros., 1931, 317 pp.

Gifts, an ornate illustrated brochure issued by the Building Program Committee of T. C. U. for the Campaign in Fort Worth in 1946, 50 pages.

Hay, Kenneth, The Life and Influence of Charles Carlton, Published privately in Fort Worth, Texas, 1940, (available at 2909 Lubbock Street, Fort Worth).

Montgomery, Riley B., Education of the Ministry of the Disciples of Christ, Bethany Press, 1931.

Osborn, Ronald, Ely Vaughn Zollars, Teacher of Preachers, Builder of Colleges: A Biography. Christian Board of Publication, Saint Louis, 1947.


## PERIODICALS

Caller, The Brite College of the Bible, a Quarterly since May, 1940. The May issue is the Catalog, except that in 1940 it was the August issue.

The Catalogs of the Institution, published each spring, listing the enrollments of the preceding and announcing the faculty and offerings for the subsequent session. All numbers are available in the T. C. U. Library except for '78, '79, '83 and '96. The first twenty-one numbers and for 1903 were donated from the stock of Mrs. Ida (Alex) Nesbit, a sister of Addison and Randolph Clark. Volumes for 1888 and 1897 were donated by Mrs. J. W. Kinsey.

The following table clarifies the early publications; after 1913 the numbers run regularly and they are fully available, printed usually by Stafford-Lowdon.

| Session Number | Volume Number | Year Printed | Announcing For: | Number of Pages | Name of the Printer |
|---|---|---|---|---|---|
| 1 | | | | | |
| 2 | 1 | 1874 | 74-75 | 16 | F. B. Marshall, Fort Worth, Epitomist Office. |
| 3 | 2 | 75 | 75-76 | 16 | Chronicle Office, Cleburne. |
| 4 | 3 | 76 | 76-77 | 16 | Chronicle Office, Cleburne. |
| 5 | 4 | 77 | 77-78 | 16 | |
| 6 | 5 | | | | |
| 7 | 6 | | | | |
| 8 | 7 | 80 | 80-81 | 16 | Tommie Clark, A. R. C. Hood Co. |
| 9 | 8 | 81 | 81-82 | 20 | Student Office, A. R. C. |
| 10 | 9 | 82 | 82-83 | 36 | Student Office, A. R. C. |
| 11 | 10 | | 83-84 | | |
| 12 | 11 | 84 | 84-85 | 36 | Loving Pub. Co., Fort Worth. |
| 13 | 12 | 85 | 85-86 | 32 | Gazette Job Office. |

| Session Number | Volume Number | Year Printed | Announcing For: | Number of Pages | Name of the Printer |
|---|---|---|---|---|---|
| 14 | 13 | 86* | 86-87 | 32 | Tex-Christian Print. |
| 15 | 14 | 87 | 87-88 | 34 | ? |
| 16 | 15 | 88* | 88-89 | 36 | Add-Ran Student Print. |
| 17 | 16 | 89 | 89-90 | 38 | Add-Ran Student Print. |
| 18 | 17 | 90* | 90-91 | 40 | Thorp Spring, Texas. |
| 19 | 18 | 91 | 91-92 | 32 | The Student Job Print. |
| 20 | 19 | 92* | 92-93 | 44 | The Student Job Print. |
| 21 | 20 | 93* | 93-94 | 52 | B. H. Simpson, Ptr., Troy, Texas. |
| 22 | 21 | 94 | 94-95 | 54 | Gospel Advocate Pub Co., Nashville. |
| 23 | | 95* | 95-96 | 60 | Standard Pub. Co., Cin. |
| 24 | | | 96-97 | | |
| 25 | | 97* | 97-98 | 80 | Knight Prt. Co., Waco. |
| 26 | | 98 | 98-99 | 80 | C. C. Womack Co., Waco. |
| 27 | | 99 | 99-1900 | 76 | C. C. Womack Co., Waco. |
| 28 | | 00* | 00-01 | 76 | B. H. Simpson, Waco. |
| 29 | | 01 | 01-02 | 98 | J. S. Hill & Co., Waco. |
| 30 | | 02 | 02-03 | 152 | ? |
| 31 | | 03 | 03-04 | 172 | ? |
| 32 | 1 | 04 | 04-05 | 208 | ? |
| 33 | 2 | 05 | 05-06 | 200 | ? |
| 34 | 3 | 06 | 06-07 | 200 | ? |
| 35 | 4 | 07 | 07-08 | 176 | J. S. Hill & Co., Waco. |
| 36 | 5 | 08 | 08-09 | 172 | |
| 37 | 6 | 09 | 09-10 | 178 | |
| 38 | 7 | 10 | 10-11 | 160 | ? |
| 39 | 8 | 11 | 11-12 | 160 | ? |
| 40 | 9 | 12 | 12-13 | 178 | T. C .U. Print S. |
| 41 | 10 | 13 | 13-14 | 158 | S. H. Taylor, Fort Worth. |

Catalog, Brite College of the Bible, 1914. From 1915 through 1939 it was a section of the T. C. U. catalog. Since 1940 it has been the May issue of the Brite College of the Bible Caller.

Catalog Add Ran Jarvis College (Thorp Spring) Announcements for 1906-'07, also one for 1908-'09. One copy each in T. C. U. Library.

Catalog Jarvis College (Thorp Spring) 1903-04, 36 pp. One copy in T. C. U. Library.

The Collegian, a monthly Literary journal published by the Add-Ran, then T. C. U. students from 1895 through 1912. Files in T. C. U. Library.

Golden Jubilee Pageant, "These Fifty Years," contributed by the English Department of T. C. U., 1923.

Christian Courier, Weekly (later monthly) newspaper of the Christian Churches in Texas. Files from 1910 complete (with some numbers prior to date) in the T. C. U. Library.

Horned Frog, The Annual of Texas Christian University. Volume I, 1897, Volume II, 1905; thereafter annually, except 1910.

The Interpreter, a monthly journal of publicity by Texas Christian University, E. W. McDiarmid, Editor, November, 1926, through May, 1931.

Millenial Harbinger, Alexander Campbell, Editor, a monthly journal of religion, 1830-1866. Complete in file in T. C. U. Library.

The Skiff, a weekly newspaper of T. C. U., published by the students. 1902———. Files in the T. C. U. Library except that the numbers prior to March, 1910, were destroyed by the fire.

Waco Times Herald, The, May 11, 1910, announcing the move of T. C. U. to Fort Worth.

## UNPUBLISHED DOCUMENTS

Breeden, Leon, Introducing the T. C. U. Horned Frog Band, 1947. Pamphlet, 20 pages. In the T. C. U. Library.

Clark, Randolph, The Life of Joseph Addison Clark. A 20-page pamphlet published privately, 1903. One copy of the original is in possession of the family of Mrs. Dr. Frank Clark, Iowa Park, Texas. Phostatic copies in the Library of Texas Christian University.

Freeman, W. W., History of the Campbell Movement. An unpublished thesis presented to the faculty of Southern Methodist University in partial fulfillment of the requirements for the degree of Master of Arts (Education) August 24, 1925, 825 pages. Largely devoted to the history of the Colleges of the Churches of Christ, with emphasis on Abilene Christian College.

Mason, Frankie Miller, Beginnings of T. C. U. An unpublished Thesis presented to the Faculty of Texas Christian University in partial fulfillment of the requirements for the degree of Master of Arts (History) 1930.

Minutes of the Board of Trustees of Add-Ran Christian University 1889-1902 and of Texas Christian University 1902—except the portion lost by the fire, 1902—March 22, 1910. All in the archives in the office of the Business Manager.

Minutes of the Board of Trustees of Brite College of the Bible, 1914————. In the archives in the office of Brite College of the Bible.

Ridings, Paul, The History of Football in Texas Christian University. A freshman Theme, on file in the Library of Texas Christian University.

## LETTERS (Bound, in T. C. U. Library)

Bass, Mrs. J. D., nee Lou Carr, B. A., 1879. Memoranda, written when she was an octogenarian, concerning the life at Thorp Spring.

Clark, Randolph. An Interview with Colby D. Hall, February, 1931.

Committee on Education, Special Report of, To the Texas Christian Missionary Convention, April 27, 1927, 8 pages.

Deed to Carr-Burdette College copied from the Court Records of Grayson County, Texas, January 13, 1894. (Courtesy of Rev. Robert Badgett and Hon. Jesse F. Holt.)

Elkin, F. F. Letter of February 20, 1945, to Colby D. Hall relating to the Presidency of Midland College, one page.

Hall, Colby D. Memoranda concerning the Burnett Trust Gift, based on his interview with Dr. Charles H. Harris and his own part in the proceedings. Written in May, 1941.

Holloway, Mrs. R. F., nee Louella Clark. Memoranda on the life of her husband, R. F. Holloway, January, 1944.

———— An Address to a Woman's Club in Brownwood, Texas, October, 1942, 20 pages.

Isaacks, Buford. Letter to Colby D. Hall concerning the history of Randolph College at Cisco, February 19, 1945, 2 pages.

Keith, Noel. A letter written March 30, 1942, when he was pastor at Marfa, Texas, concerning the baptism of Mr. and Mrs. Brite.

McClintic, James V. Letter January 4, 1946, containing information about the early football experiences, 3 pages.

McKissick, J. T. Letter dated November 25, 1944, containing some autobiographical data, and some comments.

Shirley, Douglas A. A letter dated September 30, 1944, concerning Hereford Christian College.

Wood, Archie F. A letter to L. C. Wright, asserting the facts concerning the origin of the name "Horned Frogs."

APPENDICES

*Appendix I.* Showing the spread of attendance sources, by counties, during early years. (The catalogs omit the information for some of the years.)

Column 1. The number of counties represented in the enrollment.
2. The number of students from Hood County.
3. The number of students from outside Hood County.

| Year | Col. 1 | Col. 2 | Col. 3 |
|------|--------|--------|--------|
| 1873-74 | 9 | 103 | 14 |
| -75 | 14 | 121 | 43 |
| -76 | 18 | 79 | 82 |
| -77 | 24 | 116 | 85 |
| -78 | | | |
| -79 | | | |
| -80 | 34 | 166 | 130 |
| -81 | 31 | 133 | 162 |
| -82 | 26 | 182 | 216 |
| -83 | | | |
| -84 | 54 | 219 | 216 |
| -85 | | | |
| -90 | 63 | 215 | 210 |
| -91 | | 162 | 198 |
| -92 | | 108 | 207 |
| -93 | 60 | 196 | 249 |
| -94 | 60 | 164 | 206 |
| -95 | | 97 | 197 |

*Appendix II.* The record of Enrollments.

Column 1. Over-all total for the calendar year. Each separate individual counted once. Figures in parenthesis for 1912-16 are the medical students, in addition.
2. Through 1921, the College of Arts and Sciences and the Preparatory Department, with the Prep. showing in parenthesis some years. After 1922, Column 2 shows the summer term enrollment. There were summer terms before 1922, but the enrollment was not recorded. There were summer Normals, using the buildings, but not enrolling the students in T. C. U. From 1937, the extra column (in parenthesis) is Evening College.
3. The number of ministerial students enrolled (no record prior to '95). For a few years in the catalog, this number is shown as including all students in Bible classes, but these figured here have been corrected to show only ministerial students.
4. The number of students receiving degrees.
5. The number of ministerial students receiving degrees.

| Year | Col. 1 | Col. 2 | Col. 3 | Col. 4 | Col. 5 |
|------|--------|--------|--------|--------|--------|
| 1873-74 | 117 | | | | |
| -75 | 164 | | | | |
| -76 | 161 | | | 2 | |
| -77 | 201 | | | 2 | |
| -78 | | | | | |
| -79 | | | | | |
| -80 | 296 | | | 1 | |

| Year | Col. 1 | Col. 2 | Col. 3 | Col. 4 | Col. 5 |
|---|---|---|---|---|---|
| 1880-81 | 295 | | | 5 | |
| -82 | 398 | | | 5 | |
| -83 | | | | 5 | |
| -84 | 435 | | | 3 | 1 |
| -85 | 359 | | | 1 | 1 |
| -86 | 415 | | | 7 | 1 |
| -87 | 312 | | | 2 | |
| -88 | 394 | | | 4 | |
| -89 | 395 | | | 2 | |
| -90 | 425 | | | 7 | |
| -91 | 360 | | | 4 | |
| -92 | 315 | | | 7 | |
| -93 | 445 | | | 12 | 2 |
| -94 | 370 | | | 8 | 1 |
| -95 | 294 | | 5 | 6 | 1 |
| -96 | | | | 6 | 2 |
| -97 | 193 | | 9 | 3 | 1 |
| -98 | 186 | | 16 | 5 | 1 |
| -99 | 199 | | 12 | 5 | |
| -1900 | 161 | | 7 | 4 | |
| 1900-01 | 148 | | 8 | 8 | 1 |
| -02 | | | | 4 | 2 |
| -03 | 302 | 216 | 17 | 3 | 2 |
| -04 | 428 | 290 (188) | 19 | 18 | 5 |
| -05 | 470 | 264 (166) | 22 | 19 | 4 |
| -06 | 412 | 318 | 23 | 18 | 6 |
| -07 | 340 | 295 | 17 | 12 | 3 |
| -08 | 334 | 211 | 13 | 14 | 1 |
| -09 | 379 | 279 | 13 | 16 | 1 |
| -10 | 367 | 275 | | 16 | 3 |
| -11 | 362 | 282 | 26 | 21 | 1 |
| -12 | 414 (114) | 331 | 22 | 23 | 1 |
| -13 | 495 (88) | 309 (94) | | 31 | 5 |
| -14 | 497 (75) | 345 | 37 | 22 | |
| -15 | 507 39) | 355 (101) | 38 | 17 | 2 |
| -16 | 536 (53) | 359 (107) | 41 | 29 | 2 |
| -17 | 589 | 455 (128) | 30 | 26 | 4 |
| -18 | 620 | 456 (141) | 40 | 32 | 6 |
| -19 | 805 | 677 (97) | 97 | 34 | 0 |
| -20 | 839 | 668 (179) | 60 | 47 | 8 |
| -21 | 778 | 677 (131) | 67 | 45 | 6 |
| -22 | 740 | 143 *Summer* | 84 | 49 | 8 |
| -23 | 813 | 239 | 86 | 69 | 19 |
| -24 | 1015 | 232 | 94 | 58 | 5 |
| -25 | 1186 | 265 | 86 | 103 | 4 |
| -26 | 1330 | 303 | 92 | 121 | 13 |
| -27 | 1412 | 364 | 91 | 145 | 8 |
| -28 | 1528 | 337 | 98 | 163 | 8 |
| -29 | 1687 | 337 | 111 | 167 | 9 |
| -30 | 1498 | 352 | 98 | 198 | 14 |
| -31 | 1392 | 301 | 85 | 203 | 12 |
| -32 | 1311 | 312 | 86 | 142 | 12 |
| -33 | 986 | 204 | 80 | 142 | 8 |
| -34 | 907 | 182 | 64 | 149 | 9 |
| -35 | 1040 | 269 *Evening* | 60 | 138 | 9 |
| -36 | 1161 | 300 *College* | 62 | 135 | 9 |
| -37 | 1598 | 301 (455) | 59 | 163 | 10 |

| Year | Col. 1 | Col. 2 | Col. 3 | Col. 4 | Col. 5 |
|------|--------|--------|--------|--------|--------|
| 1937-38 | 2037 | 355 (616) | 64 | 199 | 12 |
| -39 | 2042 | 411 (668) | 75 | 225 | 13 |
| -40 | 2080 | 428 (612) | 84 | 234 | 18 |
| -41 | 1734 | 407 (539) | 80 | 276 | 10 |
| -42 | 1889 | 407 (547) | 77 | 197 | 12 |
| -43 | 1625 | 454 (450) | 110 | 250 | 14 |
| -44 | 2390 | 776 (875) | 103 | 165 | 22 |
| -45 | 2633 | 574 (875) | 114 | 170 | 17 |
|  |  | est. |  |  |  |
| -46 | 3703 | 658 ( 1141) | 151 | 164 | 14 |
| -47 |  |  |  |  | 32 |

*Appendix III.* A list of the members of the Board of Trustees of Texas Christian University, showing the years of membership. Also the Officers of the Board. They are arranged in the order of their appearance on the Board. The first date is the year of coming on the Board, the second, the year of going off. The source of information is the catalog, sometimes corrected by the Minutes. "d" indicates he served until death, —— indicates he is still serving

Addison Clark, Thorp Spring, 1874-93.
Randolph Clark, Thorp Spring, 1874-93.
J. A. Clark, Thorp Spring, 1874-87.
H. D. Bantau, Milsap, 1874-82.
J. H. Harbison, Thorp Spring, 1874-77.
A. M. Arnot, 1874-75.
J. M. Brock, 1875.
T. E. Stirman, 1876-77.
J. T. Poe, 1876-77.
W. A. Stewart, 1876-77.
C. M. Wilmeth, McKinney, 1877-82.
E. Elgan, Hutchins, 1877.
W. A. George, Stephenville, 1877-80.
W. K. Hamblen, Salado, 1877-78.
R. M. Gano, Dallas, 1877-78.
T. C. Hart, Weatherford, 1880-81.
J. W. Hamblin, San Gabriel, 1880-81.
J. H. Caruthers, Palo Pinto, 1881-86.
T. F. Rawlins, Hood County, 1882-83.
W. B. Gano, Dallas, 1882-83.
C. McPherson, Waxahachie, 1883-03.
W. K. Homan, Caldwell, 1883-87; 1903-08 (Adv)
J. B. Gibson, Waxahachie, 1883-86.
C. G. Couch, Brenham, 1883-86.
G. D. Harrison, Longview, 1883-86.
R. E. McKnight, 1887.
E. C. Snow, Thorp Spring, 1887-88; 92.
A. G. Dabney, Thorp Spring, 1887-88; 92-95.
F. O. McKinsey, Thorp Spring, 1888.
R. L. Ragsdale, Denton, 1888; 93-97.
W. B. Parks, Thorp Spring, 1888.
L. A. Snow, 1888.
J. P. Smith, Fort Worth, 1889-90.

J. J. Jarvis, Fort Worth, 1889-99.
T. A. Wythe, Weatherford, 1889-95.
J. N. Votaw, Hico, 1889-92.
Alfred Irby, Thorp Spring, 1889-92.
H. G. Taylor, Palo Pinto, 1889-92.
Charles Carlton, Bonham, 1889-91.
Ed. C. Smith, Dallas, 1890.
W. C. Lemon, Dallas, 1890-92.
J. J. Collins, Dallas, 1890.
A. S. Henry, Blooming Grove, 1890-96.
H. M. Bandy, Thorp Spring, 1890-92.
C. M. Boynton, Hamilton, 1892-95.
S. N. Strange, Troy, 1893-1900.
J. B. Loving, Sherman, 1893-94.
T. M. Scott, Melissa, 1893-1903.
H. H. Smith, Dallas, 1893-94.
T. E. Shirley, Melissa, 1893-1917.
Scott Milam, Glen Rose, 1893-96.
W. I. Weatherly, Grapevine, 1894.
L. J. Caraway, Thorp Spring, 1895-96.
Louis Garver, Van Alstyne, 1895-96.
Jas. I. Moore, Waco, 1896-99.
W. B. Hays, Waco, 1896-98.
Dr. F. W. Burger, Waco, 1896-1900.
Col. J. Z. Miller, Belton, 1896-99.
R. W. Carpenter, McKinney, 1896.
C. P. Vance, Taylor, 1896.
B. B. Sanders, Austin, 1896.
W. S. Blackshear, Waco, 1896-1900.
J. H. Banton, Waco, 1896-98.
Newell Kane, Palestine, 1898.
John P. London, Gainesville, 1897-1905.
Spencer Ford, 1897-98.
Chas. W. Gibson, Waxahachie, 1899-1920 d.

S. M. Hamilton,
Waco, Ex. '93, 1899-1913.
Granville Jones, Midland, 1899-1905.
A. E. Wilkinson, Austin, 1899-1905.
W. B. Holloway, Midland, 1899-1905.
I. D. Newsome, McKinney, 1899.
G. V. McClintic, Groesbeck, 1899-1903.
C. E. Bird, Dallas, 1899.
John T. Walton, Waco, 1900.
Van Zandt Jarvis, Fort Worth, B. A., '95,
1901-40; d. 4-18-40.
J. J. Hart, Dallas, B. A. '97, 1901-10.
Joseph Blanks, Lockhart, 1902.
E. J. Mantooth, Lufkin, 1902-06.
George A. Faris, Dallas, 1902-12.
J. T. McKissick, Weatherford, B. A. '97,
1902.
J. H. Fielder, Athens, 1902.
Jas. L. White, McKinney, 1902-05.
Wm. A. Wilson, Houston, 1907-10.
J. C. Sanders, Bonham, 1907.
Charles Halsell, Bonham, 1906-07.
T. E. Tomlinson, Hillsboro, 1907-46; d.
2-1-46.
F. F. Elkin, Plano, B. A. '98, 1908-10.
F. M. Miller, Waco, 1908-14.
Dr. H. W. Gates, Waco, 1908-14.
George W. Cole, Jr., Belton, 1910-22; d.
T. W. Marse, Taylor, 1910-18.
S. P. Bush, Allen, 1910-29.
H. H. Watson, Longview, Ex., 1910-16.
Morgan Weaver, Abilene, 1910.
T. W. Marse, Taylor, 1910-18.
Dr. Bacon Saunders, Fort Worth,
1910-25; d.
R. L. Crouch, Dallas, 1910-27; d.
John L. Cassell, Fort Worth, 1910-16; d.
H. M. Durrett, Fort Worth, 1910-15;
d. '26.
James Harrison, Fort Worth, 1910-22;
d. '37.
L. C. Brite, Marfa, 1912-41; d.
H. W. Stark, Gainesville, 1912-44; d.
F. G. Jones, McKinney, B. A. '90,
1912-19.
Malcom Reed, Austin, 1912-19.
Dr. R. H. Gough, Fort Worth, 1913-17.
S. J. McFarland, Dallas, 1913—.
W. W. Mars, Fort Worth, 1914-33; d.
Dan D. Rogers, Dallas, B. A. '09,
1915—.
T. C. Morgan, Longview, Ex.
1916-23.

W. E. Gee, Amarillo, 1916-25.
R. M. Rowland, Fort Worth, 1917-21.
D. G. McFadin,
Austin, Dallas, 1917—.
J. C. Smith, Vernon, 1919-20.
Andrew Sherley, Anna, 1920-45; d.
Chas. F. Spencer,
Wichita Falls, 1920-27.
Dave C. Reed, Austin, Ex., 1920—.
J. N. Winters, Fort Worth, 1922.
H. R. Ford,
Houston, B. A. '04, 1922-23.
L. D. Anderson,
Fort Worth, B. A. '06, 1922—.
R. S. Sterling,
Houston, 1922-33; 39—.
Charles F. Wheeler,
Fort Worth, 1923—.
H. H. Rogers,
San Antonio, 1923-31.
B. S. Walker,
Breckenridge, 1924-28; d.
B. S. McKinney, Dallas, 1926.
W. Steve Cooke, Fort Worth, 1926-47.
H. C. Garrison, Austin, 1927-36; d.
M. E. Daniel,
Breckenridge, B. A. '12, 1928—.
Mrs. Ida Van Zandt Jarvis, Fort Worth,
1928-37; d.
E. E. Bewley, Fort Worth, 1928-40.
Lewis J. Ackers, Abilene, Ex., 1929—.
R. Houston Foster,
Fort Worth, B. A. '04, 1932-41;
d. 6-19-41.
L. N. D. Wells, Dallas, 1933—.
Harry Knowles, Houston, 1934—.
Bonner Frizzell, Palestine, B. A. '09, 1934—.
Mrs. Sadie T. Beckham,
Fort Worth, 1938—.
Galen McKinney,
Fort Worth, 1940—.
Stanley Thompson,
Fort Worth, 1940—.
Ed. Winton, Fort Worth, 1940—.
Charles Roesser, Fort Worth, 1940-41.
I. W. Keys, Corpus Christi, 1940—.
T. J. Brown, Fort Worth, 1941—.
Ed. A. Landreth, Fort Worth, 1941—.
R. E. Harding, Fort Worth, 1941—.
Marshall Fuller, Fort Worth, 1942—.
George F. Cuthrell, Tyler, 1942-45.
Mrs. L. C. Brite,
Marfa, 1942—.

George Kuykendall,
Lubbock, 1944—.
W. W. Woods, Buda, 1944—.
Dewey Lawrence,
Tyler, B. A., 1944—.
Ferdinand Moore, Sherman, 1944—.
Harry Mosser, Alice, 1944—.

Ralph B. Shank, Dallas, 1944—.
Granville Walker,
Fort Worth, B. A., 1945—.
Elmer Henson,
Houston, B. A., 1946—
Clyde Tomlinson,
Hillsboro, B. A. '12, 1946—

Trustees who have served 15 years or more. Their pictures are shown elsewhere, except for those unavailable.

| 1. Van Zandt Jarvis | 39 | 14. W. S. Cooke | 20 |
|---|---|---|---|
| 2. T. E. Tomlinson | 37 | 15. W. W. Mars | 19 |
| 3. L. D. Anderson* | 33 | 16. M. E. Daniel | 19 |
| 4. Dan D. Rogers | 32 | 17. S. P. Bush | 19 |
| 5. H. W. Stark | 32 | 18. Ross Sterling | 19 |
| 6. S. J. McFarland | 30 | 19. Lewis Ackers | 18 |
| 7. L. C. Brite | 29 | 20. R. L. Crouch | 17 |
| 8. J. W. Kerns BCB | 28 | 21. R. H. Foster* | 15 |
| 9. Dave Reed | 27 | 22. A. C. Parker BCB | 15 |
| 10. James Harrison | 27 | | |
| 11. Andrew Sherley | 25 | * The Brite College term was the longer. | |
| 12. T. E. Shirley | 24 | | |
| 13. C. W. Gibson | 21 | | |

*Appendix IV.* Officers of the Board of Trustees. (Prior to 1880 there is no record of the Officers.)

*President—Year.*
Addison Clark, 1881-89 (Except 1880 and 1887).
J. A. Clark, 1880 and 1887.
J. J. Jarvis, 1890-95.
Col. J. Z. Miller, 1896-99.
T. E. Shirley, 1899-1909.
T. E. Tomlinson, 1909-17.
Sam McFarland, 1917-27.
Van Zandt Jarvis, 1927-1940.
R. H. Foster, 1940-41.
L. D. Anderson, 1941—.

*Secretary—Year.*
A. Clark, 1880-81.
R. Clark, 1881, '87, '98-93.
C. McPherson, 1884-86.
F. O. McKinsey, 1888.
T. M. Scott, 1894-96.
W. K. Homan, 1896-97.
W. B. Hays, 1897-98.
F. W. Burger, 1898-99.
S. M. Hamilton, 1899-06.
Colby D. Hall, 1907-10.
E. M. Waits, 1910-16.
R. M. Rowland, 1917-18.
W. P. Jennings, 1919-21.
B. S. Smiser, 1922-32.
Colby D. Hall, 1933—.
Jerome Moore, Assoc., 1946—.

*Appendix V.* Members and Officers of the Board of Trustees of Brite College of the Bible.
*President—Year.*
Dr. Bacon Saunders, 1914-25.
L. C .Brite, 1925-41.
George Cuthrell, 1941-43.
E. D. Henson, 1943—.
*Secretary—Year.*
L. D. Anderson, 1914—.
*Members—Year.*
L. D. Anderson, Fort Worth, 1914—.
L. C. Brite, Marfa, 1914-41; d.

C. W. Gibson,
Waxahachie, 1914-19; d.
James Harrison,
Fort Worth, 1914-37; d.
Eugene H. Holmes, Plano, 1914-25; d.
Van Zandt Jarvis, Fort Worth, 1914-40; d.
John M. Kerns, Austin, 1914-42; d.
Millard Patterson, El Paso, 1914-20.
Dr. Bacon Saunders,
Fort Worth, 1914-25; d.

Bibliography

A. C. Parker, Dallas, 1919-34; d.
Andrew Sherley,
Anna, 1920-45 (Emeritus) d.
H. C. Garrison, Austin, 1926-36; d.
R. H. Foster, Fort Worth, 1926-41; d.
Thurman Morgan,
Jacksonville, Fla., 1934-45.
George Cuthrell, Tyler, 1937-43.
Tom Beauchamp, Austin, 1938—.
Lewis Ackers, Abilene, 1942—.

Mrs. L. C. Brite, Marfa, 1942—.
Elmer D. Henson,
San Angelo, 1942—.
Douglas Tomlinson,
Fort Worth, 1943—.
D. G. McFadin, Dallas, 1944—.
Granville Walker,
Fort Worth, 1945—.
W. Oliver Harrison,
Corpus Christi, 1946—.


*Appendix VI.* Roster of Faculty Members from 1873-1947.
(Including degrees obtained before leaving T. C. U.
d indicates date of death in service of T. C. U.)

Jessie R. Adams, B. A., Psych.: Personnel, 1945.
Walter S. Adkins, B. S., Biol.: Ass't. Prof., 1913-14.
Riley Aiken, A. B., M. A., Span.: Instr., 1923-25; Ass't. Prof., 1925-29.
Charles Ivan Alexander, A. B., B. S., Math.: Prof., Head, 1908-19. d., 9-19.
Charles Ivan Alexander, Jr., B. S., M. S., Ph. D., Biol.; Fellow., 1924-27; Instr., 1927-28; Ass't. Prof., 1928-34.
Margarette Alexander, Piano: Inst., 1926-27.
Mollie G. Allin, Prep. Primary: Ass't., 1881-87.
J. N. Alpin, A. B., B. B. S., Bus.: Princ., 1907-08.
Edwina Alsop: Prim. Princ., 1890-92.
L. D. Anderson, B. A., LL. D., Homiletics: Lee., 1933-39; Adj. Prof., 1939—.
Ruth Anderson, B. S. C., M. C. S., Ed. D. Educ.: Ass't. Prof., 1946.
J. F. Anderson, A. M., Biol.: Prof., Head, 1904-11; Vice-Pres., 1904-11.
Nell Andrew, Registrar. 1907-08; Librarian, 1908-24.
Lawrence D. Andrews, Piano: Prof., 1920-23.
J. J. Andujar, M. D., Med. Tech.: Prof., 1939—.
Ruth Speer Angel, B. A., M. A., Eng.; Instr., 1937-45; Ass't. Prof., 1945—.
John R. Anthony, A. B., Eng.: Assoc. Prof., 1917-18.
Albert F. Armstrong, A. M., Nat. Sc.: Prof., Head, 1901-05; Indus. Dep't. Mangr., 1905-06.
Walter Arthur, A. B., M. S., Physics: Prof., 1922-23.
Margaretha Ascher, A. B., A. M., Ph. D., Ger.: Assoc. Prof., 1928-37.
Karl E. Ashburn, A. B., M. A., Eco.: Instr., 1930-31; Ass't. Prof., 1931-33.
Lucy Ault, Voice and Piano: Instr., 1912-13.
Stockton Axson, Ph. D., (Prof. in Rice Inst.): Annual Lee., 1923-25.
Fannie Ayres, Ass't. Prep., 1896-97.
Roger W. Babcock, A. B., A. M., Eng.: Instr., 1927-28.
Alma Louise Bailey, B. A., M. A., Commer.: Instr., 1935-40, Commer. and Eng.: Instr., 1935—(on leave, 1943-46).
Dick Bailey, A. B., A. M., French: Fellow., 1927-28; Instr., 1928-30.
Katherine McKee Bailey, B. M., Piano: Assoc. Prof., 1931-35; Prof., 1935—.
Mrs. E. F. Baker, Matron, 1884-87.
Mary Louise Baker, B. A., M. A., Music: Ass't. Prof., 1946—.
Wm. Price Baker, B. A., M. A., Eng.: Instr. 1940-46; (on leave, 1943-46).
Paul Baker, A. B., A. M., Gov't.: Eco. Ass't. Prof., 1924-32.
Marie Balch, B. M., Piano: Ass't., 1925-29.

William Balch, A. B., Voice: Instr., 1929-30.
Virginia Bales, B. A., M. A., French: Instr., 1926-27; Instr., 1931-34.
Mrs. Catherine Ball, Hostess, Jarvis Hall, 1944—.
John W. Ballard, B. C. S., C. P. A., Bus. Adm.: Prof., Head, 1923-35.
H. L. Barber, Prin., College of Business, 1917-18.
Edith Slote Bartholomew, B. A., M. A., Eng.: Instr., 1945—.
William H. Batson, A. B., Ph. D., Phil., Psych.: Prof., 1913-15; Educa.: Prof., 1915-17.
Sam Adrian Baugh, B. A., Phys. Ed.: Ass't. Coach, 1937-38.
Mrs. Sadie T. Beckham, Lady Prin., 1918-29; Superv. of Woman, 1929-33; Dean of Women, 1933-37; Emeritus, 1937—.
Madison Bell, B. S., Phys. Ed.: Head Coach, 1924-28.
E. R. Bentley, Academy Science: Instr., 1912-15.
J. K. Bentley, A. B., Hist.: Instr., 1927-29.
Carl Beutel, Piano: Prof. and Direc. of Fine Arts, 1912-15.
J. Quincy Biggs, A. B., B. O., Pub. Speak.: Prof., 1919-21.
Frank E. Billington, A. B., A. M., B. D., M. R. E., Rel. Ed.: Prof., 1920-29; Chris. Min., 1929-43; Retired, 1943—.
Willie R. Birge, A. B., A. M., Biol., Prof., 1912-13.
Reka Lois Black, B. S. E., Math.: Instr., 1944-45.
Arthur Witt Blair, B. S., M. A., Educa.: Prof. Elem., 1941-46; on military leave, 1943-46.
Alvord L. Boeck, A. B., M. A., Ph. D., Bus. Adm.: Assoc. Prof., 1935-36; Prof., Head, 1936-43; Director of Even. College, 1937-43.
Mrs. Beulah Boggess: Matron, 1928-39.
Fielding Bohart, B. A., Math.: Fellow., 1925-26.
S. A. Boles, B. S., M. A., Eng.: Ass't. Prof. and Athletic Direc., 1914-15.
Henry G. Bowden, Vice-Pres., 1927-29.
Mrs. Henry G. Bowden, Hostess, 1942-45.
Beverly H. Bowman, B. S., M. S., Bus. Adm.: Instr., 1941-42.
Ethlyn Bowman, Piano: Instr., 1913-15.
Adeline Boyd, B. M., Piano: Instr., 1930-35.
Mrs. Effie Boyd, Music: Ass't., 1890-91.
Kenneth Boyle, Electronics: Spec. Ass't., 1942—.
Mrs. E. C. Boynton, Librarian, 1906-08.
Haldeen Braddy, B. A., M. A., Ph. D., Eng.: Assoc. Prof., 1938-43.
Mrs. Annie Bradley, Music: Instr., 1882-87.
Beulah Bradley, B. S., Dom. Sc.: Ass't. Prof., 1919-21.
Ina May Bramblett, A. B., M. A., Math.: Instr., 1942-45; Ass't. Prof., 46—.
Helene Brasted, B. A., Eng.: Instr., 1925-27.
Leon Breeden, B. A., Music: Band Direc., Instr., 1944—.
Thelma Breithaupt, B. A., M. A., Bus. Ad. and Eng.: Instr., 1938-41.
John Brigham, B. M., Voice: Ass't. Prof., 1939—.
Connie Garza Brockett, A. B., M. A., Span.: Instr., 1929-31; Ass't. Prof., 1931-33.
Estelle Brooks, B. A., M. A., Eco.: Instr., 1946.
Marvin H. Brown, A. B., LL. B., Law: Prof., 1916-20.
Mrs. Emma Bruhn, Ger., Fr., Needle-wk., Music: Teacher, 1877-78.
Lester Brumbelow, B. A., Phys. Ed.: Line Coach, 1936-46; (on military leave, 1943-46).
Mrs. Artemisia B. Bryson, B. A., M. A., Eng.: Instr., 1924-32; Ass't. Prof., 1932—.
Walter E. Bryson, A. M., Eng.: Prof. Head, 1917-22. d. 6-22.
Clarence A. Burch, B. A., Bible.: Adj. Prof., 1942-46; Ass't. Prof., 46—.
Vesta Burford, A. B., Domes. Sc.: Principal 1917-19.
George O. Burr, A. B., Chem.: Ass't. Prof., 1919-20.

## Bibliography

Helen Fouts Cahoon, Voice: Head, 1913-20; 1929-38.
Frederic M. Cahoon, Violin: Coach, 1913-20.
Emory C. Cameron, A. B., M. A., Bible: Old Test. Assoc. Prof., 1930-34.
Ray Camp, B. A., Eng.: Instr., 1922-24.
Mrs. Ray Camp, B. A., Eng.: Instr., 1946—.
Paul Campbell, B. A., Assistant to the President, 1945-47.
Ruth Iris Caraway, B. S. L. S., M. S., Lib.: Ass't.
Mary Leslie Cantrell, B. A., M. A., Eng.: Instr., 1945—.
Robert J. Cantrell, A. B., B. 0., Latin: Instr., 1915-17.
Bernice Carleton, B. A., Music: Violin and Theory Prof., 1922-25.
Frank Carney, A. B., Ph. D., Geography: Adj. Prof., 1929-30.
Avery L. Carlson, A. B., J. D., C. P. A., Bus. Ad.: Ass't. Prof., 1927-31.
G. E. Carpenter, S. B., Latin and Elocution: Teacher, 1880-82.
Margaret Carpenter, B. A., Biol.: Fellow., 1924-26.
Lou Carr, S. B.: Ass't. in Primary, 1880-81.
Eula Lee Carter, B. A., M. A., Span.: Instr., 1924-25; Ass't. Prof., 1925-30;
    Assoc. Prof., 1930-46; Prof. 1946—.
Hazel Carter, A. B., Speech: Instr., 1929-31.
Carrie Cartlidge, B. S., Hist.: Instr., 1946.
Clara L. Case, A. B., D. O., Span.: Prof. 1913-14.
Lewis Casperson, Piano: Instr., 1915-16.
Sallie Cayce, Prim. Art: Instr., 1890-96.
Theodora Cayce, Elocution, Ass't. Prep.: 1895-96.
Ethel Ray Cheatham, B. A., Math.: Special Instr., 1942-44.
Ione Way Chambers, A. B., Math.: Instr., 1931-32.
Leslie Chambers, B. S., M. S., Ph. D., Biol.: Ass't. Prof., 1930-32.
Rawlins Cherryhomes, A. B., B. D., Hist.: Instr., 1943-44.
Cecil F. Cheverton, B. A., M. A., Ph. D., Bible: Old Test. Prof. Head, 1944-47;
    Dep't Rel. Head, 1947—.
Joe Cinquemani, Music: Inst., 1946.
Leroy Clardy, B. A., M. S., Electronics: Instr., 1923-33.
Addison Clark, LL. D., Pres., 1873-99; Teacher, Anc. Lang., Mental Phil., Greek,
    Logic, and Metaphysics; Prin., Bible and Teachers' Dept., 1873-99; Bible, Prof.
    and Dean, 1899-1902.
Addison Clark, Jr., B. A., M. A., Eng. and Hist. 1896-98.
Adele Clark, A. B., M. A., Span.: Instr., 1928-33.
Mrs. Alice Clark, Music: Adj. Prof., 1880-82.
J. A. Clark, Prop. and Gen. Bus. Mangr., 1873-1885.
Mrs. Hettie Clark, Matron, 1873-83.
Jessie Clark, A. B., Primary: Princ., 1893-95.
Lee Clark, A. M., Prep. and Hist.: Princ., 1904-06.
Mack Clark, B. A., Phys. Ed.: Instr. and Track Coach, 1929—; (on military
    leave, 1943-45).
Randolph Clark, A. M., Vice-Pres., 1873-95; Teacher, Physics Chem., Math.,
    Nat. Sc.: Princ. of Pub. Sch. Eng., Greek Ass't., Gen. Hist., 1873-95.
T. M. Clark, Music: Vocal Instr., 1874-91; Instr., Ger., Fr., and Elocution,
    1874-91.
W. N. Clark, Chem.: Ass't., 1913-14.
C. Stanley Clifton, B. A., M. A., Sociol.: Ass't. Prof., 1944—; on leave, 46-47.
Merrill Dare Clubb, A. B., Ph. D., Eng.: Prof., 1929-36.
Owen Cobb, B. A., Physics: Instr., 1942-44.
Dura Brokaw Cockrell, A. B., A. G., A. M., Art: Prof., Head, 1899-1903;
    1906-11; 1912-22; Hostess, 1939-42.

Egbert R. Cockrell, B. A., LL. M., Hist., Pol. and Soc. Sc.: Prof., 1899-1903; 1906-11; 1912-21.
Vardaman B. Cockrell, B. A., M. A., Personnel Office, Assistant, 46—.
Frances Coldwell, B. A., B. S., Lib. Sc.: Ass't. Librarian, 1937-42.
Mary Virginia Coleman, A. B., M. A., Fr.; Ass't. Prof., 1926-31.
Lucile Coffman, A. B., Latin and Math.: Instr., 1917-20.
Josiah H. Combs, A. B., M. A., Ph. D., Mod. Lang.: Prof., Head, 1927-47.
Mrs. Josiah Combs, French: Instr., 1946.
T. Louis Comparette, B. A., Anc. Lang.: Prof., Ed., 1894-97.
Allie Merl Conger, Piano: 1914-15.
George M. Conner, LL. B., Law: Prof., 1915-20.
Nellie Cook, A. B., M. A., Eng.: Instr., 1929-30.
Bertha Ann Cooper, Voice: 1920-21.
J. J. Corliss, A. B., A. M., Math.: Ass't. Prof., 1927-28.
Frank Council, A. B., Biol.: Instr., 1922-23.
Joseph B. Cowan, B. A., M. A., Jour.: Instr., 1929-33.
Mrs. E. E. Cox, House Mother, 1938—.
Iva Sheppard Cox, Assistant Librarian, 1945—.
Mabel Crabb, M. S., Mod. Lang.: Instr., 1894-95.
Cecil Craiger, Art: Ass't. in Paint. and Draw., 1916-17.
James A. Crain, B. A., M. A., Eng.: Instr., 1915-17: Hist., Ass't. Prof., 1916-17.
Austin Lee Crouch, B. S., Eco.: Instr., 1939-40.
Albert Cruzan, Oratory: Instr., 1908-10.
Nettie Jo Cummings, B. A., M. A., Fr. and Span.: Instr., 1936-43.
B. A. Crouch, B. A., M. A., Educ.: Instr., 1928-32; Ass't. Prof., 1932-43; Assoc. Prof., 1943—.
Arthur R. Curry, A. B., B. L. S., Lib. Sc.: Librarian, 1925-33.
Frank W. Cuprien, Voice: Instr., 1910-11.
Howard B. Dabbs, A. M., Chem.: Assoc. Prof., 1913-17.
J. A. Dacus, M. Acct.: Bus.: Princ., 1905-07; 1910-12; 1917-19; Bus. Mangr., 1912-15.
Milton E. Daniel, A. B., LL. B., Law: Prof., Coach, 1915-18.
George B. Davidson, A. B., Ph. D., Fr., and Ger.: Prof., 1922-25.
J. L. Davidson, Primary: Princ., 1888-89.
A. A. Davis, B. M., M. M. E., Music: Instr., 1946.
Beatrice Davis, Primary: Ass't., 1890-92.
Garnett S. Davis, B. B. A., M. S., Acc't.: Instr., 1946-47; Ass't Prof. 47—.
John Davis, A. M., Chem.: Prof., 1919-22.
Lily R. Davis, Chem.: Instr., 1921-22.
Madge Davis, Eng.: Instr., 1920-21.
P. H. Dawson, Voice: Instr., 1875-76.
A. E. Day, Supervisor of Men, 1925-27.
L. L. Dees, Sup't of Grounds and Plant, 1920—.
Ollie Rambin Dickie, B. A., M. A., Span.: Instr., 1946.
Bailey Diffie, B. A., Hist.: Instr., 1926-27.
Paul Dinkins, B. A., M. A., Ph. D., Eng.: Instr., 1937-41; Ass't. Prof., 1943-45; Assoc. Prof., 1945-47; Prof. 47—.
Carl Rupp Doering, Piano: Prof., 1917-20.
Mrs. Carl Rupp Doering, Piano: Prof., 1917-22.
O. B. Douglas, Science: Instr., 1919-20.
Constance Donaldson, Phys. Ed.: Instr., 1924-26.
James H. Dougherty, B. S., M. S., Ph. D., Ed.: Assoc. Prof., 1937-42; Direc. of Test. Office, 1940-42.
Craig Dryden, Registrar, 1915-17.
Cora D'Spain, Princ. of Pri. School, 1884-87.

Julia Duncan, Oratory, Phys. Ed.: Instr., 1917-19.
Robert M. Duncan, A. B., A. M., Ph. D., Gov't.: Ass't. Prof., 1928-30.
L. A. Dunagan, Cashier, 1924—.
Wayne Dunlap, B. A., Music: Brass Instr., 1941-42.
G. W. Dunlavey, B. S., B. A., Hist.: Assoc. Prof., 1920-29; on leave, 1929-35.
   d. 12-4-35.
Lillian Durrett, Registrar, 1917-24.
Lucille Durrett, Piano: Instr., 1921-23.
Loraine Dutton, B. A., Biol.: Instr., 1920-21.
R. Dyksterhaus, Violin and Piano: Prof., 1905-06.
A. C. Easley, L. B., Bus.: Princ. of College of Bus., 1890-97; 1901-04.
   But see also p. 84.
Henry Elkins, B. S., Music: Ass't. in Violin, 1925-27.
A. C. Elliott, B. S.: Princ. of Normal College, 1905-06.
Edwin A. Elliott, B. A., Ph. D., Superv. of Men, 1922-24; Eco. Ass't. Prof.,
   1926-27; Assoc. Prof., 1927-31; Prof., Head, 1931-34.
Jacob Embry, A. M., Eng.: Instr., 1901-02.
Martine Emert, B. A., M. A., Ph. D., Hist.: Ass't. Prof., 1946—.
Mrs. Bessie Plummer Ellis, B. A., M. A., Span. and Latin: Fellow.,
   1927-28; Instr., 1930-33.
Susanne C. Englemann, Ph. D., For. Lang., Ass't. Prof., 1946-47.
Bonnie M. Enlow, B. S., M. A., Home Eco.: Instr., 1924-32; Ass't. Prof.,
   1932-43; Assoc. Prof., 1943—.
James B. Eskridge, A. M., Ph. D., Anc. Lang.: Prof., Head, 1898-1902; 1903-12.
Graham Estes, A. B., M. A., Math.: Instr., 1924-25; Ass't. Prof., 1928-31.
T. H. Ethridge, B. A., M. A., Psych.: Instr., 1924-27.
L. A. Eubanks, Princ. of College of Bus., 1913-14.
Mrs. L. A. Eubanks, College of Bus.: Ass't., 1913-14.
Julian F. Evans, B. S., M. A., Ph. D., Physics: Ass't. Prof., 1940-42.
A. M. Ewing, B. B. A., C. P. A., Acct.: Instr., 1936.
C. A. Exley, A. B., Philos.: Ass't. Prof., 1912-13.
Arthur Faguy-Cote, Voice: Ass't. Prof., 1929—.
Lew D. Fallis, A. B., Pub. Spk.: Prof., Head, 1924—.
Ellsworth Faris, B. S., Hist. and Philos.: Prof., 1906-11.
George Farmer, B. A. Rel.: Instr., 1946-47.
P. M. Faulkner, Academy: Ass't., 1912-13.
Betsy Feagan, B. A., Eng. Teaching Fellow, 1946.
Alexander Findlay, Director of Music, 1903-04.
Mrs. Alexander Findlay, Piano: Instr., 1903-04.
C. J. Firkins, B. S., M. A., Psych.: Instr., 1946.
George W. Fitzroy, Piano: Prof., 1909-10.
Nellie Florence Fox., A. B., Elocu.: Instr., 1899-1900.
Clyde Flowers, B. S. Athlet.: Instr., 1946—.
C. Dorsey Forrest, B. S., M. B. A., Bus. Ad.: Instr., 1940-41.
John Forsyth, B. S., Ph. D., Biol.: Instr., 1937-39; Ass't. Prof., 1946—.
E. Y. Freeland, Ath. Coach, 1915-17.
J. W. Froley, M. S., Math.: Prof., Head, 1896-99.
Newton Gaines, B. S. in E. E., A. M., Ph. D., Physics: Instr., 1924-25;
   Ass't. Prof., 1925-27; Assoc. Head, 1927-33; Prof. Head, 1933—.
Mrs. Lena Gardner, Eng.: Instr., 1915-18.
Emily Garnett, B. A., B. S. L. S., M. S. L. S., Lib.: Ref., 1944—.
Ralph Garrett, B. A., M. A., Hist.: Ass't. Prof., 1939—.
Eunice Joiner Gates, B. A., M. A., Ph. D., For. Lang.: Prof., 1946—.
W. B. Gates, B. S., M. A., Ph. D., Eng.: Prof. Head, 1946—.

James A. Gathings, M. A., Gov't.: Ass't. Prof., 1930-31.

Emma Louise Gentzke, B. A., B. S. L. S., Lib.: Ass't., 1946—.

Warner E. Gettys, A. B., A. M., Sociol.: Prof., 1921-22.

Mrs. M. B. M. Gibbons, Librarian, 1904-16.

Ernest W. Gibson, B. A., M. A., Bus. Ad.: Ass't. Prof., 1942-43.

Don Eugene Gillis, B. A., B. M., Music Theo.: Instr. and Band Direc., 1935-43.

J. A. Glaze, B. S., M. S., Ph. D., Psych.: Prof., 1928-31.

Marie Moser Glick, B. B. A., M. B. A., Sec. Sc.: Instr., 1944-46.

Eloise Golden, A. B., M. A., Eng.: Instr., 1931-31.

Nimmo Goldston, B. A., Bible: Fellow., 1936-37.

Ida Root Gordon, B. A., M. A., Oratory: Instr., 1901-02.

Herbert W. Graham, B. S., M. A., Ph. D., Biol.: Ass't. Prof., 1938-39.

Thornton Shirley Graves, A. B., A. M., Eng.: Ass't. Prof., 1908-09.

Wallace Graves, B. A., Gov't.: Teaching Fellow, 1946.

Robert H. Gregory, B. S., M. A., Ph. D. Acc't. Finance: Assoc. Prof., 1946—.

Lura Gregory, B. A., M. A., Eng.: Instr., 1946.

Perry E. Gresham, B. A., B. D., Phil.: Ass't. Prof., 1937-43.

Ernest Grey, Ph. D., Greek, German: Prof., 1945, fall.

J. T. Griffith, B. A., M. A., Hebrew and Greek: Fellow, 1926-28.

Daniel Groff, B. A., B. D., Rel. Ed.: Instr., 1945—.

Wm. Howard Grubbs, B. S., M. S., Phys. Ed.: Instr., and Manager, 1934— (on military leave, 1943-45).

Henry D. Guelick, A. B., B. M., Theory: Prof., Head, 1923-33.

Coleman Gully, A. B., M. A., Eco.: Instr., 1927-28; Superv. of Men, 1927-28.

C. C. Gumm, A. M., Ph. D., Eng.; Prof., 1914-16; Appl. Eco. Lecturer, 1920-21.

Artie Hall, Primary Dep't., 1882-86.

Bita May Hall, B. A., M. A., Fr., and Span.: Instr., 1938-45; Ass't. Prof., 1945— (on leave 45-47).

Colby D. Hall, B. A., M. A., LL. D., Latin and Greek: Prof., 1902-03; Ed. Sec., 1906-09; Univ. Chur. Pastor, 1909-10; Latin: Prof., 1912-14; Bible: Prof., 1913-28; Dean of Brite College, 1914-47; Dean of T. C. U., 1920-43; Ch. Hist. Prof., 1928—.

Colby D. Hall, Jr., B. A., M. S., Elec.: Instr., 1942-43.

Thomas H. Hamilton, A. B., Piano and Voice: Instr., 1915-17.

William L. Hamilton, B. S., LL. B., Princ. of Acad., 1908-09.

Mrs. Wm. L. Hamilton, B. Ped., Acad. Ass't., 1908-09.

John H. Hammond, B. A., M. A., Romance Lang.: Instr., 1934-36.

Margaret Forsythe Hammond, B. A., M. A., Eng.: Instr., 1925-27.

Wm. J. Hammond, B. A., M. A., Ph. D., Hist.: Instr., 1924-28; Ass't. Prof., 1929-32; Assoc. Prof., 1932-34; Prof., Head, 1934—.

W. T. Hamner, A. B., B. S., Eng.: Acad. Pric., 1897-1900; 1902-07; Eng. Instr., 1909-14; Superv. of Men, 1896-1900; 1902-07; 1909-14.

Henry Hardt, B. A., M. A., Ph. D., Chem.: Prof. Head, 1946—.

M. Greenwood Hardy, B. E., Elocu.: Instr., 1896-97.

A. J. Hargett, A. M., Math.: Prof., Head, 1920-27.

Mrs. A. H. Harle, Drawing and Painting: 1874-76.

Samuel Harper, Princ. and Adj. Teacher in Prim. Dep't., 1876-77.

Mrs. Georgia Harris, Stewardess, 1920-43; Hostess, 1943-45.

Virginia Lee Harrison, Pub. Spk.: Instr., 1925-28.

Lucy Harris, R. N., School of Nursing: Dean, 1947—.

Mrs. Minnie Lee Harrison, Hostess Foster Hall, 1946—.

J. J. Hart, A. B., LL. B., Commer.: Princ., 1908-10.

Mrs. J. J. Hart, A. B., Commer.: Ass't., 1908-10.

John B. Hawley, B. S., M. A., Engineer: Consult., 1927-41.

Kenneth Hay, B. A., B. D., Alumni Sec., 1939-41.

*Bibliography*

Basil A. Hayes, Superin. of College of Bus., 1914-15.
Leo Hendricks, B. S., M. S., Ph. D., Geol.: Ass't. Prof., 1946—.
Jean Shelly Henry, B. A., M. A., Eng.: Instr., 1937-39.
Patrick Henry, Sr., College of Business: Princp., 1913-14; Student Counselor, Brite, 1939—.
Robert G. Henry, Civil Aero.: Instr., 1941-43.
Mrs. May Henson, A. B., Eng.: Instr., 1927-28.
Willis G. Hewatt, B. S., M. S., Ph. D., Biol.: Ass't. Prof., 1933-40; Assoc. Prof., 1940-41; Prof., 1941—.
Lucian G. Hickman, A. B., A. M., Eng.: Prof., 1923-25.
W. B. Higgins, Dean of Men, Ath. Direc., 1919-20.
Benjamin H. Hill, Biol.: Instr., 1923-25.
Samuel Hill, B. S., Biol.: Fellow., 1925-26.
John J. Hinrichs, M. A., Ger. and Fr.: Instr., 1937-41.
Merrit L. Hoblit, A. B., Span. and Latin: Prof., 1921-22.
F. Woodall Hogan, B. S., M. S., Chem.: Assoc., Prof., 1920-29; Prof., 1929—.
R. F. Holloway, B. S., Math.: Adj. Prof., 1892-96.
Mrs. Eugene Holmes, Hostess, 1942—.
Cortell Holsapple, B. A., M. A., B. D., Ph. D., Philos.: Assoc. Prof., 1939-43; Prof., 1943—; Dean of Even. College, 1943—.
Merle Holsapple, Eng. and Span.: Instr., 1917-19; Prof., 1919-20.
Alex Holt, Heb. and Greek: Teacher, 1877-78.
Alpha S. Hopkins, Hostess, 1939-43.
Frank A. Horak, B. A., M. A., Math.: Instr., 1939-40.
Samuel Henry Horne, Latin and Span.: Instr., 1905-07.
C. W. Howard, A. B., Anc. Lang.: Prof., 1892-94.
Mrs. C. W. Howard, Prim. Princ., 1892-93.
E. Barton Howe, A. B., A. M., Ph. D., Eng.: Assoc. Prof., 1928-29.
Herbert L. Hughes, A. B., A. M., Ph. D., Eng.: Prof., Head, 1925-33.
Belle Hunter, B. L., Eng.: Instr., 1899-1900.
Willis C. Hunter, Violin and Harm.: Prof., 1906-10.
Mrs. W. C. Hunter, Voice: Prof., 1906-10.
Samuel Ward Hutton, A. B., B. D., Bible and Worship: Instr., 1929-31; Ass't. Prof., 1931-35; Prof., 1936—; Registrar, 1932—.
Isabel Ingalls, Voice: Instr., 1901-03.
Alfred Irby, M. D., College Phys., 1888-93.
Kate N. Jackson, Drawing: Inst., 1907-11.
Mrs. Ida Jacobs, Princ. of Prim. Dept., 1875-80.
J. E. Jarrott, Eng. and Math.: Teacher, 1875-78.
Dan Jarvis, B. A., Geol. Teaching Ass't., 1946—.
Mrs. Ida Van Zandt Jarvis, Sup't., Girls' Home, 1895-97.
Dick Jay, B. A., Eco.: Instr., 1946-47.
Q'Zella Oliver Jeffus, Organ: Ass't. Prof., 1928—.
Mrs. S. H. Jenkins, Hostess, 1938-42.
Cora Lee Jennings, Piano: Instr., 1906-08.
Walter P. Jennings, Pastor: Sec'y. Trustees, 1919-22.
Franklin G. Jones, Latin and Hist.: Adj. Prof., 1890-91; Latin and Greek Prof., 1897-98; Second. Ed., Prof., 1927-35; Emeritus, 1936-45; d. 2-2-45.
H. J. Jones, B. A., M. A., Math.: Instr., 1936-43; on military leave, 1943-44.
Leon Jones, B. A., Chem.: Instr., 1922-27; Ass't. Prof., 1927-29.
William Jones, B. A., Soc. Sc.: Ass't., 1917-18.
Frank Arthur Johnson, Direc. of Conservatory, 1910-13.
Mrs. S. L. Johnson, Hostess, 1937-42.
W. B. Juneau, A. B., Phys. Ed.: Ath. Direc., 1920-21.
Mrs. Joseph Karol, B. A., Eng.: Instr., 1946—.

Daniel Keefe, B. A., M. A., Eng.: Instr., 1946—.
Noel Keith, B. A., B. D., Rel. Instr., 1946—. Ass't. to President 1946—.
Joseph Kemp, M. D., College Physician, 1893-96.
Frederick D. Kershner, M. A., LL. D., Pres., 1911-15; Bible, Prof., 1911-14.
Mary Louise Kiber, B. A., M. A., Eng.: Instr., 1942-45.
Mrs. Terry King, Ass't. Matron, 1912-13.
John W. Kinsey, A. B., Ed.: Prof., 1909-15.
Mrs. John W. Kinsey, Academy: Instr., 1909-15.
R. P. Kirk, A. B., Prep. Princ., 1896-97.
Geraldine Kissinger, B. A., Lab. Instr., 1946-47.
Paul Klingstedt, Voice and Theo.: Instr., 1925-27; Assoc. Prof., 1927-30.
Melvin M. Knight, A. B., A. M., Hist.: Ass't. Prof., 1913-16.
Robert Knight, B. A., M. A., Ec.: Instr., 1929-30.
Mrs. Lena Knox, A. B., Eng.: Instr., 1932-33.
Walter S. Knox, A. B., Phys. Ed.: Instr., 1929-33; Ass't. Prof., 1933-35.
M. F. Knoy, A. B., Math.: Instr., 1927-28.
Abdullah Ben Kori, A. B. Mod. Lang.: Prof., 1902-06.
Edwin Kubale, A. B., Phys. Ed.: Instr., Line Coach, 1926-28.
S. Owen Lane, B. A., M. A., Eco.: Instr., 1938-40.
Lacy Lee Leftwich, A. B., A. M., B. D., Dean of Men, 1928-33.
Mary Cason Leftwich, A. B., Music: Instr., 1928-32.
Donald Leonard, B. A., B. D., Rel. Ed.: Instr., 1940-41.
Elva Lerret, B. A., Math.: Instr., 1946—.
Paul Lerret, B. A., B. S.,Math. Instr., 1946—.
John Lewis, A. B., B. S., M. E., Ed. D., Mus. Ed.: Assoc. Prof., 1944-46.
E. Florence Lewellyn, Voice, 1903-04.
G. A. Lewellyn, Ph. D., LL. D., Homil. and Chc. Hist.: Prof. 1909-11; Bible College Dean, 1910-11; d. 1911.
Harve Light, A. B., Ed.: Fellow., 1927-28.
D. Ray Lindley, B. A., B. D., M. A., Ph. D., Christ. Minis. and Rel. Ed.: Ass't. Prof., 1941-43; Assoc. Prof., 1943-44; Prof., 1944—; Dean Brite College, 1947—.
Vachael Lindsay, LL. D., Eng.: Lect. in Poetry, 1924-25.
F. M. Lisle, B. A., M. A., Chem.: Ass't. Prof., 1944—.
Cleatice A. Littlefield, B. S., M. S., Sec. Sc.: Instr., 1941-43.
Margaret M. Littlejohn, Painting: Ass't., 1914-15.
Clinton Lockhart, A. M., Ph. D., LL. D., Lit. D., Pres., 1906-11; Bible College Dean, 1906-10; Dean of Arts College, 1916-20; Prof. of Greek, Semitics, Old Test., 1906-11; 1912-43; Emeritus, 1943—.
Bess Jane Logan, A. B., Eng.: Instr., 1924-28.
Lola Lollar (Huff), B. A., M. S., Biol.: Ass't., 1942-44; Instr., 1944—.
Erskine Long, Spoken Word; Instr., 1921-23.
Orie W. Long, A. B., Mod. Lang.: Prof. Head, 1906-11.
John Lord, B. A., M. A., Ph. D., Span.: Prof., 1920-21; Pol. Sc. Gov't.: Prof. Head, 1921—. Graduate School Dean, 1924—.
Samuel S. Losh, Piano, Voice: Prof., 1910-11.
Hal Lotterman, B. F. A., M. F. A., Art: Instr., 1946—.
James W. Lowber, B. A., M. A., Ph. D., Sc. D., LL. D., F. R. G. S., R. A. S., R. S. G. S., R. S. A., A. A. A. S., M. R. A. S., Chancellor, Lecturer, 1892-1900.
Frank Edgar Lozo, B. A., M. A., Ph. D., Geol.: Instr., 1939-42; Ass't. Prof., 1943-44.
Mrs. Carrie Fletcher Luck, Music: Vocal Ass't., 1893-94.

S. T. Lyles, B. A., M. A., Th. M. Biol.: Teaching Ass't., 1946—.
Oliver L. Lyon, A. M., Ph. D., Eng.: Prof. Head, 1911-14.
J. R. Maceo, C. P. A., Acct.: Ass't. Prof., 1936-43; Assoc. Prof., 1943-1946.
Mary Anne Mack, B. A., M. A., Math.: Instr., 1946-47.
Gladys Maddocks, B. A., M. A., Eng.: Instr., 1946-47.
J. W. Mahan, Penmanship, Book-kpg.: Teacher, 1874-78.
Sadie Mahon, B. S., M. S., Biol.: Fellow., 1924-26; Instr., 1926-30.
Mabel I. Major, B. A., B. S., A. M., Eng.: Ass't. Prof., 1919-23; Assoc. Prof., 1923-38; Prof., 1938—; Acting Head, 1943-46.
L. L. Manchester, B. S., M. E., Math.: Instr., 1946-47.
Luther Mansfield, B. A., Eng.: Fellow., 1927-28.
Wm. J. Marsh, Organ: Glee Club Direc., 1934—.
Alpheus R. Marshall, B. A., M. A., Ph. D., Eco.: Assoc. Prof., 1934-37.
Frank H. Marshall, A. B., A. M., Ph. D., Rhet. and Eng.: Prof., 1899-1902; Bible College: Dean, 1901-02; Bible Prof., 1902-06.
Abe Martin, B. E., M. A., Phys. Ed.: Coach, 1945—.
A. D. Martin, A. B., Latin, Algebra: Instr., 1920-21.
Marian Douglas Martin, Piano: Ass't. Prof., 1941—.
Vera Rogers Maxwell, B. A., M. A., Span.: Instr., 1946-47.
Mrs. E. E. McAlister, B. A., M. A., Eng.: Instr., 1946—.
Olive Leaman McClintic, A. B., Elocu. and Ora.: Prof., 1901-07.
John R. McClung, A. M., Chem.: Prof., 1916-19.
Jennie V. McCulloh, A. B., Mod. Lang.: Instr., 1908-09.
Lilita McCorkle, B. M., Piano: Ass't. Prof., 1946—.
T. Smith McCorkle, B. M., M. A., Ph. D., Music: School of Fine Arts: Dean, 1943—; Prof., Violin and Mus. Ed., 1943—.
Patsy McCord, B. A., French: Instr., 1929-32.
Bruce McCully, A. M., Eng.: Prof. Head, 1902-09.
Errett Weir McDiarmid, A. B., A. M., Dean of Women, 1918-20; Philos., Psych.: Prof., 1918-39; d. 9-39.
Mrs. E. W. McDiarmid, Lady Princ., 1918-20.
John McDiarmid, A. B., M. A., Gov't.: Instr., 1932-33.
Willis McGregor, A. B., Eco.: Ass't. Prof., 1917-19.
Carroll C. McKee, Piano: Prof., Direc. of Music, 1918-20.
A. M. McKinney, Bus. Ad.: Teacher of Penmshp., Typ., 1890-91.
F. O. McKinsey, B. A., Greek and Latin: Prof., 1884-1891.
R. E. McKnight, Bursar, 1887-88.
Mrs. R. E. McKnight, Matron, 1887-88.
Alma McLendon, B. A., M. A., Educ.: Primary, Instr.; Jarvis Hall, Director, 1945—.
Anne McLendon, Piano: Instr., 1917-18.
Chalmers McPherson, Endowment Sec., 1908-11; N. T.: Prof., 1914-27; d. 9-27.
Jesse McQuigg, Prep. Dep't.: Teacher, 1880-83.
Herbert R. McQuillan, B. S., Phys. Ed.: Coach, 1941—.
Ed. R. McWilliams, B. A., Bible: Instr., 1929-30.
R. March Merrill, A. B., A. M., Fr. and Ger.: Prof., 1923-25.
Leo Meyer, A. B., Phys. Ed.: Instr., and Fresh. Coach, 1924-33; Head Coach, 1934—; Athletic Dir., 1943-44.
Dorothy Michael, B. A., M. A., Eng.: Instr., 1946-47.
James Miller, Eng.: Instr., 1912-13.
L. B. Miller, A. B., Greek: Ass't., 1881-83.
L. T. Miller, Jr., B. S., M. A., Bus. Ad.: Instr., 1935-41; Ass't. Prof., 1941-42; Even. College, 1942-44.
Mabel Annette Miller, Bus. Ad.: Instr., 1902-03.
Martha K. Miller, Shorthand: Teacher, 1899-1902; Registrar, 1902-11.
Ed Millwee, A. B., Pol. Ec.: Teacher, 1880-83.

Keith Mixson, B. A., B. N., Piano: Instr., 1934-42; (on military leave, 1942-45); Ass't. Prof., 1945-47; Assoc. Prof. 47—.

Charles B. Mohle, A. B., Bible: Instr., 1927-29.

Mateo Molina, A. B., Fr. and Span.: Ass't. Prof., 1909-11.

J. E. Montgomery, Assistant to the President, 1942—.

Jerome Moore, A. B., Span.: Instr., 1926-28; Prof. and Dean of Arts and Sc., 1943—.

Mary Lee Moore, A. B., Dom. Sc. and Home Ec.: Prin., 1915-17.

Milton Harvey Moore, A. B., Ad. Ed.: Lecturer, 1922-32.

Walter Moreman, B. S., M. S., Ph. D., Biol.: Instr., 1926-28; Ass't. Prof., 1930-33.

Edith L. Morgan, B. A., M. A., Math.: Instr., 1944—.

Herbert Bush Morgan, A. B., Eng.: Instr., 1919-20.

Joseph Morgan, B. A., M. A., Ph. D., Physics: Ass't. Prof., 1941-43; Assoc. Prof., 1943-45; Prof., 1945—.

Brooks Morris, Violin: Ass't. Prof., 1944—.

Harlee Morrison, A. M., Latin and Span.: Prof., 1918-19.

William Charles Morro, A. B., M. A., B. D., Ph. D., New Test.: Prof., Head, 1927-43; d. 3-24-43.

Daisy Morrow, A. B., Latin: Instr., 1913-14.

Eleanor Morse (Hall), B. M., Piano, Theo.: Instr., 1938-44.

Tesse Ferne Mosey, Oratory: Ass't., 1914-19; Princ., 1919-20.

Mrs. Bertie Mothershead, Lib. Sc.: Ass't. Lib., 1923-33; Acting Lib., 1933-38; Lib., 1938—.

Karl Mueller, B. A., Gov't.: Fellow., 1925-27.

Mary Elizabeth Moutray, Voice: Instr., 1923-25.

M. L. Munday, Math.: Instr., 1915-17.

Herbert R. Mundhenke, B. A., M. A., Ph. D., Ec.: Prof. Head, 1937—.

Helen Walker Murphy, B. A., Phys. Ed.: Instr., 1926-34; Ass't. Prof., 1934-45.

S. A. Myatt, M. A., Span. and Latin: Prof., 1914-16.

William Nance, Phys. Ed.: Base Ball Coach, 1925-26.

Mrs. Roger Neely, Voice: Instr., 1940—.

W. Harvey Neeley, A. B., M. S., Math.: Ass't. Prof., 1946—.

Carl W. Nelson, B. S., M. S. E., Ph. D., Math.: Ass't. Prof., 1946-47.

Frank H. Newlee, Span. and Latin: Instr., 1907-08.

Otto Nielsen, B. A., B. A., Superv. of Men, 1933-38; Dean of Men, 1938-40.

Charlie Noble, B. A., B. S., M. A., Math.: Instr., 1944-46.

Will V. Norris, M. S., Chem. and Physics: Prof., 1919-21.

Katherine Moore Norton, B. A., M. A., Speech: Instr., 1928-33; 1935-45.

Annie Nunn, Ph. B., Hist.: Prof., 1917-18.

W. C. Nunn, B. A., M. A., Ph. D., Hist.: Assoc. Prof., 1946.

W. T. O'Gara, B. A., M. S., Biol.: Ass't. Prof., 1946.

Clifton Oliver, Jr., B. A., M. A., Bus. Ad.: Instr., 1940-43; (On leave 1943-46); 1946-47.

Rowena Onderdonk, A. B., M. A., Span.: Instr., 1926-27.

Kelly O'Neal, B. A., M. A., Ph. D., Christ. Min.: Adj. Prof., 1940-41.

Mrs. Helen Orbeck, Dietician, 1945—.

Charlotte Ousley, A. B., Home Ec.: Prof., 1922-24.

Mrs. W. B. Owen, China Painting: Instr., 1920-22.

H. F. Page, A. M., Eng.: Ass't. Prof., 1912-13.

Harlan M. Page, A. B., A. M., M. D., Psych. and Biol.: Prof., 1903-04.

Mattie Wade Parks, A. M., Mod. Lang.: Instr., 1891-96; Piano Instr., 1908-09.

W. B. Parks A. M., Physics and Chem.: Prof., 1887-99; 1904-16; Dean, 1911-16.

Bettie Parker, Prep. Princ., 1889-94.

Robert C. Perry, B. A., Eng.: Instr., 1936-37.

*Bibliography*

James S. Petty, B. A., Music: Woodwind Instr., 1941-42.
Eula Burton Phares, B. A., M. A., Eng. and Latin: Instr., 1922-26; Ass't. Prof., 1926-27.
H. L. Pickerill, A. B., B. D., Rel. Ed.: Assoc. Prof., 1927-28; Prof., 1928-33.
Stella Pierce, Music School Princ., 1896-97.
Herman Riley Pittman, B. A., M. A., B. D., Dean of Men, 1940-42.
Guy Richard Pitner, Piano: Instr., 1915-16.
Austin L. Porterfield, B. A., M. A., Ph. D., Sociol.: Prof. Head, 1936—.
Marguerite Potter, B. S., M. A., Soc. Sc.: Instr., 1945—.
Leila Long Powell, Oratory: Princ., 1913-19.
J. S. Poyner, A. M., M. D., College Physician: Physics Teacher, 1879-83.
Eugenia Price, Art: Instr., 1896-97.
Leslie Proctor, A. B., Hist.: Instr., 1907-08.
Lurine Prouse, A. B., Phys. Ed.: Instr., 1945-46.
Thomas Prouse, B. A., M. A., Phys. Ed.: Ass't. Prof., 1934—.
R. L. Ragsdale, B. A., Eng. Lit. and Hist.: Instr., 1887-90.
Louis W. Ramsey, B. S. in E. E., Math.: Instr., 1927-32; Engin. Instr., 1940-41; Ass't. Prof. 1942—.
Mrs. Anna S. Ratliff, Ass't. Lady Princ., 1922-28.
Blanche Rawlins, Ass't. in Prim., 1893-94.
Harrell Rea, B. A., B. D., Bible: Instr., 1942-43.
Morris Rector, A. B., LL. B., Law: Prof., 1919-20.
Evelyn P. Redden, B. A., Physics: Instr., 1942-43.
Emmette S. Redford, A. B., M. A., Gov't.: Ass't. Prof., 1930-32.
William L. Reed, B. D., Ph. D., Rel.: Asst. Prof., 1946; O. T.: Assoc. Prof. 1947—.
Clyde Batsell Reeves, Oratory: Prof. Head, 1907-13.
C. H. Richards, Jr., B. A., M. A., Ph. D., Eco. and Gov't.: Instr., 1940-42; Ass't. Prof., 1944-46.
J. R. Richards, Ph. D., Mod. Lang.: Prof., 1917-22.
Thomas F. Richardson, B. S., M. S., Ph. D., Psych.: Ass't. Prof., 1943-44; Prof. Head and Dir. of Personnel, 1943—.
J. Willard Ridings, A. B., B. J., Journ.: Ass't. Prof., 1927-29; Assoc. Prof., 1929-31; Prof., 1931—; Dir. of Publicity, 1927—.
Pauline Rippy, B. A., M. A., Eng.: Instr., 1946—.
Walter Roach, B. A., Phys. Ed.: Instr. and Coach, 1937—; (on military leave, 1943-45).
C. H. Roberts, A. B., A. M., Hist.: Princ., 1912-19; Prof., Head, 1919-33; d. '33.
Mrs. Ethyl Harshberger Roberts, Hist.: Instr., 1919-21; Librarian Ass't., 1921-28.
J. C. Roberts, Phys. Ed.: Instr., 1922-24.
Jessie Robinson, Bus. Ad.: Ass't., 1907-08.
J. B. Rogers, Prep. Dep't.: Teacher, 1884-85.
Wm. V Roosa, B. A., M. A., Ph. D., Old Test.: Assoc. Prof., 1937-43; N. Test. Prof, 143-48, on leave 1947-48.
Theodore Rosenthal, Music: Wind Inst. Instr., 1920-21.
Walter Lee Ross, A. M., Hist. and Pol. Sc.: Prof. Head, 1903-06.
Augustus C. Rothe, Piano and Theo.: Instr., 1910-11.
Rhinehart E. Rouer, LL. B., Law: Prof., 1919-20.
R. M. Rowland, LL. B., Law: Sec. of Trustees, 1917-18; Attorney, 1922—.
Lucy Rutherford, Mod. Lang.: Teacher, 1876-77.
Clarence M. Sale, A. B., Math.: Ass't. Prof., 1946—.
Retha Sale, B. S., M. A., Art: Ass't. Prof., 1945—.
Claude Sammis, B. M., Music: Violin Instr., 1925-27; Prof. Head,

1927-42; Band Dir., 1925-35; Mus. Fac. Dir., 1934-42; d. 8-42.
Pauline Hensley Sammis, A. B., Music, Theory: Ass't., 1927-28.
Perry A. Sandefer, A. B., M. A., Span.: Instr., 1936-38.
Clois J. Sanders, A. B., M. A., Physics: Acting Prof., 1929-30.
Lillian Sansom, Oratory: Prof. of Phys. Ed., 1920-21.
Margaret L. Sargent, Mod. Lang.: Prof., 1912-18.
Mamie Schafer, A. B., Primary: Princ., 1900-01.
W. B. Schimmelpfennig, Music Dir., 1901-03.
Francis Schmidt, LL. B., Phys. Ed.: Instr. and Head Coach, 1929-33.
Mattie Schultz, Ger. and Fr.: Instr., 1888-89.
Gayle Scott, M. S., Dr. es Sc., Biol. and Geo.: Ass't. Prof., 1920-25; Prof., 1926—.
Marvin J. Scott, A. B., Comm., Bus. Ad.: Instr., 1924-25; Ass't. Prof., 1925-27.
David Scoular, Voice: Instr., 1930-34; Glee Club Dir., 1930-34.
Ottis Sears, M. A., Ph. D., Eng.: Prof., 1909-11.
John H. Sewell, M. S., Med. Direc., 1922-42.
Elizabeth Shelburne, B. A., M. A., Math.: Instr., 1929-38; Ass't. Prof., 1938—;
Dean of Women, 1937—.
Henry Shepherd, B. A., Gov't.: Instr., 1927-28.
Hilton Shepherd, Ed. D., Bus. Adm.: Prof., 1946—.
Jasmine Shepherd (Smoot), B. A., M. A., Span.: Instr., 1946—.
Robert Evans Sheppard, A. B., A. M., B. D., Sociol. and Eco.: Prof., 1922-24.
Charles R. Sherer, A. B., A. M., Math.: Prof. Head, 1928—.
Mirth W. Sherer, B. A., M. A., Educa.: Instr., 1929-31; Gov't., Soc. Sc. Instr., 1931-33; Ass't. Prof., 1933—.
Loraine Sherley, A. B., M. A., Eng.: Instr., 1927-37; Ass't. Prof., 1937-46; Assoc. Prof., 46—.
Mrs. Cephas Shelburne, House Mother, 1933-44; d. '44.
Mrs. Clover Shore, B. A., M. A., Art Ass't. Prof., 1946—.
Eva Wall Singleton, B. A., M. A., Educ. Instr., 1946—.
A. Skidmore, Latin, Greek, Heb.: Instr., 1890-92.
Douglas E. Shirley, A. B., Ass't. Treas., 1905-08.
Bess Shoemake, Phys. Ed.: Instr., 1922-23.
George Elliott Simpson, Piano: Instr., 1914-15.
Mrs. George Elliott Simpson, Piano: Instr., 1914-15.
Church H. Smiley, B. A., M. A., Rel.: Instr., 1945-47.
Nell Simpson Smiley, B. A., Greek: Instr., 1946-47.
B. S. Smiser, B. A., Ass't. Bus. Mangr., 1921-22; Bus. Mangr., 1922-33.
Clifford Smith, B. A., Physics: Fellow., 1927-28.
Harriet Frances Smith, Music: Piano Prof., 1905-08.
Raymond A. Smith, A. B., M. A., B. D., Educ.: Prof., Head, 1920—;
Dean of Sch. of Ed., 1943—.
Rebecca Smith (Lee), A. M., Ph. D., Eng.: Ass't. Prof., 1919-22; Assoc. Prof., 1922-30; Prof., 1931-45; Prof., Head, 1933-45; (on military leave, 1943-45).
W. C. Smith, Ph. D., Sociol.: Prof., 1929-33.
T. V. Smith, A. M., Eng.: Prof., 1916-17; Phil. Prof., 1917-18.
E. C. Snow, A. M., Math.: Teach., 1884-93; 1900-08; Act. Pres., 1900-02.
Dessie Pickens Snow, M. B., Music: Instr., 1887-93.
L. A. Snow, Bursar, 1888-89.
Ellis M. Sowell, B. S., M. S., Ph. D., Acc't.: Prof., Head, 1944—; Dean of Sch. of Bus., 1944—.
Katherine Prater Spearman, B. A., Phys. Ed.: Instr., 1941-43.

August O. Spain, B. A., M. A., Ph. D., Eco.: Ass't. Prof., 1946—.
Lyde Spraggins, A. B., A. M., Eng.: Ass't. Prof., 1928-37; Ass't.
Dean of Women, 1931-37.
Walter Stairs, A. M., Greek and New Test.: Prof., 1906-09.
Frank J. Stangl, B. A., M. S., Biol.: Fellow., 1927-28; Instr., 1928-29.
Ruth Stapp, B. M., M. M., Music: Instr., 1946—.
Ann Barham Stephens, B. A., Speech: Act. Instr., 1946—.
James Clark Street, Jr., B. A., M. A., Ph. D., Biol.: Instr., 1939-42; Ass't. Prof.,
1942-46; (on military leave, 1943-45).
P. E. Stearns, B. A., LL. B., Law: Prof., 1919-20.
J. B. Stev<ill/>ns, Voice: Instr., 1899-1900.
Charlotte June Stevenson, B. M., M. M., Music: Instr., 1945—.
Laurene Stong, B. A., M. A., Bus. Adm.: Act. Instr., 1947—.
Mary Strange, Painting: Instr., 1920-21.
W. O. Suiter, B. A., M. A., Eco.: Ass't. Prof., 1929-30.
Hazel Summers, B. A., M. A., Eng.: Fellow., 1927-31.
Harry Trumbell Sutton, A. B., B. S., Homil. and Ora.: Prof., 1910-14.
J. B. Sweeney, A. M., Sacred Hist. and Lit.: Prof., Dean of Bible College,
1895-99.
Mrs. J. B. Sweeney, Stewardess, 1914-20.
Shirley Sweeney, A. B., Biol.: Instr., 1917-19.
Robert H. Talbert, B. A., M. A., Ph. D., Sociol.: Ass't. Prof., 1946—.
Mrs. R. H. Talbert, B. A., M. A., Hist.: Instr., 1946—.
Mrs. Annie Taylor, Boys Matron, 1904-05.
A. Taylor, A. M., Mod. Lang.: Prep. Princ., 1896-97; Mod. Lang., 1896-97.
Bernaid U. Taylor, Voice: Adj. Prof., 1922-23.
Mrs. M. Taliaferro, Matron, 1888-91; 1904-05.
Anna Mae Tanner, Painting: Instr., 1916-18.
Harold R. Techau, Music: Instr., 1905-06; Dir., 1910-14.
A. P. Thomas, A. B., Prep. Princ., 1881-83.
Mrs. Anna Coghill Thomason, A. B., Pub. Spk.: Instr., 1924-25.
Olah Thompson, Art: Instr., 1882-89.
W. L. Thornton, A. B., B. O., Acad. Sc.: Instr., 1916-17.
W. L. Thornton, B. A., M. A., Soc. Sc.: Prof., 1920-21.
Wm. Edward Thrash, Music: Princ., 1899-1900.
Jeanette Tillett, Piano: Ass't. Prof., 1938—.
Maybelle Tinkle, M. Ed., Phys. Ed.: Ass't. Prof., 1946—.
E. M. Tipton, A. M., LL. D., Law: Prof., 1918-19; Athlet. Coach, 1918-19.
Elliott Todhunter, B. A., Spk. Word: Prof., 1921-22.
Douglas Tomlinson, A. B., LL. B., Jour.: Lecturer, 1922-42.
Ruth Towne, B. A., M. A., Rel. Ass't. Prof., 1946—.
Margaret Trippet, A. B., M. A., Psych.: Instr., 1931-33.
C. Allen True, B. A., M. A., Ph. D., Hist.: Instr., 1928-31; Assoc. Prof., 1934-43.
Jessie Dean Crenshaw Trulove, B. M., Piano: Assoc. Prof., 1923-26; 1935-39.
Ernest R. Tucker, A. B., M. A., Math.: Assoc. Prof., 1920-32; Registrar,
1924-32; d. 6-32.
Gladys Turner, A. B., Dom. Sc.: Princ., 1919-22.
Donald Tweedy, A. B., A. M., Music: Assoc. Prof., 1945.
Paul Tyson, A. B., Biol.: Ass't. Prof., 1909-10; Prof., 1913-14.
Ralph Uniacke, Violin: Prof., 1920-22.
Bruce Underwood, B. S., Eng.: Instr., 1946.

Fanny Vaden, Ass't. Princ. of Prim. Sch., 1886-87.
Nancy Jane Vance, B. A., M. A., Eng.: Instr., 1946.
I. L. Van Zandt, M. D., College Physician, 1884-86.
Nell Van Zandt, B. S., In Commer. and Lib. Sc.: Lib. Ass't., 1941—.
Don Ver Duin, B. A., B. D., Director of Men's Dormitories, 1945—.
Winifred Vickery, A. B., Eng. and Math.: Instr., 1913-14.
Walthat Volbach, Ph. D., Speech-Drama: Assoc. Prof., 1946—.
Mary Bell Waddill, B. A., Eng.: Instr., 1946—.
Gertrude Wade, Music: Princ., 1893-96.
Marjorie Sewalt Waits, B. A., M. A., Eng.: Instr., 1941-43.
Mary Elizabeth Waits (Scott), B. A., M. A., Educa.: Instr., 1924-28;
   Eng. Instr., 1928-30.
Edward McShane Waits, B. A., LL. D., President, 1916-41; Emeritus and Prof.
Christian Ministries, 1941—.
Granville Walker, B. A., B. D., Greek and Bible: Fellow., 1936-37;
   Ass't. Bible Prof., 1939-41.
Erline Walker, B. A., M. A., Educa.: Instr., 1939-40.
S. A. Wall, B. A., M. A., Ph. D., Educa.: Ass't. Prof., 1944; Assoc. Prof.,
   1947—.
Mabel Wallace, Piano: Instr., 1908-09.
Gussie Ward, A. B., Voice: Prof., 1905-06.
Lucretia Ward, B. A. L. S., Lib.: Ass't., 1946—.
Lottie Watson, Matron, 1908-10.
Catherine Weaver, A. B., M. A., Eng.: Instr., 1929-33.
Clifford Weaver, A. M., Chancellor, 1916-19.
W. A. Welsh, Jr., B. A., B. D., Greek and Bible: Instr., 1938-43; N. T., Ass't. Prof.,
   1945-46; Assoc. Prof., 1946—.
Anna Mary Wells, B. A., M. A., Eng.: Instr., 1927-29.
Carl D. Wells, A. B., A. M., B. D., Sociol.; Assoc. Prof., 1926-29.
Raymond L. Welty, B. S., M. A., Ph. D., Hist.: Assoc. Prof., 1928-36.
Fred West, B. A., B. D., Ph. D., Religion: Ass't. Prof., 1943-44; Prof., Head,
   1944-46.
I. V. West, B. S. in C. E., Math.: Instr., 1946-47.
Ruth White (Echols), B. A., B. S., Lib. Sc.: Ass't. Lib., 1941—.
Naomi J. Whitehurst, Director of Band, 1942-43.
Anna W. Whitlock, Music: Instr., 1920-22.
E. Clyde Whitlock, Violin: Ass't. Prof., 1944—.
Lenora May Williams, B. A., M. A., Biol.: Instr., 1929-30.
James L. Whitman, A. B., M. A., Ph. D., Chem.: Prof., Head, 1928-45;
   d. 11-30-45.
Marian Whitney, B. A., M. A., Ph. D., Geol: Assoc. Prof., 1946—.
R. B. Whitten, Comm. Dep't.: Instr., 1882-87.
R. B. Whitten, LL. B., Bus. Ad.: Ass't., 1910-11.
Mrs. M. E. Wideman, Matron, 1891-97.
Tyler Wilkinson, Matron, 1905-08; 10-11; 13-18.
Lenora May Williams, B. A., M. S., Biol. Instr., 1929-30.
W. M. Williams, Endowment Sec., 1912-14.
Ruth Williamson, B. B. A., Comm.: Instr., 1921-23.
Elsie Willis, B. M., Piano: Ass't. Prof., 1927-31.
J. R. Wilmeth, Prep. Princ., 1882-83.
Mrs. Clara Wilmeth, Ger. and Fr.: Instr., 1881-83.
E. C. Wilson, B. A., Ph. D., Educ. and Philos.: Prof., 1915-17;
   Educa. Prof., 1917-19.
Fred W. Wimberly, Music: Prof., 1907-10.
Michael Winesanker, B. A., M. A., Ph. D., Music: Assoc. Prof., 1946—.

Aline Weir Wilson, Piano: Instr., 1915-18.
Kitty Wingo, B. S., Phys. Ed.: 1946—.
Hortense Winton, Biol.: Instr. and Curator of Museum, 1916—.
William McClain Winton, B. S., M. S., Biol. and Geo.: Prof., Head, 1913—.
Catherine Wisdom, B. A., Span.: Fellow., 1927-28.
John William Woldt, B. M., M. M., Music Theo.: Horn, Ass't. Prof., Dir. of Band, 1943-44.
Raymond Wolf, B. A., Phys. Ed.: Instr. and Line Coach, 1929-36.
Warren Wood, A. B., A. M., Ph. D., Eng. and Ass't. Prof., 1946—.
Mrs. Celeste Coursey Woodard, B. A., Educa.: Instr., 1925-30.
John Woodard, B. A., M. A., Educa.: Instr., 1922-26; Ass't. Prof., 1926-30.
Harriet Woodward, Art: Instr., 1903-04.
Hazel Tucker Woodward, B. A., M. A., Philos. and Psych.: Fellow., 1927-33; Ass't. Prof., 1933—.
Samuel Andrew Woodward, M. D., F. A. C. S., Med. Direc., 1918-22.
Alla Wright, Piano: Instr., 1919-20.
L. C. Wright, B. A., Phys. Ed.: Dir. of Phys. Ed., 1924-33; Bus. Mangr., 1933—.
Hal Wright, A. B., Eco.: Instr., 1933-35.
Verna Wyatt, B. A., Eng.: Instr., 1946—.
Henriette J. Siegel, Art: Prof., 1904-06.
S. P. Ziegler, Harmony: Prof., 1917-19; Art, Prof., Head, 1925—.
Charles Zlatkovich, B. S., M. A. B., Bus. Ad.: Instr., 1939-41.
Ely V. Zollars, A. M., LL. D., Pres. and Dean of Bible College, 1902-06.

Teachers and Officers who have served as many as 20 years. An endeavor has been to include the pictures of these; some were not available.

| | | | | | |
|---|---|---|---|---|---|
| 1. Colby D. Hall | 40 | | 18. Bertie Mothershead | 24 |
| 2. Clinton Lockhart | 36 | | 19. S. P. Ziegler | 24 |
| 3. W. M. Winton | 34 | | 20. Bonnie M. Enlow | 24 |
| 4. E. M. Waits | 31 | | 21. F. E. Billington | 23 |
| (As Pres. 25) | | | 22. Artemisia Bryson | 23 |
| 6. Mrs. W. M. Winton | 31 | | 23. Eula Lee Carter | 23 |
| 7. Addison Clark | 29 | | 24. L. D. Fallis | 23 |
| (As Pres. 26) | | | 25. W. J. Hammond | 23 |
| 8. Raymond A. Smith | 27 | | 26. Newton Gaines | 23 |
| 9. F. W. Hogan | 27 | | 27. L. A. Dunagan | 23 |
| 10. Gayle Scott | 27 | | 28. Dura Brokaw Cockrell | 22 |
| 11. L. L. Dees | 27 | | 29. E. W. McDiarmid | 21 |
| 12. Rebecca Smith Lee | 26 | | 30. C. H. Roberts | 21 |
| 13. L. C. Wright | 25 | | 31. Loraine Sherley | 20 |
| 14. Georgia Harris | 25 | | 32. Hazel Tucker Woodward | 20 |
| 15. R. M. Rowland | 25 | | 33. Josiah Combs | 20 |
| 16. W. B. Parks | 24 | | 34. J. Willard Ridings | 20 |
| 17. L. R. Meyer | 23 | | | |

The following have served nearly 20 years. Their pictures, for the most part were crowded out.

| | | | | | |
|---|---|---|---|---|---|
| 1. Sadie Beckham | 19 | | 9. Mack Clark | 18 |
| 2. Charles Sherer | 19 | | 10. E. C. Snow | 17 |
| 3. Mirth Sherer | 19 | | 11. Claude Sammis | 17 |
| 4. B. A. Crouch | 19 | | 12. J. L. Whitman | 17 |
| 5. Helen Murphy | 19 | | 13. Katherine Norton | 17 |
| 6. Helen Fouts Cahoon | 18 | | 14. Katherine Bailey | 16 |
| 7. E. R. Cockrell | 18 | | 15. Chalmers McPherson | 16 |
| 8. S. W. Hutton | 18 | | | |

*Appendix VII.* Lists of Student Officers (as available).

| Year | President of Students | Editor of Skiff | Bus. Mgr. Skiff |
|------|----------------------|-----------------|-----------------|
| 02-03 | | Ed S. McKinney | |
| -04 | | Ed S. McKinney | |
| -05 | | Alonzo Ashmore | L. Edwin Brannin |
| -06 | | Gordon B. Hall | M. Gary Smith |
| -07 | | Howell G. Knight | H. G. Knight |
| -08 | | Herbert Bozeman | Bonner Frizzell |
| -09 | | Herbert Bozeman | Dan D. Rogers |
| -10 | | G. W. Stevenson | Barney Halbert |
| -11 | | Howard B. Dabbs | W. C. Ferguson |
| -12 | Clarence M. Hall | W. C. Ferguson | Roy Tomlinson |
| -13 | Charles Bussey | Robert Lines | W. Boyd Wilson |
| -14 | E. Carl Tomlinson | Edwin R. Bentley | R. Cecil Bevan |
| -15 | Crawford Reeder | Horace Jones | Homer Tomlinson |
| -16 | John Keith | Horace Jones | Homer Tomlinson |
| -17 | Willis McGregor | Chas. Christenberry | H. Tomlinson |
| -18 | William Jones | Jesse Martin | Wm. Jones |
| -19 | Shelby Faulkner | Beatrice Mabry | Myra Peacock |
| -20 | Cecil Bradford | T. E. Dudney | Loy Ledbetter |
| -21 | J. W. Boultinghouse | T. E. Dudney | Forest McCutcheon |
| -22 | Judge Green | T. E. Dudney | Vernon Bradley |
| -23 | T. E. Dudney | Jerome Moore | Henry E. Fussell |
| -24 | Judge Green | Nimmo Goldston | Karl Mueller |
| -25 | Hubert Robison | Philip Ayres | Sterling P. Clark |
| -26 | Carlos Ashley | Richard Gaines | Herd Wimberly |
| -27 | Hubert Anderson | Henry L. Shepherd | Ted Brown |
| -28 | Jerome Smiser | Amos Melton | Bill Adkinson |
| -29 | Weir McDiarmid | Amos Melton | Bill Adkinson |
| -30 | Hugh Buck | Pauline Barnes | Sam Frankrich |
| -31 | A. T. Barrett | Jay Williams | Sam Frankrich |
| -32 | Alf Roark | Lawrence Coulter | Ed Van Orden |
| -33 | Marion Hicks | Ernestine Scott | Ed Van Orden |
| -34 | Roy O'Brien | Jo Sargent | Atys Gardner |
| -35 | Jack Langdon | Ben Sargent | Atys Gardner |
| -36 | Melvin Diggs | Raymond Michero | Paul Ridings |
| -37 | Harry Roberts | Walter Pridemore | Paul Ridings |
| -38 | Richard Poll | Paul Ridings | James Matthews |
| -39 | Guy Daniel | Ernest Peyton | James Matthews |
| -40 | Wm. Chappell | Bill Hayworth | Cleland Early |
| -41 | Malvern Stevenson | V. G. Smylie | Cleland Early |
| -42 | Ronald Brumbaugh | Margaret Ramage | Wilson Baugh, Jr. |
| -43 | Dunny Sims | Lois Jean Cayce | Janice Conley |
| -44 | Clyde Foltz | Billy Jean Boney | Janice Conley |
| | Z. Chronister | | |
| | Ed Cornelius | | |
| -45 | Joan Gardner | Dixie Belle Williams | Mary Lou Slay |
| | David Hibbard | Mary Lou Slay | |
| -46 | Norman Hoffman | Bobby Reinlander | Mary Frances Potter |
| | Nell Epperson | | |
| | Chas. Matthews | | |
| -47 | David Bunn | Richard Moore | Lynn Fleming |
| | Darrel Tipps | | |

| Yr. | Horned Frog Ed. | Football Captain | Baseball Captain | Football Coach |
|---|---|---|---|---|
| 97-98 | A. Clark, Jr. | | | Joe J. Field |
| -99 | | | | James Morrison |
| -00 | | J. V. McClintic | | |
| -01 | | C. I. Alexander | | |
| -02 | | Tom Reed | | |
| -03 | | Homer Rowe | | H. E. Hildebrand |
| -04 | | H. H. Watson | | |
| -05 | Elster M. Haile | Jack Muse | Ben Mouldin | C. E. Cronk |
| -06 | | H. G. Knight | Ben Mouldin | E. J. Hyde |
| -07 | W. Hanneford | B. Frizzell | L. C. Proctor | E. J. Hyde |
| -08 | Gordon B. Hall | L. C. Wright | | E. J. Hyde |
| -09 | H. G. Knight | Manley Thomas | Elmer Randall | J. R. Langley |
| -10 | | L. C. Wright | M. Baldwin | J. R. Langley |
| -11 | Earl X. Gough | J. W. Massie | M. Baldwin | Kemp Lewis |
| -12 | C. M. Hall | Milton Daniel | | Henry Lever |
| -13 | H. N. Bussey | Bryant Ware | Clark Campbell | W. T. Stewart |
| -14 | R.A.Highsmith | Blue Rattan | Jim McKowan | Fred Cahoon |
| -15 | E. R. Bentley | C. Reeder | Jim McKowan | S. A. Boles |
| -16 | R. E. Cox | John P. Cox | | E. Y. Freeland |
| -17 | S. Sweeney | Ralph Martin | | M. E. Daniel |
| -18 | E. B. Sewell | O. Hawes | Howard Vaughn | M. E. Daniel |
| -19 | Mary Hefner | Will Hill Acker | | E. M. Tipton |
| -20 | Beth Combs | Will Hill Acker | Leo Meyer | T. E. D. Hackney |
| -21 | F. McCutchon | A. S. Douglas | Chester Fowler | W. L. Driver |
| -22 | Judge Green | Chester Fowler | Chili McDaniel | W. L. Driver |
| -23 | L. Sherley | Judge Green | Chili McDaniel | Jno. McKnight |
| -24 | W. L. Page | Blair Cherry | | Madison Bell |
| -25 | Girard Dokey | Lindsay Jacks | | Madison Bell |
| -26 | C. L. Waller | Herman Clark | | Madison Bell |
| -27 | D. Pruden | John Washman | Hezzie Carson | Madison Bell |
| -28 | Everett Shipp | B. Williams | Jimmie Grant | Madison Bell |
| -29 | | Jake Williams | Howard Grubbs | Madison Bell |
| -30 | R. Z. Dallas | M. Brumbelow | Ralph Walker | Francis Schmidt |
| -31 | Sterling Brown | Noble Adkins | Buster Walker | Francis Schmidt |
| -32 | Lillian Eylers | Harlos Green | Hal Wright | Francis Schmidt |
| -33 | L. O. Dallas | Johnny Vauht | | Francis Schmidt |
| -34 | Roy Bacus | Jack Graves | | Francis Schmidt |
| -35 | Anna Harness | Joe Coleman | Jimmy Jacks | Leo R. Meyer |
| -36 | Jones Bacus | Darrell Lester | Jimmy Jacks | Leo R. Meyer |
| -37 | Hays Bacus | Walter Roach | Sam Baugh | Leo R. Meyer |
| -38 | Robert Belzner | Mason Mayne | L. D. Meyer | Leo R. Meyer |
| -39 | Frances Taylor | I. B. Hale | | Leo R. Meyer |
| -40 | Sam Jackson | Don Looney | | Leo R. Meyer |
| | | Bud Taylor | | |
| -41 | Mildred Smith | C. Alexander | | Leo R. Meyer |
| -42 | Harry R. Davis | Bill Crawford | | Leo R. Meyer |
| -43 | V. Tomme | Bruce Alford | | Leo R. Meyer |
| -44 | Bettie Baker | Clyde Flowers | | Leo R. Meyer |
| -45 | S. Glasscock | Clyde Flowers | | Leo R. Meyer |
| -46 | Marylou Miller | Merle Gibson | | Leo R. Meyer |
| -47 | Perry Gandy | Fred Taylor | | Leo R. Meyer |

375

*Appendix VIII*

CHARTER
Add-Ran Male and Female College
At Thorp Springs, Hood County, Texas.
Under the General Law for Private Incorporation Approved
December 2, 1871

This charter is for the incorporation of "Add-Ran Male and Female College," at Thorp Springs, Hood County, Texas. The place for the transaction of business shall be at Thorp Springs, Hood County, Texas.

The purpose of said College shall be for the support and promotion of Literary and scientific Education.

This charter shall be in force for forty years.

The following named persons shall be trustees to hold and use the College ground and buildings in trust for the legal owners of said property, for the purpose of education as above mentioned, to-wit: J. A. Clark and A. Clark, of Tarrant County, R. Clark and J. H. Harbison, of Hood County, James Brock, of Parker County, H. D. Bantau, of Johnson County, and A. M. Arnot, of Hill County.

Said trustees shall have succession, shall have power to maintain and defend judicial proceedings; shall be privileged to make and use common seal; shall have power to purchase and hold real and personal estate in trust as aforesaid, as the purpose of the corporation may require; to make by-laws, not inconsistent with existing laws, for the management of its property and the regulation of its affairs; to enter into contract or obligation essential to the transaction of its ordinary affairs; to increase or diminish the number of its trustees to not more than thirteen nor less than three; provided, that no one shall be a trustee who is not a member in good standing of the Christian Church; to fill vacancies in the board; to appoint such officers as they may deem necessary for the corporation; and to alter or amend the by-laws.

The President, Vice-President and Professors of said College shall constitute a Faculty, and shall have power to enforce the rules and regulations enacted by the trustees for the government and discipline of the students as may be necessary; and shall have power to confer degrees and grant diplomas.

This charter shall take effect and be in force from and after the time of the filing of the same in the office of the Secretary of State.

Note.—The above charter went into effect April 11, 1874.

376

# INDEX

Also, see Appendix for list of Trustees and Teachers

Page

Page

# HISTORY OF TEXAS CHRISTIAN UNIVERSITY

# Index

Page

Page

# Index

# A World-Wide Outlook

Long before the modern citizen or even statesmen were awakened to the consciousness of the "one world," there was in Add-Ran a world-wide outlook. In the early 1890's when the campus was in an obscure village and the students were gathered from far-scattered homes of the frontier, there was a Student Volunteer Band, dedicated to the task of carrying the Christian Gospel to the ends of the earth. Out of this modest company came one who pioneered the evangelistic and educational program of the Disciples in Mexico and another who went to the savages of the Belgian Congo, wrote down their language, devised their grammar, baptized their early converts and helped to lay the foundations for the marvelous transformation from a barbaric to a Christian civilization.

Now that the experiences of our boys in World War II have startled the average American citizen into an appreciation of the practical, beneficent effects of foreign missions on the social order, it is fitting that the last page of this volume should be devoted to those students who, through the years, have represented their alma mater in this world-unifying enterprise of foreign missions. Here is the list (probably incomplete) of those we thus delight to honor.

Kenneth Bonham, M. D., B. A., '26. India.
Mrs. Esther Shepherd Bonham, B. A., '27. India.
Miss Nona Boegeman, B. A., '08. India, several years.
Frank Buck, B. D., '07. Jamaica, several years.
Arturo Macias Campirano, B. A., '33. Mexico.
George Cherryhomes, B. A., '37, B. D., '39. China.
Mrs. Margaret May Cherryhomes, 1947. China.
Miss Vida Elliot, B. A., '25. India.
Ellsworth E. Faris, B. A., '94. Belgian Congo, Africa.
Bertha Mason Fuller, B. A., '96. Mexico, several years.
Joe A. Fowler, M. D., B. A., '26.
Mrs. Thelma Collins Fowler, B. A., '25.
Miss Pearl Gibbons, 1909-11. Mexico.
Miss Leona Hood, B. A., '23. Mexican Christian Institute, San Antonio.
Mrs. Ida Tobin Hopper, B. A., '23. Paraguay, several years.
Eulalia Luna, B. A., '30, M. A., '32, Mexican Christian Institute, San Antonio, Texas.

Samuel Guy Inman, 1897-99, LL. D., '23, Mexico; Director Commission on Cooperation in Latin America, many years.
Miss Ruth Musgraves, B. A., '16. Africa.
Fred Norris, M. D., B. A., '21. Porto Rico, a few years.
Nabunda Oda, B. A., '27, Dean Girls' College, Japan.
Miss Katherine Schutze, B. A., '27, China, until the war.
Mrs. Nell Simpson Smiley, B. A., '27. India.
Miss Hallie Strange, Missionary Diploma, '21. Mexico.
Tadishi Tominaga, B. A., '29, M. R. E., '30. President of a College in Japan.
Katherine Wisdom (later Mrs. Burnett), M. A., '33. Mexico.